"This wonderful book is essential reading not only for those committed to genuine Catholic education, but also for all those who refuse to acquiesce in the reigning educational paradigm that merely trains students in various utilitarian competencies. It clarifies the true ends of education in the Christian tradition and it sheds notable light on the means to accomplish them. *Renewing the Mind* is a crucial text for those who understand that through Christian learning truths can be made to shine more brightly so that souls may be attracted to that which is Truth itself. It will benefit greatly all who appreciate that authentic Christian education does not train the mind at the expense of the heart."

—FR. WILSON D. MISCAMBLE, CSC, Professor of History, University of Notre Dame

❖

"There are many books about education. Topping's book is one of the few that presents the first principles of Catholic education. Arguably, this book is simply the finest compendium of the best that has been written or said about education in Western Civilization. If only one book were to be placed in the hands of teachers, administrators, and board members, it should be this book."

—DR. WILLIAM EDMUND FAHEY, Fellow & President, Thomas More College of Liberal Arts, Merrimack, N.H.

❖

"Dr. Topping has provided a most timely work, certainly for a wide Catholic readership, but particularly for those who research and teach in the area of the Catholic philosophy of education. Education, says Jacques Maritain, is ultimately for personal freedom, and the texts Dr. Topping has chosen demonstrate the simplicity and sophistication of education as an essential source of freedom."

—FR. MARIO O. D'SOUZA, CSB, Dean Emeritus, Faculty of Theology, Basilian Fathers Chair in Religion and Education, University of Toronto

❖

"This much-needed anthology of writings in the philosophy of Catholic education is a timely publication. As the Church embarks on its New Evangelization, it is essential to revisit our work in the field of education. Dr. Topping has done Catholic educators a tremendous service with this volume packed with interesting and relevant insights from those on whose shoulders we stand today."

—DR. LEONARDO FRANCHI, Head of the St. Andrew's Foundation, School of Education, University of Glasgow

❖

"Many approaches to education concentrate on the learnables, to the virtual exclusion of the developmentals. In this volume Topping has wisely selected readings that stress the need for the formation of the whole person through the cultivation of virtue—intellectual and moral. The discussion questions provided for these readings will help educators keep their focus on the maturation of the person, not just the communication of information or the refinement of skills apart from moral values."

—FR. JOSEPH W. KOTERSKI, SJ, Philosophy Department, Fordham University

❖

"*Renewing the Mind* offers a wide range of key texts in classical and Catholic educational thought. There are some old favourites and some unknown gems. The four-part division into 'Aims,' 'Matter,' 'Methods,' and 'Renewal' is helpful and the framing discussions and questions excellent. This book will be very useful to students and newcomers to the field, and will delight those already familiar with the area."

—DR. HAYDEN RAMSAY, Senior Deputy Vice Chancellor, University of Notre Dame, Australia

❖

"When so many anthologies of educational readings jump from the classical to the renaissance worlds, here at last is a rich and rewarding selection that provides access to what we might want to describe as the perennial tradition in Western educational thought. Here we meet Athens and Jerusalem united, the crowning of the classical liberal arts tradition with Christian wisdom. It is to be hoped that this anthology from Ryan Topping will be widely used in universities and colleges to help reacquaint a new generation of students, thirsty for a recovery of this wisdom, with the contours of this little-trodden path."

—DR PETROC WILLEY, Professor of Catechetics, Francsican University of Steubenville; Reader in the New Evangelization, School of the Annunciation, Buckfast Abbey, England

❖

"Christian educational reflection of any depth and substance stands in need of engagement with the rich history of Christian wrestling with key questions regarding educational aims, content, and processes. This valuable collection offers readers broad exposure to important strands of Catholic thinking about education, as well as some of their roots and influences. It is recommended to any who desire to step beyond the tyranny of the present and glimpse a larger, longer conversation."

—DAVID I. SMITH, Director of Graduate Studies in Education and Director of the Kuyers Institute for Christian Teaching and Learning, Calvin College, Mich.

❖

"One ongoing task of the New Evangelization is to present anew an authentically Catholic education rooted in a Christian anthropology. And so along comes Ryan Topping's *Renewing the Mind*, a book both timely and timeless. This collection of readings is timely because it is well suited to this task, containing as it does over two thousand years of human thinking on the truths about God, humanity, and the mind. It is timeless in that, like a good liberal arts education, this book promises to liberate students (and not a few faculty) from the narrow, presentist bigotry of our age. For those in the Catholic Studies movement who face the task not so much of preserving but rather of restoring the Catholic intellectual tradition at their colleges and universities, *Renewing the Mind* will be especially welcome."

—DR. JOHN C. PINHEIRO, Director of Catholic Studies, Aquinas College, Grand Rapids, Mich.

RENEWING *the* MIND

RENEWING *the* MIND

A Reader in the Philosophy of Catholic Education

EDITED BY RYAN N. S. TOPPING

Foreword by Don J. Briel

 THE CATHOLIC UNIVERSITY OF AMERICA
PRESS | WASHINGTON, D.C.

Library of Congress Cataloging-in-Publication Data
Renewing the mind : a reader in the philosophy of Catholic edu-
cation / edited by Ryan N.S. Topping ; foreword by Don J. Briel.
    pages cm
Includes bibliographical references and index.
ISBN 978-0-8132-2731-3 (pbk. : alk. paper)   1. Catholic
Church—Education—Philosophy.   2. Catholic schools.
3. Catholic universities and colleges.   I. Topping, Ryan N. S.
(Ryan Nathan Scott), 1977–
LC473.R46 2015
371.071'2—dc23   2015010030

publication aided by a university press grant
Figure Foundation
school thy philosophy, join truth to revelation

❖

I dedicate this work to my students, present and past.
Non multa, sed multum. Oremus pro invicem.
Thomas More College, New Hampshire
Feast of St. Thomas More

❖

❖ CONTENTS

Part III. The Methods of Teaching

Part IV. On Renewal in Our Time

❖ ILLUSTRATIONS

All illustrations are courtesy of the National Gallery of Art, Washington, D.C.

The loss of the sense that all true enculturation ultimately requires a religious foundation has not been without dramatic effects on contemporary education, both secular and religious. In the absence of this basic assumption it is perhaps inevitable that education is today no longer understood in terms of an incorporation into a specific tradition introducing both integral accounts of the nature of the virtues and fundamental claims about the truth. What replaces this classical account of education is one which stresses instead the necessity of civility and tolerance, of the importance of applied skills and therapeutic self-esteem.

Ryan Topping's *Renewing the Mind: A Reader in the Philosophy of Catholic Education* provides both a judicious selection of primary texts expressive of a broad humanist educational tradition and an insightful and often provocative reflection on the modern educational crisis. He reminds us that our current situation, one in which for the first time "Western civilization has not shared a common mind either with itself or about its past," marks a unique break with a common tradition that allowed debates about the nature of education, which were vital not in spite of but rather because of a certain unanimity about the first principles of education. In doing so, he confronts the contemporary tendency to reduce education to an instrumental technique. At the same time he confronts the modern tendency to describe education as the art of teaching students to explore their own values. In fact, he insists, to teach is to shape a human being, and this necessarily involves a certain violence, for "every act of instruction is an incursion upon a living organism that you hope to change through the encounter." Of course this requires that the ends one has in mind need to be both clear and publicly stated, for "to educate is to act, and to act is to work from the basis of some principle stated or implied."

Topping assumes Newman's basic principle that the end of education is not primarily the advancement of knowledge, the acquisition of practical skills, or a claustrophobic self-contemplation but rather the formation of a habit of mind allowing the student to see things in relation, to form a view, to be able to judge rightly the complex state of things. In assuming this classical principle, he assumes as well its moral implications, for as he rightly insists, "the same cradle can beget monsters and tyrants as well as saints and citizens," echoing Newman's point that the gentleman, the chief expression of liberal education, can be marked either by holiness or by profligacy.

The general introduction rightly identifies the reductionism of many aspects of contemporary education which is so tied to the naive confidence of the social sciences in the inevitability of progress, a naivete analyzed by Christopher Dawson in *Progress and Religion* nearly ninety years earlier. The modern preoccupation with the latest discoveries and the neglect of a broad and robust intellectual humanist tradition produces what Topping calls a fundamentally flawed disposition, for "the study of education is not like cancer research for the reason that men are not merely molecules." Genuine education's progress is not simply linear. Instead, it requires a consistent reappropriation of the past as well as an anticipation of the future, neither of which is reducible to mechanical formula.

Topping's approach is at once insightful and challenging. His selection of works from the great humanist traditions of education focuses not only on classical sources but also on contemporary theory. The anthology's strength is not only the comprehensive range of the readings but also the conscious and explicit use of Christian principles in judging the means and ends of education. For, as he notes, the modern crisis in education arises largely because in the removal of God from the universe one loses the university, a point equally stressed by Newman in *The Idea of a University*. The choice not only of individual texts but of specific selections from those texts has been handled with unusual skill and discrimination and his suggestions for further reading related to and contextualizing these texts makes this a very useful reference tool for students, teachers and parents. *Renewing the Mind: A Reader in the Philosophy of Catholic Education* is an important and timely contribution to the work of renewing the great and enduring tradition of Catholic education.

Don J. Briel
Blessed John Henry Newman Chair of
Liberal Arts, University of Mary, Bismarck

✦ ACKNOWLEDGMENTS

It is a joy to record my thanks to those who helped toward the completion of this project. Foremost, I register my debt to two research assistants, Conal Tanner and Tyler Worthy, as well as to a number of generous friends and relatives who provided support for this project at various stages: Drs. Thomas and Carolyn Barry, Dr. Thomas and Jill Bateman, John and Eileen Dunlop, Drs. Pat and Darlene Kelly, Colin and Margaret Phillips, Dave and Laurice Sidloski, John and Beatrice Sidloski, Robert and Leah Sidloski, Dan and Carol Seibert, Dr. Michael Tobin, and Ken and Tonya Wiebe.

Institutional support by St. Thomas University, Fredericton, New Brunswick, and Thomas More College of the Liberal Arts, New Hampshire, I here gratefully acknowledge. I wish to thank my colleagues-in-arms at Thomas More College for their friendship; it is a rare privilege to work in a community where festivity, sanctity, and scholarship breathe easily together. The book has benefitted immensely from the diligent efforts of James Kruggel, Susan Needham, Theresa Walker, and the staff at the CUA Press.

It is a great honor for me to have Dr. Don J. Briel write the foreword; I thank him not only for his encouragement of this book, but more importantly, for his example and generous fidelity to the cause of the renewal of Catholic education in our time. I have been privileged to teach many wonderful students over the years. I became interested in education, however, chiefly because of the prospect of raising my own children. Special thanks, therefore, is owed to my wife, Anna Topping, an excellent teacher, with whom I am blessed to share that work.

I thank the publishing houses and literary estates that have allowed me to reprint selections from their works. Formal acknowledgment with bibliographical details can be found in the Sources and Permissions section at the back of the book. On that score, effort has been made to contact copyright holders; any omissions or errors will be corrected in subsequent printings if notice is given to the editor. Images were made possible through the National Gallery's (Washington, D.C.) generous benefaction.

Lastly, the introduction grew out of an article first published as "Great Books, Great Questions, Great God" in *Convivium* (September/October

2012): 27–31, which itself grew out of the conference "Great Books Education" at King's College, Halifax. I thank the editors for permission to reproduce elements of that essay below and the conference organizers for allowing a theologian into their midst.

RENEWING *the* MIND

The Annunciation

Introduction

Let a father, then, as soon as his son is born, conceive first of all the best possible hopes of him, for he will thus grow the more solicitous about his improvement from the very beginning.

QUINTILIAN

Do not be conformed to this world but be transformed by the renewing of your mind ...

ST. PAUL

For all its hostility to the faith, the modern West still bears the marks of fifteen solid centuries of being cradled in the arms of the Church. For too long Christian schools and their administrators have thrown a false cloak of shame over their tradition. Given the Church's contribution to learning, this is odd. One literally cannot conceive of Western civilization apart from the dazzling influence of Christianity upon education. To begin to measure the Church's civilizing impact upon the culture of the mind one need only think, for instance, of the educational mission of the early Irish monks, the invention of the Cyrillic alphabet, the birth of Oxford and Cambridge, the poetry of Dante, the philosophy of Thomas, the labor of the Jesuits and Salesians, the discoveries of Pascal and Pasteur, or the hundreds of parochial schools that dot every continent of the globe.

The purpose of this book is to introduce students and teachers to a noble tradition of debate over the first principles of education. This debate arose in Athens, was joined by the early Christians, was extended by the scholastics, and then ended with the moderns. A debate, at its best, is like any dance. It requires a level of agreement about times and places and terms, even if after too many drinks the tango ends up looking more like a duel. Between the best minds of antiquity and the Catholic philosophers who came after them, on the nature, methods, and ends of education there has always existed a great deal of sympathy. There was debate because there was unanimity.

Already by the time of Plato and Aristotle, the Greeks had developed a pattern of education based on the study of liberal disciplines. "Liberal" these would be called because their mastery served the aim of freedom. They liberated because they lifted ignorance. In training the mind to think with rigor they offered a man the chance to step out from under the tutelage of others, so as to direct his own affairs, to know his own good. If done adequately, such an education would allow a boy or girl to know the difference between a good argument, a bad argument, and one that needed more evidence. As Aristotle explained, a liberally educated man should be able to form reasonable judgments as to the goodness or badness of the method used in any exposition. His general study would acquaint him with the principles and methods of a range of subjects, to the end that he might become competent "in all or nearly all branches of knowledge."[1] It is in this sense that liberal education contrasts with servile.

Servile education, training in technique—the sort of preparation that contemporary academies excel in—is not unimportant. More so than in any period of human history, American, Chinese, and Indian graduates can manipulate medicines that heal, build machines that serve, and produce commercials that sell. A healthy society cannot function without craftsmen. But it requires more than craftsmen. Mechanical disciplines, from carpentry to medicine, to engineering, or economics, hardly prepare students to think about the ends of their activity, the purposes toward which buildings or profit should be directed. A classical liberal education does.

In the time of the Roman Republic, a boy or girl typically began formal education, if it was available, at age seven. After an early training in music and gymnastics, the student would turn to subjects like literature, arithmetic, and music as a means of forming their intelligence in the first principles of thought and action. Students would pass through three stages. The first lasted from about ages seven to ten. Instruction in this period was given by the *ludi magister*, the elementary tutor, literally a teacher of games. Next, and most importantly, came the five years under a *grammaticus*, or grammarian. Here students were introduced to the history, geography, and poetry contained in classical texts, such as the *Iliad* or the *Aeneid*. Finally, if students went on, before beginning their career they might spend two or three years with a professional rhetorician. These years often acted as a sort of finishing school for young men on their way to law or other public careers. It was here that students also encountered philosophy, as Augustine did at age eighteen, through his study of Cicero.[2]

Christians inherited the ideal of the liberal arts from Greece and Rome, and through adaptation, transformed this pattern into their own. Under the influence of St. Augustine in particular, but also St. Basil, Cassiadorus, and others, the normal course of preparatory education would eventually include a core of seven disciplines: grammar, logic, rhetoric, arithmetic, geometry, astronomy, music. The first three study the world through language, the rest through number. All of this was in the service of producing a person capable of thinking not only of means but also of ends.

Nobody supposed that the new faith required the end of the old learning. Rather, what the Incarnation provided was a new lens. It gave Christians a new point of view from which to judge the past. Eventually, what Christians came to criticize was not so much the structure and methods of classical education, for it excelled at perfecting man's natural abilities. Where the ancients failed was to live up to their own measure. By the Christian period, pagan philosophy was plagued by self-doubt. It had become politically irrelevant. Educated Romans no longer believed in the old gods. Roman legions could still fight under the banner of Mars; but what increasingly fed the spiritual appetites of pagans were irrational mystery cults imported from the East. In the ancient world, Paganism, like Islam, failed to unite the God of the philosophers to the God of experiential religion. To Christians, the Incarnation showed how to link head with heart. Our image of God, to be sure, needed to be purified. But the Prime Mover, the divine Logos or creative reason behind the cosmos, was also the son of Mary. Reason now had a face.

How did the coming of Jesus Christ advance thinking about liberal education? For one thing, it provided Christians with a moral certainty that there need be no conflict between reason and revelation. The material world, as an ordered expression of the mind of God, was worthy of esteem and study. Science could explore nature with the faith that all learning ultimately is unified in the Mind of the Maker. It is instructive in this regard to recall that "catholic" means universal. All truth, which belongs to the Father, is also rightfully claimed by his children. It was the Church's confidence in the goodness of knowledge that encouraged European scholars to extend and far surpass the achievements of ancient science and philosophy, which they did.

Besides confidence, the Incarnation gave to study a new focus. Learning should rightly serve our temporal welfare; most of all it should promote our eternal good: happiness with God. More than love of knowledge, which the Greeks always nurtured, Christians also learned knowledge of *love*. "God is love," announced St. John.[3] Pagan audacity never reached such a pitch.

The classical ideal of the wise man was now made concrete in the person and teachings of Jesus Christ. St. Paul warned against being taken captive by deceptive philosophy "according to human tradition."[4] This son of a Pharisee was not afraid of dialectic. At the Areopagus he vigorously debated the Greeks, appealing even to their own poets and customs in defense of his cause. What Paul warned against was apathy. Christianity presented a new fact: the resurrection of a dead man. The old prophesies were fulfilled. The world had been made anew. Any philosophy that refused the testimony of apostles, that ignored the miracle of the martyrs, that despised the conversion of sinners, was a regression and a barrier to wisdom. For believers, the task of Christian *paideia* would entail nothing less than the "renewal of your mind,"[5] the long process of the elevation of nature through the effects of grace. How might this be done?

The Incarnation taught to the nations what St. Augustine would term the true *ordo amoris*, the order of love, the right ordering of our affections.[6] The wise man works backwards in accord with the end. Our end is happiness. Christ's resurrection justified our hope of lasting happiness. For this reason, winning eternal life with God, not money, or honor, or even knowledge of nature, would be for Christians the true mark of success. We should see this insight not as contradicting but as extending the best thought of the Greeks. As Cicero remarks, Socrates brought ancient philosophy down from the heavens into the city.[7] By this he meant that Socrates turned his disciples from the study of nature also to include the study of human nature. Plato and Aristotle, at least, always knew that contemplation of God was the highest form of activity.[8] Then again, not everyone can be Plato or Aristotle. And only revelation gave to men and women the confidence we need to direct our efforts toward spiritual, and not only material, goods. Thus, while Christianity encouraged knowledge, it also clarified the ultimate ends toward which knowledge ought to be directed. One mark of the de-Christianization of our schools and colleges in our time is the narrowing of our ambitions for our students, and this narrowing has led, naturally enough, to the abandonment of liberal study for the sake of mere economy.

The tradition of Catholic liberal arts education found its crowning expression, arguably, in the development of the university, a community of scholars devoted to universal knowledge from molecules to metaphysics. We still have universities. But for two hundred years now Western civilization has not shared a common mind either with itself or about its past. Is man a clever monkey or a dull angel? Is the mind suited for reality? Does freedom have a purpose? Can we perfect society? To these questions and more, classical philosophy and orthodox Christian theology gave common replies: neither, yes, yes, and, no. Though it is true that Augustine's *City of God* adds much to Plato's *Republic*, and St. Thomas's *Summa* to the *Ethics* of Aristotle, the dramatic break, from the point of view of educational theory and practice, is not between pagans and Christians, but between the moderns and everybody else. The ancients before Christ were like expectant virgins who found in the Bridegroom, we might say, the fulfillment of their hope. Contemporary agnostics, it has been observed, are more like embittered divorcees. Neither has (or had) faith; but the one came to think life never could be so good, while the other tries to forget the past like a nightmare. With the modern era, agreement dissolved and the dance came to a halt.

Who turned off the music? Long before John Dewey and R. S. Peters argued for "progressive" education, two philosophical ideas—one medieval, one early modern—had eroded confidence in the principles that justified this European tradition of education. First, was the heresy of the nominalists, second, that of the utopians. Where nominalists declared the mind had no access to heaven, utopian philosophers made it their aim, through the schools, to bring heaven down to earth. Both trends remain. Both deliver false expectations about the enterprise of education, at once diminishing and exaggerating the potential of learning to serve human happiness.

We begin with the nominalists. This school is best seen against the backdrop of the philosopher whom it originally denied and the teaching that it subsequently displaced: St. Thomas and his metaphysical realism. Since about fifty years after his death, popes have consistently held up St. Thomas Aquinas (1225–74) as the model of learning in the Church. The Fathers of Trent placed his *Summa* on the altar beside the Bible during their conclave. In 1880 he was declared Patron of Catholic Schools and Universities. St. John Paul II called him a "master of thought."[9] He is the "doctor communis" not because he made no mistakes (though he rarely did) but because his doctrine and method contain, as Leo XIII memorably said, "the seeds of almost infinite truths."[10] All this praise is for good reason. St. Thomas constructed a scaffold upon which others could build. Perhaps most importantly, from the view of the contemporary renewal of educational philosophy, is Thomas's defense of common sense: hence, his metaphysical realism. Like Aristotle, though unlike Descartes, Kant, and Hegel, Thomas begins from our ordinary experience. He is called the philosopher of common sense because his teaching explores, explains, and, better than others, defends our conviction that the mind is made to know *things*. We know, said Thomas the realist, neither as the angels know, who see without sensation, nor as the beasts know, who sense without seeing. We know like men. In us, sense and reason combine. In harmonizing Plato and Aristotle, Thomas demonstrated a way to bind together the sound insights of both the rationalist and empiricist tendencies of ancient thought, thereby saving the appearances without enslaving us to them. And here is a crucial difference between Thomas and the nominalists. While the Thomist (or realist) philosopher agrees that knowledge must begin in sensible experience, he shows how it does not end there. We can know objects not merely as they appear to the taste and touch, but also their *essence*, the form which unites my sons Peter and Joseph to my other children and to all other children of Adam. We perceive objects through sense; we proceed by reason to understand their cause, even up to their first cause.

William of Ockham (c. 1285–1347) and his followers denied this. For Ockham, there are no classes. Objects are merely discrete entities with no tie between them. Nature presents herself to sense without rhyme or reason, without, we might say, disclosing the patterns that would allow us to unite and divide between classes and establish causal links. Medieval and modern nominalists will not admit universals, not even in the mind of God. One consequence of this late medieval turn away from realism is that the human mind found itself rather alone in the universe. Without universals in things (as Aristotelians taught), without forms in the mind of God (as Platonists taught), material objects hold nothing in common, either with themselves or, as signs, with their creator. Reason has no rope to heaven. Traditional proofs for God, as well as the rational arguments against murder, theft and adultery, are no longer properly objects of knowledge, but, at best, matters of faith.[11] We might say that after the synthesis of reason and revelation that Thomas labored to achieve—the rescue of Aristotle from the Arabs and the resuscitation of Augustine from the mystical Augustinians—Ockham pushed Western philosophy back into the old natural pagan superstition, which is to believe this: that God is not only above reason but beyond reach. The influence of Ockham spread far beyond his native British shores. We find it transmitted to Luther through the German scholastic Gabriel Biel (c. 1420–95); Kant meets Ockham twice, once in his own pietistic Lutheran education, later in the Scottish nominalist David Hume.

The chief difficulty with this negative view of reason, from the point of view of education, is that it dries up confidence. In one of his last sermons, Luther famously called reason a whore.[12] The image tells. It is not that reason for him is ugly, but that it seduces. It fools men into falling into the wrong arms, when we were meant for a better mistress, theology. The wish to see faith triumph over reason is not unique to Luther. Among Christians, the temptation has always been present, popping up now with Tertullian in the third century, then again among the Franciscans in the twelfth, and in our own time with the followers of Karl Barth. The triumph of faith over reason may entice. But such a conquest would prove in the long run only a Pyrrhic victory. Faith flounders without reason for the same reason that legs fall flat without feet. The higher builds upon the lower. "Grace does not destroy nature but perfects it" (*gratia non tollat naturam, sed perficiat*).[13]

By the time we come to Immanuel Kant (1724–1804), Aquinas's famous Five Ways are abandoned and the existence of the divine is reduced to a hypothetical postulant of practical reason, assumed, but unknowable. With nominalism, and its bastard cousins, scientism and positivism, the world closes in. Reason is no longer entrusted with the full range of her powers. The mind must be content with physical causes. "Facts," by which we mean empirical observations or inferences, stand as the whole of knowledge. Anything outside of the senses is relegated to values, that is, to opinion. Such a division of knowledge is antithetical to the Catholic view of the world. For, if faith is reduced to mere opinion, if God, freedom, and immortality, and along with them, the natural law, cannot be the objects of proof, then faith is reduced to feeling and science itself is stripped of all grandeur. When schools and colleges accept such a division, when Catholics retreat into the subjective language of "values," they will find no way to defend the rationality of faith or, ultimately, the unity of the curriculum. Take God from the universe and you lose the university.

The first educational heresy is the medieval retreat from metaphysics and the concomitant lessening of our expectation for the life of the mind; the second is the modern blunder in morals, the dream of a perfect society. Once philosophers lost hope in heaven, attention naturally fell back upon the earth. Here we require a distinction. Against each of the world-denying philosophies of the East, against the Manicheans, Albigensians, and New Age gnostics of our time, Catholic culture has always affirmed the goodness of this world. Secular is not bad. It comes from the Latin, *saeculum*, which simply means age, as in the age of the Church, the time before the return of Christ. St. Benedict's monks, Paris's Notre Dame Cathedral, and Mother Teresa's sisters are evidence enough that to love the next world, in the Catholic spirit, does not mean that you abandon this one. The renewal of the mind means that you learn to love this life in the light of the Heavenly City. We may draw a contrast. For the worldly philosophers of the modern era, in the long trajectory of thinking about learning from Francis Bacon to

Machiavelli to J. S. Mill to Karl Marx, all aspirations must settle on the City of Man. And, next to bloody revolution, education became the chief instrument for its reform.

We may take Jean-Jacques Rousseau's approach to education in the *Emile* (1762) as exemplary. In this work he declared himself the originator of an entirely new approach to instruction, an approach based upon a novel view of man. Rejecting original sin, Rousseau located evil not in the individual will but in "society." Systems, not sinners, impede progress. "Man is born free," he declared at the beginning of the *Social Contract*, "and is everywhere in chains." Through his *Emile,* Rousseau proposed to Europeans and the rest of the world how we might take off our shackles. Both the problem and the remedy Rousseau proposes are distinctively modern. The ancient sage sought knowledge to overcome ignorance. The saint sought the *imitatio Christi* to recover grace. Rousseau preached authenticity. In place of the struggle over ignorance and vice, modern educational philosophers would set before their mirror the self-regarding man. Without original sin, without heaven, his fictitious model student "Emile" learned neither obedience to others nor respect for tradition, but only how to know his own mind. Nature would be Emile's teacher. Yet it is a disenchanted human nature; it is a nature that needs no grace, and one that prompts through the stirrings only of enlightened self-interest. It is through Rousseau's work, transmitted by the sociologists and psychologists who popularized him, that contemporary educators learn to value self-esteem over virtue and self-expression over obedience.

Departments of Education rarely encourage enquiry into the origins of their discipline. In my experience, young teachers tend to roll out of college and into classrooms having had precious little opportunity to reflect on the principles that are to guide their life-long practice. This can only bring disaster. For the school, from kindergarten to college, is the first front in the battle of the culture wars in our time, as in every time. And for a long time already, the dominant currents of Western culture have run downstream.

Education is not a thing. It is a method. *Educo* means to instruct, or to draw out. It is a process by which potentiality is transformed into act, by which a boy or girl becomes a man or woman. As a discipline, education takes its lead from other masters, namely philosophy and theology; "education" can no more act on its own than a hammer apart from a hand. This is to say nothing against a hammer. It is only that where it should strike, how it should pull, or when it should stay—these are derived wholly from the mind of its master, from the plan of the builder. So, when we teach or study, what do we intend to build? That is easy: man. To teach is to shape a human being. What is a human being? If we have spoken thus far of two modern heresies in education, we may now add a third lazy mental habit which we must confront in ourselves at once: the wish to avoid the question.

So, what is man? If you are Catholic, you have an answer. A man is a child of God. We are free because intelligent, responsible because free, impaired because of sin, glorious because of redemption. Buddhists, atheists, and others will take quite other views. In education you have no choice but to choose. Education is and always has been a battle between the gods. For a generation already, teachers have been taught to say that they wish children to explore their own values. This is cowardly. Teaching is violent. Every act of instruction is an incursion upon a living organism that you hope to change through the encounter. Whether your school preaches multiculturalism or militarism, whether you wish boys to be tolerant or tough, you cannot avoid preaching your cause. In short, to educate is to act, and to act is to work from the basis of some principle stated or implied. For unlike monkeys and spirits or rocks and stars for that matter, neither Sally, nor Peter, nor Billy contain within themselves all that is needed for their perfection. Homo sapiens is almost endlessly malleable. The same cradle can beget monsters and tyrants as well as saints and citizens. The boy or girl—and to a lesser extent the college freshman—is, we might say, still half-formed. My hope is that the following selections can help us form wisely.

❖

In bringing together the present collection my aim has been to make accessible some of the finest thinking about the principles of learning. I offer a few words on my choice of texts and their method of organization.

1. First, on the texts themselves. In selecting these readings I have had in mind the needs of homeschooling parents, school teachers and administrators, and above all, Catholics in teacher colleges. Drawn from a range of historical periods, these readings illustrate or argue about the first principles of education. This Reader aims to instruct in first principles, not in all principles. Another very useful approach to the Catholic tradition of education would be to focus upon particular examples of great teachers and great schools. The art of education, like the art of music, involves both theory and practice. In addition to principles, every Catholic teacher needs to grow in their experience of institutions (beginning with the family); we need to become familiar with exemplary teachers of the faith, present and past (such as St. Angela Merici, St. John Bosco, or Blessed John Henry Newman); they need practice; and they need prayer. And yet, theory deserves its due.

My aim has been to represent the Catholic tradition, not every tradition. Catholics, by definition and rather presumptuously, conceive of their tradition as containing something of "the whole." It should not surprise, then, that we would include readings from among the ancients (e.g., Plato) and our contemporaries (e.g., C. S. Lewis) who, though not confessing communion with the Catholic Church, nevertheless perceive truth about man. Should a Catholic interested in education read Kant or Rousseau? By all means. Many of the readings (e.g., Gerdil) can be adequately judged only against the background of the claims and counter-claims of the deist, secularist, or atheistic writers with whom they debate.

2. I have not produced an exhaustive "historical catalogue." There remains, nevertheless, an advantage to including texts from the past. By examining a generous selection of the best thinking about education through the ages, one can view the progression of contexts and at the same time observe that the fundamental questions of education have remained the same. For contemporary readers, direct knowledge of the past can impart confidence. The tradition of Catholic thinking about learning is long. Our memory is short. Catholic teachers today face constant agitation to upgrade their classroom technologies and techniques. And so, forewarned is forearmed. Contemporary educational practice, being wed to the often fickle social sciences, assumes that our knowledge of education, like our knowledge of the common cold or the computer chip, should advance progressively, that is to say, inevitably. This is why school-board trustees and university presidents have no qualm about imposing upon teachers (and their students) the latest "discoveries" from child-psychology and educational laboratories. In some modern academies, curricula are replaced sooner than the light bulbs. This is precisely the wrong disposition. The study of education is not like cancer research, for the reason that men are not merely molecules. Men have free will. We are born into society. And, as in other endeavors, where there is most at stake, men should move with most caution. The hubris of much modern education is made plain by the fact that so few are allowed to experiment on so many. As G. K. Chesterton once wisely put it, "it ought to be the oldest things that are taught to the youngest people, the assured and experienced truths that are put first to the baby."[14] This book offers an introduction to the "oldest things" of education.

3. The selections that form Parts One, Two, and Three take up the causes of education, the essential characteristics that define all learning activity: its purpose (or aim), its form and content (or curriculum), its method (or pedagogy). The texts of Part Four illustrate the contemporary renewal of

Temple of Concord and Roman Forum

Catholic education. Since at least the time of Pope Leo XIII, Catholics have been aware of a breakdown in modern philosophy, a breakdown that has turned education on its head. Readings in this final section are drawn from Catholics and other Christian writers who offer compelling descriptions of the problem our civilization faces and the prospects of renewal in our time. Included are selections that speak not only to liberal or general education but to a variety of contexts in which Catholics are called to study or teach: at home, at school, in college, or at the seminary.

4. Finally, a word about the introductions and study questions. As my aim has been to allow the texts to speak for themselves, my own comments are minimal. Beyond brief historical and biographical introductions, at the head of every text I offer a guide to further reading. These bibliographies are illustrative rather than exhaustive, and an interested student can use them to start, but not finish, research on a topic. Questions at the close of each selection can serve for private review or as the basis of a group discussion.

❖ PART I

The Aims of Education

Christ among the Doctors

❖ I

PLATO (427–347 BC)

The Republic

> Moreover, I said, you must not wonder that those who attain to this beatific vision are unwilling to descend to human affairs; for their souls are ever hastening into the upper world where they desire to dwell ...

As Socrates' student and Aristotle's long-time teacher, Plato was also Greece's greatest philosopher of education. The central problem of the *Republic* is how to bring forth justice in the soul and in the city. Plato's solution is prayer and education. Books 2–4 of the dialogue outline his views on early education; there he stresses the orderly habituation of the passions through music, the arts, and physical training. Books 6–7 turn to formation through philosophy. The Allegory of the Cave, given below, is Plato's most celebrated image. Here Socrates introduces his young friends Glaucon and Adiemantus to his vision of learning. Like the scriptural story of Adam and Eve in the Garden of Eden, Plato's image purports to explain how everyman recapitulates a primordial fall from innocence to ignorance, from freedom to captivity. By means of the analogy we learn that it is not politicians who most shape public opinion, but artists. It is from artists—singers, playwrights, directors—that we learn what to love and fear. Are poets the best teachers? Freedom of thought requires, in the first instance, liberation from our habitual indignation, not so that we care for nothing, but so that we might learn to care for truth over our own received opinions. Here, then, is the ultimate aim of study: to turn the soul from attachment to the shadows of opinion toward the quest for knowledge.

Further Reading: Allan Bloom, *The Republic of Plato*, second edition, with introduction and commentary (New York: Basic Books 1991); Julia Annas, *An Introduction to Plato's* Republic (Oxford: Oxford University Press, 1981); Simone Weil, *Gravity and Grace* (New York: Putnam and Sons, 1952).

❖

And now, I said, let me show in a figure how far our nature is enlightened or unenlightened: Behold! human beings living in a underground den, which has a mouth open towards the light and reaching all along the den; here they have been from their childhood, and have their legs and necks chained so that they cannot move, and can only see before them, being prevented by the chains from turning round their heads. Above and behind them a fire is blazing at a distance, and between the fire and the prisoners there is a raised way; and you will see, if you look, a low wall built along the way, like the screen which marionette players have in front of them, over which they show the puppets.

I see.

And do you see, I said, men passing along the wall carrying all sorts of vessels, and statues and figures of animals made of wood and stone and various materials, which appear over the wall? Some of them are talking, others silent.

You have shown me a strange image, and they are strange prisoners.

Like ourselves, I replied; and they see only their own shadows, or the shadows of one another, which the fire throws on the opposite wall of the cave?

True, he said; how could they see anything but the shadows if they were never allowed to move their heads?

And of the objects which are being carried in like manner they would only see the shadows?

Yes, he said.

And if they were able to converse with one another, would they not suppose that they were naming what was actually before them?

Very true.

And suppose further that the prison had an echo which came from the other side, would they not be sure to fancy when one of the passers-by spoke that the voice which they heard came from the passing shadow?

No question, he replied.

To them, I said, the truth would be literally nothing but the shadows of the images.

That is certain.

And now look again, and see what will naturally follow if the prisoners are released and disabused of their error. At first, when any of them is liberated and compelled suddenly to stand up and turn his neck round and walk and look towards the light, he will suffer sharp pains; the glare will distress him, and he will be unable to see the realities of which in his former state he

had seen the shadows; and then conceive some one saying to him, that what
he saw before was an illusion, but that now, when he is approaching nearer
to being and his eye is turned towards more real existence, he has a clearer
vision—what will be his reply? And you may further imagine that his in-
structor is pointing to the objects as they pass and requiring him to name
them—will he not be perplexed? Will he not fancy that the shadows which
he formerly saw are truer than the objects which are now shown to him?

Far truer.

And if he is compelled to look straight at the light, will he not have a
pain in his eyes which will make him turn away to take refuge in the objects of vision which he can see, and which he will conceive to be in reality
clearer than the things which are now being shown to him?

True, he said.

[And suppose once more, that he is reluctantly dragged up a steep and
rugged ascent, and held fast until he is forced into the presence of the sun
himself, is he not likely to be pained and irritated? When he approaches the
light his eyes will be dazzled, and he will not be able to see anything at all of
what are now called realities.]

inability to go back to ignorance

Not all in a moment, he said.

[He will require to grow accustomed to the sight of the upper world.
And first he will see the shadows best, next the reflections of men and other objects in the water, and then the objects themselves; then he will gaze
upon the light of the moon and the stars and the spangled heaven; and he
will see the sky and the stars by night better than the sun or the light of the
sun by day?

Certainly.

Last of all he will be able to see the sun, and not mere reflections of
him in the water, but he will see him in his own proper place, and not in
another; and he will contemplate him as he is.] *← not what we wish we were*

Certainly.

He will then proceed to argue that this is he who gives the season and
the years, and is the guardian of all that is in the visible world, and in a certain way the cause of all things which he and his fellows have been accustomed to behold?

Clearly, he said, he would first see the sun and then reason about him.

And when he remembered his old habitation, and the wisdom of the
den and his fellow-prisoners, do you not suppose that he would felicitate
himself on the change, and pity them?

Certainly, he would.

Plato: form of good = good of good = sun

leaving our prison

And if they were in the habit of conferring honours among themselves on those who were quickest to observe the passing shadows and to remark which of them went before, and which followed after, and which were together; and who were therefore best able to draw conclusions as to the future, do you think that he would care for such honours and glories, or envy the possessors of them? Would he not say with Homer, "Better to be the poor servant of a poor master," and to endure anything, rather than think as they do and live after their manner?

Yes, he said, I think that he would rather suffer anything than entertain these false notions and live in this miserable manner.

Imagine once more, I said, such an one coming suddenly out of the sun to be replaced in his old situation; would he not be certain to have his eyes full of darkness?

To be sure, he said.

And if there were a contest, and he had to compete in measuring the shadows with the prisoners who had never moved out of the den, while his sight was still weak, and before his eyes had become steady (and the time which would be needed to acquire this new habit of sight might be very considerable), would he not be ridiculous? Men would say of him that up he went and down he came without his eyes; and that it was better not even to think of ascending; and if any one tried to loose another and lead him up to the light, let them only catch the offender, and they would put him to death.

No question, he said.

This entire allegory, I said, you may now append, dear Glaucon, to the previous argument; the prison-house is the world of sight, the light of the fire is the sun, and you will not misapprehend me if you interpret the journey upwards to be the ascent of the soul into the intellectual world according to my poor belief, which, at your desire, I have expressed—whether rightly or wrongly God knows. But, whether true or false, my opinion is that in the world of knowledge the idea of good appears last of all, and [the good] is seen only with an effort; and, when seen, is also inferred to be the universal author of all things beautiful and right, parent of light and of the lord of light in this visible world, and the immediate source of reason and truth in the intellectual; and that this is the power upon which he who would act rationally either in public or private life must have his eye fixed.

I agree, he said, as far as I am able to understand you.

Moreover, I said, you must not wonder that those who attain to this beatific vision are unwilling to descend to human affairs; for their souls are

Idea of Good is a standard

ever hastening into the upper world where they desire to dwell; which desire of theirs is very natural, if our allegory may be trusted.

Yes, very natural.

And is there anything surprising in one who passes from divine contemplations to the evil state of man, misbehaving himself in a ridiculous manner; if, while his eyes are blinking and before he has become accustomed to the surrounding darkness, he is compelled to fight in courts of law, or in other places, about the images or the shadows of images of justice, and is endeavouring to meet the conceptions of those who have never yet seen absolute justice?

Anything but surprising, he replied.

Any one who has common sense will remember that the bewilderments of the eyes are of two kinds, and arise from two causes, either from coming out of the light or from going into the light, which is true of the mind's eye, quite as much as of the bodily eye; and he who remembers this when he sees any one whose vision is perplexed and weak, will not be too ready to laugh; he will first ask whether that soul of man has come out of the brighter life, and is unable to see because unaccustomed to the dark, or having turned from darkness to the day is dazzled by excess of light. And he will count the one happy in his condition and state of being, and he will pity the other; or, if he have a mind to laugh at the soul which comes from below into the light, there will be more reason in this than in the laugh which greets him who returns from above out of the light into the den.

That, he said, is a very just distinction.

But then, if I am right, certain professors of education must be wrong when they say that they can put a knowledge into the soul which was not there before, like sight into blind eyes.

They undoubtedly say this, he replied.

[Whereas, our argument shows that the power and capacity of learning exists in the soul already; and that just as the eye was unable to turn from darkness to light without the whole body, so too the instrument of knowledge can only by the movement of the whole soul be turned from the world of becoming into that of being, and learn by degrees to endure the sight of being, and of the brightest and best of being, or in other words, of the good.

Very true.

And must there not be some art which will effect conversion in the easiest and quickest manner; not implanting the faculty of sight, for that exists already, but has been turned in the wrong direction, and is looking away from the truth?]

Yes, he said, such an art may be presumed.

And whereas the other so-called virtues of the soul seem to be akin to bodily qualities, for even when they are not originally innate they can be implanted later by habit and exercise, the virtue of wisdom more than anything else contains a divine element which always remains, and by this conversion is rendered useful and profitable; or, on the other hand, hurtful and useless. Did you never observe the narrow intelligence flashing from the keen eye of a clever rogue—how eager he is, how clearly his paltry soul sees the way to his end; he is the reverse of blind, but his keen eye-sight is forced into the service of evil, and he is mischievous in proportion to his cleverness?

Very true, he said.

But what if there had been a circumcision of such natures in the days of their youth; and they had been severed from those sensual pleasures, such as eating and drinking, which, like leaden weights, were attached to them at their birth, and which drag them down and turn the vision of their souls upon the things that are below—if, I say, they had been released from these impediments and turned in the opposite direction, the very same faculty in them would have seen the truth as keenly as they see what their eyes are turned to now.

Very likely.

Yes, I said; and there is another thing which is likely, or rather a necessary inference from what has preceded, that neither the uneducated and uninformed of the truth, nor yet those who never make an end of their education, will be able ministers of State; not the former, because they have no single aim of duty which is the rule of all their actions, private as well as public; nor the latter, because they will not act at all except upon compulsion, fancying that they are already dwelling apart in the islands of the blest.

Very true, he replied.

Then, I said, the business of us who are the founders of the State will be to compel the best minds to attain that knowledge which we have already shown to be the greatest of all—they must continue to ascend until they arrive at the good; but when they have ascended and seen enough we must not allow them to do as they do now.

What do you mean?

I mean that they remain in the upper world: but this must not be allowed; they must be made to descend again among the prisoners in the den, and partake of their labours and honours, whether they are worth having or not.

But is not this unjust? he said; ought we to give them a worse life, when they might have a better?

You have again forgotten, my friend, I said, the intention of the legislator, who did not aim at making any one class in the State happy above the rest; the happiness was to be in the whole State, and he held the citizens together by persuasion and necessity, making them benefactors of the State, and therefore benefactors of one another; to this end he created them, not to please themselves, but to be his instruments in binding up the State.

True, he said, I had forgotten.

Observe, Glaucon, that there will be no injustice in compelling our philosophers to have a care and providence of others; we shall explain to them that in other States, men of their class are not obliged to share in the toils of politics: and this is reasonable, for they grow up at their own sweet will, and the government would rather not have them. Being self-taught, they cannot be expected to show any gratitude for a culture which they have never received. But we have brought you into the world to be rulers of the hive, kings of yourselves and of the other citizens, and have educated you far better and more perfectly than they have been educated, and you are better able to share in the double duty. [Wherefore each of you, when his turn comes, must go down to the general underground abode, and get the habit of seeing in the dark. When you have acquired the habit, you will see ten thousand times better than the inhabitants of the den, and you will know what the several images are, and what they represent, because you have seen the beautiful and just and good in their truth.] And thus our State, which is also yours, will be a reality, and not a dream only, and will be administered in a spirit unlike that of other States, in which men fight with one another about shadows only and are distracted in the struggle for power, which in their eyes is a great good. Whereas the truth is that the State in which the rulers are most reluctant to govern is always the best and most quietly governed, and the State in which they are most eager, the worst.

Quite true, he replied.

And will our pupils, when they hear this, refuse to take their turn at the toils of State, when they are allowed to spend the greater part of their time with one another in the heavenly light?

Impossible, he answered; for they are just men, and the commands which we impose upon them are just; there can be no doubt that every one of them will take office as a stern necessity, and not after the fashion of our present rulers of State.

Yes, my friend, I said; and there lies the point. You must contrive for

not just about getting out of cave, but going back down with the ability to see reality.

your future rulers another and a better life than that of a ruler, and then you may have a well-ordered State; for only in the State which offers this, will they rule who are truly rich, not in silver and gold, but in virtue and wisdom, which are the true blessings of life. Whereas if they go to the administration of public affairs, poor and hungering after their own private advantage, thinking that hence they are to snatch the chief good, order there can never be; for they will be fighting about office, and the civil and domestic broils which thus arise will be the ruin of the rulers themselves and of the whole State.

Most true, he replied.

And the only life which looks down upon the life of political ambition is that of true philosophy. Do you know of any other?

Indeed, I do not, he said.

And those who govern ought not to be lovers of the task? For, if they are, there will be rival lovers, and they will fight.

No question.

Who then are those whom we shall compel to be guardians? Surely they will be the men who are wisest about affairs of State, and by whom the State is best administered, and who at the same time have other honours and another and a better life than that of politics?

They are the men, and I will choose them, he replied.

And now shall we consider in what way such guardians will be produced, and how they are to be brought from darkness to light—as some are said to have ascended from the world below to the gods?

By all means, he replied.

Review and Discussion Questions

1. "The Cave" is an image. What does Socrates say it represents?

2. Describe four details of the image (e.g., chains) and tell what they signify.

3. What makes escape difficult?

4. Often philosophers are represented as impractical and useless to political life. In what senses might Plato both agree and disagree with this view?

❖ 2

ARISTOTLE (384–22 BC)

On the Parts of Animals

In the foregoing we have an example of the method which we must adopt,
and also an example of the kind of phenomena, the causes of which we have
to investigate.

If, in the Cave Allegory, Plato turns our minds upward to the study of ultimate causes, in this selection Aristotle defends the value of having our feet
planted firmly upon the earth. Though metaphysics (the study of being as
being) yields the highest satisfaction, the human body, snails, and stones,
are not without their own attraction. As he argues, no part of nature should
be shunned "for each and all will reveal to us something natural and something beautiful." The liberally educated man distinguishes himself not only
by this heathy curiosity but by an assured sense of method. Just as he is interested in all parts of nature, so too he understands how each part should
be approached. Mastery of all fields is impossible; but a liberal education
gives familiarity with the basic principles of each science. Along the way, Aristotle introduces us to the four causes, a refutation of a naturalistic (i.e., ma-
terialistic) science, and a sturdy defense of the view that nature acts for ends.

Further Reading: Aristotle's *Metaphysics* [Book 1] in *The Complete Works of Aristotle:* Volume 2,
ed. Jonathan Barnes (Princeton, N.J.: Princeton University Press, 1984); Marie I. George, "The
Notion of Paideia in Aristotle's *De Partibus Animalium,*" *American Catholic Philosophical Quar-
terly* 67, no. 3 (Summer 1993): 299–319; Ralph McInerny, Preambula Fidei: *Thomism and the God
of Philosophy* (Washington, D.C.: The Catholic University of America Press, 2006).

❖

Every systematic science, the humblest and the noblest alike, seems to
admit of two distinct kinds of proficiency; one of which may be properly
called scientific knowledge of the subject, while the other is a kind of educational acquaintance with it. For an educated man should be able to form
a fair off-hand judgement as to the goodness or badness of the method used

by a professor in his exposition. To be educated is in fact to be able to do this; and even the man of universal education we deem to be such in virtue of his having this ability. It will, however, of course, be understood that we only ascribe universal education to one who in his own individual person is thus critical in all or nearly all branches of knowledge, and not to one who has a like ability merely in some special subject. For it is possible for a man to have this competence in some one branch of knowledge without having it in all.

It is plain then that, as in other sciences, so in that which inquires into nature, there must be certain canons, by reference to which a hearer shall be able to criticize the method of a professed exposition, quite independently of the question whether the statements made be true or false. Ought we, for instance (to give an illustration of what I mean), to begin by discussing each separate species—man, lion, ox, and the like—taking each kind in hand independently of the rest, or ought we rather to deal first with the attributes which they have in common in virtue of some common element of their nature, and proceed from this as a basis for the consideration of them separately? For genera that are quite distinct yet oftentimes present many identical phenomena, sleep, for instance, respiration, growth, decay, death, and other similar affections and conditions, which may be passed over for the present, as we are not yet prepared to treat of them with clearness and precision. Now it is plain that if we deal with each species independently of the rest, we shall frequently be obliged to repeat the same statements over and over again; for horse and dog and man present, each and all, every one of the phenomena just enumerated. A discussion therefore of the attributes of each such species separately would necessarily involve frequent repetitions as to characters, themselves identical but recurring in animals specifically distinct. (Very possibly also there may be other characters which, though they present specific differences, yet come under one and the same category. For instance, flying, swimming, walking, creeping, are plainly specifically distinct, but yet are all forms of animal progression.) We must, then, have some clear understanding as to the manner in which our investigation is to be conducted; whether, I mean, we are first to deal with the common or generic characters, and afterwards to take into consideration special peculiarities; or whether we are to start straight off with the ultimate species. For as yet no definite rule has been laid down in this matter. So also there is a like uncertainty as to another point now to be mentioned. Ought the writer who deals with the works of nature to follow the plan adopted by the mathematicians in their astronomical demonstrations, and after considering the phenomena presented by animals, and their several parts, proceed subsequently to treat of the causes and the reason why; or ought he to follow some other method? And when these questions are answered, there yet remains another. The causes concerned in the generation of the works of nature are, as we see, more than one. There is the final cause and there is the motor cause. Now we must decide which of these two causes comes first, which second. Plainly, however, that cause is the first which we call the final one. For this is the Reason, and the Reason forms the starting-point, alike in the works of art and in works of nature. For consider how the physician or how the builder sets about his work. He starts by forming for himself a definite picture, in the one case perceptible to mind, in the other to sense, of his end—the physician of health, the builder of a house—and this he holds forward as the reason and explanation of each subsequent step that he takes, and of his acting in this or that way as the case may be. Now in the works of nature the good end and the final cause is still more dominant than in works of art such as these, nor is necessity a factor with the same significance in them all; though almost all writers, while they try to refer their origin to this cause, do so without distinguishing the various senses in which the term necessity is used. For there is absolute necessity, manifested in eternal phenomena; and there is hypothetical necessity, manifested in everything that is generated by nature as in everything that is produced by art, be it a house or what it may. For if a house or other such final object is to be realized, it is necessary that such and such material shall exist; and it is necessary that first this then that shall be produced, and first this and then that set in motion, and so on in continuous succession, until the end and final result is reached, for the sake of which each prior thing is produced and exists. As with these productions of art, so also is it with the productions of nature. The mode of necessity, however, and the mode of ratiocination are different in natural science from what they are in the theoretical sciences, of which we have spoken elsewhere. For in the latter the starting-point is that which is; in the former that which is to be. For it is that which is yet to be— health, let us say, or a man—that, owing to its being of such and such character, necessitates the pre-existence or previous production of this and that antecedent; and not this or that antecedent which, because it exists or has been generated, makes it necessary that health or a man is in, or shall come into, existence. Nor is it possible to track back the series of necessary antecedents to a starting-point, of which you can say that, existing itself from eternity, it has determined their existence as its consequent. These however again, are matters that have been dealt with in another treatise. There too it was stated in what cases absolute and hypothetical necessity exist; in what cases also the proposition expressing hypothetical necessity is simply convertible, and what cause it is that determines this convertibility.

Another matter which must not be passed over without consideration is, whether the proper subject of our exposition is that with which the ancient writers concerned themselves, namely, what is the process of formation of each animal; or whether it is not rather, what are the characters of a given creature when formed. For there is no small difference between these two views. The best course appears to be that we should follow the method already mentioned, and begin with the phenomena presented by each group of animals, and, when this is done, proceed afterwards to state the causes of those phenomena, and to deal with their evolution [generation]. For elsewhere, as for instance in house building, this is the true sequence. The plan of the house, or the house, has this and that form; and because it has this and that form, therefore is its construction carried out in this or that manner. For the process of evolution [i.e., generation] is for the sake of the thing finally evolved, and not this for the sake of the process. Empedocles, then, was in error when he said that many of the characters presented by animals were merely the results of incidental occurrences during their development; for instance, that the backbone was divided as it is into vertebrae, because it happened to be broken owing to the contorted position of the fetus in the womb. In so saying he overlooked the fact that propagation implies a creative seed endowed with certain formative properties. Secondly, he neglected another fact, namely, that the parent animal pre-exists, not only in idea, but actually in time. For man is generated from man; and thus it is the possession of certain characters by the parent that determines the development of like characters in the child. The same statement holds good also for the operations of art, and even for those which are apparently spontaneous. For the same result as is produced by art may occur spontaneously. Spontaneity, for instance, may bring about the restoration of health. The products of art, however, require the pre-existence of an efficient cause homogeneous with themselves, such as the statuary's art, which must necessarily precede the statue; for this cannot possibly be produced spontaneously. Art indeed consists in the conception of the result to be produced before its realization in the material. As with spontaneity, so with chance; for this also produces the same result as art, and by the same process.

The fittest mode, then, of treatment is to say, a man has such and such parts, because the conception of a man includes their presence, and because they are necessary conditions of his existence, or, if we cannot quite say this, which would be best of all, then the next thing to it, namely, that it is either quite impossible for him to exist without them, or, at any rate, that it is better for him that they should be there; and their existence involves the existence of other antecedents. Thus we should say, because man is an animal with such and such characters, therefore is the process of his development necessarily such as it is; and therefore is it accomplished in such and such an order, this part being formed first, that next, and so on in succession; and after a like fashion should we explain the evolution of all other works of nature.

Now that with which the ancient writers, who first philosophized about Nature, busied themselves, was the material principle and the material cause. They inquired what this is, and what its character; how the universe is generated out of it, and by what motor influence, whether, for instance, by antagonism or friendship, whether by intelligence or spontaneous action, the substratum of matter being assumed to have certain inseparable properties; fire, for instance, to have a hot nature, earth a cold one; the former to be light, the latter heavy. For even the genesis of the universe is thus explained by them. After a like fashion do they deal also with the development of plants and of animals. They say, for instance, that the water contained in the body causes by its currents the formation of the stomach and the other receptacles of food or of excretion; and that the breath by its passage breaks open the outlets of the nostrils; air and water being the materials of which bodies are made; for all represent nature as composed of such or similar substances.

But if men and animals and their several parts are natural phenomena, then the natural philosopher must take into consideration not merely the ultimate substances of which they are made, but also flesh, bone, blood, and all other homogeneous parts; not only these, but also the heterogeneous parts, such as face, hand, foot; and must examine how each of these comes to be what it is, and in virtue of what force. For to say what are the ultimate substances out of which an animal is formed, to state, for instance, that it is made of fire or earth, is no more sufficient than would be a similar account in the case of a couch or the like. For we should not be content with saying that the couch was made of bronze or wood or whatever it might be, but should try to describe its design or mode of composition in preference to the material; or, if we did deal with the material, it would at any rate be with the concretion of material and form. For a couch is such and such a form embodied in this or that matter, or such and such a matter with this or that form; so that its shape and structure must be included in our description. For the formal nature is of greater importance than the material nature.

Does, then, configuration and colour constitute the essence of the various animals and of their several parts? For if so, what Democritus says will be strictly correct. For such appears to have been his notion. At any rate he says that it is evident to every one what form it is that makes the man, seeing that he is recognizable by his shape and colour. And yet a dead body has exactly the same configuration as a living one; but for all that is not a man. So also no hand of bronze or wood or constituted in any but the appropriate way can possibly be a hand in more than name. For like a physician in a painting, or like a flute in a sculpture, in spite of its name it will be unable to do the office which that name implies. Precisely in the same way no part of a dead body, such I mean as its eye or its hand, is really an eye or a hand. To say, then, that shape and colour constitute the animal is an inadequate statement, and is much the same as if a woodcarver were to insist that the hand he had cut out was really a hand. Yet the physiologists, when they give an account of the development and causes of the animal form, speak very much like such a craftsman. What, however, I would ask, are the forces by which the hand or the body was fashioned into its shape? The woodcarver will perhaps say, by the axe or the auger; the physiologist, by air and by earth. Of these two answers the artificer's is the better, but it is nevertheless insufficient. For it is not enough for him to say that by the stroke of his tool this part was formed into a concavity, that into a flat surface; but he must state the reasons why he struck his blow in such a way as to effect this, and what his final object was; namely, that the piece of wood should develop eventually into this or that shape. It is plain, then, that the teaching of the old physiologists is inadequate, and that the true method is to state what the definitive characters are that distinguish the animal as a whole; to explain what it is both in substance and in form, and to deal after the same fashion with its several organs; in fact, to proceed in exactly the same way as we should do, were we giving a complete description of a couch.

If now this something that constitutes the form of the living being be the soul, or part of the soul, or something that without the soul cannot exist; as would seem to be the case, seeing at any rate that when the soul departs, what is left is no longer a living animal, and that none of the parts remain what they were before, excepting in mere configuration, like the animals that in the fable are turned into stone; if, I say, this be so, then it will come within the province of the natural philosopher to inform himself concerning the soul, and to treat of it, either in its entirety, or, at any rate, of that part of it which constitutes the essential character of an animal; and it will be his duty to say what this soul or this part of a soul is; and to discuss the attributes that attach to this essential character, especially as nature is spoken of in two senses, and the nature of a thing is either its matter or its essence; nature as essence including both the motor cause and the final cause. Now it is in the latter of these two senses that either the whole soul or some part of it constitutes the nature of an animal; and inasmuch as it is the presence of the soul that enables matter to constitute the animal nature, much more than it is the presence of matter which so enables the soul, the inquirer into nature is bound on every ground to treat of the soul rather than of the matter. For though the wood of which they are made constitutes the couch and the tripod, it only does so because it is capable of receiving such and such a form.

What has been said suggests the question, whether it is the whole soul or only some part of it, the consideration of which comes within the province of natural science. Now if it be of the whole soul that this should treat, then there is no place for any other philosophy beside it. For as it belongs in all cases to one and the same science to deal with correlated subjects—one and the same science, for instance, deals with sensation and with the objects of sense—and as therefore the intelligent soul and the objects of intellect, being correlated, must belong to one and the same science, it follows that natural science will have to include the whole universe in its province. But perhaps it is not the whole soul, nor all its parts collectively, that constitutes the source of motion; but there may be one part, identical with that in plants, which is the source of growth, another, namely the sensory part, which is the source of change of quality, while still another, and this not the intellectual part, is the source of locomotion. I say not the intellectual part; for other animals than man have the power of locomotion, but in none but him is there intellect. Thus then it is plain that it is not of the whole soul that we have to treat. For it is not the whole soul that constitutes the animal nature, but only some part or parts of it. Moreover, it is impossible that any abstraction can form a subject of natural science, seeing that everything that Nature makes is means to an end. For just as human creations are the products of art, so living objects are manifest in the products of an analogous cause or principle, not external but internal, derived like the hot and the cold from the environing universe. And that the heaven, if it had an origin, was evolved [generated] and is maintained by such a cause, there is therefore even more reason to believe, than that mortal animals so originated. For order and definiteness are much more plainly manifest in the celestial bodies than in our own frame; while change and chance are characteristic of the perishable things of earth. Yet there are some who, while they allow that every animal exists and was generated by nature, nevertheless hold that the heaven was constructed to be what it is by chance and spontaneity; the heaven, in which not the faintest sign of haphazard or of disorder is discernible! Again, whenever there is plainly some final end, to which a motion tends should nothing stand in the way, we always say that such final end is the aim or purpose of the motion; and from this it is evident that there must be a something or other really existing, corresponding to what we call by the name of Nature. For a given germ [or seed] does not give rise to any chance living being, nor spring from any chance one; but each germ springs from a definite parent and gives rise to a definite progeny. And thus it is the germ that is the ruling influence and fabricator of the offspring. For these it is by nature, the offspring being at any rate that which in nature will spring from it. At the same time the offspring is anterior to the germ; for germ and perfected progeny are related as the developmental process and the result. Anterior, however, to both germ and product is the organism from which the germ was derived. For every germ implies two organisms, the parent and the progeny. For germ or seed is both the seed of the organism from which it came, of the horse, for instance, from which it was derived, and the seed of the organism that will eventually arise from it, of the mule, for example, which is developed from the seed of the horse. The same seed then is the seed both of the horse and of the mule, though in different ways as here set forth. Moreover, the seed is potentially that which will spring from it, and the relation of potentiality to actuality we know.

There are then two causes, namely, necessity and the final end. For many things are produced, simply as the results of necessity. It may, however, be asked, of what mode of necessity are we speaking when we say this. For it can be of neither of those two modes which are set forth in the philosophical treatises. There is, however, the third mode, in such things at any rate as are generated. For instance, we say that food is necessary; because an animal cannot possibly do without it. This third mode is what may be called hypothetical necessity. Here is another example of it. If a piece of wood is to be split with an axe, the axe must of necessity be hard; and, if hard, must of necessity be made of bronze or iron. Now exactly in the same way the body, which like the axe is an instrument—for both the body as a whole and its several parts individually have definite operations for which they are made—just in the same way, I say, the body, if it is to do its work, must of necessity be of such and such a character, and made of such and such materials.

It is plain then that there are two modes of causation, and that both of these must, so far as possible, be taken into account in explaining the works of nature, or that at any rate an attempt must be made to include them both; and that those who fail in this tell us in reality nothing about nature. For primary cause constitutes the nature of an animal much more than does its matter. There are indeed passages in which even Empedocles hits upon this, and following the guidance of fact, finds himself constrained to speak of the ratio (logos) as constituting the essence and real nature of things. Such, for instance, is the case when he explains what is a bone. For he does not merely describe its material, and say it is this one element, or those two or three elements, or a compound of all the elements, but states the ratio (logos) of their combination. As with a bone, so manifestly is it with the flesh and all other similar parts.

The reason why our predecessors failed in hitting upon this method of treatment was, that they were not in possession of the notion of essence, nor of any definition of substance. The first who came near it was Democritus, and he was far from adopting it as a necessary method in natural science, but was merely brought to it, in spite of himself, by constraint of facts. In the time of Socrates a nearer approach was made to the method. But at this period men gave up inquiring into the works of nature, and philosophers diverted their attention to political science and to the virtues which benefit mankind.

Of the method itself the following is an example. In dealing with respiration we must show that it takes place for such or such a final object; and we must also show that this and that part of the process is necessitated by this and that other stage of it. By necessity we shall sometimes mean hypothetical necessity, the necessity, that is, that the requisite antecedents shall be there, if the final end is to be reached; and sometimes absolute necessity, such necessity as that which connects substances and their inherent properties and characters. For the alternate discharge and re-entrance of heat and the inflow of air are necessary if we are to live. Here we have at once a necessity in the former of the two senses. But the alternation of heat and refrigeration produces of necessity an alternate admission and discharge of the outer air, and this is a necessity of the second kind.

In the foregoing we have an example of the method which we must adopt, and also an example of the kind of phenomena, the causes of which we have to investigate.

...

Of things constituted by nature some are ungenerated, imperishable, and eternal, while others are subject to generation and decay. The former are excellent beyond compare and divine, but less accessible to knowledge. The evidence that might throw light on them, and on the problems which we long to solve respecting them, is furnished but scantily by sensation; whereas respecting perishable plants and animals we have abundant information, living as we do in their midst, and ample data may be collected concerning all their various kinds, if only we are willing to take sufficient pains. Both departments, however, have their special charm. The scanty conceptions to which we can attain of celestial things give us, from their excellence, more pleasure than all our knowledge of the world in which we live; just as a half glimpse of persons that we love is more delightful than a leisurely view of other things, whatever their number and dimensions. On the other hand, in certitude and in completeness our knowledge of terrestrial things has the advantage. Moreover, their greater nearness and affinity to us balances somewhat the loftier interest of the heavenly things that are the objects of the higher philosophy. Having already treated of the celestial world, as far as our conjectures could reach, we proceed to treat of animals, without omitting, to the best of our ability, any member of the kingdom, however ignoble. For if some have no graces to charm the sense, yet even these, by disclosing to intellectual perception the artistic spirit that designed them, give immense pleasure to all who can trace links of causation, and are inclined to philosophy. Indeed, it would be strange if mimic representations of them were attractive, because they disclose the mimetic skill of the painter or sculptor, and the original realities themselves were not more interesting, to all at any rate who have eyes to discern the reasons that determined their formation. We therefore must not recoil with childish aversion from the examination of the humbler animals. Every realm of nature is marvellous: and as Heraclitus, when the strangers who came to visit him found him warming himself at the furnace in the kitchen and hesitated to go in, reported to have bidden them not to be afraid to enter, as even in that kitchen divinities were present, so we should venture on the study of every kind of animal without distaste; for each and all will reveal to us something natural and something beautiful. Absence of haphazard and conduciveness of everything to an end are to be found in Nature's works in the highest degree, and the resultant end of her generations and combinations is a form of the beautiful.

If any person thinks the examination of the rest of the animal kingdom an unworthy task, he must hold in like disesteem the study of man. For no one can look at the primordia of the human frame—blood, flesh, bones, vessels, and the like—without much repugnance. Moreover, when any one of the parts or structures, be it which it may, is under discussion, it must not be supposed that it is its material composition to which attention is being directed or which is the object of the discussion, but the relation of such part to the total form. Similarly, the true object of architecture is not bricks, mortar, or timber, but the house; and so the principal object of natural philosophy is not the material elements, but their composition, and the totality of the form, independently of which they have no existence.

The course of exposition must be first to state the attributes common to whole groups of animals, and then to attempt to give their explanation. Many groups, as already noticed, present common attributes, that is to say, in some cases absolutely identical affections, and absolutely identical organs—feet, feathers, scales, and the like—while in other groups the affections and organs are only so far identical as that they are analogous. For instance, some groups have lungs, others have no lung, but an organ analogous to a lung in its place; some have blood, others have no blood, but a fluid analogous to blood, and with the same office. To treat of the common attributes in connexion with each individual group would involve, as already suggested, useless iteration. For many groups have common attributes. So much for this topic....

Review and Discussion Questions

1. What are the two types of proficiency that Aristotle names? Reflect upon your own education up to this point. Identify where you have proficiency in one type, and where in the other.

2. What is the chief benefit that a liberal education can impart?

3. For what reason does Aristotle reject a strictly material account of causation?

4. With reference to the causes of a house, describe and illustrate each of its four causes (material, formal, efficient, and final).

5. Aristotle proposes that nature acts for "ends." Cite evidence for this view from your own experience of nature.

❖ 3

QUINTILIAN (35–C. 100)

The Institutes of Oratory

I would express a wish that even the lines that are set him for his imitation in
writing should not contain useless sentences, but such as convey some moral
instruction.

Along with Cicero, Quintilian was Rome's eminent philosopher of education. His *Institutes of Oratory* comprise ten books that set forth his theoretical and practical reflections on the art of rhetoric. Combining both the
philosophical and rhetorical traditions of the ancients, Quintilian's ideal
wise-man is an orator, or public philosopher. In this view, the orator is not
a sophist. Effective speech is his aim, but so is wisdom. The political community depends upon men and women who can defend justice before a
crowd. The *Institutes* suggests how such leaders are formed. In the following
excerpt Quintilian stresses the formative influence of habit, especially upon
the young. The young soul imitates. Teachers, therefore, should model correct diction and demand legible script; more important than sound technique, though, is the witness of a teacher's own noble conduct.

Further Reading: Plato, *Republic*, Book 4, trans. Allan Bloom (New York: Basic Books, 1991);
Cicero, *On Invention*, Loeb Classical Library no. 386, trans. H. M. Hubbell (Cambridge, Mass.:
Harvard University Press, 1949); Stanley Bonner, *Education in Ancient Rome* (Berkeley: University of California Press, 1977); George A. Kennedy, *Classical Rhetoric and Its Christian and Secular Tradition from Ancient to Modern Times* (London: Croom Helm, 1980).

❖

Let a father, then, as soon as his son is born, conceive first of all the best
possible hopes of him, for he will thus grow the more solicitous about his
improvement from the very beginning. It is a complaint without foundation that "to very few people is granted the faculty of comprehending what
is imparted to them, and that most, through dullness of understanding,
lose their labor and their time." On the contrary, you will find the greater

number of men both ready in conceiving and quick in learning, since such quickness is natural to man. As birds are born to fly, horses to run, and wild beasts to show fierceness, so to us peculiarly belong activity and sagacity of understanding; hence the origin of the mind is thought to be from heaven. But dull and unteachable persons are no more produced in the course of nature than are persons marked by monstrosity and deformities; such are certainly but few. It will be a proof of this assertion that among boys, good promise is shown in the far greater number; and if it passes off in the progress of time, it is manifest that it was not natural ability, but care, that was wanting. But one surpasses another, you will say, in ability. I grant that this is true, but only so far as to accomplish more or less; there is no one who has not gained something by study. Let him who is convinced of this truth, bestow, as soon as he becomes a parent, the most vigilant possible care on cherishing the hopes of a future orator.

Before all things, let the talk of the child's nurses not be ungrammatical. Chrysippus wished them, if possible, to be women of some knowledge; at any rate he would have the best chosen, as far as circumstances would allow. To their morals, doubtless, attention is first to be paid, but let them also speak with propriety. It is they that the child will hear first; it is their words that he will try to form by imitation. We are by nature most tenacious of what we have imbibed in our infant years, as the flavor with which you scent vessels when new remains in them, nor can the colors of wool, for which its plain whiteness has been exchanged, be effaced. Those very habits, which are of a more objectionable nature, adhere with the greater tenacity, for good ones are easily changed for the worse, but when will you change bad ones into good? Let the child not be accustomed, therefore, even while he is yet an infant, to phraseology which must be unlearned.

In parents I should wish that there should be as much learning as possible. Nor do I speak, indeed, merely of fathers, for we have heard that Cornelia, the mother of the Gracchi (whose very learned writing in her letters has come down to posterity), contributed greatly to their eloquence; the daughter of Laelius is said to have exhibited her father's elegance in her conversation; and the oration of the daughter of Quintus Hortensius, delivered before the Triumviri, is read not merely as an honor to her sex. Nor let those parents, who have not had the fortune to get learning themselves, bestow the less care on the instruction of their children, but let them, on this very account, be more solicitous as to other particulars.

Of the boys, among whom he who is destined to this prospect is to be educated, the same may be said as concerning nurses.

Of *paedagogi* this further may be said, that they should either be men of acknowledged learning, which I should wish to be the first object, or that they should be conscious of their want of learning; for none are more pernicious than those who, having gone some little beyond the first elements, clothe themselves in a mistaken persuasion of their own knowledge. Since they disdain to yield to those who are skilled in teaching and, growing imperious, and sometimes fierce, in a certain right, as it were, of exercising their authority (with which that sort of men are generally puffed up), they teach only their own folly. Nor is their misconduct less prejudicial to the manners of their pupils; for Leonides, the tutor of Alexander, as is related by Diogenes of Babylon, tinctured him with certain bad habits, which adhered to him, from his childish education, even when he was grown up and become the greatest of kings.

If I seem to my reader to require a great deal, let him consider that it is an orator that is to be educated, an arduous task even when nothing is deficient for the formation of his character; and that more and more difficult labours yet remain. There is need of constant study, the most excellent teachers, and a variety of mental exercises. The best of rules, therefore, are to be laid down, and if any one shall refuse to observe them, the fault will lie not in the method, but in the man.

If, however, it should not be the good fortune of children to have such nurses as I should wish, let them at least have one attentive *paedagogus*, not unskilled in language, who, if anything is spoken incorrectly by the nurse in the presence of his pupil, may at once correct it and not let it settle in his mind. But let it be understood that what I prescribed at first is the right course, and this only a remedy.

I prefer that a boy should begin with the Greek language, because he will acquire the Latin in general use, even though we tried to prevent him, and because, at the same time, he ought first to be instructed in Greek learning, from which ours is derived. Yet I should not wish this rule to be so superstitiously observed that he should for a long time speak or learn only Greek, as is the custom with most people; for hence arise many faults of pronunciation, which is viciously adapted to foreign sounds, and also of language, in which when Greek idioms have become inherent by constant usage, they keep their place most pertinaciously even when we speak a different tongue. The study of Latin ought, therefore, to follow at no long interval, and soon after to keep pace with the Greek; thus it will happen that when we have begun to attend to both tongues with equal care, neither will impede the other.

Some have thought that boys, as long as they are under seven years of age, should not be set to learn, because that is the earliest age that can understand what is taught, and endure the labor of learning. Of which opinion a great many writers say that Hesiod was, at least such writers as lived before Aristophanes the grammarian, for he was the first to deny that the *Hypothecae,* in which this opinion is found, was the work of that poet. But other writers likewise, among whom is Erastothenes, have given the same advice. Those, however, advise better, who, like Chrysippus, think that no part of a child's life should be exempt from tuition; for Chrysippus, though he has allowed three years to the nurses, is of the opinion that the minds of children may be imbued with excellent instruction even by them. And why should not that age, which is now confessedly subject to moral influence, be under the influence of learning? I am not indeed ignorant that during the whole time of which I am speaking, scarcely as much can be done as one year may afterwards accomplish. Yet those who are of the opinion which I have mentioned appear, with regard to this part of life, to have spared not so much the learners as the teachers. What else, after they are able to speak, will children do better, for they must do something? Or why should we despise the gain, how little so ever it be, previous to the age of seven years? For certainly, small as may be the proficiency which an earlier age exhibits, the child will yet learn something greater during the very year in which he would have been learning something less. This advancement, extended through each year, is a profit on the whole, and whatever is gained in infancy is an acquisition to youth. The same rule should be prescribed as to the following years, so that what every boy has to learn, he may not be too late in beginning to learn. Let us not then lose even the earliest period of life, and so much the less, as the elements of learning depend on the memory alone, which not only exists in children, but is at that time of life even most tenacious.

Yet I am not so unacquainted with differences of age as to think that we should urge those of tender years severely or exact a full complement of work from them. For it will be necessary, above all things, to take care lest the child should conceive a dislike to the application which he cannot yet love, and continue to dread the bitterness which he has once tasted, even beyond the years of infancy. Let his instruction be an amusement to him; let him be questioned and praised; let him never feel pleased that he does not know a thing; and sometimes, if he is unwilling to learn, let another be taught before him, of whom he may be envious. Let him strive for victory now and then, and generally suppose that he gains it; and let his powers be called forth by rewards such as that age prizes.

We are giving small instructions, while professing to educate an orator. But even studies have their infancy, and as the rearing of the very strongest bodies commenced with milk and the cradle, so he, who was to be the most eloquent of men, once uttered cries, tried to speak at first with a stuttering voice, and hesitated at the shapes of the letters. Nor, if it is impossible to learn a thing completely, is it therefore unnecessary to learn it at all. If no one blames a father who thinks that these matters are not to be neglected in regard to his son, why should he be blamed who communicates to the public what he would practice to advantage in his own house? And this is so much more the case, as younger minds more easily take in small things. And as bodies cannot be formed to certain flexures of the limbs unless while they are tender, so even strength itself makes our minds likewise more unyielding to most things. Would Philip, king of Macedonia, have wished the first principles of learning to be communicated to his son Alexander by Aristotle, the greatest philosopher of that age, or would Aristotle have undertaken that office if they had not both thought that the first rudiments of instruction are best treated by the most accomplished teacher and have an influence on the whole course? Let us suppose, then, that Alexander were committed to me, and laid in my lap, an infant worthy of so much solicitude (though every man thinks his own son worthy of similar solicitude), should I be ashamed, even in teaching him his very letters, to point out some compendious methods of instruction?

For that which I see practiced in regard to most children by no means pleases me, namely, that they learn the names and order of the letters before they learn their shapes. This method hinders their recognition of them, as, while they follow their memory that takes the lead, they do not fix their attention on the forms of the letters. This is the reason why teachers, even when they appear to have fixed them sufficiently in the minds of children, in the straight order in which they are usually first written, make them go over them again the contrary way, and confuse them by variously changing the arrangement, until their pupils know them by their shape, not by their place. It will be best for children therefore, to be taught the appearances and names of the letters at once, as they are taught those of men. But that which is hurtful with regard to letters, will be no impediment with regard to syllables. I do not disapprove, however, the practice, which is well known, of giving children, for the sake of stimulating them to learn, ivory figures of letters to play with, or whatever else can be invented, in which that infantine age may take delight, and which may be pleasing to handle, look at, or name.

But as soon as the child shall have begun to trace the forms of the letters, it will not be improper that they should be cut for him, as exactly as possible, on a board, that his stylus may be guided along them as along grooves, for he will then make no mistakes, as on wax (since he will be kept in by the edge on each side, and will be unable to stray beyond the boundary). By following these sure traces rapidly and frequently, he will form his hand and not require the assistance of a person to guide his hand with his own hand placed over it. The accomplishment of writing well and expeditiously, which is commonly disregarded by people of quality, is by no means an indifferent matter. Writing itself is the principal thing in our studies, and by it alone sure proficiency, resting on the deepest roots, is secured. A too slow way of writing retards thought, and a rude and confused hand cannot be read; and hence follows another task, that of reading off what is to be copied from the writing. At all times, therefore, and in all places, and especially in writing private and familiar letters, it will be a source of pleasure to us not to have neglected even this acquirement.

For learning syllables there is no short way. They must all be learned throughout, nor are the most difficult of them, as is the general practice, to be postponed, that children may be at a loss, forsooth, in writing words. Moreover, we must not even trust to the first learning by heart; it will be better to have syllables repeated and to impress them long upon the memory; and in reading too, not to hurry on, in order to make it continuous or quick, until the clear and certain connection of the letters become familiar, without at least any necessity to stop for recollection. Let the pupil then begin to form words from syllables and to join phrases together from words. It is incredible how much retardation is caused to reading by haste; for hence arise hesitation, interruption, and repetition, as children attempt more than they can manage; and then, after making mistakes, they become distrustful even of what they know. Let reading, therefore, be at first sure, then continuous, and for a long time slow, until, by exercise, a correct quickness is gained. For to look to the right, as everybody teaches, and to look forward, depends not merely on rule, but on habit, since, while the child is looking to what follows, he has to pronounce what goes before, and, what is very difficult, the direction of his thoughts must be divided, so that one duty may be discharged with his voice, and another with his eyes.

When the child shall have begun, as is the practice, to write words, it will cause no regret if we take care that he may not waste his efforts on common words, and such as perpetually occur. For he may readily learn the explanations of obscure terms, which the Greeks call *glossai* [glosses], while some other occupation is before him, and acquire, amidst his first rudiments, a knowledge of that which would afterwards demand a special time for it. Since, too, we are still attending to small matters, I would express a wish that even the lines that are set him for his imitation in writing should not contain useless sentences, but such as convey some moral instruction. The remembrance of such admonitions will attend him to old age and will be of use even for the formation of his character. It is possible for him, also, to learn the sayings of eminent men, and select passages, chiefly from the poets (for the reading of poets is more pleasing to the young), in his playtime. Memory (as I shall show in its proper place) is most necessary to an orator and is eminently strengthened and nourished by exercise; and, at the age of which we are now speaking, and which cannot, as yet, produce anything of itself, it is almost the only faculty that can be improved by the aid of teachers. It will not be improper, however, to require of boys of this age (in order that their pronunciation may be fuller and their speech more distinct) to roll forth, as rapidly as possible, certain words and lines of studied difficulty, composed of several syllables, and those roughly clashing together, and, as it were, rugged-sounding; the Greeks call them *calinoi* [chalinoi]. This may seem a trifling matter to mention, but when it is neglected, many faults of pronunciation, unless they are removed in the years of youth, are fixed by incorrigible ill habit for the rest of life.

Review and Discussion Questions

1. In what sense are children "imitative"?

2. Quintilian suggests that a child's teacher must keep careful watch of his or her habits. What justification does he offer for this advice?

3. What various purposes of education are identified?

4. List in order the topics discussed in this passage. In what ways are Quintilian's concerns like and unlike those commonly discussed today?

❖ 4

ST. AUGUSTINE (354–430)

On Christian Teaching

> But because words pass away as soon as they stike upon the air, and last
> no longer than their sound, men have by means of letters formed signs
> and words.

As a young Catholic, Augustine set out to rewrite a Christianized liberal
arts curriculum. His aim: "to show how the mind could move from corporeal to incorporeal realities." Besides writing a few books on music, dialectic, and the theory of liberal education (see his *On Order*), the project was
left unfinished. In place of a series of textbooks, Augustine left *On Christian
Teaching*. The second half of book two offers a vision of how Scripture, re-
placing Homer and Virgil, might stand as the basis for a new core curriculum. The first part of book II, offered below, is a reflection on the purpose
of language. Postmodern philosophers despair of finding a connection between signs and things. If langauge is only a web of signifiers, words about
words, education's aim will be entirely rhetorical. To say this another way:
without access to truth, study is little more than an apprenticeship in adver-
tising, an exercise in the techniques of the will to power. Augustine provides
reasons for us to reject that postmodern despair. Far from being trapped inside a self-referential web of signs, the careful interpreter of Scripture—and
poetry, philosophy, and history, for that matter—can, through attention to
the multiple uses of words, attain true insight. Ultimately, when the gift of
language is joined to piety, the mind can even be carried into contact with
the silent Word which is the source of wisdom.

Further Reading: Edward D. English, ed., *Reading and Wisdom: The* De doctrina christiana *of
Augustine in the Middle Ages* (Notre Dame, Ind.: University of Notre Dame Press, 1994); Ryan
Topping, *St. Augustine*, Bloomsbury Library of Educational Thought (London: Bloomsbury
Press, 2014); Henri de Lubac, *Medieval Exegesis* (Grand Rapids, Mich.: Wm. B. Eerdmans Pub-
lishing, 2000).

❖

Signs, Their Nature and Variety

As when I was writing about things, I introduced the subject with a warning against attending to anything but what they are in themselves, even though they are signs of something else, so now, when I come in its turn to discuss the subject of signs, I lay down this direction, not to attend to what they are in themselves, but to the fact that they are signs, that is, to what they signify. For a sign is a thing which, over and above the impression it makes on the senses, causes something else to come into the mind as a consequence of itself: as when we see a footprint, we conclude that an animal whose footprint this is has passed by; and when we see smoke, we know that there is fire beneath; and when we hear the voice of a living man, we think of the feeling in his mind; and when the trumpet sounds, soldiers know that they are to advance or retreat, or do whatever else the state of the battle requires.

Now some signs are natural, others conventional. Natural signs are those which, apart from any intention or desire of using them as signs, do yet lead to the knowledge of something else, as, for example, smoke when it indicates fire. For it is not from any intention of making it a sign that it is so, but through attention to experience we come to know that fire is beneath, even when nothing but smoke can be seen. And the footprint of an animal passing by belongs to this class of signs. And the countenance of an angry or sorrowful man indicates the feeling in his mind, independently of his will: and in the same way every other emotion of the mind is betrayed by the tell-tale countenance, even though we do nothing with the intention of making it known. This class of signs, however, it is no part of my design to discuss at present. But as it comes under this division of the subject, I could not altogether pass it over. It will be enough to have noticed it thus far.

Conventional signs, on the other hand, are those which living beings mutually exchange for the purpose of showing, as well as they can, the feelings of their minds, or their perceptions, or their thoughts. Nor is there any reason for giving a sign except the desire of drawing forth and conveying into another's mind what the giver of the sign has in his own mind. We wish, then, to consider and discuss this class of signs so far as men are concerned with it, because even the signs which have been given us of God, and which are contained in the Holy Scriptures, were made known to us through men—those, namely, who wrote the Scriptures. The beasts, too, have certain signs among themselves by which they make known the desires in their mind. For when the poultry-cock has discovered food, he signals with his voice for the hen to run to him, and the dove by cooing calls his mate, or is called by her in turn; and many signs of the same kind are matters of common observation. Now whether these signs, like the expression or the cry of a man in grief, follow the movement of the mind instinctively and apart from any purpose, or whether they are really used with the purpose of signification, is another question, and does not pertain to the matter in hand. And this part of the subject I exclude from the scope of this work as not necessary to my present object.

Among Signs, Words Hold the Chief Place

Of the signs, then, by which men communicate their thoughts to one another, some relate to the sense of sight, some to that of hearing, a very few to the other senses. For, when we nod, we give no sign except to the eyes of the man to whom we wish by this sign to impart our desire. And some convey a great deal by the motion of the hands: and actors by movements of all their limbs give certain signs to the initiated, and, so to speak, address their conversation to the eyes: and the military standards and flags convey through the eyes the will of the commanders. And all these signs are as it were a kind of visible words. The signs that address themselves to the ear are, as I have said, more numerous, and for the most part consist of words. For though the bugle and the flute and the lyre frequently give not only a sweet but a significant sound, yet all these signs are very few in number compared with words. For among men words have obtained far and away the chief place as a means of indicating the thoughts of the mind. Our Lord, it is true, gave a sign through the odor of the ointment which was poured out upon His feet; and in the sacrament of His body and blood He signified His will through the sense of taste; and when by touching the hem of His garment the woman was made whole, the act was not wanting in significance. But the countless multitude of the signs through which men express their thoughts consist of words. For I have been able to put into words all those signs, the various classes of which I have briefly touched upon, but I could by no effort express words in terms of those signs.

Origin of Writing

But because words pass away as soon as they strike upon the air, and last no longer than their sound, men have by means of letters formed signs of words. Thus the sounds of the voice are made visible to the eye, not of course as sounds, but by means of certain signs. It has been found impossible, however, to make those signs common to all nations owing to the sin of discord among men, which springs from every man trying to snatch the chief place for himself. And that celebrated tower which was built to reach to heaven was an indication of this arrogance of spirit; and the ungodly men concerned in it justly earned the punishment of having not their minds only, but their tongues besides, thrown into confusion and discordance.

Scripture Translated into Various Languages

And hence it happened that even Holy Scripture, which brings a remedy for the terrible diseases of the human will, being at first set forth in one language, by means of which it could at the fit season be disseminated through the whole world, was interpreted into various tongues, and spread far and wide, and thus became known to the nations for their salvation. And in reading it, men seek nothing more than to find out the thought and will of those by whom it was written, and through these to find out the will of God, in accordance with which they believe these men to have spoken.

Use of the Obscurities in Scripture Which Arise from Its Figurative Language

But hasty and careless readers are led astray by many and manifold obscurities and ambiguities, substituting one meaning for another; and in some places they cannot hit upon even a fair interpretation. Some of the expressions are so obscure as to shroud the meaning in the thickest darkness. And I do not doubt that all this was divinely arranged for the purpose of subduing pride by toil, and of preventing a feeling of satiety in the intellect, which generally holds in small esteem what is discovered without difficulty. For why is it, I ask, that if any one says that there are holy and just men whose life and conversation the Church of Christ uses as a means of redeeming those who come to it from all kinds of superstitions, and making them through their imitation of good men members of its own body; men who, as good and true servants of God, have come to the baptismal font laying down the burdens of the world, and who rising thence do, through the implanting of the Holy Spirit, yield the fruit of a two-fold love, a love, that is, of God and their neighbor; how is it, I say, that if a man says this, he does not please his hearer so much as when he draws the same meaning from that passage in Canticles [4:2], where it is said of the Church, when it is being praised under the figure of a beautiful woman, "Thy teeth are like a flock of sheep that are shorn which came up from the washing, whereof every one bears twins, and none is barren among them"?" Does the hearer learn anything more than when he listens to the same thought expressed in the plainest language, without the help of this figure? And yet, I don't know why, I feel greater pleasure in contemplating holy men, when I view them as the teeth of the Church, tearing men away from their errors, and bringing them into the Church's body, with all their harshness softened down, just as if they had been torn off and masticated by the teeth. It is with the greatest pleasure, too, that I recognize them under the figure of sheep that have been shorn, laying down the burthens of the world like fleeces, and coming up from the washing, i.e., from baptism, and all bearing twins, i.e., the twin commandments of love, and none among them barren in that holy fruit.

But why I view them with greater delight under that aspect than if no such figure were drawn from the sacred books, though the fact would remain the same and the knowledge the same, is another question, and one very difficult to answer. Nobody, however, has any doubt about the facts, both that it is pleasanter in some cases to have knowledge communicated through figures, and that what is attended with difficulty in the seeking gives greater pleasure in the finding. For those who seek but do not find suffer from hunger. Those, again, who do not seek at all because they have what they require just beside them often grow languid from satiety. Now weakness from either of these causes is to be avoided. Accordingly the Holy Spirit has, with admirable wisdom and care for our welfare, so arranged the Holy Scriptures as by the plainer passages to satisfy our hunger, and by the more obscure to stimulate our appetite. For almost nothing is dug out of those obscure passages which may not be found set forth in the plainest language elsewhere.

Steps to Wisdom: First, Fear; Second, Piety; Third, Knowledge; Fourth, Resolution; Fifth, Counsel; Sixth, Purification of Heart; Seventh, Stop or Termination, Wisdom

First of all, then, it is necessary that we should be led by the fear of God to seek the knowledge of His will, what He commands us to desire and what to avoid. Now this fear will of necessity excite in us the thought of our mortality and of the death that is before us, and crucify all the motions of pride as if our flesh were nailed to the tree. Next it is necessary to have our hearts subdued by piety, and not to run in the face of Holy Scripture, whether when understood it strikes at some of our sins, or, when not understood, we feel as if we could be wiser and give better commands ourselves. We must rather think and believe that whatever is there written, even though it be hidden, is better and truer than anything we could devise by our own wisdom.

After these two steps of fear and piety, we come to the third step, knowledge, of which I have now undertaken to treat. For in this every earnest student of the Holy Scriptures exercises himself, to find nothing else in them but that God is to be loved for His own sake, and our neighbor for God's sake; and that God is to be loved with all the heart, and with all the soul, and with all the mind, and one's neighbor as one's self—that is, in such a way that all our love for our neighbor, like all our love for ourselves, should have reference to God. And on these two commandments I touched in the previous book when I was treating about things. It is necessary, then, that each man should first of all find in the Scriptures that he, through being entangled in the love of this world—i.e., of temporal things—has been drawn far away from such a love for God and such a love for his neighbor as Scripture enjoins. Then that fear which leads him to think of the judgment of God, and that piety which gives him no option but to believe in and submit to the authority of Scripture, compel him to bewail his condition. For the knowledge of a good hope makes a man not boastful, but sorrowful. And in this frame of mind he implores with unremitting prayers the comfort of the Divine help that he may not be overwhelmed in despair, and so he gradually comes to the fourth step—that is, strength and resolution—in which he hungers and thirsts after righteousness. For in this frame of mind he extricates himself from every form of fatal joy in transitory things, and turning away from these, fixes his affection on things eternal, to wit, the unchangeable Trinity in unity.

And when, to the extent of his power, he has gazed upon this object shining from afar, and has felt that owing to the weakness of his sight he cannot endure that matchless light, then in the fifth step—that is, in the counsel of compassion—he cleanses his soul, which is violently agitated, and disturbs him with base desires, from the filth it has contracted. And at this stage he exercises himself diligently in the love of his neighbor; and when he has reached the point of loving his enemy, full of hopes and unbroken in strength, he mounts to the sixth step, in which he purifies the eye itself which can see God, so far as God can be seen by those who as far as possible die to this world. For men see Him just so far as they die to this world; and so far as they live to it they see Him not. But yet, although that light may begin to appear clearer, and not only more tolerable, but even more delightful, still it is only through a glass darkly that we are said to see, because we walk by faith, not by sight, while we continue to wander as strangers in this world, even though our conversation be in heaven. And at this stage, too, a man so purges the eye of his affections as not to place his neighbor before, or even in comparison with, the truth, and therefore not himself, because not him whom he loves as himself. Accordingly, that holy man will be so single and so pure in heart, that he will not step aside from the truth, either for the sake of pleasing men or with a view to avoid any of the annoyances which beset this life. Such a son ascends to wisdom, which is the seventh and last step, and which he enjoys in peace and tranquillity. For the fear of God is the beginning of wisdom. From that beginning, then, till we reach wisdom itself, our way is by the steps now described.

Review and Discussion Questions

1. What are the types of signs?

2. How does Augustine define a sign?

3. If you utilize only the literal interpretation of Scriptural texts, what sorts of mistakes might you make?

4. Illustrate why a knowledge of the varieties of signs—and hence the various uses of language—is valuable to one's education more generally?

5. What is the ordering principle behind Augustine's seven-fold steps to wisdom?

ST. THOMAS AQUINAS (1225–74)

Summa Contra Gentiles

… they are called wise who order things rightly and govern them well.

In fewer than one thousand words, St. Thomas outlines the nature, purpose, and activity of the wise man. The wise man orders according to his knowledge of the causes. Such is his activity because the purpose of the created universe is to manifest truth. In what sense does the wise man order? He orders by teaching and by refuting error. If St. Thomas is correct, then all Catholic study, indeed every enquiry into atoms or angels, must keep wisdom as its criterion. Wisdom is a proportion or rule of thought which enables the mind to sift, to divide, and to judge aright. The wise man does not approach learning in the manner of a technician. His curiosity does not extend only as far as his power. But neither is knowledge merely "for its own sake." Every study is an invitation to pilgrimage. Despite setbacks in our understanding, Christian hope affirms that we inhabit not a chaos but a cosmos. In this selection St. Thomas encourages us not to grow weary.

Further Reading: Aristotle, *On the Parts of Animals* [Book 1], in *The Complete Works of Aristotle: Volume 1*, ed. Jonathan Barnes (Princeton, N.J.: Princeton University Press, 1984); St. Thomas Aquinas, *Summa Theologiae* [Part I, question 1, article 1], in *Summa of the Summa*, edited and annotated by Peter Kreeft (San Francisco: Ignatius Press, 1990); A. G. Sertillanges, *On the Intellectual Life*, trans. Mary Ryan, with foreword by James V. Schall, S.J. (Washington, D.C.: The Catholic University of America Press, 1998).

❖

The Office of the Wise Man

My mouth shall discuss truth, and my lips shall detest the ungodly
(Proverbs 7:7)

According to established popular usage, which the Philosopher considers should be our guide in the naming of things, they are called "wise" who put things in their right order and control them well. Now, in all things that are to be controlled and put in order to an end, the measure of control and order must be taken from the end in view; and the proper end of everything is something good. Hence we see in the arts that art A governs and, as it were, lords it over art B, when the proper end of art B belongs to A. Thus the art of medicine lords it over the art of the apothecary, because health, the object of medicine, is the end of all drugs that the apothecary's art compounds. These arts that lord it over others are called "master-building," or "masterful arts"; and the "master-builders" who practice them arrogate to themselves the name of "wise men." But because these persons deal with the ends in view of certain particular things, without attaining to the general end of all things, they are called "wise in this or that particular thing," as it is said, "*As a wise architect I have laid the foundation*" (1 Cor. iii, 10); while the name of "wise" without qualification is reserved for him alone who deals with the last end of the universe, which is also the first beginning of the order of the universe. Hence, according to the Philosopher, it is proper to the wise man to consider the highest causes.

Now the last end of everything is that which is intended by the prime author or mover thereof. The prime author and mover of the universe is intelligence, as will be shown later. Therefore the last end of the universe must be the good of the intelligence, and that is truth. Truth then must be the final end of the whole universe; and about the consideration of that end wisdom must primarily be concerned. And therefore the Divine Wisdom, clothed in flesh, testifies that He came into the world for the manifestation of truth: *For this was I born, and unto this I came into the World, to give testimony to the truth* (John xvii, 37). The Philosopher also rules that the first philosophy is the science of truth, not of any and every truth, but of that truth which is the origin of all truth, and appertains to the first principle of the being of all things; hence its truth is the principle of all truth, for things are in truth as they are in being.

It is one and the same office to embrace either of two contraries and to repel the other. Hence, as it is the office of the wise man to discuss truth, particularly of the first beginning, so it is his also to impugn the contrary error. Suitably therefore is the double function of the wise man displayed in the words above quoted from the Sapiential Book, namely, to study, and upon study to speak out the truth of God, which of all other is most properly called truth, and this is referred to in the words, *My mouth shall discuss truth*, and to impugn error contrary to truth, as referred to in the words, *And my lips shall detest the ungodly*.

Review and Discussion Questions

1. What two qualities mark the wise man, according to St. Thomas?

2. What does Thomas mean by his claim that, for all things, "the measure of control and order must be taken from the end"?

3. Why is a master craftsman, properly speaking, not "wise"?

4. Refer back to Aristotle's discussion of the value of a liberal education. How does this "general" or "liberal" education equip a wise person for his "two-fold" office?

❖ 6

THOMAS À KEMPIS (1380–1471)

The Imitation of Christ

> Not that learning is to be blamed ... but a good conscience and a holy life is
> better than all.

Over the past five hundred years perhaps no other spiritual book has been
read as often, outside of Scripture, as *The Imitation of Christ*. Composed by
a fifteenth-century German monk, the work both reflects its age and sums
up the best of the Medieval Catholic mystical tradition. Written two centuries after St. Thomas's *Summa* and just decades before Luther's launch of the
Reformation (1517), the *Imitation* echoes the wisdom of the early monks of
the Egyptian desert: learning without love is straw. In his opposition to arid
definitions, à Kempis likely has in view not St. Thomas or St. Bonaventure
but another tradition of scholastic formation—represented by Abelard, and
later William of Ockham—which seemed to delight without moderation in
controversy and distinctions. Erasmus in his *Praise of Folly* will echo similar
complaints against the Medieval Schools. And yet, for all his caution of for-
malized study, Thomas is neither Ockham nor Luther. *The Imitation* is neither drunk on logic nor allergic to it. Rather, what he sets before our mind
is that the *ordo studendi* ought to reflect the *ordo amoris*, that study should
be directed not to the ends of power, nor to the ends of idle curiosity, but to
the ends of love.

Further Reading: St. Athanasius, *Life of Antony and Letter to Marcellinus*, trans. R. C. Gregg
(Mahwah, N.J.: Paulist Press, 1980); St. Augustine, *Confessions*, Books 1–3, trans. Maria Bould-
ing, O.S.B., ed. David Meconi, S.J. (San Francisco: Ignatius Press, 2012); Erasmus, *The Praise of
Folly*, trans. B. Radice, introduction by A. J. T. Levi (London: Penguin, 1988).

❖

Of the Imitation of Christ, and of Contempt of the World and All Its Vanities

He that followeth me shall not walk in darkness, saith the Lord (John 8:12). These are the words of Christ; and they teach us how far we must imitate His life and character, if we seek true illumination, and deliverance from all blindness of heart. Let it be our most earnest study, therefore, to dwell upon the life of Jesus Christ.

His teaching surpasseth all teaching of holy men, and such as have His Spirit find therein the hidden manna (Revelation 2:17). But there are many who, though they frequently hear the Gospel, yet feel but little longing after it, because they have not the mind of Christ. He, therefore, that will fully and with true wisdom understand the words of Christ, let him strive to conform his whole life to that mind of Christ.

What doth it profit thee to enter into deep discussion concerning the Holy Trinity, if thou lack humility, and be thus displeasing to the Trinity? For verily it is not deep words that make a man holy and upright; it is a good life which maketh a man dear to God. I had rather feel contrition than be skilful in the definition thereof. If thou knewest the whole Bible, and the sayings of all the philosophers, what should all this profit thee without the love and grace of God? Vanity of vanities, all is vanity, save to love God, and Him only to serve. That is the highest wisdom, to cast the world behind us, and to reach forward to the heavenly kingdom.

It is vanity then to seek after, and to trust in, the riches that shall perish. It is vanity, too, to covet honours, and to lift up ourselves on high. It is vanity to follow the desires of the flesh and be led by them, for this shall bring misery at the last. It is vanity to desire a long life, and to have little care for a good life. It is vanity to take thought only for the life which now is, and not to look forward to the things which shall be hereafter. It is vanity to love that which quickly passeth away, and not to hasten where eternal joy abideth.

Be ofttimes mindful of the saying, The eye is not satisfied with seeing, nor the ear with hearing (Ecclesiastes 1:8). Strive, therefore, to turn away thy heart from the love of the things that are seen, and to set it upon the things that are not seen. For they who follow after their own fleshly lusts, defile the conscience, and destroy the grace of God.

Of Thinking Humbly of Oneself

There is naturally in every man a desire to know, but what profiteth knowledge without the fear of God? Better of a surety is a lowly peasant who serveth God, than a proud philosopher who watcheth the stars and neglecteth the knowledge of himself. He who knoweth himself well is vile in his own sight; neither regardeth he the praises of men. If I knew all the things that are in the world, and were not in charity, what should it help me before God, who is to judge me according to my deeds?

Rest from inordinate desire of knowledge, for therein is found much distraction and deceit. Those who have knowledge desire to appear learned, and to be called wise. Many things there are to know which profiteth little or nothing to the soul. And foolish out of measure is he who attendeth upon other things rather than those which serve to his soul's health. Many words satisfy not the soul, but a good life refresheth the mind, and a pure conscience giveth great confidence towards God.

The greater and more complete thy knowledge, the more severely shalt thou be judged, unless thou hast lived holily. Therefore be not lifted up by any skill or knowledge that thou hast; but rather fear concerning the knowledge which is given to thee. If it seemeth to thee that thou knowest many things, and understandest them well, know also that there are many more things which thou knowest not. Be not high-minded, but rather confess thine ignorance. Why desirest thou to lift thyself above another, when there are found many more learned and more skilled in the Scripture than thou? If thou wilt know and learn anything with profit, love to be thyself unknown and to be counted for nothing.

That is the highest and most profitable lesson, when a man truly knoweth and judgeth lowly of himself. To account nothing of one's self, and to think always kindly and highly of others, this is great and perfect wisdom. Even shouldest thou see thy neighbor sin openly or grievously, yet thou oughtest not to reckon thyself better than he, for thou knowest not how long thou shalt keep thine integrity. All of us are weak and frail; hold thou no man more frail than thyself.

Of the Knowledge of Truth

Happy is the man whom Truth by itself doth teach, not by figures and transient words, but as it is in itself. Our own judgment and feelings often deceive us, and we discern but little of the truth. What doth it profit to argue about hidden and dark things, concerning which we shall not be even reproved in the judgment, because we knew them not? Oh, grievous folly, to neglect the things which are profitable and necessary, and to give our minds to things which are curious and hurtful! Having eyes, we see not.

And what have we to do with talk about genus and species! He to whom the Eternal Word speaketh is free from multiplied questionings. From this One Word are all things, and all things speak of Him; and this is the Beginning which also speaketh unto us (Numbers 12:8). No man without Him understandeth or rightly judgeth. The man to whom all things are one, who bringeth all things to one, who seeth all things in one, he is able to remain steadfast of spirit, and at rest in God. O God, who art the Truth, make me one with Thee in everlasting love. It wearieth me oftentimes to read and listen to many things; in Thee is all that I wish for and desire. Let all the doctors hold their peace; let all creation keep silence before Thee: speak Thou alone to me.

The more a man hath unity and simplicity in himself, the more things and the deeper things he understandeth; and that without labour, because he receiveth the light of understanding from above. The spirit which is pure, sincere, and steadfast, is not distracted though it hath many works to do, because it doth all things to the honour of God, and striveth to be free from all thoughts of self-seeking. Who is so full of hindrance and annoyance to thee as thine own undisciplined heart? A man who is good and devout arrangeth beforehand within his own heart the works which he hath to do abroad; and so is not drawn away by the desires of his evil will, but subjecteth everything to the judgment of right reason. Who hath a harder battle to fight than he who striveth for self-mastery? And this should be our endeavour, even to master oneself, and thus daily to grow stronger than self, and go on unto perfection.

All perfection hath some imperfection joined to it in this life, and all our power of sight is not without some darkness. A lowly knowledge of thyself is a surer way to God than the deep searching of man's learning. Not that learning is to be blamed, nor the taking account of anything that is good; but a good conscience and a holy life is better than all. And because many seek knowledge rather than good living, therefore they go astray, and bear little or no fruit.

O if they would give that diligence to the rooting out of vice and the planting of virtue which they give unto vain questionings: there had not been so many evil doings and stumbling-blocks among the laity, nor such ill living among houses of religion. Of a surety, at the Day of Judgment it will be demanded of us, not what we have read, but what we have done; not how well we have spoken, but how holily we have lived. Tell me, where now are all those masters and teachers, whom thou knewest well, whilst they were yet with you, and flourished in learning? Their stalls are now filled by others, who perhaps never have one thought concerning them. Whilst they lived they seemed to be somewhat, but now no one speaks of them.

Oh how quickly passeth the glory of the world away! Would that their life and knowledge had agreed together! For then would they have read and inquired unto good purpose. How many perish through empty learning in this world, who care little for serving God. And because they love to be great more than to be humble, therefore they "have become vain in their imaginations." He only is truly great, who hath great charity. He is truly great who deemeth himself small, and counteth all height of honour as nothing. He is the truly wise man, who counteth all earthly things as dung that he may win Christ. And he is the truly learned man, who doeth the will of God, and forsaketh his own will.

Of Prudence in Action

We must not trust every word of others or feeling within ourselves, but cautiously and patiently try the matter, whether it be of God. Unhappily we are so weak that we find it easier to believe and speak evil of others, rather than good. But they that are perfect, do not give ready heed to every newsbearer, for they know man's weakness that it is prone to evil and unstable in words.

This is great wisdom, not to be hasty in action, or stubborn in our own opinions. A part of this wisdom also is not to believe every word we hear, nor to tell others all that we hear, even though we believe it. Take counsel with a man who is wise and of a good conscience; and seek to be instructed by one better than thyself, rather than to follow thine own inventions. A good life maketh a man wise toward God, and giveth him experience in many things. The more humble a man is in himself, and the more obedient towards God, the wiser will he be in all things, and the more shall his soul be at peace.

Of the Reading of Holy Scriptures

It is Truth which we must look for in Holy Writ, not cunning of words. All Scripture ought to be read in the spirit in which it was written. We must rather seek for what is profitable in Scripture, than for what ministereth to subtlety in discourse. Therefore we ought to read books which are devotional and simple, as well as those which are deep and difficult. And let not the weight of the writer be a stumbling-block to thee, whether he be of little or much learning, but let the love of the pure Truth draw thee to read. Ask not, who hath said this or that, but look to what he says.

Men pass away, but the truth of the Lord endureth for ever. Without respect of persons God speaketh to us in divers manners. Our own curiosity often hindereth us in the reading of holy writings, when we seek to understand and discuss, where we should pass simply on. If thou wouldst profit by thy reading, read humbly, simply, honestly, and not desiring to win a character for learning. Ask freely, and hear in silence the words of holy men; nor be displeased at the hard sayings of older men than thou, for they are not uttered without cause.

Of Inordinate Affections

Whensoever a man desireth aught above measure, immediately he becometh restless. The proud and the avaricious man are never at rest; while the poor and lowly of heart abide in the multitude of peace. The man who is not yet wholly dead to self, is soon tempted, and is overcome in small and trifling matters. It is hard for him who is weak in spirit, and still in part carnal and inclined to the pleasures of sense, to withdraw himself altogether from earthly desires. And therefore, when he withdraweth himself from these, he is often sad, and easily angered too if any oppose his will.

But if, on the other hand, he yield to his inclination, immediately he is weighed down by the condemnation of his conscience; for that he hath followed his own desire, and yet in no way attained the peace which he hoped for. For true peace of heart is to be found in resisting passion, not in yielding to it. And therefore there is no peace in the heart of a man who is carnal, nor in him who is given up to the things that are without him, but only in him who is fervent towards God and living the life of the Spirit.

Of Fleeing from Vain Hope and Pride

Vain is the life of that man who putteth his trust in men or in any created Thing. Be not ashamed to be the servant of others for the love of Jesus Christ, and to be reckoned poor in this life. Rest not upon thyself, but build thy hope in God. Do what lieth in thy power, and God will help thy good intent. Trust not in thy learning, nor in the cleverness of any that lives, but rather trust in the favour of God, who resisteth the proud and giveth grace to the humble.

Boast not thyself in thy riches if thou hast them, nor in thy friends if they be powerful, but in God, who giveth all things, and in addition to all things desireth to give even Himself. Be not lifted up because of thy strength or beauty of body, for with only a slight sickness it will fail and wither away. Be not vain of thy skilfulness or ability, lest thou displease God, from whom cometh every good gift which we have.

Count not thyself better than others, lest perchance thou appear worse in the sight of God, who knoweth what is in man. Be not proud of thy good works, for God's judgments are of another sort than the judgments of man, and what pleaseth man is ofttimes displeasing to Him. If thou hast any good, believe that others have more, and so thou mayest preserve thy humility. It is no harm to thee if thou place thyself below all others; but it is great harm if thou place thyself above even one. Peace is ever with the humble man, but in the heart of the proud there is envy and continual wrath.

Of the Inward Voice of Christ to the Faithful Soul

I will hearken what the Lord God shall say within me. Blessed is the soul which heareth the Lord speaking within it, and receiveth the word of consolation from His mouth. Blessed are the ears which receive the echoes of the soft whisper of God, and turn not aside to the whisperings of this world. Blessed truly are the ears which listen not to the voice that soundeth without, but to that which teacheth truth inwardly. Blessed are the eyes which are closed to things without, but are fixed upon things within. Blessed are they who search inward things and study to prepare themselves more and more by daily exercises for the receiving of heavenly mysteries. Blessed are they who long to have leisure for God, and free themselves from every hindrance of the world. Think on these things, O my soul, and shut the doors of thy carnal desires, so mayest thou hear what the Lord God will say within thee.

These things saith thy Beloved, "I am thy salvation, I am thy peace and thy life. Keep thee unto Me, and thou shalt find peace." Put away from thee all transitory things, seek those things that are eternal. For what are all temporal things but deceits, and what shall all created things help thee if thou be forsaken by the Creator? Therefore put all things else away, and give thyself to the Creator, to be well pleasing and faithful to Him, that thou mayest be able to attain true blessedness.

Review and Discussion Questions

1. What sort of learning does Thomas think worthless?

2. Why is the philosopher who is knowledgeable in cosmology, but ignorant of human nature, to be pitied?

3. Interpret his claim: "All Scripture ought to be read in the spirit in which it was written."

4. In what ways do à Kempis's reflections on the value of learning complement or contradict St. Thomas's statement on the office of the wise man?

H. S. GERDIL (1718–1803)

The Anti-Emile

> But reason requires culture for it to develop. It resembles the fire concealed in the flint, which only shows itself when struck by steel.

Emile (1762) signaled the first rupture in the philosophy of Western education. Rousseau's call for the education of the "natural man" was based on his view of an unspoiled human nature. To Rousseau, culture is the great enemy of learning. True education is a long war against convention. It was through Rousseau, or at least partly through Rousseau, that moderns would acquire a distrust of rote learning, of deference to authority, of trust in tradition. For his reply, the Italian priest Fr. Gerdil admits that much in Rousseau is wise, many of his observations keen, all of his suggestions provocative; it is only his principles that are corrupt. Rousseau's philosophy of learning, and his severing the bonds of authority that tie father to son, assume the absence of original sin. Gerdil argues that, far from undermining liberty, the cultivation of reason within a community is necessary to man's perfection. Wreck authority, and you ruin the child.

Further Reading: Jean-Jacques Rousseau, *Emile: Or, On Education*, translation with introduction and notes by Allan Bloom (New York: Basic Books, 1979); Michel de Montaigne, "On Educating Children," in *The Essays: A Selection*, translated by M. A. Screech (London: Penguin Books, 2004); James Bowen, *A History of Western Education* (New York: St. Martin's Press, 1981).

❖

Whether Laws and Society Reduce Man to a Servile State of Dependency

Another deprivation of society, according to the author [Rousseau], is that born from dependency:

There are two sorts of dependence: dependence on things, which is from nature; dependence on men, which is from society. Dependence on things, since it has no morality, is in no way detrimental to freedom and engenders no vices. Dependence on men, since it is without order, engenders all the vices, and by it, master and slave are mutually corrupted.[1]

To say that the dependence of men established in all governments of which history takes any notice is a disordered dependency that gives rise to every vice overtly contradicts Holy Scripture, which authorizes and recommends in a thousand places this kind of dependency. "Be obedient," says St. Peter, "for the love of God to the order which is established among men: Be obedient to the king, as being possessed of the supreme power, and to those to whom he gives his authority." St. Paul speaks the same language. Know that Rousseau considers vile slaves those who have not the so-called courage to think as he does. Yet we dare to say that the first apostles of Christianity did not lack courage and that they were by no means possessed of that flattery and cowardliness that Rousseau makes the mark of slaves.

This dependence is inevitable and cannot be avoided even in our author's ideal system. By the social pact "each of us puts his person and all his power in common under the supreme control of the general will...." Yet Rousseau at the same time is obliged to acknowledge that every individual can have, as a man, a particular will contrary to the general will.

His private interest may speak to him quite differently from the common interest; his absolute and naturally independent existence may make him envision what he owes to the common cause as a gratuitous contribution, the loss of which will be less harmful to others than its payment is burdensome to him, ... injustice that would bring about the ruin of the body politic, were it to spread. In order, therefore, that the social pact may not be an empty formula, it tacitly includes the commitment, which alone can give force to the others, that anyone who refuses to obey the general will shall be compelled to do so by the entire body; this means nothing else than that he will be forced to be free....[2]

Thus in a system imagined precisely for the maintenance of liberty, a man is obliged to be dependent and submit to the authority of a body that can force him to obey despite himself. It is true that Rousseau has found an admirable expedient to remedy this inconvenience. The City, in constraining a man to obey despite himself, makes no attempt upon his liberty, but to the contrary, it forces him to be free. The fact is clear. As Rousseau understands it, liberty consists in doing what we want. Therefore to force a man to be free, by compelling him to obey despite what he wants, is to do that which he wants, precisely while compelling him to do that which he does not want to do. Who does not understand such a claim? But besides the City which limits itself to making laws, it is still necessary in Rousseau's system that there be a magistracy charged with all the particular acts of government. Here, therefore, there is a particular body, or sometimes a single man, on whom it is necessary to depend.

The dependence of men is not contrary to the nature of man. Nature did not make men in order to live alone, and therefore they were not made to live independently. Society and dependence are correlative ideas, for no society can subsist without order, and there can be no order without dependency. Sick persons submit to the prescriptions of their physician, travelers to the directions of their guide, and soldiers to the orders of their commander. They are persuaded that the physician, the guide, and the general know better than they what is to their advantage. Men know by nature that it is necessary for them to live in society, and they must certainly know it naturally, since everywhere they are established in societies; the multitude also know it must be governed. The people who have been the most jealous of their liberty have seen that they cannot do so without a leader authorized to maintain the laws and armed with the public strength to oppose those whose particular interests set them against the general interest. Rousseau says that the multitude desire what is good, but do not know it. He admits that the best and most natural order is that in which the multitude are governed by the wise. Upon this principle, the Medes, worn out by anarchy, voluntarily submitted themselves to be governed by Deioces, whose wisdom and integrity they knew well. In doing this, they followed the impulse of nature, which requires order in society as well as in everything else. The savage, whom Robinson Crusoe saved from death (I cite an instance to which Rousseau can have no objection), delivered himself up without conditions to his benefactor, not only out of gratitude for the benefit he had received from him, but because he recognized that Robinson was superior to him in wisdom and could teach him to be a better man. One has never seen a dependence more absolute that that of this man in regard to the master that he had given himself. Yet this man was a savage, that is to say, one of those wild souls in whom Rousseau so complaisantly admires the original independence of nature. In sum, because men must live together, it is necessary that some should command and others obey. One might try to evade the fact, but after a few twists and turns, we must either come back to this conclusion or say with Rousseau that when the city or its magistrates commit a man to prison, it is that they want him dependent, but they force him to be free. The Egyptian, with good reason, said, "O Hellenes! Will you always be children?"

Rousseau represents neither the state of nature nor the state of society in their true light. He says that "we were made to be men; laws and society have plunged us once more into childhood." He adds that "whoever does what he wants is happy if he is self-sufficient; this is the case of the man living in the state of nature." First of all, it does not occur to him that without laws and society there would be no education, and without education men would be either simpletons or ferocious, or both the one and the other, according as their passions were calm or agitated. Rousseau paints the state of nature as his imagination represents it to him. A more solid writer will depict it according to nature with features drawn from the testaments of history. This writer is the author of an excellent treatise *On the Origin of Laws, Arts, Science,* etc. There was a time, he says, when almost the whole world was plunged in an extreme state of barbarity. Men were then seen to wander in the woods and plains, without laws, without regulated order, without any leader: here is the state of nature, properly characterized. Their ferociousness became so great that in some cases it brought them to the point of eating one another. They so far neglected even common knowledge that some even forgot the use of fire. It is these unhappy times the profane historians refer to when they relate the miseries that the world labored under in the beginning. We shall find no difficulty in believing these accounts, if we turn our attention to the state into which the ancient historians say that several countries had fallen in their own times, conditions the reality of which we find confirmed by modern studies. Travelers tell us that even at this day in some parts of the world there are men so cruel and ferocious in their nature that they enter into neither society nor commerce with one another; they wage perpetual war, seeking to destroy and even to eat each other. Devoid of all principles of humanity, these people live without laws, without regulated order, without any form of government. So little different from the wild beasts, their only shelter is in rocks and caverns. Their food consists in a few fruits and roots, which the woods supply them. For want of knowledge and industry they are seldom able to procure more solid nourishment for themselves. Deprived of even the most simple and commonplace notions, these people are men only in their appearances.

Here are two pictures drawn from quite different testimonies. On one hand, Rousseau affirms that the law and society have returned men to a state of childhood and that the condition of man in the state of nature is to be sufficient unto himself and to live happily. This he asserts, but he does not provide the least proof. On the other hand, the author of *On the Origin of Laws* affirms that the want of laws and government plunges men into the most horrible barbarity, and he proves it with the facts. With which of these two should we agree?

On the Natural Love of Order and Origins of Society

We must not, however, imagine that men are born wicked, as Hobbes thinks. If this were the case, the sum of unjust actions of every people would infinitely surpass the sum of humanly just actions. Instead, however, the sum of just actions is incomparably superior to the evil, or else no society could possibly subsist. This would be easy to verify in particular cases. What usually convinces us to the contrary is that ordinary acts of justice and goodness are little noticed because they are in the natural order of things. We do not feel the pulse of the heart and the arteries so long as they occur in conformity to that state of health that is natural to man. But we acutely feel every displacement of the parts that run contrary to the natural condition. Every particular motion in bodies is determined by the general order and tends toward this order. It is the result of the combinations of all the moving forces of the universe, and it tends to maintain the harmony between all the moving forces. Whatever is done in nature is directed by those principles ordered among themselves and tends toward the maintenance of the order in these principles. The regularity of the primitive combination of the whole system has determined a regular course in all the movements of the parts, and this regular course holds together the regularity of the system. In organic bodies, which have a principle of sensation, their preservation and well-being depend on the natural harmony of their parts; pain and misery is tied to the derangement of parts that disrupts this harmony. Such is the plan of nature.

If we turn our attention from sensitive to intelligent beings, we shall find that the idea of their order is in some way natural and common to the species, and that it is a powerful inclination, which induces them to act in a manner consistent with their perfection and happiness. Man is naturally a friend of order, and wherever he finds it he approves it and delights in it. He can know nothing except because of the order discerned in his perceptions; he can do nothing except because of the order that he puts into his operations. The more disposed he is to seize the order and perceive it in the different intelligible objects, the greater is his genius and his talent. It is from the order of our affections that a calmness and serenity of soul proceeds; the contrary condition, which consists in the disrupted harmony, produces disquiet, rage, and despair. If a given number of men find themselves assembled for a purpose of some sort, a certain impression of order will immediately lead them to arrange themselves in a manner suitable to the object for which they gathered.

Thus it is neither fear alone, nor utility alone, nor benevolence alone, which has disposed men to assemble in social bodies. Each one of these causes is in itself inadequate, and it is this that renders defective those systems that pretend to establish the foundation of society exclusively on either the one or the other. It is then necessary that all three should be held together, since they naturally tend toward the same end. We must join to them the ruling impression of order, which serves as their common bond, and then we shall have the true principle of every civil society. Benevolence is in effect the first sentiment which connects men to each other, as seems evident from the state of the family, from the pleasure we take in the fellowship of our friends, from the satisfaction we feel when we are able to oblige others, and from the gratitude we express to those who oblige us. These sentiments may be opposed or even overpowered and smothered by selfishness, but they are not on that account less natural. Utility is the second motive that inclines individual men and families to join together. Without this assembly, they would often want for necessities. By virtue of it, however, they are able to provide for themselves not only indispensable needs but also the more agreeable things of life. Fear is the third motivation for associations. For cupidity, in the process of breaking the first bonds of nature, arms wicked men against those who are good, and so requires these latter to unite their forces in order to repel the attacks of the former.

These are the causes that bring men to assemble. But they are no sooner gathered than the impression of order prompts them to give an arrangement, a suitable form to their association. This arrangement requires the rules which are called laws. The establishment of laws leads to the establishment of the authority charged with their maintenance. Such is the origin of the civil order.

Thus man, naturally a friend to order, is not by nature wicked, but becomes so by rivalry and by the clashing of interests which stir up his passions. At first sight it might seem as if society by increasing interests increases the causes of this clashing and thereby the sources of evil, but in this matter there are two obvious considerations. The first is that in the state of society the division of interests does not proceed from the first needs of life. With respect to things necessary for life, the civil state furnishes sufficiently for all and even an abundance for many. In the state of nature, on the contrary, or in those states that approximate it, men are frequently exposed to all the horrors of hunger and famine. It is to these severe extremities that the author of *On the Origin of Laws* attributes the horrid barbarism into which men can be plunged by the state of nature, for it can provoke them to destroy and even to devour each other. The civil state, by securing for men the sure means of subsistence, has banished the horrid custom of devouring each other, which for want of such a state, still subsists in certain savage and barbarous nations. Let the clashing of civil interests in a state of society be ever so great, it can never excite passions comparable to that which carries men to the extremes of cruelty and ferocity. The second observation to be made this: It is true that society multiplies interests by increasing wealth and the conveniences of life. Yet it lessens the clashing and the effects of this clashing by the laws, which set limits to pretensions and fix the rights of each man. Men living in the state of nature will have greater contests about a little wild fruit than the greatest interests are capable of exciting in well-ordered states.

To this we may add that by virtue of their natural constitutions some men have from birth limited spirits and calm passions, others have spirits more lively and passions more ardent. If uncultivated, the first will remain imbeciles, and the other sort become ferocious if they are not governed or restrained. There are others who are born with a physical disorder of their organs, a derangement which does not produce an absolute folly, but which causes an irregularity of ideas which gives rise to uneasy, bungling, turbulent characters that delight in disorder and mischief making. People of such dispositions can only be kept in order by the natural fear they have of the chastisements and corrections which alone can restrain the impetuous sallies occasioned by the confusion of their brains. Now the assistance required in order to rear and guide men in conformity to their respective characters is only to be found in the state of society. Therefore, it was only from caprice that Rousseau took it into his head to say that laws and society again reduce men to a state of childhood. Does he himself not acknowledge that men are indebted to their education for all that which they lack when they are born and which they want when they are grown up?

Now I am absolutely certain that no reasonable plan of education can be formed that does not have some connection or other with laws and society. Rousseau would not have been able to outline his new system, except by virtue of the insight he acquired from society, and which he abused in order to undermine that same society. He pretends that society debases man. He apparently imagines that men in the state of nature would generally have those elevated sentiments which people of birth find within themselves, and furthermore, that they would be able to give them freer rein if they were to live in total independence. But this is sheer illusion. That nobility and generosity of sentiment that characterizes well-born souls scarcely ever develop in children who would, if I may so put it, educate themselves. These sentiments, though natural, require culture in order to develop themselves. This culture is the fruit of a civil education and of a solicitous care that early on impresses on the spirit of children the ideas of virtue and honor.

Man's Reason, the Natural Analogue to Animal Instinct, Requires Education

It pleases Rousseau to suppose that in the state of nature man would be stronger, because his strength would be proportionate to his desires and his desires to his needs, and that in the state of society he becomes feeble, because his desires increase beyond his power. I dare to say that this thought is more specious than solid. Either man in the state of nature would have only perception purely sensitive of heat, cold, pleasure, pain, and the like, without anything that could properly be called an idea, which is to say in Rousseau's language, without notions determined by relations; or else in the state of nature he would be able to raise his sensation to the knowledge of objects and of their relations, thereby making some use of his reason. If in the state of nature man was limited to what was merely sensitive, without any settled idea of things, without having any use of his reason, it is quite true that his desires would be as limited as those of the beasts of the field. He would feel no other want than to satisfy his hunger, to defend himself from heat and cold, and the like. But however limited these desires and these wants may be, it is no less true that a man deprived of the use of his reason would be absolutely unable to gratify and supply them. For as we have already observed, man has not, like other animals, received from nature an instinct destined to one particular kind of work and furnished with organs or instruments solely adapted to particular operations. The sensation of want and the impression of sensible objects suffice both to trigger this instinct that nature has conferred as a guide to animals, and to make them punctually execute all the successive movements and operations by which she has provided for their preservation and defense. It is not this way with man. Nature has not limited him to one particular kind of work or to one particular order of operations that are, so to say, mechanical. The mere sensation of want or the mere impression of sensible objects does not suffice to determine his organs to the actions necessary for his defense and preservation. This sensation, this impression only give him, as it were, notice of his wants and rouse his knowledge and reason to think of some means of satisfying them. He must learn to know the objects that surround him, to discern their relative fitness or unfitness with respect to himself, to imagine ways of acquiring or avoiding them, and the manner of using them.

Reason is like a universal art, which for man takes the place of all the particular arts by enabling him to vary his industry in a manner best suited to the circumstances he finds himself in. Also, as Galen observes following Aristotle, nature has given him hands as a universal instrument adapted for making and using the particular instruments that are necessary to secure his ends. I would, at this point, willingly ask a philosophical materialist what is this nature that has made a being whose species needs to perpetuate itself and yet whose preservation essentially depends on intellectual ideas. It is then certain that if in the state of nature man could be limited to having only purely sensible perceptions, far from being strong, he would be the most wretched of all beings and would perish through the absolute want of power to procure himself the least support.

From this it follows that man could never exist in the way that Rousseau describes him in his book on the inequality of man. Therefore, in order that man may be able to support himself in the state of nature, we must allow him some degree of knowledge and some use of reason. Accordingly, his reason would either remain in that coarse and imperfect state that was always the lot of people living without laws and without government, and we know that men, so far from acquiring power or strength in this state, are reduced to the most wretched necessity without the power of supplying even the most urgent wants of nature. Or else, which is contrary to all experience, reason would acquire in the state of nature as much lucidity, force, and extension as in a well-ordered society, but in this case man would have new desires and new wants, with less means for satisfying them. The order and development of man's inclinations correspond exactly to the order and development of his perception and knowledge. Does he have only sensations? Then all his desires are limited to the sphere of the sensible. Does he have ideas in the proper sense of notions determined by relations? Does he understand by means these relations the fitness or unfitness of objects? Then from these intellectual notions will immediately arise a new order of inclinations relative to the idea that reason gives us of perfection and happiness.

How little reason there is to Rousseau's notion that laws and society have reduced man to a state of childhood—as if man springing from the bosom of nature, as it were, was furnished with whatever would be necessary to preserve, defend, and maintain himself in his natural independence, to supply all his wants, and thus to live contented and happy. Nothing is less reasonable than such a thought.

For we have seen, first of all, that without the guidance of reason man is utterly incapable of making the least use of his own strength, to the extent that we may say that he has only so much strength as he has reason, because the application of his strength always presupposes a choice which cannot exist without some degree of knowledge and some use of reason. But reason requires culture for it to develop. It resembles the fire concealed in the flint, which only shows itself when struck by the steel. The culture of reason necessarily requires a communication of intelligence, which can only be had in society.

And secondly, even reason itself, enlightened as it may be, does not suffice to procure man all the assistance he may want. Rousseau might have been convinced of this by the real or symbolic adventures of Robinson Crusoe on his island. Notwithstanding the knowledge and experience he had acquired in society, notwithstanding the assistance he received from the wreck of his ship, still what labor he expended and what fatigue he suffered in order to procure himself a moderate subsistence. But all of his industriousness would not have been sufficient to save himself from certain death if the island had been less temperate or if it had been infested with wild beasts.

Reason was not given to a man so that he might supply his own partial wants. It was given to men so that they might learn to unite and in a mutual commerce of reciprocal duties and assistance find everything that would be necessary to live in a manner suitable to the dignity of their nature.

There is no necessity for us to travel as far as the countries of the Hurons or Hottentots to see a troop of men living together nearly in the state of nature. Every country of Europe offers us the image of it in the class of wandering beggars. This class forms as a separate body within the state. They live without care on the daily alms they receive from the rich, in the same manner as savages live on the fruits they gather, with this difference, however, that they find at the foundations of humanity characteristic of every civil society more certain resources against want than savages generally find in the productions of nature. They also derive from society the advantage that the fear of punishment prevents them from giving way to those excesses that might otherwise disrupt the general order. Apart from these exceptions, they feel very little influence of the laws. No bond ties them to the country; they lack property, commerce, arts, and industry. They possess nothing. They have no rank, no place in the state, no civil interests, nor any share in the civil institutions. They aspire to nothing, their desires being fully satisfied if they can drink, eat, and do nothing. These men, flocked together purely by chance, represent rather well the state of nature, isolated from the greater body of citizens, and living in a total independence from one another. Here are men who have not been corrupted by social institutions; they educate themselves and follow without restraint the propensities of nature. These are the men, therefore, in whom we should find sound reason, pure manners, hardy souls, with noble and generous sentiments. But this is far from being the case. Most of them lead the greatest part of their lives in an utter ignorance of the duties of man and of the most common principles of religion and morality, without culture, without any of that knowledge that honors and perfects reason. Their only thought is to take advantage of people's compassion, and for this purpose they use every kind of cunning and fraud and sometimes the most criminal artifices when they think they will not be discovered. With a suppliant air, affecting a mild and hypocritical maner, they beg their alms, but if you refuse them, they soon utter the vilest invectives. The distribution of some pieces of money often occasions sharp quarrels among them, at which times they breathe forth all the festering bitterness of their soul. Indolence and laziness constitute the pleasures of their life, and they are said to abandon themselves in secret to debauchery and the most shameful lewdness. Such are the wretched who, detached from the bonds of society, fully enjoy their natural liberty. Such are not the poor who are taken into hospitals, where they are brought up in the fear of God, are accustomed to labor, and are taught the sentiments of a just subordination. We may hence conclude that natural independence is not so favorable to the perfection, as Rousseau thinks. For man's nature is such that he cannot make progress of any sort without the cooperation of others like him, a cooperation that necessarily entails a society, a society to which a certain order is indispensable, an order that can only subsist through laws, laws that can only be maintained through a government, which comprehends within its essence the correlative ideas of authority and subordination.

Yet one more reflection on an observation of Rousseau: "all animals have exactly the faculties necessary to preserve themselves. Man alone has superfluous faculties," and he pretends that "this superfluity [is] the instrument of his unhappiness." Whence he concludes that "if man were wise enough to count his superfluity for nothing, he would always have what is necessary." To this he adds that "any man who only wanted to live would live happily."[3]

Even if the observation is philosophical, the conclusion is hardly so. It is from nature, or rather from the author of nature, that man derives all his faculties. If he has some that are superfluous to his preservation, does it follow that they are in every respect superfluous? It would be absurd to think so. Animals only possess the faculties necessary for their preservation because the animal life they lead can have no other object. But the life of man should be reasonable and sociable. Man does not live merely with a view of existing; he lives to cultivate his reason, in order to enjoy the inestimable fruits of wisdom, and to fulfill the immensity of his duties to God, to himself, and to his own kind. If nature has given to man alone more faculties than are necessary for his preservation, it is a clear proof that she did not mean to limit him, like other animals, to the care of his preservation alone. It is in vain for us to count this superfluity for nothing. Man will never attain to happiness by aiming short of the goal that the author of nature has appointed. Sound reason will always tell us that man cannot attain to happiness except by making a good use, not by a chimerical curtailment, of those faculties that he has received from nature.

Whether Children Are Capable of Understanding Moral Categories

To Rousseau's two principles which have already examined, namely (1) that the first movements of nature are always right and there is no original perversity in the heart of man and (2) that the dependence of man is disordered, we must add another, namely, (3) that at the age of ten or twelve years, or even more, reason is not sufficiently developed in children to render them capable of morality. These three principles are the foundation of his practical education until nearly the age of fifteen years. From these principles Rousseau concludes:

1. One ought not to get involved with raising a child if one does not know how to guide him where one wants by the laws of the possible and the impossible alone.... Do not give your pupil any kind of verbal lessons; he ought to receive them only from experience. Inflict no kind of punishment on him, for he does not know what it is to be at fault. Never make him beg pardon, for he could not know how to offend you.[4]

2. It is necessary that he be dependent and not that he obey. He is only subject to others by virtue of his needs. No one not even the father has a right to command the child what is not for his good.[5] Keep the child in dependence only on things.... Never present to his undiscriminating will anything but physical obstacles or punishments which stem from the actions themselves and which he will recall on the proper occasion.... Experience or impotence alone ought to take the place of law for him.[6]

3. I return to practice. I have already said that your child ought to get a thing not because he asks for it but because he needs it, and do a thing not

out of obedience but only out of necessity. Thus the words obey and command will be proscribed from his lexicon, and even more so duty and obligation. But strength, impotence, and constraint should play a great role in it.[7]

4. The weakness of the first age enchains children in so many ways that it is barbarous to add to this subjection a further subjection—that of our caprices—by taking from them a freedom so limited, which they are so little capable of abusing.[8] Why do you want to deprive these little innocents of the enjoyment of a time so short which escapes them and of a good so precious which they do not know how to abuse?[9] Let us ... leave to childhood the exercise of natural freedom that keeps at a distance, for a time at least, vices contracted in slavery.[10]

It is needless to observe how different this practice is from that recommended in the Holy Scriptures. Rousseau would not have children obey but only be dependent, because they have need for assistance. St. Paul would have children obey because it is right in the sight of God. Rousseau forbids fathers giving their children any verbal instructions or ever speaking to them of duty or obligation. Moses, whose legislation Rousseau admires, commands fathers to instruct their children in the law of God from their earliest years.

Rousseau says that fathers should not chastise their children. Yet Eli is punished for not having chastised his children. Rousseau would have us leave children the full enjoyment of their natural liberty. The wise man recommends that they should be accustomed to the yoke from their infancy. Even if this method had not been warranted by the word of God, still the experience of many ages would be a sufficient guarantee of its solidity.

This is not to say that one cannot take advantage of physical obstacles to oppose the indiscreet volitions of a child and, as much as possible, to make them find in them the punishment of their faults as a natural consequence of their disorder. But the absolute exclusion of every prohibition and of every chastisement is an untenable paradox. To be praised and blamed are the natural consequences of good and bad actions in society. It would be proper for the child to feel these effects from all those who are connected with him. He would begin to feel through direct experience the consequences of a good or a bad reputation. Such a matter is not an indifferent concern; it is a plan to be sagely arranged.

Rousseau supposes that until the age of fifteen years, children do not have enough reason to distinguish moral good from evil. Is it Rousseau who speaks this language, he who is persuaded that the sentiment of the just and the unjust is innate in the heart of man? Let us recall what he says on this subject.

I shall never forget having seen one of these difficult criers thus struck by his nurse. He immediately kept quiet. I believed he was intimidated. I said to myself, "This will be a servile soul from which one will get nothing except severity." I was mistaken. The unfortunate was suffocating with anger; he had lost his breath; I saw him become violent. A moment after came sharp screams; all the signs of the resentment, fury, and despair of this age were in his accents. I feared he would expire in this agitation. If I had doubted that the sentiment of the just and the unjust were innate in the heart of man, this example alone would have convinced me. I am sure that a live ember fallen by chance on this child's hand would have made less of an impression than this blow, rather light but given in the manifest intention of offending him.[11]

What! An infant at the breast can discern in a slight blow an intention of offending him, and the sentiment of this offense wounds him more forcefully than would a hot firebrand. And yet one is to say that a child of ten, twelve, or even fifteen years of age is still at this point incapable of distinguishing actions in terms of their morality!

But let us pass over infants at the breast and consider children at the age of seven or eight years of age. Let us examine their conduct and see whether there does not appear some discernment of moral good and evil. Suppose two children quarrel; you need only ask those who witnessed the event, and they will know to tell you who was in the wrong and who in the right. The strictest inquiry will only serve to further convince you of the equity of their judgment.

Children know quite well when one rewards or punishes rightly or wrongly. On this point they never deceive themselves. But to distinguish actions as deserving reward or punishment is to be able to discern moral good from moral evil.

Horace, the poet of reason, does not hesitate to summon men to deeds of rectitude, which is visible even in children's play. "At pueri ludentes, 'Rex eris,' aiunt, 'si recte facies' (But boys at their game would cry out, 'You will be king, if you do the right thing')" Yes, children in their play confer royalty on those who do the best. They are cognizant that merit should correspond to preference. Is this what it means to be deprived of all ideas of morality?

Children distinguish the evil that was done inadvertently from that which was done by design. They excuse the one, but do not pardon the other. They therefore know to hold one culpable only for those deeds done with evil intention.

When a child would take for his own the book or playthings of one of his companions, all the rest declare him to be in the wrong. They have already this sentiment of equity that it is only just that everyone should enjoy what belongs to him or what has been appropriated to his use. Children of seven or eight years of age are capable of possessing all these ideas of morality, and their conduct continually furnishes the proof and examples.[12]

I would like as little to insist that a ten-year-old be five feet tall as that he possess judgment. Actually, what would reason do for him at that age? It is the bridle of strength, and the child does not need this bridle.[13]

It would be absurd to require that a child of ten years old should be five feet high; it would be equally absurd to require that he should at that age have as ripe a judgment as a man of thirty. Judgment is a faculty that develops and forms itself little by little. We see this faculty first begin to appear in children from the age of seven or eight years, and at ten years old it has made perceptible progress. "Reason," says Rousseau, "is the bridle of strength." I would rather say that it should serve as a bridle to the first interior movements which incline us to use our strength. A child of ten years of age has a lively sentiment of his nascent strength, a sentiment active and vigorous prompting him to be in act, to be continually fidgeting, to take those objects that are near at hand, and to turn them about and work them in every manner. It is in this fashion that by a hidden impulse of nature the young bull shakes his proud head and strikes his impotent blows, testing the weapons that he does not yet possess. This nascent strength in animals is governed by a certain and unalterable instinct that guides them, but in man there is no immediate rule other than reason. Why then should reason be entirely useless to a child of ten years old? This interior propensity that stirs and agitates him, which prompts him to continual action and keeps him always out of breath—does it not need some restraint? It is true that at this age reason is too weak to suffice by itself. It needs to be assisted and fortified by precepts, examples, and appropriate practices. "We are born weak ... we need judgment ... [and it is] given us by education."[14]

Review and Discussion Questions

1. Why does Rousseau wish to free students from "dependence on men," and why does Gerdil think the attempt foolish?

2. Contrast Rousseau's from Gerdil's view of the purpose of liberty?

3. Gerdil accepts the doctrine of original sin. How does this doctrine contribute to his account of the nature and purpose of education?

4. According to Gerdil, why was reason given to man?

5. What evidence does Gerdil offer to support his claim that children are capable of grasping moral categories?

❖ 8

BL. JOHN HENRY NEWMAN (1801–90)

The Idea of a University

> If they are nothing more than well-read men, or men of information, they
> have not what specially deserves the name of culture of mind, or fulfills the
> type of Liberal Education.

As a hospital aims at health, and the gymnasium fitness, so the university
aims at the improvement of the mind. In this selection, Newman searches
for a definition of intellectual excellence. Though liberal education has for
its end knowledge, further specification is needed. The enlargement of the
mind aims to instill, in addition, the capacity for synthesis. Details count,
but so too does a grasp of how parts relate to wholes. Only a mind cultivated to grasp "the natural and true relations" among things can be said to be
liberally formed. More than a century before schools gave themselves over
to "careerism," Cardinal Newman had anticipated the problem and offered
a solution.

Further reading: Arthur Dwight Culler, *The Imperial Intellect: A Study of Newman's Educational
Ideal* (Oxford: Oxford University Press, 1955); Ian Ker, *John Henry Newman: A Biography* (Ox-
ford: Clarendon Press, 1988); Frederick D. Aquino, *An Integrative Habit of Mind: John Henry
Newman on the Path to Wisdom* (De Kalb, Ill.: Northern Illinois University Press, 2012). Paul
Shrimpton, *The 'Making of Men': The* Idea *and Reality of Newman's University in Oxford and
Dublin* (Leominister, Herefordshire: Gracewing Publishing, 2014).

❖

I.

It were well if the English, like the Greek language, possessed some definite word to express, simply and generally, intellectual proficiency or perfection, such as "health," as used with reference to the animal frame, and
"virtue," with reference to our moral nature. I am not able to find such a
term;—talent, ability, genius, belong distinctly to the raw material, which
is the subject-matter, not to that excellence which is the result of exercise

and training. When we turn, indeed, to the particular kinds of intellectual perfection, words are forthcoming for our purpose, as, for instance, judgment, taste, and skill; yet even these belong, for the most part, to powers or habits bearing upon practice or upon art, and not to any perfect condition of the intellect, considered in itself. Wisdom, again, is certainly a more comprehensive word than any other, but it has a direct relation to conduct, and to human life. Knowledge, indeed, and Science express purely intellectual ideas, but still not a state or quality of the intellect; for knowledge, in its ordinary sense, is but one of its circumstances, denoting a possession or a habit; and science has been appropriated to the subject-matter of the intellect, instead of belonging in English, as it ought to do, to the intellect itself. The consequence is that, on an occasion like this, many words are necessary, in order, first, to bring out and convey what surely is no difficult idea in itself, that of the cultivation of the intellect as an end; next, in order to recommend what surely is no unreasonable object; and lastly, to describe and make the mind realize the particular perfection in which that object consists. Every one knows practically what are the constituents of health or of virtue; and every one recognizes health and virtue as ends to be pursued; it is otherwise with intellectual excellence, and this must be my excuse, if I seem to any one to be bestowing a good deal of labour on a preliminary matter.

In default of a recognized term, I have called the perfection or virtue of the intellect by the name of philosophy, philosophical knowledge, enlargement of mind, or illumination; terms which are not uncommonly given to it by writers of this day: but, whatever name we bestow on it, it is, I believe, as a matter of history, the business of a University to make this intellectual culture its direct scope, or to employ itself in the education of the intellect,—just as the work of a Hospital lies in healing the sick or wounded, of a Riding or Fencing School, or of a Gymnasium, in exercising the limbs, of an Almshouse, in aiding and solacing the old, of an Orphanage, in protecting innocence, of a Penitentiary, in restoring the guilty. I say, a University, taken in its bare idea, and before we view it as an instrument of the Church, has this object and this mission; it contemplates neither moral impression nor mechanical production; it professes to exercise the mind neither in art nor in duty; its function is intellectual culture; here it may leave its scholars, and it has done its work when it has done as much as this. It educates the intellect to reason well in all matters, to reach out towards truth, and to grasp it.

2.

This, I said in my foregoing Discourse, was the object of a University, viewed in itself, and apart from the Catholic Church, or from the State, or from any other power which may use it; and I illustrated this in various ways. I said that the intellect must have an excellence of its own, for there was nothing which had not its specific good; that the word "educate" would not be used of intellectual culture, as it is used, had not the intellect had an end of its own; that, had it not such an end, there would be no meaning in calling certain intellectual exercises "liberal," in contrast with "useful," as is commonly done; that the very notion of a philosophical temper implied it, for it threw us back upon research and system as ends in themselves, distinct from effects and works of any kind; that a philosophical scheme of knowledge, or system of sciences, could not, from the nature of the case, issue in any one definite art or pursuit, as its end; and that, on the other hand, the discovery and contemplation of truth, to which research and systematizing led, were surely sufficient ends, though nothing beyond them were added, and that they had ever been accounted sufficient by mankind.

Here then I take up the subject; and, having determined that the cultivation of the intellect is an end distinct and sufficient in itself, and that, so far as words go it is an enlargement or illumination, I proceed to inquire what this mental breadth, or power, or light, or philosophy consists in. A Hospital heals a broken limb or cures a fever: what does an Institution effect, which professes the health, not of the body, not of the soul, but of the intellect? What is this good, which in former times, as well as our own, has been found worth the notice, the appropriation, of the Catholic Church?

I have then to investigate, in the Discourses which follow, those qualities and characteristics of the intellect in which its cultivation issues or rather consists; and, with a view of assisting myself in this undertaking, I shall recur to certain questions which have already been touched upon. These questions are three: viz. the relation of intellectual culture, first, to *mere* knowledge; secondly, to *professional* knowledge; and thirdly, to *religious* knowledge. In other words, are *acquirements* and *attainments* the scope of a University Education? or *expertness in particular arts and pursuits?* or *moral and religious proficiency?* or something besides these three? These questions I shall examine in succession, with the purpose I have mentioned; and I hope to he excused, if, in this anxious undertaking, I am led to repeat what, either in these Discourses or elsewhere, I have already put upon paper. And first, of *Mere Knowledge*, or Learning, and its connexion with intellectual illumination or Philosophy.

3.

I suppose the *prima-facie* view which the public at large would take of a University, considering it as a place of Education, is nothing more or less than a place for acquiring a great deal of knowledge on a great many subjects. Memory is one of the first developed of the mental faculties; a boy's business when he goes to school is to learn, that is, to store up things in his memory. For some years his intellect is little more than an instrument for taking in facts, or a receptacle for storing them; he welcomes them as fast as they come to him; he lives on what is without; he has his eyes ever about him; he has a lively susceptibility of impressions; he imbibes information of every kind; and little does he make his own in a true sense of the word, living rather upon his neighbours all around him. He has opinions, religious, political, and literary, and, for a boy, is very positive in them and sure about them; but he gets them from his schoolfellows, or his masters, or his parents, as the case may be. Such as he is in his other relations, such also is he in his school exercises; his mind is observant, sharp, ready, retentive; he is almost passive in the acquisition of knowledge. I say this in no disparagement of the idea of a clever boy. Geography, chronology, history, language, natural history, he heaps up the matter of these studies as treasures for a future day. It is the seven years of plenty with him: he gathers in by handfuls, like the Egyptians, without counting; and though, as time goes on, there is exercise for his argumentative powers in the Elements of Mathematics, and for his taste in the Poets and Orators, still, while at school, or at least, till quite the last years of his time, he acquires, and little more; and when he is leaving for the University, he is mainly the creature of foreign influences and circumstances, and made up of accidents, homogeneous or not, as the case may be. Moreover, the moral habits, which are a boy's praise, encourage and assist this result; that is, diligence, assiduity, regularity, despatch, persevering application; for these are the direct conditions of acquisition, and naturally lead to it. Acquirements, again, are emphatically producible, and at a moment; they are a something to show, both for master and scholar; an audience, even though ignorant themselves of the subjects of an examination, can comprehend when questions are answered and when they are not. Here again is a reason why mental culture is in the minds of men identified with the acquisition of knowledge.

The same notion possesses the public mind, when it passes on from the thought of a school to that of a University: and with the best of reasons so far as this, that there is no true culture without acquirements, and that philosophy presupposes knowledge. It requires a great deal of reading, or a wide range of information, to warrant us in putting forth our opinions on any serious subject; and without such learning the most original mind may be able indeed to dazzle, to amuse, to refute, to perplex, but not to come to any useful result or any trustworthy conclusion. There are indeed persons who profess a different view of the matter, and even act upon it. Every now and then you will find a person of vigorous or fertile mind, who relies upon his own resources, despises all former authors, and gives the world, with the utmost fearlessness, his views upon religion, or history, or any other popular subject. And his works may sell for a while; he may get a name in his day; but this will be all. His readers are sure to find on the long run that his doctrines are mere theories, and not the expression of facts, that they are chaff instead of bread, and then his popularity drops as suddenly as it rose.

Knowledge then is the indispensable condition of expansion of mind, and the instrument of attaining to it; this cannot be denied, it is ever to be insisted on; I begin with it as a first principle; however, the very truth of it carries men too far, and confirms to them the notion that it is the whole of the matter. A narrow mind is thought to be that which contains little knowledge; and an enlarged mind, that which holds a great deal; and what seems to put the matter beyond dispute is, the fact of the great number of studies which are pursued in a University, by its very profession. Lectures are given on every kind of subject; examinations are held; prizes awarded. There are moral, metaphysical, physical Professors; Professors of languages, of history, of mathematics, of experimental science. Lists of questions are published, wonderful for their range and depth, variety and difficulty; treatises are written, which carry upon their very face the evidence of extensive reading or multifarious information; what then is wanting for mental culture to a person of large reading and scientific attainments? what is grasp of mind but acquirement? where shall philosophical repose be found, but in the consciousness and enjoyment of large intellectual possessions?

And yet this notion is, I conceive, a mistake, and my present business is to show that it is one, and that the end of a Liberal Education is not mere knowledge, or knowledge considered in its *matter*; and I shall best attain my object, by actually setting down some cases, which will be generally granted to be instances of the process of enlightenment or enlargement of mind, and others which are not, and thus, by the comparison, you will be able to judge for yourselves, Gentlemen, whether Knowledge, that is, acquirement, is after all the real principle of the enlargement, or whether that principle is not rather something beyond it.

4.

For instance, let a person, whose experience has hitherto been confined to the more calm and unpretending scenery of these islands, whether here or in England, go for the first time into parts where physical nature puts on her wilder and more awful forms, whether at home or abroad, as into mountainous districts; or let one, who has ever lived in a quiet village, go for the first time to a great metropolis—then I suppose he will have a sensation which perhaps he never had before. He has a feeling not in addition or increase of former feelings, but of something different in its nature. He will perhaps be borne forward, and find for a time that he has lost his bearings. He has made a certain progress, and he has a consciousness of mental enlargement; he does not stand where he did, he has a new centre, and a range of thoughts to which he was before a stranger.

Again, the view of the heavens which the telescope opens upon us, if allowed to fill and possess the mind, may almost whirl it round and make it dizzy. It brings in a flood of ideas, and is rightly called an intellectual enlargement, whatever is meant by the term.

And so again, the sight of beasts of prey and other foreign animals, their strangeness, the originality (if I may use the term) of their forms and gestures and habits and their variety and independence of each other, throw us out of ourselves into another creation, and as if under another Creator, if I may so express the temptation which may come on the mind. We seem to have new faculties, or a new exercise for our faculties, by this addition to our knowledge; like a prisoner, who, having been accustomed to wear manacles or fetters, suddenly finds his arms and legs free.

Hence Physical Science generally, in all its departments, as bringing before us the exuberant riches and resources, yet the orderly course, of the Universe, elevates and excites the student, and at first, I may say, almost takes away his breath, while in time it exercises a tranquilizing influence upon him.

Again, the study of history is said to enlarge and enlighten the mind, and why? because, as I conceive, it gives it a power of judging of passing events, and of all events, and a conscious superiority over them, which before it did not possess.

And in like manner, what is called seeing the world, entering into active life, going into society, travelling, gaining acquaintance with the various classes of the community, coming into contact with the principles and modes of thought of various parties, interests, and races, their views, aims, habits and manners, their religious creeds and forms of worship—gaining experience how various yet how alike men are, how low-minded, how bad, how opposed, yet how confident in their opinions; all this exerts a perceptible influence upon the mind, which it is impossible to mistake, be it good or be it bad, and is popularly called its enlargement.

And then again, the first time the mind comes across the arguments and speculations of unbelievers, and feels what a novel light they cast upon what he has hitherto accounted sacred; and still more, if it gives in to them and embraces them, and throws off as so much prejudice what it has hitherto held, and, as if waking from a dream, begins to realize to its imagination that there is now no such thing as law and the transgression of law, that sin is a phantom, and punishment a bugbear, that it is free to sin, free to enjoy the world and the flesh; and still further, when it does enjoy them, and reflects that it may think and hold just what it will, that "the world is all before it where to choose," and what system to build up as its own private persuasion; when this torrent of wilful thoughts rushes over and inundates it, who will deny that the fruit of the tree of knowledge, or what the mind takes for knowledge, has made it one of the gods, with a sense of expansion and elevation—an intoxication in reality, still, so far as the subjective state of the mind goes, an illumination? Hence the fanaticism of individuals or nations, who suddenly cast off their Maker. Their eyes are opened; and, like the judgment-stricken king in the Tragedy, they see two suns, and a magic universe, out of which they look back upon their former state of faith and innocence with a sort of contempt and indignation, as if they were then but fools, and the dupes of imposture.

On the other hand, Religion has its own enlargement, and an enlargement, not of tumult, but of peace. It is often remarked of uneducated persons, who have hitherto thought little of the unseen world, that, on their turning to God, looking into themselves, regulating their hearts, reforming their conduct, and meditating on death and judgment, heaven and hell, they seem to become, in point of intellect, different beings from what they were. Before, they took things as they came, and thought no more of one thing than another. But now every event has a meaning; they have their own estimate of whatever happens to them; they are mindful of times and seasons, and compare the present with the past; and the world, no longer dull, monotonous, unprofitable, and hopeless, is a various and complicated drama, with parts and an object, and an awful moral.

5.

Now from these instances, to which many more might be added, it is plain, first, that the communication of knowledge certainly is either a condition or the means of that sense of enlargement or enlightenment, of which at this day we hear so much in certain quarters: this cannot be denied; but next, it is equally plain, that such communication is not the whole of the process. The enlargement consists, not merely in the passive reception into the mind of a number of ideas unknown to it, but in the mind's energetic and simultaneous action upon and towards and among those new ideas, which are rushing in upon it. It is the action of a formative power, reducing to order and meaning the matter of our acquirements; it is a making the objects of our knowledge subjectively our own, or, to use a familiar word, it is a digestion of what we receive, into the substance of our previous state of thought; and without this no enlargement is said to follow. There is no enlargement, unless there be a comparison of ideas one with another, as they come before the mind, and a systematizing of them. We feel our minds to be growing and expanding *then*, when we not only learn, but refer what we learn to what we know already. It is not the mere addition to our knowledge that is the illumination; but the locomotion, the movement onwards, of that mental centre, to which both what we know, and what we are learning, the accumulating mass of our acquirements, gravitates. And therefore a truly great intellect, and recognized to be such by the common opinion of mankind, such as the intellect of Aristotle, or of St. Thomas, or of Newton, or of Goethe (I purposely take instances within and without the Catholic pale, when I would speak of the intellect as such) is one which takes a connected view of old and new, past and present, far and near, and which has an insight into the influence of all these one on another; without which there is no whole, and no centre. It possesses the knowledge, not only of things, but also of their mutual and true relations; knowledge, not merely considered as acquirement, but as philosophy.

Accordingly, when this analytical, distributive, harmonizing process is away, the mind experiences no enlargement, and is not reckoned as enlightened or comprehensive, whatever it may add to its knowledge. For instance, a great memory, as I have already said, does not make a philosopher, any more than a dictionary can be called a grammar. There are men who embrace in their minds a vast multitude of ideas, but with little sensibility about their real relations towards each other. These may be antiquarians, annalists, naturalists; they may be learned in the law; they may be versed in statistics; they are most useful in their own place; I should shrink from speaking disrespectfully of them; still, there is nothing in such attainments to guarantee the absence of narrowness of mind. If they are nothing more than well-read men, or men of information, they have not what specially deserves the name of culture of mind, or fulfils the type of Liberal Education.

In like manner, we sometimes fall in with persons who have seen much of the world, and of the men who, in their day, have played a conspicuous part in it, but who generalize nothing, and have no observation, in the true sense of the word. They abound in information in detail, curious and entertaining, about men and things; and, having lived under the influence of no very clear or settled principles, religious or political, they speak of every one and every thing, only as so many phenomena, which are complete in themselves, and lead to nothing, not discussing them, or teaching any truth, or instructing the hearer, but simply talking. No one would say that these persons, well informed as they are, had attained to any great culture of intellect or to philosophy.

The case is the same still more strikingly where the persons in question are beyond dispute men of inferior powers and deficient education. Perhaps they have been much in foreign countries, and they receive, in a passive, otiose, unfruitful way, the various facts which are forced upon them there. Seafaring men, for example, range from one end of the earth to the other; but the multiplicity of external objects, which they have encountered, forms no symmetrical and consistent picture upon their imagination; they see the tapestry of human life, as it were on the wrong side, and it tells no story. They sleep, and they rise up, and they find themselves, now in Europe, now in Asia; they see visions of great cities and wild regions; they are in the marts of commerce, or amid the islands of the South; they gaze on Pompey's Pillar, or on the Andes; and nothing which meets them carries them forward or backward, to any idea beyond itself. Nothing has a drift or relation; nothing has a history or a promise. Every thing stands by itself, and comes and goes in its turn, like the shifting scenes of a show, which leave the spectator where he was. Perhaps you are near such a man on a particular occasion, and expect him to be shocked or perplexed at something which occurs; but one thing is much the same to him as another, or, if he is perplexed, it is as not knowing what to say, whether it is right to admire, or to ridicule, or to disapprove, while conscious that some expression of opinion is expected from him; for in fact he has no standard of judgment at all, and no landmarks to guide him to a conclusion. Such is mere acquisition, and, I repeat, no one would dream of calling it philosophy.

Review and Discussion Questions

1. What English terms does Newman consider and reject in his search for an adequate description of "intellectual excellence"?

2. What, most importantly, ought a boy to learn?

3. Newman settles on the term "enlargement of mind" as the end of liberal education. What instances indicating this process does Newman offer?

4. How, in Newman's view, does liberal education aid the mind in forming a "connected view of old and new"?

5. Newman contrasts the man of culture with the man of "mere acquisition." What is deficient in the intellect of the latter?

❖ 9

ST. JOHN PAUL II (1920–2005)

On Faith and Reason

> The ultimate purpose of personal existence, then, is the theme of philosophy
> and theology alike ... lasting joy of the contemplation of the Triune God.

As St. John Paul II judges it, modern philosophy has long concentrated
upon the knowing subject rather than upon the external world. This turn
away from what thought can discover toward what it is that conditions
thought—class, sex, race, temperament—has often led our attention away
from philosophy's proper vocation: truth itself. Wonder finds completion
in wisdom, and the task of critical thought is not to see through the world,
not to explain it away, but to comprehend its fullness, to direct men's paths
"towards a truth which transcends them." Against the temptations to skepticism and cynicism, *Fides et Ratio* calls Catholic intellectuals to reclaim
their vocation as lovers of truth. Truth is why we study; truth is why we
teach. Armed with confidence that reason's quest is not fruitless, men and
women in our time can find in study the God of joy.

Further reading: D. R. Foster and J. W. Koterski, S.J., eds., *The Two Wings of Catholic Thought:
Essays on* Fides et Ratio (Washington, D.C.: The Catholic University of America Press, 2003);
Benedict XVI, *Spes Salvi* (Saved in Hope) (San Francisco: Ignatius Press, 2008); Fergus Kerr,
Twentieth-Century Catholic Theologians (Oxford: Blackwell Publishing, 2007).

❖

My Venerable Brother Bishops,
Health and the Apostolic Blessing!

Faith and reason are like two wings on which the human spirit rises to
the contemplation of truth; and God has placed in the human heart a desire
to know the truth—in a word, to know himself—so that, by knowing and
loving God, men and women may also come to the fullness of truth about
themselves (cf. Ex 33:18; Ps 27:8–9; 63:2–3; Jn 14:8; 1 Jn 3:2).

"Know Yourself"

1. In both East and West, we may trace a journey which has led humanity down the centuries to meet and engage truth more and more deeply. It is a journey which has unfolded—as it must—within the horizon of personal self-consciousness: the more human beings know reality and the world, the more they know themselves in their uniqueness, with the question of the meaning of things and of their very existence becoming ever more pressing. This is why all that is the object of our knowledge becomes a part of our life. The admonition *Know yourself* was carved on the temple portal at Delphi, as testimony to a basic truth to be adopted as a minimal norm by those who seek to set themselves apart from the rest of creation as "human beings," that is as those who "know themselves."

Moreover, a cursory glance at ancient history shows clearly how in different parts of the world, with their different cultures, there arise at the same time the fundamental questions which pervade human life: *Who am I? Where have I come from and where am I going? Why is there evil? What is there after this life?* These are the questions which we find in the sacred writings of Israel, as also in the Veda and the Avesta; we find them in the writings of Confucius and Lao-Tze, and in the preaching of Tirthankara and Buddha; they appear in the poetry of Homer and in the tragedies of Euripides and Sophocles, as they do in the philosophical writings of Plato and Aristotle. They are questions which have their common source in the quest for meaning which has always compelled the human heart. In fact, the answer given to these questions decides the direction which people seek to give to their lives.

2. The Church is no stranger to this journey of discovery, nor could she ever be. From the moment when, through the Paschal Mystery, she received the gift of the ultimate truth about human life, the Church has made her pilgrim way along the paths of the world to proclaim that Jesus Christ is "the way, and the truth, and the life" (Jn 14:6). It is her duty to serve humanity in different ways, but one way in particular imposes a responsibility of a quite special kind: the *diakonia of the truth*.[1] This mission on the one hand makes the believing community a partner in humanity's shared struggle to arrive at truth;[2] and on the other hand it obliges the believing community to proclaim the certitudes arrived at, albeit with a sense that every truth attained is but a step towards that fullness of truth which will appear with the final Revelation of God: "For now we see in a mirror dimly, but then face to face. Now I know in part; then I shall understand fully" (1 Cor 13:12).

3. Men and women have at their disposal an array of resources for generating greater knowledge of truth so that their lives may be ever more human. Among these is *philosophy*, which is directly concerned with asking the question of life's meaning and sketching an answer to it. Philosophy emerges, then, as one of noblest of human tasks. According to its Greek etymology, the term philosophy means "love of wisdom." Born and nurtured when the human being first asked questions about the reason for things and their purpose, philosophy shows in different modes and forms that the desire for truth is part of human nature itself. It is an innate property of human reason to ask why things are as they are, even though the answers which gradually emerge are set within a horizon which reveals how the different human cultures are complementary.

Philosophy's powerful influence on the formation and development of the cultures of the West should not obscure the influence it has also had upon the ways of understanding existence found in the East. Every people has its own native and seminal wisdom which, as a true cultural treasure, tends to find voice and develop in forms which are genuinely philosophical. One example of this is the basic form of philosophical knowledge which is evident to this day in the postulates which inspire national and international legal systems in regulating the life of society.

4. Nonetheless, it is true that a single term conceals a variety of meanings. Hence the need for a preliminary clarification. Driven by the desire to discover the ultimate truth of existence, human beings seek to acquire those universal elements of knowledge which enable them to understand themselves better and to advance in their own self-realization. These fundamental elements of knowledge spring from the *wonder* awakened in them by the contemplation of creation: human beings are astonished to discover themselves as part of the world, in a relationship with others like them, all sharing a common destiny. Here begins, then, the journey which will lead them to discover ever new frontiers of knowledge. Without wonder, men and women would lapse into deadening routine and little by little would become incapable of a life which is genuinely personal.

Through philosophy's work, the ability to speculate which is proper to the human intellect produces a rigorous mode of thought; and then in turn, through the logical coherence of the affirmations made and the organic unity of their content, it produces a systematic body of knowledge. In different cultural contexts and at different times, this process has yielded results which have produced genuine systems of thought. Yet often enough in history this has brought with it the temptation to identify one single stream with the whole of philosophy. In such cases, we are clearly dealing with a "philosophical pride" which seeks to present its own partial and imperfect view as the complete reading of all reality. In effect, every philosophical *system*, while it should always be respected in its wholeness, without any instrumentalization, must still recognize the primacy of philosophical *enquiry*, from which it stems and which it ought loyally to serve.

Although times change and knowledge increases, it is possible to discern a core of philosophical insight within the history of thought as a whole. Consider, for example, the principles of non-contradiction, finality and causality, as well as the concept of the person as a free and intelligent subject, with the capacity to know God, truth and goodness. Consider as well certain fundamental moral norms which are shared by all. These are among the indications that, beyond different schools of thought, there exists a body of knowledge which may be judged a kind of spiritual heritage of humanity. It is as if we had come upon an *implicit philosophy*, as a result of which all feel that they possess these principles, albeit in a general and unreflective way. Precisely because it is shared in some measure by all, this knowledge should serve as a kind of reference-point for the different philosophical schools. Once reason successfully intuits and formulates the first universal principles of being and correctly draws from them conclusions which are coherent both logically and ethically, then it may be called right reason or, as the ancients called it, *orthós logos, recta ratio*.

5. On her part, the Church cannot but set great value upon reason's drive to attain goals which render people's lives ever more worthy. She sees in philosophy the way to come to know fundamental truths about human life. At the same time, the Church considers philosophy an indispensable help for a deeper understanding of faith and for communicating the truth of the Gospel to those who do not yet know it.

Therefore, following upon similar initiatives by my Predecessors, I wish to reflect upon this special activity of human reason. I judge it necessary to do so because, at the present time in particular, the search for ultimate truth seems often to be neglected. Modern philosophy clearly has the great merit of focusing attention upon man. From this starting-point, human reason with its many questions has developed further its yearning to know more and to know it ever more deeply. Complex systems of thought have thus been built, yielding results in the different fields of knowledge and fostering the development of culture and history. Anthropology, logic, the natural sciences, history, linguistics and so forth—the whole universe of knowledge has been involved in one way or another. Yet the positive results achieved must not obscure the fact that reason, in its one-sided concern to investigate human subjectivity, seems to have forgotten that men and women are always called to direct their steps towards a truth which transcends them. Sundered from that truth, individuals are at the mercy of caprice, and their state as person ends up being judged by pragmatic criteria based essentially upon experimental data, in the mistaken belief that technology must dominate all. It has happened therefore that reason, rather than voicing the human orientation towards truth, has wilted under the weight of so much knowledge and little by little has lost the capacity to lift its gaze to the heights, not daring to rise to the truth of being. Abandoning the investigation of being, modern philosophical research has concentrated instead upon human knowing. Rather than make use of the human capacity to know the truth, modern philosophy has preferred to accentuate the ways in which this capacity is limited and conditioned.

This has given rise to different forms of agnosticism and relativism which have led philosophical research to lose its way in the shifting sands of widespread scepticism. Recent times have seen the rise to prominence of various doctrines which tend to devalue even the truths which had been judged certain. A legitimate plurality of positions has yielded to an undifferentiated pluralism, based upon the assumption that all positions are equally valid, which is one of today's most widespread symptoms of the lack of confidence in truth. Even certain conceptions of life coming from the East betray this lack of confidence, denying truth its exclusive character and assuming that truth reveals itself equally in different doctrines, even if they contradict one another. On this understanding, everything is reduced to opinion; and there is a sense of being adrift. While, on the one hand, philosophical thinking has succeeded in coming closer to the reality of human life and its forms of expression, it has also tended to pursue issues—existential, hermeneutical or linguistic—which ignore the radical question of the truth about personal existence, about being and about God. Hence we see among the men and women of our time, and not just in some philosophers, attitudes of widespread distrust of the human being's great capacity for knowledge. With a false modesty, people rest content with partial and provisional truths, no longer seeking to ask radical questions about the meaning and ultimate foundation of human, personal and social existence. In short, the hope that philosophy might be able to provide definitive answers to these questions has dwindled.

6. Sure of her competence as the bearer of the Revelation of Jesus Christ, the Church reaffirms the need to reflect upon truth. This is why I have de-

cided to address you, my venerable Brother Bishops, with whom I share the mission of "proclaiming the truth openly" (2 Cor 4:2), as also theologians and philosophers whose duty it is to explore the different aspects of truth, and all those who are searching; and I do so in order to offer some reflections on the path which leads to true wisdom, so that those who love truth may take the sure path leading to it and so find rest from their labours and joy for their spirit.

I feel impelled to undertake this task above all because of the Second Vatican Council's insistence that the Bishops are "witnesses of divine and catholic truth."[3] To bear witness to the truth is therefore a task entrusted to us Bishops; we cannot renounce this task without failing in the ministry which we have received. In reaffirming the truth of faith, we can both restore to our contemporaries a genuine trust in their capacity to know and challenge philosophy to recover and develop its own full dignity.

There is a further reason why I write these reflections. In my Encyclical Letter *Veritatis Splendor*, I drew attention to "certain fundamental truths of Catholic doctrine which, in the present circumstances, risk being distorted or denied."[4] In the present Letter, I wish to pursue that reflection by concentrating on the theme of *truth* itself and on its *foundation* in relation to *faith*. For it is undeniable that this time of rapid and complex change can leave especially the younger generation, to whom the future belongs and on whom it depends, with a sense that they have no valid points of reference. The need for a foundation for personal and communal life becomes all the more pressing at a time when we are faced with the patent inadequacy of perspectives in which the ephemeral is affirmed as a value and the possibility of discovering the real meaning of life is cast into doubt. This is why many people stumble through life to the very edge of the abyss without knowing where they are going. At times, this happens because those whose vocation it is to give cultural expression to their thinking no longer look to truth, preferring quick success to the toil of patient enquiry into what makes life worth living. With its enduring appeal to the search for truth, philosophy has the great responsibility of forming thought and culture; and now it must strive resolutely to recover its original vocation. This is why I have felt both the need and the duty to address this theme so that, on the threshold of the third millennium of the Christian era, humanity may come to a clearer sense of the great resources with which it has been endowed and may commit itself with renewed courage to implement the plan of salvation of which its history is part.

The Revelation of God's Wisdom

Jesus, Revealer of the Father

7. Underlying all the Church's thinking is the awareness that she is the bearer of a message which has its origin in God himself (cf. 2 Cor 4:1–2). The knowledge which the Church offers to man has its origin not in any speculation of her own, however sublime, but in the word of God which she has received in faith (cf. 1 Th 2:13). At the origin of our life of faith there is an encounter, unique in kind, which discloses a mystery hidden for long ages (cf. 1 Cor 2:7; Rom 16:25–26) but which is now revealed: "In his goodness and wisdom, God chose to reveal himself and to make known to us the hidden purpose of his will (cf. Eph 1:9), by which, through Christ, the Word made flesh, man has access to the Father in the Holy Spirit and comes to share in the divine nature."[5] This initiative is utterly gratuitous, moving from God to men and women in order to bring them to salvation. As the source of love, God desires to make himself known; and the knowledge which the human being has of God perfects all that the human mind can know of the meaning of life.

8. Restating almost to the letter the teaching of the First Vatican Council's Constitution *Dei Filius*, and taking into account the principles set out by the Council of Trent, the Second Vatican Council's Constitution *Dei Verbum* pursued the age-old journey of *understanding faith*, reflecting on Revelation in the light of the teaching of Scripture and of the entire Patristic tradition. At the First Vatican Council, the Fathers had stressed the supernatural character of God's Revelation. On the basis of mistaken and very widespread assertions, the rationalist critique of the time attacked faith and denied the possibility of any knowledge which was not the fruit of reason's natural capacities. This obliged the Council to reaffirm emphatically that there exists a knowledge which is peculiar to faith, surpassing the knowledge proper to human reason, which nevertheless by its nature can discover the Creator. This knowledge expresses a truth based upon the very fact of God who reveals himself, a truth which is most certain, since God neither deceives nor wishes to deceive.[6]

9. The First Vatican Council teaches, then, that the truth attained by philosophy and the truth of Revelation are neither identical nor mutually exclusive: "There exists a twofold order of knowledge, distinct not only as regards their source, but also as regards their object. With regard to the source, because we know in one by natural reason, in the other by divine faith. With regard to the object, because besides those things which natural

reason can attain, there are proposed for our belief mysteries hidden in God which, unless they are divinely revealed, cannot be known."[7] Based upon God's testimony and enjoying the supernatural assistance of grace, faith is of an order other than philosophical knowledge which depends upon sense perception and experience and which advances by the light of the intellect alone. Philosophy and the sciences function within the order of natural reason; while faith, enlightened and guided by the Spirit, recognizes in the message of salvation the "fullness of grace and truth" (cf. Jn 1:14) which God has willed to reveal in history and definitively through his Son, Jesus Christ (cf. 1 Jn 5:9; Jn 5:31–32).

10. Contemplating Jesus as revealer, the Fathers of the Second Vatican Council stressed the salvific character of God's Revelation in history, describing it in these terms: "In this Revelation, the invisible God (cf. Col 1:15; 1 Tim 1:17), out of the abundance of his love speaks to men and women as friends (cf. Ex 33:11; Jn 15:14–15) and lives among them (cf. Bar 3:38), so that he may invite and take them into communion with himself. This plan of Revelation is realized by deeds and words having an inner unity: the deeds wrought by God in the history of salvation manifest and confirm the teaching and realities signified by the words, while the words proclaim the deeds and clarify the mystery contained in them. By this Revelation, then, the deepest truth about God and human salvation is made clear to us in Christ, who is the mediator and at the same time the fullness of all Revelation."[8]

11. God's Revelation is therefore immersed in time and history. Jesus Christ took flesh in the "fullness of time" (Gal 4:4); and two thousand years later, I feel bound to restate forcefully that "in Christianity time has a fundamental importance."[9] It is within time that the whole work of creation and salvation comes to light; and it emerges clearly above all that, with the Incarnation of the Son of God, our life is even now a foretaste of the fulfilment of time which is to come (cf. Heb 1:2).

The truth about himself and his life which God has entrusted to humanity is immersed therefore in time and history; and it was declared once and for all in the mystery of Jesus of Nazareth. The Constitution *Dei Verbum* puts it eloquently: "After speaking in many places and varied ways through the prophets, God 'last of all in these days has spoken to us by his Son' (Heb 1:1–2). For he sent his Son, the eternal Word who enlightens all people, so that he might dwell among them and tell them the innermost realities about God (cf. Jn 1:1–18). Jesus Christ, the Word made flesh, sent as 'a human being to human beings', 'speaks the words of God' (Jn 3:34), and completes the work of salvation which his Father gave him to do (cf.

Jn 5:36; 17:4). To see Jesus is to see his Father (Jn 14:9). For this reason, Jesus perfected Revelation by fulfilling it through his whole work of making himself present and manifesting himself: through his words and deeds, his signs and wonders, but especially though his death and glorious Resurrection from the dead and finally his sending of the Spirit of truth."[10]

For the People of God, therefore, history becomes a path to be followed to the end, so that by the unceasing action of the Holy Spirit (cf. Jn 16:13) the contents of revealed truth may find their full expression. This is the teaching of the Constitution *Dei Verbum* when it states that "as the centuries succeed one another, the Church constantly progresses towards the fullness of divine truth, until the words of God reach their complete fulfilment in her."[11]

12. History therefore becomes the arena where we see what God does for humanity. God comes to us in the things we know best and can verify most easily, the things of our everyday life, apart from which we cannot understand ourselves.

In the Incarnation of the Son of God we see forged the enduring and definitive synthesis which the human mind of itself could not even have imagined: the Eternal enters time, the Whole lies hidden in the part, God takes on a human face. The truth communicated in Christ's Revelation is therefore no longer confined to a particular place or culture, but is offered to every man and woman who would welcome it as the word which is the absolutely valid source of meaning for human life. Now, in Christ, all have access to the Father, since by his Death and Resurrection Christ has bestowed the divine life which the first Adam had refused (cf. Rom 5:12–15). Through this Revelation, men and women are offered the ultimate truth about their own life and about the goal of history. As the Constitution *Gaudium et Spes* puts it, "only in the mystery of the incarnate Word does the mystery of man take on light."[12] Seen in any other terms, the mystery of personal existence remains an insoluble riddle. Where might the human being seek the answer to dramatic questions such as pain, the suffering of the innocent and death, if not in the light streaming from the mystery of Christ's Passion, Death and Resurrection?

Reason before the Mystery

13. It should nonetheless be kept in mind that Revelation remains charged with mystery. It is true that Jesus, with his entire life, revealed the countenance of the Father, for he came to teach the secret things of God.[13] But our vision of the face of God is always fragmentary and impaired by the

limits of our understanding. Faith alone makes it possible to penetrate the mystery in a way that allows us to understand it coherently.

The Council teaches that "the obedience of faith must be given to God who reveals himself."[14] This brief but dense statement points to a fundamental truth of Christianity. Faith is said first to be an obedient response to God. This implies that God be acknowledged in his divinity, transcendence and supreme freedom. By the authority of his absolute transcendence, God who makes himself known is also the source of the credibility of what he reveals. By faith, men and women give their *assent* to this divine testimony. This means that they acknowledge fully and integrally the truth of what is revealed because it is God himself who is the guarantor of that truth. They can make no claim upon this truth which comes to them as gift and which, set within the context of interpersonal communication, urges reason to be open to it and to embrace its profound meaning. This is why the Church has always considered the act of entrusting oneself to God to be a moment of fundamental decision which engages the whole person. In that act, the intellect and the will display their spiritual nature, enabling the subject to act in a way which realizes personal freedom to the full.[15] It is not just that freedom is part of the act of faith: it is absolutely required. Indeed, it is faith that allows individuals to give consummate expression to their own freedom. Put differently, freedom is not realized in decisions made against God. For how could it be an exercise of true freedom to refuse to be open to the very reality which enables our self-realization? Men and women can accomplish no more important act in their lives than the act of faith; it is here that freedom reaches the certainty of truth and chooses to live in that truth.

To assist reason in its effort to understand the mystery there are the signs which Revelation itself presents. These serve to lead the search for truth to new depths, enabling the mind in its autonomous exploration to penetrate within the mystery by use of reason's own methods, of which it is rightly jealous. Yet these signs also urge reason to look beyond their status as signs in order to grasp the deeper meaning which they bear. They contain a hidden truth to which the mind is drawn and which it cannot ignore without destroying the very signs which it is given.

In a sense, then, we return to the *sacramental* character of Revelation and especially to the sign of the Eucharist, in which the indissoluble unity between the signifier and signified makes it possible to grasp the depths of the mystery. In the Eucharist, Christ is truly present and alive, working through his Spirit; yet, as Saint Thomas said so well, "what you neither see nor grasp, faith confirms for you, leaving nature far behind; a sign it is that now appears, hiding in mystery realities sublime."[16] He is echoed by the philosopher Pascal: "Just as Jesus Christ went unrecognized among men, so does his truth appear without external difference among common modes of thought. So too does the Eucharist remain among common bread."[17]

In short, the knowledge proper to faith does not destroy the mystery; it only reveals it the more, showing how necessary it is for people's lives: Christ the Lord "in revealing the mystery of the Father and his love fully reveals man to himself and makes clear his supreme calling,"[18] which is to share in the divine mystery of the life of the Trinity.[19]

14. From the teaching of the two Vatican Councils there also emerges a genuinely novel consideration for philosophical learning. Revelation has set within history a point of reference which cannot be ignored if the mystery of human life is to be known. Yet this knowledge refers back constantly to the mystery of God which the human mind cannot exhaust but can only receive and embrace in faith. Between these two poles, reason has its own specific field in which it can enquire and understand, restricted only by its finiteness before the infinite mystery of God.

Revelation therefore introduces into our history a universal and ultimate truth which stirs the human mind to ceaseless effort; indeed, it impels reason continually to extend the range of its knowledge until it senses that it has done all in its power, leaving no stone unturned. To assist our reflection on this point we have one of the most fruitful and important minds in human history, a point of reference for both philosophy and theology: Saint Anselm. In his *Proslogion*, the Archbishop of Canterbury puts it this way: "Thinking of this problem frequently and intently, at times it seemed I was ready to grasp what I was seeking; at other times it eluded my thought completely, until finally, despairing of being able to find it, I wanted to abandon the search for something which was impossible to find. I wanted to rid myself of that thought because, by filling my mind, it distracted me from other problems from which I could gain some profit; but it would then present itself with ever greater insistence ... Woe is me, one of the poor children of Eve, far from God, what did I set out to do and what have I accomplished? What was I aiming for and how far have I got? What did I aspire to and what did I long for? ... O Lord, you are not only that than which nothing greater can be conceived (*non solum es quo maius cogitari nequit*), but you are greater than all that can be conceived (*quiddam maius quam cogitari possit*) ... If you were not such, something greater than you could be thought, but this is impossible."[20]

15. The truth of Christian Revelation, found in Jesus of Nazareth, en-

Saint Cecilia and an Angel

ables all men and women to embrace the "mystery" of their own life. As absolute truth, it summons human beings to be open to the transcendent, whilst respecting both their autonomy as creatures and their freedom. At this point the relationship between freedom and truth is complete, and we understand the full meaning of the Lord's words: "You will know the truth, and the truth will make you free" (Jn 8:32).

Christian Revelation is the true lodestar of men and women as they strive to make their way amid the pressures of an immanentist habit of mind and the constrictions of a technocratic logic. It is the ultimate possibility offered by God for the human being to know in all its fullness the seminal plan of love which began with creation. To those wishing to know the truth, if they can look beyond themselves and their own concerns, there is given the possibility of taking full and harmonious possession of their lives, precisely by following the path of truth. Here the words of the Book of Deuteronomy are pertinent: "This commandment which I command you is not too hard for you, neither is it far off. It is not in heaven that you should say, 'Who will go up for us to heaven, and bring it to us, that we may hear it and do it?' Neither is it beyond the sea, that you should say, 'Who will go over the sea for us, and bring it to us, that we may hear and do it?' But the word is very near you; it is in your mouth and in your heart, that you can do it" (30:11–14). This text finds an echo in the famous dictum of the holy philosopher and theologian Augustine: "Do not wander far and wide but return into yourself. Deep within man there dwells the truth" (*Noli foras ire, in te ipsum redi. In interiore homine habitat veritas*).[21]

These considerations prompt a first conclusion: the truth made known to us by Revelation is neither the product nor the consummation of an argument devised by human reason. It appears instead as something gratuitous, which itself stirs thought and seeks acceptance as an expression of love. This revealed truth is set within our history as an anticipation of that ultimate and definitive vision of God which is reserved for those who believe in him and seek him with a sincere heart. The ultimate purpose of personal existence, then, is the theme of philosophy and theology alike. For all their difference of method and content, both disciplines point to that "path of life" (Ps 16:11) which, as faith tells us, leads in the end to the full and lasting joy of the contemplation of the Triune God.

Review and Discussion Questions

1. Why would John Paul II open with a meditation on a pagan oracle?
2. What characterizes a philosophical or "fundamental" question?
3. What is meritorious in modern philosophy? What is lacking?
4. How does the Incarnation of Christ illumine or energize the project of philosophy?
5. In what sense(s) do philosophy and theology share the same end(s)?

PART II

The Matter of Learning

Geometria

PLATO (427–347 BC)

The Republic

And when reason comes, he will recognize and salute the friend with whom his education has made him long familiar.

What do young children need to know? Very little, according to Plato. Their work is not so much to fill their heads as it is to tighten their muscles, and attune their ears. Early education, as Plato argued and ancient Greek practice presumed, ought to form the soul through both music and exercise. Music, which in the ancient view encompasses poetry, helps to harmonize the passions of the soul. Gymnastics, dance, and athletic competition disciplines the body, and most importantly, the will. Underlying Plato's conception of the early curriculum is the premise that the soul is imitative. Ugly images encourage ugly souls. Coarse music begets rough minds. Before the soul is capable to grasp the good it must first be habituated to desire the good. It is this foundational principle which shapes Plato's vision of the early curriculum.

Further Reading: Plato, *Seventh Letter*, in *The Complete Works of Plato*, ed. John M. Cooper (Indianapolis, Ind.: Hackett Publishing, 1997); Aristotle, *On Rhetoric* in *The Complete Works of Aristotle*, volume 2, ed. Jonathan Barnes (Princeton, N.J.: Princeton University Press, 1984); Augustine, *Confessions* [Books I–IV], trans. Maria Boulding, O.S.B., ed. David Meconi, S.J. (San Francisco: Ignatius Press, 2012).

❖

The preferring of Apollo and his instruments to Marsyas and his instruments is not at all strange, I [Socrates] said.

Not at all, he [Glaucon] replied.

And so, by the dog of Egypt, we have been unconsciously purging the State, which not long ago we termed luxurious.

And we have done wisely, he replied.

Then let us now finish the purgation, I said. Next in order to harmonies, rhythms will naturally follow, and they should be subject to the same rules, for we ought not to seek out complex systems of metre, or metres of every kind, but rather to discover what rhythms are the expressions of a courageous and harmonious life; and when we have found them, we shall adapt the foot and the melody to words having a like spirit, not the words to the foot and melody. To say what these rhythms are will be your duty—you must teach me them, as you have already taught me the harmonies.

But, indeed, he replied, I cannot tell you. I only know that there are some three principles of rhythm out of which metrical systems are framed, just as in sounds there are four notes (i.e. the four notes of the tetrachord.) out of which all the harmonies are composed; that is an observation which I have made. But of what sort of lives they are severally the imitations I am unable to say.

Then, I said, we must take Damon into our counsels; and he will tell us what rhythms are expressive of meanness, or insolence, or fury, or other unworthiness, and what are to be reserved for the expression of opposite feelings. And I think that I have an indistinct recollection of his mentioning a complex Cretic rhythm; also a dactylic or heroic, and he arranged them in some manner which I do not quite understand, making the rhythms equal in the rise and fall of the foot, long and short alternating; and, unless I am mistaken, he spoke of an iambic as well as of a trochaic rhythm, and assigned to them short and long quantities. Also in some cases he appeared to praise or censure the movement of the foot quite as much as the rhythm; or perhaps a combination of the two; for I am not certain what he meant. These matters, however, as I was saying, had better be referred to Damon himself, for the analysis of the subject would be difficult, you know? [Translator's Note: Socrates expresses himself carelessly in accordance with his assumed ignorance of the details of the subject. In the first part of the sentence he appears to be speaking of paeonic rhythms which are in the ratio of 3/2; in the second part, of dactylic and anapaestic rhythms, which are in the ratio of 1/1; in the last clause, of iambic and trochaic rhythms, which are in the ratio of 1/2 or 2/1.]

Rather so, I should say.

But there is no difficulty in seeing that grace or the absence of grace is an effect of good or bad rhythm.

None at all.

And also that good and bad rhythm naturally assimilate to a good and bad style; and that harmony and discord in like manner follow style; for our principle is that rhythm and harmony are regulated by the words, and not the words by them.

Just so, he said, they should follow the words.

And will not the words and the character of the style depend on the temper of the soul?

Yes.

And everything else on the style?

Yes.

Then beauty of style and harmony and grace and good rhythm depend on simplicity—I mean the true simplicity of a rightly and nobly ordered mind and character, not that other simplicity which is only an euphemism for folly?

Very true, he replied.

And if our youth are to do their work in life, must they not make these graces and harmonies their perpetual aim?

They must.

And surely the art of the painter and every other creative and constructive art are full of them—weaving, embroidery, architecture, and every kind of manufacture; also nature, animal and vegetable—in all of them there is grace or the absence of grace. And ugliness and discord and inharmonious motion are nearly allied to ill words and ill nature, as grace and harmony are the twin sisters of goodness and virtue and bear their likeness.

That is quite true, he said.

But shall our superintendence go no further, and are the poets only to be required by us to express the image of the good in their works, on pain, if they do anything else, of expulsion from our State? Or is the same control to be extended to other artists, and are they also to be prohibited from exhibiting the opposite forms of vice and intemperance and meanness and indecency in sculpture and building and the other creative arts; and is he who cannot conform to this rule of ours to be prevented from practising his art in our State, lest the taste of our citizens be corrupted by him? We would not have our guardians grow up amid images of moral deformity, as in some noxious pasture, and there browse and feed upon many a baneful herb and flower day by day, little by little, until they silently gather a festering mass of corruption in their own soul. Let our artists rather be those who are gifted to discern the true nature of the beautiful and graceful; then will our youth dwell in a land of health, amid fair sights and sounds, and receive the good in everything; and beauty, the effluence of fair works, shall flow into the eye and ear, like a health-giving breeze from a purer region, and insensibly draw the soul from earliest years into likeness and sympathy with the beauty of reason.

There can be no nobler training than that, he replied.

And therefore, I said, Glaucon, musical training is a more potent instrument than any other, because rhythm and harmony find their way into the inward places of the soul, on which they mightily fasten, imparting grace, and making the soul of him who is rightly educated graceful, or of him who is ill-educated ungraceful; and also because he who has received this true education of the inner being will most shrewdly perceive omissions or faults in art and nature, and with a true taste, while he praises and rejoices over and receives into his soul the good, and becomes noble and good, he will justly blame and hate the bad, now in the days of his youth, even before he is able to know the reason why; and when reason comes he will recognise and salute the friend with whom his education has made him long familiar.

Yes, he said, I quite agree with you in thinking that our youth should be trained in music and on the grounds which you mention.

Just as in learning to read, I said, we were satisfied when we knew the letters of the alphabet, which are very few, in all their recurring sizes and combinations; not slighting them as unimportant whether they occupy a space large or small, but everywhere eager to make them out; and not thinking ourselves perfect in the art of reading until we recognise them wherever they are found:

True—

Or, as we recognise the reflection of letters in the water, or in a mirror, only when we know the letters themselves; the same art and study giving us the knowledge of both:

Exactly—

Even so, as I maintain, neither we nor our guardians, whom we have to educate, can ever become musical until we and they know the essential forms of temperance, courage, liberality, magnificence, and their kindred, as well as the contrary forms, in all their combinations, and can recognise them and their images wherever they are found, not slighting them either in small things or great, but believing them all to be within the sphere of one art and study.

Most assuredly.

And when a beautiful soul harmonizes with a beautiful form, and the two are cast in one mould, that will be the fairest of sights to him who has an eye to see it?

The fairest indeed.

And the fairest is also the loveliest?

That may be assumed.

And the man who has the spirit of harmony will be most in love with the loveliest; but he will not love him who is of an inharmonious soul?

That is true, he replied, if the deficiency be in his soul; but if there be any merely bodily defect in another he will be patient of it, and will love all the same.

I perceive, I said, that you have or have had experiences of this sort, and I agree. But let me ask you another question: Has excess of pleasure any affinity to temperance?

How can that be? he replied; pleasure deprives a man of the use of his faculties quite as much as pain.

Or any affinity to virtue in general?

None whatever.

Any affinity to wantonness and intemperance?

Yes, the greatest.

And is there any greater or keener pleasure than that of sensual love?

No, nor a madder.

Whereas true love is a love of beauty and order—temperate and harmonious?

Quite true, he said.

Then no intemperance or madness should be allowed to approach true love?

Certainly not.

Then mad or intemperate pleasure must never be allowed to come near the lover and his beloved; neither of them can have any part in it if their love is of the right sort?

No, indeed, Socrates, it must never come near them.

Then I suppose that in the city which we are founding you would make a law to the effect that a friend should use no other familiarity to his love than a father would use to his son, and then only for a noble purpose, and he must first have the other's consent; and this rule is to limit him in all his intercourse, and he is never to be seen going further, or, if he exceeds, he is to be deemed guilty of coarseness and bad taste.

I quite agree, he said.

Thus much of music, which makes a fair ending; for what should be the end of music if not the love of beauty?

I agree, he said.

After music comes gymnastic, in which our youth are next to be trained.

Certainly.

Gymnastic as well as music should begin in early years; the training in it should be careful and should continue through life. Now my belief is—and this is a matter upon which I should like to have your opinion in confirmation of my own, but my own belief is—not that the good body by any bodily excellence improves the soul, but, on the contrary, that the good soul, by her own excellence, improves the body as far as this may be possible. What do you say?

Yes, I agree.

Then, to the mind when adequately trained, we shall be right in handing over the more particular care of the body; and in order to avoid prolixity we will now only give the general outlines of the subject.

Very good.

That they must abstain from intoxication has been already remarked by us; for of all persons a guardian should be the last to get drunk and not know where in the world he is.

Yes, he said; that a guardian should require another guardian to take care of him is ridiculous indeed.

But next, what shall we say of their food; for the men are in training for the great contest of all—are they not?

Yes, he said.

And will the habit of body of our ordinary athletes be suited to them?

Why not?

I am afraid, I said, that a habit of body such as they have is but a sleepy sort of thing, and rather perilous to health. Do you not observe that these athletes sleep away their lives, and are liable to most dangerous illnesses if they depart, in ever so slight a degree, from their customary regimen?

Yes, I do.

Then, I said, a finer sort of training will be required for our warrior athletes, who are to be like wakeful dogs, and to see and hear with the utmost keenness; amid the many changes of water and also of food, of summer heat and winter cold, which they will have to endure when on a campaign, they must not be liable to break down in health.

That is my view.

The really excellent gymnastic is twin sister of that simple music which we were just now describing.

How so?

Why, I conceive that there is a gymnastic which, like our music, is simple and good; and especially the military gymnastic.

What do you mean?

My meaning may be learned from Homer; he, you know, feeds his heroes at their feasts, when they are campaigning, on soldiers' fare; they have no fish, although they are on the shores of the Hellespont, and they are not allowed boiled meats but only roast, which is the food most convenient for soldiers, requiring only that they should light a fire, and not involving the trouble of carrying about pots and pans.

True.

And I can hardly be mistaken in saying that sweet sauces are nowhere mentioned in Homer. In proscribing them, however, he is not singular; all professional athletes are well aware that a man who is to be in good condition should take nothing of the kind.

Yes, he said; and knowing this, they are quite right in not taking them.

Then you would not approve of Syracusan dinners, and the refinements of Sicilian cookery?

I think not.

Nor, if a man is to be in condition, would you allow him to have a Corinthian girl as his fair friend?

Certainly not.

Neither would you approve of the delicacies, as they are thought, of Athenian confectionary?

Certainly not.

All such feeding and living may be rightly compared by us to melody and song composed in the panharmonic style, and in all the rhythms.

Exactly.

There complexity engendered licence, and here disease; whereas simplicity in music was the parent of temperance in the soul; and simplicity in gymnastic of health in the body.

Most true, he said.

But when intemperance and diseases multiply in a State, halls of justice and medicine are always being opened; and the arts of the doctor and the lawyer give themselves airs, finding how keen is the interest which not only the slaves but the freemen of a city take about them.

Of course.

And yet what greater proof can there be of a bad and disgraceful state of education than this, that not only artisans and the meaner sort of people need the skill of first-rate physicians and judges, but also those who would profess to have had a liberal education? Is it not disgraceful, and a great sign of want of good-breeding, that a man should have to go abroad for his law and physic because he has none of his own at home, and must therefore surrender himself into the hands of other men whom he makes lords and judges over him?

Of all things, he said, the most disgraceful.

Would you say "most," I replied, when you consider that there is a further stage of the evil in which a man is not only a life-long litigant, passing all his days in the courts, either as plaintiff or defendant, but is actually led by his bad taste to pride himself on his litigiousness; he imagines that he is a master in dishonesty; able to take every crooked turn, and wriggle into and out of every hole, bending like a withy and getting out of the way of justice: and all for what?—in order to gain small points not worth mentioning, he not knowing that so to order his life as to be able to do without a napping judge is a far higher and nobler sort of thing. Is not that still more disgraceful?

Yes, he said, that is still more disgraceful.

Well, I said, and to require the help of medicine, not when a wound has to be cured, or on occasion of an epidemic, but just because, by indolence and a habit of life such as we have been describing, men fill themselves with waters and winds, as if their bodies were a marsh, compelling the ingenious sons of Asclepius to find more names for diseases, such as flatulence and catarrh; is not this, too, a disgrace?

Yes, he said, they do certainly give very strange and newfangled names to diseases.

Review and Discussion Questions

1. In what ways are the souls of the young "imitative"?

2. Socrates claims that certain rhythms express "a courageous and harmonious life." In your observation, are there any types of music that accompany a base life?

3. Socrates claims that beautiful works "insensibly" draw the soul into "sympathy with the beauty of reason." Have you ever had such an experience (say, in the presence of a noble building, painting, or song)?

4. For the young student, Socrates recommends music and physical play (gymnastics). What happens to the soul if either is lacking?

5. If the young are badly educated, what happens to the state?

❖ II

ST. BASIL THE GREAT (330–79)

Address to Young Men on the Reading of Greek Literature

After the manner of the bees must we use these writings, for the bees do not visit all flowers without discrimination.

Is pagan wisdom still wisdom? In this remarkable letter, St. Basil outlines a Christian philosophy of culture. He names principles by which we may evaluate the "spoils of the Egyptians." By the fourth century A.D., Christians had received from the Greeks and Romans an established canon of authors whose works defined the bulk of the liberal arts curriculum. Classical authors (Homer, Virgil, and Cicero) can still be read. But the curriculum is relativized. Instead of serving as ends in themselves, or as the means to social promotion, the old books should be read as primers for the New Testament, as milk before the meat. Just as Moses learned from the Egyptians, and David from the Babylonians, so Christians are to take what is noble in the past dispensation and submit it to the scrutiny of a higher wisdom, the Gospel of Christ.

Further Reading: St. Augustine, *On Christian Teaching* [Book 2], trans. R. P. H Green (Oxford: Oxford University Press, 1995); E. L. Fortin, "Hellenism and Christianity in Basil the Great's *Ad Adulsescentes,*" in H. J. Blumenthal and R. A. Markus, eds., *Neoplatonism and Early Christian Thought: Essays in Honour of A. H. Armstrong* (London: Variorum Publications, 1981); Harvey and Laurie Bluedorn, *Teaching the Trivium: Christian Homeschooling in a Classical Style* (Muscatine, Iowa: Trivium Pursuit, 2001).

❖

Many considerations, young men, prompt me to recommend to you the principles which I deem most desirable, and which I believe will be of use to you if you will adopt them. For my time of life, my many-sided training, yea, my adequate experience in those vicissitudes of life which teach their lessons at every turn, have so familiarized me with human affairs, that

I am able to map out the safest course for those just starting upon their careers. By nature's common bond I stand in the same relationship to you as your parents, so that I am no whit behind them in my concern for you. Indeed, if I do not misinterpret your feelings, you no longer crave your parents when you come to me. Now if you should receive my words with gladness, you would be in the second class of those who, according to Hesiod, merit praise; if not, I should say nothing disparaging, but no doubt you yourselves would remember the passage in which that poet says: "He is best who, of himself, recognizes what is his duty, and he also is good who follows the course marked out by others, but he who does neither of these things is of no use under the sun."

Do not be surprised if to you, who go to school every day, and who, through their writings, associate with the learned men of old, I say that out of my own experience I have evolved something more useful. Now this is my counsel, that you should not unqualifiedly give over your minds to these men, as a ship is surrendered to the rudder, to follow whither they list, but that, while receiving whatever of value they have to offer, you yet recognize what it is wise to ignore. Accordingly, from this point on I shall take up and discuss the pagan writings, and how we are to discriminate among them.

We Christians, young men, hold that this human life is not a supremely precious thing, nor do we recognize anything as unconditionally a blessing which benefits us in this life only. Neither pride of ancestry, nor bodily strength, nor beauty, nor greatness, nor the esteem of all men, nor kingly authority, nor, indeed, whatever of human affairs may be called great, do we consider worthy of desire, or the possessors of them as objects of envy; but we place our hopes upon the things which are beyond, and in preparation for the life eternal do all things that we do. Accordingly, whatever helps us towards this we say that we must love and follow after with all our might, but those things which have no bearing upon it should be held as naught. But to explain what this life is, and in what way and manner we shall live it, requires more time than is at our command, and more mature hearers than you.

And yet, in saying thus much, perhaps I have made it sufficiently clear to you that if one should estimate and gather together all earthly weal from the creation of the world, he would not find it comparable to the smallest part of the possessions of heaven; rather, that all the precious things in this life fall further short of the least good in the other than the shadow or the dream fails of the reality. Or rather, to avail myself of a still more natural comparison, by as much as the soul is superior to the body in all things, by so much is one of these lives superior to the other.

Into the life eternal the Holy Scriptures lead us, which teach us through divine words. But so long as our immaturity forbids our understanding their deep thought, we exercise our spiritual perceptions upon profane writings, which are not altogether different, and in which we perceive the truth as it were in shadows and in mirrors. Thus we imitate those who perform the exercises of military practice, for they acquire skill in gymnastics and in dancing, and then in battle reap the reward of their training. We must needs believe that the greatest of all battles lies before us, in preparation for which we must do and suffer all things to gain power. Consequently we must be conversant with poets, with historians, with orators, indeed with all men who may further our soul's salvation. Just as dyers prepare the cloth before they apply the dye, be it purple or any other color, so indeed must we also, if we would preserve indelible the idea of the true virtue, become first initiated in the pagan lore, then at length give special heed to the sacred and divine teachings, even as we first accustom ourselves to the sun's reflection in the water, and then become able to turn our eyes upon the very sun itself.

If, then, there is any affinity between the two literatures, a knowledge of them should be useful to us in our search for truth; if not, the comparison, by emphasizing the contrast, will be of no small service in strengthening our regard for the better one. With what now may we compare these two kinds of education to obtain a simile? Just as it is the chief mission of the tree to bear its fruit in its season, though at the same time it puts forth for ornament the leaves which quiver on its boughs, even so the real fruit of the soul is truth, yet it is not without advantage for it to embrace the pagan wisdom, as also leaves offer shelter to the fruit, and an appearance not untimely. That Moses, whose name is a synonym for wisdom, severely trained his mind in the learning of the Egyptians,and thus became able to appreciate their deity. Similarly, in later days, the wise Daniel is said to have studied the lore of the Chaldaeans while in Babylon, and after that to have taken up the sacred teachings.

Perhaps it is sufficiently demonstrated that such heathen learning is not unprofitable for the soul; I shall then discuss next the extent to which one may pursue it. To begin with the poets, since their writings are of all degrees of excellence, you should not study all of their poems without omitting a single word. When they recount the words and deeds of good men, you should both love and imitate them, earnestly emulating such conduct. But when they portray base conduct, you must flee from them and stop up your ears, as Odysseus is said to have fled past the song of the sirens, for familiarity with evil writings paves the way for evil deeds. Therefore the soul must be guarded with great care, lest through our love for letters it receive some contamination unawares, as men drink in poison with honey. We shall not praise the poets when they scoff and rail, when they represent fornicators and winebibbers, when they define blissfulness by groaning tables and wanton songs. Least of all shall we listen to them when they tell us of their gods, and especially when they represent them as being many, and not at one among themselves. For, among these gods, at one time brother is at variance with brother, or the father with his children; at another, the children engage in truceless war against their parents. The adulteries of the gods and their amours, and especially those of the one whom they call Zeus, chief of all and most high, things of which one cannot speak, even in connection with brutes, without blushing, we shall leave to the stage. I have the same words for the historians, and especially when they make up stories for the amusement of their hearers. And certainly we shall not follow the example of the rhetoricians in the art of lying. For neither in the courts of justice nor in other business affairs will falsehood be of any help to us Christians, who, having chosen the straight and true path of life, are forbidden by the gospel to go to law. But on the other hand we shall receive gladly those passages in which they praise virtue or condemn vice. For just as bees know how to extract honey from flowers, which to men are agreeable only for their fragrance and color, even so here also those who look for something more than pleasure and enjoyment in such writers may derive profit for their souls. Now, then, altogether after the manner of bees must we use these writings, for the bees do not visit all the flowers without discrimination, nor indeed do they seek to carry away entire those upon which they light, but rather, having taken so much as is adapted to their needs, they let the rest go. So we, if wise, shall take from heathen books whatever befits us and is allied to the truth, and shall pass over the rest. And just as in culling roses we avoid the thorns, from such writings as these we will gather everything useful, and guard against the noxious. So, from the very beginning, we must examine each of their teachings, to harmonize it with our ultimate purpose, according to the Doric proverb, "testing each stone by the measuring-line."

Since we must needs attain to the life to come through virtue, our attention is to be chiefly fastened upon those many passages from the poets, from the historians, and especially from the philosophers, in which virtue itself is praised. For it is of no small advantage that virtue become a habit with a youth, for the lessons of youth make a deep impression, because the soul is then plastic, and therefore they are likely to be indelible. If not to incite youth to virtue, pray what meaning may we suppose that Hesiod had in those universally admired lines, of which the sentiment is as follows: "Rough is the start and hard, and the way steep, and full of labor and pain, that leads toward virtue. Wherefore, on account of the steepness, it is not granted to every man to set out, nor, to the one having set out, easily to reach the summit. But when he has reached the top, he sees that the way is smooth and fair, easy and light to the foot, and more pleasing than the other, which leads to wickedness"—of which the same poet said that one may find it all around him in great abundance. Now it seems to me that he had no other purpose in saying these things than so to exhort us to virtue, and so to incite us to bravery, that we may not weaken our efforts before we reach the goal. And certainly if any other man praises virtue in a like strain, we will receive his words with pleasure, since our aim is a common one.

Now as I have heard from one skillful in interpreting the mind of a poet, all the poetry of Homer is a praise of virtue, and with him all that is not merely accessory tends to this end. There is a notable instance of this where Homer first made the princess reverence the leader of the Cephallenians, though he appeared naked, shipwrecked, and alone, and then made Odysseus as completely lack embarrassment, though seen naked and alone, since virtue served him as a garment. And next he made Odysseus so much esteemed by the other Phaeacians that, abandoning the luxury in which they lived, all admired and emulated him, and there was not one of them who longed for anything else except to be Odysseus, even to the enduring of shipwreck. The interpreter of the poetic mind argued that, in this episode, Homer very plainly says: "Be virtue your concern, O men, which both swims to shore with the shipwrecked man, and makes him, when he comes naked to the strand, more honored than the prosperous Phaeacians." And, indeed, this is the truth, for other possessions belong to the owner no more than to another, and, as when men are dicing, fall now to this one, now to that. But virtue is the only possession that is sure, and that remains with us whether living or dead. Wherefore it seems to me that Solon had the rich in mind when he said: "We will not exchange our virtue for their gold, for virtue is an everlasting possession, while riches are ever changing owners." Similarly Theognis said that the god, whatever he might mean by the god, inclines the balances for men, now this way, now that, giving to some riches, and to others poverty. Also Prodicus, the sophist of Ceos, whose opinion we must respect, for he is a man not to be slighted, somewhere in his writings expressed similar ideas about virtue and vice. I do not remember the exact words, but as far as I recollect the sentiment, in plain prose it ran somewhat as follows: While Hercules was yet a youth, being about your age, as he was debating which path he should choose, the one leading through toil to virtue, or its easier alternate, two women appeared before him, who proved to be Virtue and Vice. Though they said not a word, the difference between them was at once apparent from their mien. The one had arranged herself to please the eye, while she exhaled charms, and a multitude of delights swarmed in her train. With such a display, and promising still more, she sought to allure Hercules to her side. The other, wasted and squalid, looked fixedly at him, and bespoke quite another thing. For she promised nothing easy or engaging, but rather infinite toils and hardships, and perils in every land and on every sea. As a reward for these trials, he was to become a god, so our author has it. The latter, Hercules at length followed.

Almost all who have written upon the subject of wisdom have more or less, in proportion to their several abilities, extolled virtue in their writings. Such men must one obey, and must try to realize their words in his life. For he, who by his works exemplifies the wisdom which with others is a matter of theory alone, "breathes; all others flutter about like shadows." I think it is as if a painter should represent some marvel of manly beauty, and the subject should actually be such a man as the artist pictures on the canvas. To praise virtue in public with brilliant words and with long drawn out speeches, while in private preferring pleasures to temperance, and self-interest to justice, finds an analogy on the stage, for the players frequently appear as kings and rulers, though they are neither, nor perhaps even genuinely free men. A musician would hardly put up with a lyre which was out of tune, nor a choregus with a chorus not singing in perfect harmony. But every man is divided against himself who does not make his life conform to his words, but who says with Euripides, "The mouth indeed hath sworn, but the heart knows no oath." Such a man will seek the appearance of virtue rather than the reality. But to seem to be good when one is not so, is, if we are to respect the opinion of Plato at all, the very height of injustice.

After this wise, then, are we to receive those words from the pagan authors which contain suggestions of the virtues. But since also the renowned deeds of the men of old either are preserved for us by tradition, or are cherished in the pages of poet or historian, we must not fail to profit by them. A fellow of the street rabble once kept taunting Pericles, but he, meanwhile, gave no heed; and they held out all day, the fellow deluging him with reproaches, but he, for his part, not caring. Then when it was evening and dusk, and the fellow still clung to him, Pericles escorted him with a light, in order that he might not fail in the practice of philosophy. Again, a man in a passion threatened and vowed death to Euclid of Megara, but he in turn vowed that the man should surely be appeased, and cease from his hostility to him.

How invaluable it is to have such examples in mind when a man is seized with anger! On the other hand, one must altogether ignore the tragedy which says in so many words: "Anger arms the hand against the enemy"; for it is much better not to give way to anger at all. But if such restraint is not easy, we shall at least curb our anger by reflection, so as not to give it too much rein.

But let us bring our discussion back again to the examples of noble deeds. A certain man once kept striking Socrates, the son of Sophroniscus, in the face, yet he did not resent it, but allowed full play to the ruffian's anger, so that his face was swollen and bruised from the blows. Then when he stopped striking him, Socrates did nothing more than write on his forehead, as an artisan on a statue, who did it, and thus took out his revenge. Since these examples almost coincide with our teachings, I hold that such men are worthy of emulation. For this conduct of Socrates is akin to the precept that to him who smites you upon the one cheek, you shall turn the other also—thus much may you be avenged; the conduct of Pericles and of Euclid also conforms to the precept: "Submit to those who persecute you, and endure their wrath with meekness"; and to the other: "Pray for your enemies and curse them not." One who has been instructed in the pagan examples will no longer hold the Christian precepts impracticable. But I will not overlook the conduct of Alexander, who, on taking captive the daughters of Darius, who were reputed to be of surpassing beauty, would not even look at them, for he deemed it unworthy of one who was a conqueror of men to be a slave to women. This is of a piece with the statement that he who looks upon a woman to lust after her, even though he does not commit the act of adultery, is not free from its guilt, since he has entertained impure thoughts.It is hard to believe that the action of Cleinias, one of the disciples of Pythagoras, was in accidental conformity to our teachings, and not designed imitation of them. What, then, was this act of his? By taking an oath he could have avoided a fine of three talents, yet rather than do so he paid the fine, though he could have sworn truthfully. I am inclined to think that he had heard of the precept which forbids us to swear.

But let us return to the same thought with which we started, namely, that we should not accept everything without discrimination, but only what is useful. For it would be shameful should we reject injurious foods, yet should take no thought about the studies which nourish our souls, but as a torrent should sweep along all that came near our path and appropriate it. If the helmsman does not blindly abandon his ship to the winds, but guides it toward the anchorage; if the archer shoots at his mark; if also the metal-worker or the carpenter seeks to produce the objects for which his craft exists, would there be rime or reason in our being outclassed by these men, mere artisans as they are, in quick appreciation of our interests? For is there not some end in the artisan's work, is there not a goal in human life, which the one who would not wholly resemble unreasoning animals must keep before him in all his words and deeds? If there were no intelligence sitting at the tiller of our souls, like boats without ballast we should be borne hither and thither through life, without plan or purpose,

An analogy may be found in the athletic contests, or, if you will, in the musical contests; for the contestants prepare themselves by a preliminary training for those events in which wreaths of victory are offered, and no one by training for wrestling or for the pancratium would get ready to play the lyre or the flute. At least Polydamas would not, for before the Olympic games he was wont to bring the rushing chariot to a halt, and thus hardened himself. Then Milo could not be thrust from his smeared shield, but, shoved as he was, clung to it as firmly as statues soldered by lead. In a word, by their training they prepared themselves for the contests. If they had meddled with the airs of Marsyas or of Olympus, the Phrygians, abandoning dust and exercise, would they have won ready laurels or crowns, or would they have escaped being laughed at for their bodily incapacity? On the other hand, certainly Timotheus the musician did not spend his time in the schools for wrestling, for then it would not have been his to excel all in music, he who was so skilled in his art that at his pleasure he could arouse the passions of men by his harsh and vehement strains, and then by gentle ones, quiet and soothe them. By this art, when once he played Phrygian airs on the flute to Alexander, he is said to have incited the general to arms in the midst of feasting, and then, by milder music, to have restored him to his carousing friends. Such power to compass one's end, either in music or in athletic contests, is developed by practice.

I have called to mind the wreaths and the fighters. These men endure hardships beyond number, they use every means to increase their strength, they sweat ceaselessly at their training, they accept many blows from the master, they adopt the mode of life which he prescribes, though it is most unpleasant, and, in a word, they so rule all their conduct that their whole life before the contest is preparatory to it. Then they strip themselves for the arena, and endure all and risk all, to receive the crown of olive, or of parsley, or some other branch, and to be announced by the herald as victor.

Will it then be possible for us, to whom are held out rewards so wondrous in number and in splendor that tongue can not recount them, while we are fast asleep and leading care-free lives, to make these our own by half-hearted efforts? Surely, were an idle life a very commendable thing, Sardanapalus would take the first prize, or Margites if you will, whom Homer, if indeed the poem is by Homer, put down as neither a farmer, nor a vine-dresser, nor anything else that is useful. Is there not rather truth in the maxim of Pittacus which says, "It is hard to be good"? For after we have actually endured many hardships, we shall scarcely gain those blessings to which, as said above, nothing in human experience is comparable. Therefore we must not be light-minded, nor exchange our immortal hopes for momentary idleness, lest reproaches come upon us, and judgment befall us, not forsooth here among men, although judgment here is no easy thing for the man of sense to bear, but at the bar of justice, be that under the earth, or wherever else it may happen to be. While he who unintentionally violates his obligations perchance receives some pardon from God, he who designedly chooses a life of wickedness doubtless has a far greater punishment to endure.

"What then are we to do?" perchance some one may ask. What else than to care for the soul, never leaving an idle moment for other things? Accordingly, we ought not to serve the body any more than is absolutely necessary, but we ought to do our best for the soul, releasing it from the bondage of fellowship with the bodily appetites; at the same time we ought to make the body superior to passion. We must provide it with the necessary food, to be sure, but not with delicacies, as those do who seek everywhere for waiters and cooks, and scour both earth and sea, like those bringing tribute to some stern tyrant. This is a despicable business, in which are endured things as unbearable as the torments of hell, where wool is combed into the fire, or water is drawn in a sieve and poured into a perforated jar, and where work is never done. Then to spend more time than is necessary on one's hair and clothes is, in the words of Diogenes, the part of the unfortunate or of the sinful. For what difference does it make to a sensible man whether he is clad in a robe of state or in an inexpensive garment, so long as he is protected from heat and cold? Likewise in other matters we must be governed by necessity, and only give so much care to the body as is beneficial to the soul. For to one who is really a man it is no less a disgrace to be a fop or a pamperer of the body than to be the victim of any other base passion. Indeed, to be very zealous in making the body appear very beautiful is not the mark of a man who knows himself, or who feels the force of the wise maxim: "Not that which is seen is the man," for it requires a higher faculty for any one of us, whoever he may be, to know himself. Now it is harder for the man who is not pure in heart to gain this knowledge than for a blear-eyed person to look upon the sun.

To speak generally and so far as your needs demand, purity of soul embraces these things: to scorn sensual pleasures, to refuse to feast the eyes on the senseless antics of buffoons, or on bodies which goad one to passion, and to close one's ears to songs which corrupt the mind. For passions which are the offspring of servility and baseness are produced by this kind of music. On the other hand, we must employ that class of music which is better in itself and which leads to better things, which David, the sacred psalmist, is said to have used to assuage the madness of the king. Also tradition has it that when Pythagoras happened upon some drunken revelers, he commanded the flute-player, who led the merry-making, to change the tune and to play a Doric air, and that the chant so sobered them that they threw down their wreaths, and shamefacedly returned home. Others at the sound of the flute rave like Corybantes and Bacchantes. Even so great a difference does it make whether one lends his ear to healthy or to vicious music. Therefore you ought to have still less to do with the music of such influence than with other infamous things. Then I am ashamed to forbid you to load the air with all kinds of sweet-smelling perfumes, or to smear yourselves with ointment. Again, what further argument is needed against seeking the gratification of one's appetite than that it compels those who pursue it, like animals, to make of their bellies a god?

In a word, he who would not bury himself in the mire of sensuality must deem the whole body of little worth, or must, as Plato puts it, pay only so much heed to the body as is an aid to wisdom, or as Paul admonishes somewhere in a similar passage: "Let no one make provision for the flesh, to fulfill the lusts thereof." Wherein is there any difference between those who take pains that the body shall be perfect, but ignore the soul, for the use of which it is designed, and those who are scrupulous about their tools, but neglectful of their trade? On the contrary, one ought to discipline the flesh and hold it under, as a fierce animal is controlled, and to quiet, by the lash of reason, the unrest which it engenders in the soul, and not, by giving full rein to pleasure, to disregard the mind, as a charioteer is run away with by unmanageable and frenzied horses. So let us bear in mind the remark of Pythagoras, who, upon learning that one of his followers was growing very fleshy from gymnastics and hearty eating, said to him, "Will you not stop making your imprisonment harder for yourself?" Then it is said that since

Plato foresaw the dangerous influence of the body, he chose an unhealthy part of Athens for his Academy, in order to remove excessive bodily comfort, as one prunes the rank shoots of the vines. Indeed I have even heard physicians say that over-healthiness is dangerous. Since, then, this exaggerated care of the body is harmful to the body itself, and a hindrance to the soul, it is sheer madness to be a slave to the body, and serve it.

If we were minded to disregard attention to the body, we should be in little danger of prizing anything else unduly. For of what use, now, are riches, if one scorns the pleasures of the flesh? I certainly see none, unless, as in the case of the mythological dragons, there is some satisfaction in guarding hidden treasure. Of a truth, one who had learned to be independent of this sort of thing would be loath to attempt anything mean or low, either in word or deed. For superfluity, be it Lydian gold-dust, or the work of the gold-gathering ants, he would disdain in proportion to its needlessness, and of course he would make the necessities of life, not its pleasures, the measure of need. Forsooth, those who exceed the bounds of necessity, like men who are sliding down an inclined plane, can nowhere gain a footing to check their precipitous flight, for the more they can scrape together, so much or even more do they need for the gratification of their desires. As Solon, the son of Execestides, puts it, "No definite limit is set to a man's wealth." Also, one should hear Theognis, the teacher, on this point: "I do not long to be rich, nor do I pray for riches, but let it be given me to live with a little, suffering no ill."

I also admire the wholesale contempt of all human possessions which Diogenes expressed, who showed himself richer than the great Persian king, since he needed less for living. But we are wont to be satisfied with nothing save with the talents of the Mysian Pythius, with limitless acres of land, and more herds of cattle than may be counted. Yet I believe that if riches fail us we should not mourn for them, and if we have them, we should not think more of possessing them than of using them rightly. For Socrates expressed an admirable thought when he said that a rich, purse-proud man was never an object of admiration with him until he learned that the man knew how to use his wealth. If Phidias and Polycletus had been very proud of the gold and ivory with which the one constructed the statue of the Jupiter of Elis, the other the Juno of Argos, they would have been laughed at, because priding themselves in treasure produced by no merit of theirs, and overlooking their art, from which the gold gained greater beauty and worth. Then shall we think that we are open to less reproach if we hold that virtue is not, in and of itself, a sufficient ornament? Again, shall we, while manifestly ignoring riches and scorning sensual pleasures, court adulation and fulsome praise, vying with the fox of Archilochus in cunning and craft? Of a truth there is nothing which the wise man must more guard against than the temptation to live for praise, and to study what pleases the crowd. Rather truth should be made the guide of one's life, so that if one must needs speak against all men, and be in ill-favor and in danger for virtue's sake, he shall not swerve at all from that which he considers right; else how shall we say that he differs from the Egyptian sophist, who at pleasure turned himself into a tree, an animal, fire, water, or anything else? Such a man now praises justice to those who esteem it, and now expresses opposite sentiments when he sees that wrong is in good repute; this is the fawner's trick. Just as the polypus is said to take the color of the ground upon which it lies, so he conforms his opinions to those of his associates.

To be sure, we shall become more intimately acquainted with these precepts in the sacred writings, but it is incumbent upon us, for the present, to trace, as it were, the silhouette of virtue in the pagan authors. For those who carefully gather the useful from each book are wont, like mighty rivers, to gain accessions on every hand. For the precept of the poet which bids us add little to little must be taken as applying not so much to the accumulation of riches, as of the various branches of learning. In line with this Bias said to his son, who, as he was about to set out for Egypt, was inquiring what course he could pursue to give his father the greatest satisfaction: "Store up means for the journey of old age." By *means* he meant virtue, but he placed too great restrictions upon it, since he limited its usefulness to the earthly life. For if any one mentions the old age of Tithonus, or of Arganthonius, or of that Methuselah who is said to have lacked but thirty years of being a millenarian, or even if he reckons the entire period since the creation, I will laugh as at the fancies of a child, since I look forward to that long, undying age, of the extent of which there is no limit for the mind of man to grasp, any more than there is of the life immortal. For the journey of this life eternal I would advise you to husband resources, leaving no stone unturned, as the proverb has it, whence you might derive any aid. From this task we shall not shrink because it is hard and laborious, but, remembering the precept that every man ought to choose the better life, and expecting that association will render it pleasant, we shall busy ourselves with those things that are best. For it is shameful to squander the present, and later to call back the past in anguish, when no more time is given.

In the above treatise I have explained to you some of the things which I deem the most to be desired; of others I shall continue to counsel you so

long as life is allowed me. Now as the sick are of three classes, according to
the degrees of their sickness, may you not seem to belong to the third, or
incurable, class, nor show a spiritual malady like that of their bodies! For
those who are slightly indisposed visit physicians in person, and those who
are seized by violent sickness call physicians, but those who are suffering
from a hopelessly incurable melancholy do not even admit the physicians
if they come. May this now not be your plight, as would seem to be the case
were you to shun these right counsels!

Review and Discussion Questions

1. Name the three classes of men identified by the ancient Greek poet
Hesiod.

2. Basil offers principles by which to judge an ancient text. How does
he begin?

3. Basil compares reading a pagan text to looking at "the sun's reflection in the water." What is it about select pagan texts that can strengthen a
Christian's vision?

4. What is it about a pagan curriculum or text that a Christian reader
should avoid?

5. Imagine you are a principal of a Christian high school developing
a new curriculum. What is one way that you might apply Basil's advice to
your curriculum?

❖ 12

HUGH OF ST. VICTOR (1096–1141)

Didascalicon

> It is in the seven liberal arts … that all the foundation of learning is to
> be found.

Medieval reflection on the nature and value of the seven liberal arts reached
maturity by the twelfth century. Anticipating St. Thomas and St. Bonaventure, Hugh of St. Victor's *Didascalicon* outlines a universal course of study.
Education, as conceived by Hugh and other scholastics, need not be universal in content; that was the ambition of the eighteenth-century Encyclope-
dists. Its aim, rather, is to be universal in its principles. Every branch of inquiry is contained at least virtually within Hugh's scheme of learning. Grammar,
logic, rhetoric (trivium), arithmetic, geometry, astronomy, and music (quadrivium) constitute this universal study, as he tells us, because, by them, the
mind grasps the elementary principles of order underlying creation; through
the arts, "a quick mind enters into the secret places of wisdom."

Further Reading: Jerome Taylor's "Introduction" at the head of his translation of *The Didascalicon of Hugh of St. Victor* (New York: Columbia University Press, 1991); Paul Rorem, *Hugh of St.
Victor* (Oxford: Oxford University Press, 2009); Thomas Aquinas, *The Divisions and Methods of
the Sciences*, trans. Armand Maurer (Toronto: Pontifical Institute of Mediaeval Studies, 1986).

❖

Which Arts Are Principally to Be Read

Out of all the sciences above named, however, the ancients, in their
studies, especially selected seven to be mastered by those who were to be
educated. These seven they considered so to excel all the rest in usefulness
that anyone who had been thoroughly schooled in them might afterward
come to a knowledge of the others by his own inquiry and effort rather than
by listening to a teacher. For these, one might say, constitute the best instruments, the best rudiments, by which the way is prepared for the mind's

complete knowledge of philosophic truth. Therefore they are called by the name trivium and quadrivium, because by them, as by certain ways (*viae*), a quick mind enters into the secret places of wisdom.

In those days, no one was thought worthy the name of master who was unable to claim knowledge of these seven. Pythagoras, too, is said to have maintained the following practice as a teacher: for seven years, according to the number of the seven liberal arts, no one of his pupils dared ask the reason behind statements made by him; instead, he was to give credence to the words of the master until he had heard him out, and then, having done this, he would be able to come at the reason of those things himself. We read that some men studied these seven with such zeal that they had them completely in memory, so that whatever writings they subsequently took in hand or whatever questions they proposed for solution or proof, they did not thumb the pages of books to hunt for rules and reasons which the liberal arts might afford for the resolution of a doubtful matter, but at once had the particulars ready by heart. Hence, it is a fact that in that time there were so many learned men that they alone wrote more than we are able to read. But the students of our day, whether from ignorance or from unwillingness, fail to hold to a fit method of study, and therefore we find many who study but few who are wise. Yet it seems to me that the student should take no less care not to expend his effort in useless studies than he should to avoid a lukewarm pursuit of good and useful ones. It is bad to pursue something good negligently; it is worse to expend many labors on an empty thing. But because not everyone is mature enough to know what is of advantage to him, I shall briefly indicate to the student which writings seem to me more useful than others, and then I shall add a few words on the method of study.

Concerning the Two Kinds of Writings

There are two kinds of writings. The first kind comprises what are properly called the arts; the second, those writings which are appendages of the arts. The arts are included in philosophy: they have, that is, some definite and established part of philosophy for their subject matter, as do grammar, dialectic, and others of this sort. The appendages of the arts, however, are only tangential to philosophy. What they treat is some extra-philosophical matter. Occasionally, it is true, they touch in a scattered and confused fashion upon some topics lifted out of the arts, or, if their narrative presentation is simple, they prepare the way for philosophy. Of this sort are all the songs of the poets—tragedies, comedies, satires, heroic verse and lyric, iambics, certain didactic poems, fables and histories, and also the writings of those fellows whom today we commonly call "philosophers" and who are always taking some small matter and dragging it out through long verbal detours, obscuring a simple meaning in confused discourses—who, lumping even dissimilar things together, make, as it were, a single "picture" from a multitude of "colors" and forms. Keep in mind the two things I have distinguished for you—the arts and the appendages of the arts.

Between these two, however, there is in my view such distance as the poet describes when he says:

> As much as the wiry willow cedes to the pale olive,
> Or the wild nard to roses of Punic red.

It is a distance such that the man wishing to attain knowledge, yet who willingly deserts truth in order to entangle himself in these mere byproducts of the arts, will find, I shall not say infinite, but exceedingly great pains and meager fruit. Finally, the arts themselves, without these things that border on them, are able to make the student perfect, while the latter things, without the arts, are capable of conferring no perfection: and this the more especially since the latter have nothing desirable with which to tempt the student except what they have taken over and adapted from the arts; and no one should seek in them anything but what is of the arts. For this reason it appears to me that our effort should first be given to the arts, in which are the foundation stones of all things and in which pure and simple truth is revealed—and especially to the seven already mentioned, which comprise the tools of all philosophy; afterwards, if time affords, let these other things be read, for sometimes we are better pleased when entertaining reading is mixed with serious, and rarity makes what is good seem precious. Thus, we some times more eagerly take up a thought we come upon in the midst of a story.

It is in the seven liberal arts, however, that the foundation of all learning is to be found. Before all others these ought to be had at hand, because without them the philosophical discipline does not and cannot explain and define anything. These, indeed, so hang together and so depend upon one another in their ideas that if only one of the arts be lacking, all the rest cannot make a man into a philosopher. Therefore, those persons seem to me to be in error who, not appreciating the coherence among the arts, select certain of them for study, and, leaving the rest untouched, think they can become perfect in these alone.

That to Each Art Should Be Given What Belongs to It

There is still another error, hardly less serious than that just mentioned, and it must be avoided with the greatest care: certain persons, while they omit nothing which ought to be read, nonetheless do not know how to give each art what belongs to it, but, while treating one, lecture on them all. In grammar they discourse about the theory of syllogisms; in dialectic they inquire into inflectional cases; and what is still more ridiculous, in discussing the title of a book they practically cover the whole work, and, by their third lecture, they have hardly finished with the incipit. It is not the teaching of others that they accomplish in this way, but the showing off of their own knowledge. Would that they seemed to everyone as they seem to me! Only consider how perverse this practice is. Surely the more you collect superfluous details the less you are able to grasp or to retain useful matters.

Two separate concerns, then, are to be recognized and distinguished in every art: first, how one ought to treat of the art itself, and second, how one ought to apply the principles of that art in all other matters whatever. Two distinct things are involved here: treating of the art and treating by means of the art. Treating of an art is treating, for instance, of grammar; but treating by means of that art is treating some matter grammatically. Note the difference between these two—treating of grammar, and treating some matter grammatically. We treat of grammar when we set forth the rules given for words and the various precepts proper to this art; we treat grammatically when we speak or write according to rule. To treat of grammar, then, belongs only to certain books, like Priscian, Donatus, or Servius; but to treat grammatically belongs to all books.

When, therefore, we treat of any art—and especially in teaching it, when everything must be reduced to outline and presented for easy understanding—we should be content to set forth the matter in hand as briefly and as clearly as possible, lest by excessively piling up extraneous considerations we distract the student more than we instruct him. We must not say everything we can, lest we say with less effect such things as need saying. Seek, therefore, in every art what stands established as belonging specifically to it. Later, when you have studied the arts and come to know by disputation and comparison what the proper concern of each of them is, then, at this stage, it will be fitting for you to bring the principles of each to bear upon all the others, and, by a comparative and back-and-forth examination of the arts, to investigate the things in them which you did not well understand before. Do not strike into a lot of by-ways until you know the main roads: you will go along securely when you are not under the fear of going astray.

What Is Necessary for Study

Three things are necessary for those who study: natural endowment, practice, and discipline. By natural endowment is meant that they must be able to grasp easily what they hear and to retain firmly what they grasp; by practice is meant that they must cultivate by assiduous effort the natural endowment they have; and by discipline is meant that, by leading a praiseworthy life, they must combine moral behavior with their knowledge. Of these three in turn we shall now set forth a few remarks by way of introduction.

Concerning Aptitude as Related to Natural Endowment

Those who work at learning must be equipped at the same time with aptitude and with memory, for these two are so closely tied together in every study and discipline that if one of them is lacking, the other alone cannot lead anyone to perfection, just as earnings are useless if there is no saving of them, and storage equipment is useless if there is nothing to preserve. Aptitude gathers wisdom, memory preserves it.

Aptitude is a certain faculty naturally rooted in the mind and empowered from within. It arises from nature, is improved by use, is blunted by excessive work, and is sharpened by temperate practice. As someone has very nicely said:

Please! Spare yourself for my sake—there's only drudgery in those papers! Go run in the open air!

Aptitude gets practice from two things—reading and meditation. Reading consists of forming our minds upon rules and precepts taken from books, and it is of three types : the teacher's, the learner's, and the independent reader's. For we say, "I am reading the book to him," "I am reading the book under him," and "I am reading the book." Order and method are what especially deserve attention in the matter of reading.

Concerning Order in Expounding a Text

One kind of order is observed in the disciplines, when I say, for instance, that grammar is more ancient than dialectic, or arithmetic comes before music; another kind in codices or anthologies, when I declare, for instance, that the Catilinarian orations are ahead of the Jugurtha; another kind in narration, which moves in continuous series; and another kind in the exposition of a text.

Order in the disciplines is arranged to follow nature. In books it is arranged according to the person of the author or the nature of the subject matter. In narration it follows an arrangement which is of two kinds—either natural, as when deeds are recounted in the order of their occurrence, or artificial, as when a subsequent event is related first and a prior event is told after it. In the exposition of a text, the order followed is adapted to inquiry.

Exposition includes three things: the letter, the sense, and the inner meaning. The letter is the fit arrangement of words, which we also call construction; the sense is a certain ready and obvious meaning which the letter presents on the surface; the inner meaning is the deeper understanding which can be found only through interpretation and commentary. Among these, the order of inquiry is first the letter, then the sense, and finally the inner meaning. And when this is done, the exposition is complete.

Concerning the Method of Expounding a Text

The method of expounding a text consists in analysis. Every analysis begins from things which are finite, or defined, and proceeds in the direction of things which are infinite, or undefined. Now every finite or defined matter is better known and able to be grasped by our knowledge; teaching, moreover, begins with those things which are better known and, by acquainting us with these, works its way to matters which lie hidden. Furthermore, we investigate with our reason (the proper function of which is to analyze) when, by analysis and investigation of the natures of individual things, we descend from universals to particulars. For every universal is more fully defined than its particulars : when we learn, therefore, we ought to begin with universals, which are better known and determined and inclusive; and then, by descending little by little from them and by distinguishing individuals through analysis, we ought to investigate the nature of the things those universals contain.

Concerning Meditation

Meditation is sustained thought along planned lines: it prudently investigates the cause and the source, the manner and the utility of each thing. Meditation takes its start from reading but is bound by none of reading's rules or precepts. For it delights to range along open ground, where it fixes its free gaze upon the contemplation of truth, drawing together now these, now those causes of things, or now penetrating into profundities, leaving nothing doubtful, nothing obscure. The start of learning, thus, lies in reading, but its consummation lies in meditation; which, if any man will learn to love it very intimately and will desire to be engaged very frequently upon it, renders his life pleasant indeed, and provides the greatest consolation to him in his trials. This especially it is which takes the soul away from the noise of earthly business and makes it have even in this life a kind of fore-taste of the sweetness of the eternal quiet. And when, through the things which God has made, a man has learned to seek out and to understand him who has made them all, then does he equally instruct his mind with knowledge and fill it with joy. From this it follows that in meditation is to be found the greatest delight.

There are three kinds of meditation: one consists in a consideration of morals, the second in a scrutiny of the commandments, and the third in an investigation of the divine works. Morals are found in virtues and vices. The divine command either orders, or promises, or threatens. The work of God comprises what his power creates, what his wisdom disposes, and what his grace co-effects. And the more a man knows how great is the admiration which all these things deserve, the more intently does he give himself to continual meditation upon the wonders of God.

Concerning Memory

Concerning memory I do not think one should fail to say here that, just as aptitude investigates and discovers through analysis, so memory re-tains through gathering. The things which we have analyzed in the course of learning and which we must commit to memory we ought, therefore, to gather. Now "gathering" is reducing to a brief and compendious outline things which have been written or discussed at some lengths. The ancients called such an outline an "epilogue," that is, a short restatement, by head-ings, of things already said. Now every exposition has some principle upon which the entire truth of the matter and the force of its thought rest, and to this principle everything else is traced back. To look for and consider this principle is to "gather." The fountainhead is one, but its derivative streams are many: why follow the windings of the latter? Lay hold upon the source and you have the whole thing. I say this because the memory of man is dull and likes brevity, and, if it is dissipated upon many things, it has less to be-stow upon each of them. We ought, therefore, in all that we learn, to gather brief and dependable abstracts to be stored in the little chest of the memory, so that later on, when need arises, we can derive everything else from them. These one must often turn over in the mind and regurgitate from the stom-ach of one's memory to taste them, lest by long inattention to them, they disappear.

I charge you, then, my student, not to rejoice a great deal because you may have read many things, but because you have been able to retain them. Otherwise there is no profit in having read or understood much. And for this reason I call to mind again what I said earlier: those who devote themselves to study require both aptitude and memory.

Concerning Discipline

A certain wise man, when asked concerning the method and form of study, declared:

> A humble mind, eagerness to inquire, a quiet life,
> Silent scrutiny, poverty, a foreign soil.
> These, for many, unlock the hidden places of learning.

He had heard, I should judge, the saying, "Morals equip learning." Therefore he joined rules for living to rules for study, in order that the student might know both the standard of his life and the nature of his study. Unpraiseworthy is learning stained by a shameless life. Therefore, let him who would seek learning take care above all that he not neglect discipline.

Concerning Humility

Now the beginning of discipline is humility. Although the lessons of humility are many, the three which follow are of especial importance for the student: first, that he hold no knowledge and no writing in contempt; second, that he blush to learn from no man; and third, that when he has attained learning himself, he not look down upon everyone else.

Many are deceived by the desire to appear wise before their time. They therefore break out in a certain swollen importance and begin to simulate what they are not and to be ashamed of what they are; and they slip all the farther from wisdom in proportion as they think, not of being wise, but of being thought so. I have known many of this sort who, although they still lacked the very rudiments of learning, yet deigned to concern themselves only with the highest problems, and they supposed that they themselves were well on the road to greatness simply because they had read the writings or heard the words of great and wise men. "We," they say, "have seen them. We have studied under them. They often used to talk to us. Those great ones, those famous men, they know us." Ah, would that no one knew me and that I but knew all things! You glory in having seen, not in having understood, Plato. As a matter of fact, I should think it not good enough for you to listen to me. I am not Plato. I have not deserved to see him. Good for you!

You have drunk at the very fount of philosophy—but would that you thirsted still! "The king, having drunk from a goblet of gold, drinks next from a cup of clay!" Why are you blushing? You have heard Plato!—may you hear Chrysippus too! The proverb says, "What you do not know, maybe Ofellus knows." There is no one to whom it is given to know all things, no one who has not received his special gift from nature. The wise student, therefore, gladly hears all, reads all, and looks down upon no writing, no person, no teaching. From all indifferently he seeks what he sees he lacks, and he considers not how much he knows, but of how much he is ignorant. For this reason men repeat Plato's saying: "I would rather learn with modesty what another man says than shamelessly push forward my own ideas." Why do you blush to be taught, and yet not blush at your ignorance? The latter is a greater shame than the former. Or why should you affect the heights when you are still lying in the depths? Consider, rather, what your powers will at present permit: the man who proceeds stage by stage moves along best. Certain fellows, wishing to make a great leap of progress, sprawl headlong. Do not hurry too much, therefore; in this way you will come more quickly to wisdom. Gladly learn from all what you do not know, for humility can make you a sharer in the special gift which natural endowment has given to every man. You will be wiser than all if you are willing to learn from all.

Finally, hold no learning in contempt, for all learning is good. Do not scorn at least to read a book, if you have the time. If you gain nothing from it, neither do you lose anything; especially since there is, in my judgment, no book which does not set forth something worth looking for, if that book is taken up at the right place and time; or which does not possess some thing even special to itself which the diligent scrutinizer of its contents, having found it nowhere else, seizes upon gladly in proportion as it is the more rare.

Nothing, however, is good if it eliminates a better thing. If you are not able to read everything, read those things which are more useful. Even if you should be able to read them all, how ever, you should not expend the same labor upon all. Some things are to be read that we may know them, but others that we may at least have heard of them, for sometimes we think that things of which we have not heard are of greater worth than they are, and we estimate more readily a thing whose fruit is known to us.

You can now see how necessary to you is that humility which will prompt you to hold no knowledge in contempt and to learn gladly from all. Similarly, it is fitting for you that when you have begun to know something, you not look down upon everyone else. For the vice of an inflated ego attacks some men because they pay too much fond attention to their own knowledge, and when they seem to themselves to have become something, they think that others whom they do not even know can neither be nor become as great. So it is that in our days certain peddlers of trifles come fuming forth; glorying in I know not what, they accuse our forefathers of simplicity and suppose that wisdom, having been born with themselves, with themselves will die. They say that the divine utterances have such a simple way of speaking that no one has to study them under masters, but can sufficiently penetrate to the hidden treasures of Truth by his own mental acumen. They wrinkle their noses and purse their lips at lecturers in divinity and do not understand that they themselves give offense to God, whose words they preach—words simple to be sure in their verbal beauty, but lacking savor when given a distorted sense. It is not my advice that you imitate men of this kind.

The good student, then, ought to be humble and docile, free alike from vain cares and from sensual indulgences, diligent and zealous to learn willingly from all, to presume never upon his own knowledge, to shun the authors of perverse doctrine as if they were poison, to consider a matter thoroughly and at length before judging of it, to seek to be learned rather than merely to seem so, to love such words of the wise as he has grasped, and ever to hold those words before his gaze as the very mirror of his countenance. And if some things, by chance rather obscure, have not allowed him to understand them, let him not at once break out in angry condemnation and think that nothing is good but what he himself can understand. This is the humility proper to a student's discipline.

Concerning Eagerness to Inquire

Eagerness to inquire relates to practice and in it the student needs encouragement rather than instruction. Whoever wishes to inspect earnestly what the ancients in their love of wisdom have handed down to us, and how deserving of posterity's remembrance are the monuments which they left of their virtue, will see how inferior his own earnestness is to theirs. Some of them scorned honors, others cast aside riches, others rejoiced in injuries received, others despised hardships, and still others, deserting the meeting places of men for the farthest withdrawn spots and secret haunts of solitude, gave themselves over to philosophy alone, that they might have greater freedom for undisturbed contemplation insofar as they subjected their minds to none of the desires which usually obstruct the path of virtue. We read that the philosopher Parmenides dwelt on a rock in Egypt for fifteen years. And Prometheus, for his unrestrained love of thinking, is recorded to have been exposed to the attacks of a vulture on Mount Caucasus. For they knew that the true good lies not in the esteem of men but is hidden in a pure conscience and that those are not truly men who, clinging to things destined to perish, do not recognize their own good. Therefore, seeing that they differed in mind and understanding from all the rest of men, they displayed this fact in the very far removal of their dwelling places, so that one community might not hold men not associated by the same objectives. A certain man retorted to a philosopher, saying, "Do you not see that men are laughing at you?" To which the philosopher replied, "They laugh at me, and the asses bray at them." Think if you can how much he valued the praise of those men whose vituperation, even, he did not fear. Of another man we read that after studying all the disciplines and attaining the very peaks of all the arts he turned to the potter's trade. Again, the disciples of a certain other man, when they exalted their master with praises, gloried in the fact that among all his other accomplishments he even possessed that of being a shoemaker.

I could wish that our students possessed such earnestness that wisdom would never grow old in them. None but Abisag the Sunamitess warmed the aged David, because the love of wisdom, though the body decay, will not desert her lover. "Almost all the powers of the body are changed in aged men; while wisdom alone increases, all the rest fade away" [Jerome, *Ep.* 52, iii.2]. "The old age of those who have formed their youth upon creditable pursuits becomes wiser with the years, acquires greater polish through experience, greater wisdom with the passage of time, and reaps the sweetest fruits of former studies. That wise and well-known man of Greece, Themistocles, when he had lived a full one hundred seven years and saw that he was about to die, is said to have declared that he was sad to depart this life when he had just begun to be wise. Plato died writing in his eighty-first year. Socrates's filled ninety-nine years with the pain and labor of teaching and writing. I pass over in silence all the other philosophers—Pythagoras, Democritus, Xenocrates, Zeno, and the Elean (Parmenides)—who flourished throughout a long life spent in the pursuit of wisdom. I come now to the poets Homer, Hesiod, Simonides, and Tersichorus [Stesichorus], who, when advanced in years, sang, with the approach of death—how shall I say it?—a swan-song sweeter than even their former wont. When Sophocles, after an exceedingly old age and a long neglect of his family affairs, was accused by his sons of madness, he declaimed to the judge the story of Oedipus which he had only recently composed, and gave such a specimen of his wisdom in these already broken years that he moved the austere dignity of the courtroom to the applause of the theatre. Nor is this a matter for wonder, when even Cato the censor, most erudite of the Romans, neither blushed nor despaired to learn Greek when he was already an old man. And, indeed, Homer reports that from the tongue of Nestor, who was already stooped with age and nearly decrepit, flowed speech sweeter than honey" [Jerome, *Ep.* 52, iii.2]. Consider, then, how much these men loved wisdom when not even decrepit age could call them away from its quest.

The greatness of that love of wisdom, therefore, and the abundance of judgment in elderly men is aptly inferred from the interpretation of that very name "Abisag" which I mentioned above. "For 'Abisag' means 'father mine, superabounding' or again 'my father's deep-voiced cry,' whence it is most abundantly shown that, with the aged, the thunder of divine discourse tarries beyond human speech. For the word 'superabounding' here signifies fullness, not redundance. And indeed, 'Sunamitess' in our language means 'scarlet woman'" [Jerome, *Ep.* 52, iii.2], an expression which can aptly enough signify zeal for wisdom.

Concerning the Four Remaining Precepts

The four following precepts are so arranged that they alternately refer first to discipline and next to practice.

On Quiet

Quiet of life—whether interior, so that the mind is not distracted with illicit desires, or exterior, so that leisure and opportunity are provided for creditable and useful studies—is in both senses important to discipline.

On Scrutiny

Now, scrutiny, that is, meditation, has to do with practice. Yet it seems that scrutiny belongs under eagerness to inquire, and if this is true, we are here repeating ourselves needlessly, since we mentioned the latter above. It should, however, be recognized that there is a difference between these two. Eagerness to inquire means insistent application to one's work; scrutiny means earnestness in considering things. Hard work and love make you carry out a task; concern and alertness make you well-advised. Through hard work you keep matters going; through love you bring them to perfection. Through concern you look ahead; through alertness you pay close attention. These are the four footmen who carry the chair of Philology, for they give practice to the mind over which Wisdom sits ruler. The chair of

Philology is the throne of Wisdom, and it is said to be carried by these bearers because it is carried forward when one practices these things. Therefore, the two front bearers, because of their power, are neatly designated as the youths Philos and Kophos, that is Love and Hard Work, because they bring a task to external perfection; the two rear bearers are with equal neatness designated as the maidens Philemia and Agrimnia (Epimeleia and Agrypnia), that is Concern and Alertness, because they inspire interior and secret reflection. There are some who suppose that by the Chair of Philology is meant the human body, over which the rational soul presides, and which four footmen carry—that is, the four elements of which the two upper ones, namely fire and air, are masculine in function and in gender, and the two lower, earth and water, feminine.

On Parsimony

Men have wished to persuade students to be content with slender means, that is, not to hanker after superfluities. This is a matter of especial importance for their discipline. "A fat belly," as the saying goes, "does not produce a fine perception." But what will the students of our time be able to say for themselves on this point? Not only do they despise frugality in the course of their studies, but they even labor to appear rich beyond what they are. Each one boasts not of what he has learned but of what he has spent. But perhaps the explanation of this lies in their wish to imitate their masters, concerning whom I can find nothing worthy enough to say!

On a Foreign Soil

Finally, a foreign soil is proposed, since it too gives a man practice. All the world is a foreign soil to those who philosophize. However, as a certain poet says:

> I know not by what sweetness native soil attracts a man
> And suffers not that he should never forget.

It is, therefore, a great source of virtue for the practiced mind to learn, bit by bit, first to change about in visible and transitory things, so that afterwards it may be able to leave them behind altogether. The man who finds his homeland sweet is still a tender beginner; he to whom every soil is as his native one is already strong; but he is perfect to whom the entire world is as a foreign land. The tender soul has fixed his love on one spot in the world; the strong man has extended his love to all places; the perfect man has extinguished his. From boyhood, I have dwelt on foreign soil, and I know with what grief sometimes the mind takes leave of the narrow hearth of a peasant's hut, and I know, too, how frankly it afterwards disdains marble firesides and panelled halls.

Review and Discussion Questions

1. Hugh observes that, in his day, there are "many who study but few who are wise." What marks the difference between a wise and a foolish student?

2. What is the difference between "treating of an art" and treating a topic "by means of that art"?

3. Summarize Hugh's advice on the right method or approach to study.

4. Hugh claims, provocatively: "Order in the disciplines is arranged to follow nature." How might you defend that claim?

5. Hugh proposes not only an order to the curriculum but also an order to the scholar's life. How are these two types of order related?

❖ 13

ST. BONAVENTURE (1221–74)

Reduction of the Arts to Theology

Let us see, therefore, how the other illuminations of knowledge are to be
brought back to the light of Sacred Scripture.

Compact in structure, expansive in scope, Bonaventure's essay "Reduction
of the Arts to Theology" asserts the integration of all knowledge. Drawing
upon Hugh of St. Victor, and anticipating Jacques Maritain's later work
The Degrees of Knowledge, Bonaventure's concept of the "four lights" signifies the ascending levels of human cognition. The four types of knowledge correspond to four species of objects: artifical bodies (works of men),
natural bodies (works of nature), speculative objects (principles or causes
of things), and finally, revealed objects (the eternal reasons in the mind of
God). Since God is both the beginning and the end of creation, it is fitting
that we should view all science in the light of its source; speculative and
practical sciences thus serve as handmaidens to the highest study, theology.

Further Reading: Bonaventure, *Journey of the Mind to God*, trans. Philotheus Boehner, O.F.M.,
and ed. Stephen F. Brown (Indianapolis, Ind.: Hackett Publishing, 1993); Illin Delic, O.F.M.,
Simply Bonaventure: An Introduction to His Life, Thought, and Writings (Hyde Park, N.Y.: New
City Press, 2001); E. Gilson, *The Philosophy of St. Bonaventure*, trans. I. Trethowan and F. J. Sheed
(Paterson, N.J.: Franciscan Press, 1965).

❖

*Every good gift and every perfect gift is from above, coming down from the
Father of Lights,* says James in the first chapter of his epistle. These words of
Sacred Scripture not only indicate the source of all illumination but they
likewise point out the generous flow of the manifold rays which issue from
that Fount of light. Notwithstanding the fact that every illumination of
knowledge is within, still we can with reason distinguish what we may call
the *external* light, or the light of mechanical art; the *lower* light, or the light
of sense perception; the *inner* light, or the light of philosophical knowl-

134

edge; and the *higher* light, or the light of grace and of Sacred Scripture. The first light illumines in regard to structure of *artifacts;* the second, in regard to *natural forms;* the third, in regard to *intellectual truth;* the fourth and last, in regard to *saving truth.*

The first light, then, since it enlightens the mind in reference to structure of *artifacts,* which are, as it were, exterior to man and intended to supply the needs of the body, is called the light of *mechanical art.* Being, in a certain sense, servile and of a lower nature than philosophical knowledge, this light can rightly be termed external. It has seven divisions corresponding to the seven mechanical arts enumerated by Hugh in his *Didascalicon,* namely, weaving, armour-making, agriculture, hunting, navigation, medicine, and the dramatic art. That the above-mentioned arts *suffice* (for us) is shown in the following way. Every mechanical art is intended for man's *consolation* or for his comfort; its purpose, therefore, is to banish either *sorrow* or *want;* it either *benefits* or *delights,* according to the words of Horace:

Either to serve or to please is the wish of the poets.

And again:

He hath gained universal applause who hath combined the profitable with the pleasing.

If its aim is to afford *consolation* and amusement, it is *dramatic art,* or the art of exhibiting plays, which embraces every form of entertainment, be it song, music, poetry, or pantomime. If, however, it is intended for the *comfort* or betterment of the exterior man, it can accomplish its purpose by providing either *covering or food, or* by *serving as an aid in the acquisition of either.* In the *matter* of *covering,* if *it* provides a *soft* and light material, it is *weaving; if* a strong and hard material, it is *armour-making* or metalworking, an art which extends to every tool or implement fashioned either of iron or of any metal whatsoever, or of stone, or of wood.

In the matter *of food,* mechanical art may benefit us in two ways, for we derive our sustenance *from vegetables* and *from animals.* As *regards vegetables,* it *is farming; as regards flesh meats,* it is *hunting.* Or again, *as regards food,* mechanical *art has a* twofold advantage: it aids either in the *production* and multiplication of crops, in which case it is agriculture, or in the various ways of preparing food, under which aspect it is hunting, an art which extends to every conceivable way of preparing foods, drinks, and delicacies—a task with which bakers, cooks, and innkeepers are concerned.

The term "hunting" *(venatio),* however, is used for all these things because it has a certain excellence and courtliness.

Furthermore, as an aid in the acquisition of each (clothing and food), the mechanical arts contribute to the welfare of man in two ways: either by *supplying a want,* and in this case it is *navigation,* which includes all *commerce of articles* of covering or of food; or by *removing impediments* and ills of the body, under which aspect it is *medicine,* whether it is concerned with the preparation of drugs, potions, or ointments, with the healing of wounds, or with the amputation of members, in which latter case it is called surgery. Dramatic art, on the other hand, is the only one of its kind. Thus the sufficiency (of the mechanical arts) is evident.

The second light, which enables us to discern *natural forms, is* the light of *sense perception.* Rightly is it called the *lower* light because sense perception begins with a material object and takes place by the aid of corporeal light. It has five divisions corresponding to the five senses. In his *Third Book on Genesis,* Saint Augustine bases the *adequacy* of the senses on the nature of the light present in the elements in the following way. If the light or brightness which makes possible the discernment of things corporeal exists in a *high degree of its own property* and in a certain purity, it is the sense of *sight; commingled with the air,* it is *hearing; with vapor,* it is *smell; with fluid,* it is *taste; with solidity of earth,* it is *touch.* Now the sensitive life of the body partakes of the nature of light for which reason it thrives in the nerves, which are naturally unobstructed and capable of transmitting impressions, and in these five senses it possesses more or less vigor according to the greater or less soundness of the nerves. And so, since there are in the world five simple substances, namely, the four elements and the fifth essence, man has for the perception of all these corporeal forms five senses well adapted to these substances, because, on account of the well-defined nature of each sense, apprehension can take place only when there is a certain conformity and fitness between the organ and the object. There is another way of determining the adequacy of the senses, but Saint Augustine sanctions this method and it seems reasonable, since corresponding elements on the part of the organ, the medium, and the object lend joint support to the proof.

The third light, which enlightens man in the investigation of *intelligible truths,* is the light of *philosophical knowledge.* It is called inner because it inquires into inner and hidden causes through principles of learning and natural truth, which are inherent in man. There is a triple diffusion of this light in *rational, natural,* and *moral* philosophy, which seems adequate, since it covers the three aspects of truth—truth of *speech,* truth of *things,* and truth of *morals. Rational* philosophy considers the truth of *speech; natural* philosophy, the truth of *things;* and *moral* philosophy, the truth of *conduct.* Or we may consider it in a different light. Just as we find in the Most High God efficient, formal or exemplary, and final causality, since "He is the Cause of being, the Principle of knowledge, and the Pattern of human life," so do we find it in the illumination of philosophy, which enlightens the mind to discern the *causes of being,* in which case it is *physics;* or to grasp the *principles of understanding,* in which case it is *logic;* or to learn the *right way of living,* in which case it is *moral* or practical philosophy. We are now considering it under its third aspect. The light of philosophical knowledge illumines the intellectual faculty itself and this enlightenment may be threefold: if it governs the *motive power,* it is *moral* philosophy; if it *rules itself* it is *natural* philosophy; if it directs *interpretation,* it is *discursive* philosophy. As a result, man is enlightened as regards the truth of life, the truth of knowledge, and the truth of doctrine.

And since one may, through the medium of *speech,* give expression to what he has in mind with a threefold purpose in view: namely, to manifest his thought, to induce someone to believe, or to arouse love or hatred, for this reason, *discursive* or rational philosophy has three sub-divisions: *grammar, logic,* and *rhetoric.* Of these sciences the first aims to express; the second, teach; the third, to persuade. The first considers the reasoning faculty as *apprehending;* the second, as *judging;* the third, as *persuading.* Since the mind apprehends by means of *correct* speech, judges by means of *true* speech, and persuades by means of *embellished* speech, with good reason does this triple science consider these three qualities in speech.

Again, since our intellect must be guided in its judgment by formal principles, these principles, likewise, can be considered under three aspects: in relation to *matter,* they are *termed formal;* in relation to the *mind,* they are termed *intellectual;* and in relation to *Divine Wisdom,* they are called *ideal. Natural* philosophy, therefore, is subdivided into *physics* proper, *mathematics,* and *metaphysics.* Thus *physics* treats of the generation and corruption of things according to natural powers and seminal causes; *mathematics* considers forms that can be abstracted in their pure intelligibility; *metaphysics* treats of the cognition of all beings, which it leads back to one first Principle from which they proceeded according to the *ideal causes,* that is, to God, since He is the *Beginning,* the *End,* and the *Exemplar.* Concerning these ideal causes, however, there has been some controversy among metaphysicians.

Since the government of the motive power is to be considered in a threefold way, namely, as regards the *individual,* the *family,* and the *state, so* there are three corresponding divisions of *moral* philosophy: namely, *ethical, economic,* and *political,* the content of each being clearly indicated by its name.

Now the fourth light, which illumines the mind for the understanding of *saving truth, is* the light of *Sacred Scripture.* This light is called *higher* because it leads to things above by the manifestation of truths which are beyond reason and also because it is not acquired by human research, but comes down by inspiration from the *"Father of Lights."* Although in its *literal* sense it is *one,* still, in its spiritual and *mystical* sense, it *is threefold,* for in all the books of Sacred Scripture, in addition to the literal meaning which the words outwardly express, there is understood a threefold spiritual meaning: namely, the *allegorical,* by which we are taught what to believe concerning the Divinity and humanity; the *moral,* by which we are taught how to live; and the *anagogical,* by which we are taught how to be united to God. Hence all Sacred Scripture teaches these three truths: namely, the eternal generation and Incarnation of Christ, the pattern of human life, and the union of the soul with God. The first regards *faith;* the second, *morals;* and the third, the *ultimate end of both.* The doctors should labor at the study of the first; the preachers, at the study of the second; the contemplatives, at the study of the third. The first is taught chiefly by Augustine; the second, by Gregory; the third, by Dionysius. Anselm follows Augustine; Bernard follows Gregory; Richard (of Saint Victor) follows Dionysius. For Anselm excels in reasoning; Bernard, in preaching; Richard, in contemplating; but Hugh (of Saint Victor) in all three.

From the foregoing statements it can be inferred that, although according to our first classification the light coming down from above *is fourfold,* it still admits of six modifications: namely, the light of *Sacred Scripture,* the light of *sense perception,* the light of *mechanical art,* the light of *rational philosophy,* the light of *natural philosophy,* and the light of *moral philosophy.* And for that reason there are in this life six illuminations, and they have their twilight, for all *knowledge will be destroyed;* for that reason too there follows a seventh day of rest, a day which knows no evening, *the illumination of glory.*

Wherefore, very fittingly may these six illuminations be related to the six days of creation or illumination in which the world was made, the knowledge of Sacred Scripture corresponding to the creation of the first day, that is, to the creation of light, and so on, one after the other in order. Moreover, just as all those creations had their origin in one light, so too are all these branches of knowledge ordained for the knowledge of Sacred Scripture; they are contained in it; they are perfected by it; and by means of it they are ordained for eternal illumination. Wherefore, all our knowledge should end in the knowledge of Sacred Scripture, and especially is this true of the *anagogical* knowledge through which the illumination is reflected back to God whence it came. And there the cycle ends; the number six is complete and consequently there is rest.

Let us see, therefore, how the other illuminations of knowledge are to be brought back to the light of Sacred Scripture. First of all, let us consider the illumination of *sense perception,* which is concerned exclusively with the cognition of sense objects, a process in which there are three phases to be considered: namely, the *medium* of perception, the *exercise* of perception, and the *delight* of perception. If we consider the *medium* of perception, we shall see therein the Word begotten from all eternity and made man in time. Indeed, a sense object can stimulate a cognitive faculty only through the medium of a similitude which proceeds from the object as an offspring from its parent, and this by generation, by reality, or by exemplarily, for every sense. This similitude, however, does not complete the act of perception unless it is brought into contact with the sense organ and the sense faculty, and once that contact is established, there results a new percept. Through this percept the mind is led back to the object by means of the similitude. And even though the object is not always present to the senses, still the fact remains that the object by itself, when in its finished state, begets a similitude. In like manner, know that from the mind of the Most High, Who is knowable by the interior senses of our mind, from all eternity there emanated a Similitude, an Image, and an Offspring; and afterwards, when "the fullness of time came," He was united to a mind and a body and assumed the form of man, which had never been before. Through Him the minds of all of us which receive that Similitude of the Father through faith in our hearts, are brought back to God.

If we consider the *exercise* of sense perception, we shall see therein *the pattern of human life,* for each sense applies itself to its proper object, shrinks from what may harm it, and does not usurp what does not belong to it. In like manner, the *spiritual sense* lives in an orderly way when it exercises itself for its own purpose, against *negligence;* when it refrains from what is harmful, against *concupiscence;* and when it refrains from usurping what does not belong to it, against *pride.* Of a truth, every disorder springs from negligence, from concupiscence, or from pride. Surely then, he who lives a prudent, temperate, and submissive life leads a well-ordered life, for thereby he avoids negligence in things to be done, concupiscence in things to be desired, and pride in things that are excellent.

Furthermore, if we consider the *delight of* sense perception, we shall see therein the union of God and the soul. Indeed every sense seeks its proper sense object with longing, finds it with delight, and never wearied, seeks it again and again, because "the eye is not filled with seeing, neither is the ear filled with hearing." In the same way, our spiritual senses must seek with longing, find with joy, and time and again experience the beautiful, the harmonious, the fragrant, the sweet, or the delightful to the touch. Behold how the Divine Wisdom lies hidden in sense perception and how wonderful is the contemplation of the five spiritual senses in the light of their conformity to the senses of the body.

By the same process of reasoning is Divine Wisdom to be found in the illumination of the *mechanical arts,* the sole purpose of which is the *production of artifacts.* In this illumination we can see the *eternal generation and Incarnation of the Word,* the *pattern of human life,* and the *union of the soul with God.* And this is true if we consider the *production,* the *effect,* and *the fruit* of a work, or if we consider *the skill of the artist, the quality of the effect produced,* and *the utility of the product derived therefrom.*

If we consider the production, we shall see that the work of art proceeds from the artificer according to a similitude existing in his mind; this pattern or model the artificer studies carefully before he produces and then he produces as he has predetermined. The artificer, moreover, produces an exterior work bearing the closest possible resemblance to the interior exemplar, and if it were in his power to produce an effect which would know and love him, this he would assuredly do; and if that effect could know its maker, it would be by means of the similitude according to which it came from the hands of the artificer; and if the eyes of the understanding were so darkened that it could not elevate itself to things above itself in order to bring itself to a knowledge of its maker, it would be necessary for the similitude according to which the effect was produced to lower itself even to that nature which the effect could grasp and know. In like manner, understand that no creature has proceeded from the Most High Creator except through the Eternal Word, "in Whom He ordered all things," and by which Word He produced creatures bearing not only the nature of His *vestige* but also of His *image* so that through knowledge they might become like unto Him. And since by sin the rational creature had dimmed the eye of contemplation, it was most fitting that the Eternal and Invisible should become visible and take flesh that He might lead us back to the Father. Indeed, this is what is related in the fourteenth chapter of Saint John: "No one comes to the Father but through Me," and in the eleventh chapter of Saint Matthew: "No one knows the Son except the Father; nor does anyone know the Father except the Son, and him to whom the Son chooses to reveal him." For that reason, then, it is said, "the Word was made flesh." Therefore, considering the illumination of mechanical art as regards the production of the work, we shall see therein the Word begotten and made incarnate, that is, the Divinity and the Humanity and the integrity of all faith.

If we consider the *effect,* we shall see therein the *pattern of human life,* for every artificer, indeed, aims to produce a work that is beautiful, useful, and enduring, and only when it possesses these three qualities is the work highly valued and acceptable. Corresponding to the above-mentioned qualities, in the pattern of life there must be found three elements: *"knowledge, will,* and *unaltering* and *persevering toil." Knowledge* renders the work beautiful; the *will* renders it useful; *perseverance* renders it lasting. The first resides in the rational, the second in the concupiscible, and the third in the irascible appetite.

If we consider *the fruit,* we shall find therein *the union of the soul with God,* for every artificer who fashions a work does so that he may derive *praise, benefit,* or *delight* therefrom—a threefold purpose which corresponds to the three formal objects of the appetites: namely, a *noble* good, a *useful* good, and an *agreeable* good. It was for this threefold reason that God made the soul rational, namely, that of its own accord, it might *praise* Him, *serve* Him, *find delight* in Him, and be at rest; and this takes place through charity. "He who abides in it, abides in God, and God in him," in such a way that there is found therein a kind of wondrous union and from that union comes a wondrous delight, for in the Book of Proverbs it is written, "My delights were to be with the children of men." Behold how the illumination of mechanical art is the path to the illumination of Sacred Scripture. There is nothing therein which does not bespeak true wisdom and for this reason Sacred Scripture quite rightly makes frequent use of such similitudes.

In like manner is Divine Wisdom to be found in the illumination of *rational philosophy,* the main concern of which is *speech.* Here are to be considered three elements corresponding to the three aspects of speech itself: namely, the *person speaking,* the *delivery* of the speech, and its final purpose or its effect upon the *hearer.*

Considering speech in the light of the *speaker,* we see that all speech signifies a *mental concept.* That inner concept is the word of the mind and its offspring which is known to the person conceiving it; but that it may become known to the hearer, it assumes the form of the voice, and clothed therein, the intelligible word becomes sensible and is heard without; it is received into the ear of the person listening and still it does not depart from the mind of the person uttering it. Practically the same procedure is seen in the begetting of the Eternal Word, because the Father conceived Him, begetting Him from all eternity, as it is written in the eighth chapter of the Book of Proverbs, "The depths were not as yet, and I was already conceived." But that He might be known by man who is endowed with senses, He assumed the nature of flesh, and "the Word was made flesh and dwelt amongst us," and yet He remained "in the bosom of the Father."

Considering speech in the light of its *delivery,* we shall see therein the pattern of *human life,* for three essential qualities work together for the perfection of speech: namely, *suitability, truth,* and *ornament.* Corresponding to these three qualities, every act of ours should be characterized by *measure, beauty,* and *order so* that it may be *controlled* by its proper measure in its external work, *rendered beautiful* by purity of affection, and *regulated* and adorned by uprightness of intention. For then truly does one live an upright and well-ordered life when his intention is upright, his affection pure, and his activity within its proper limit.

Considering speech in the light of its *purpose,* we find that it aims to *express,* to *instruct,* and to *persuade;* but it never *expresses* except by means of a likeness; it never *teaches* except by means of a clear light; it never *persuades* except by power; and it is evident that these effects are accomplished only by means of an inherent likeness, light, and power intrinsically *united to the soul.* Therefore, Saint Augustine concludes that he alone is a true teacher who can impress a likeness, shed light, and grant power to the heart of his hearer. Hence it is that "he who teaches within hearts has his Chair in heaven." Now as perfection of speech requires the union of power, light, and a likeness within the soul, so, too, for the instruction of the soul in the knowledge of God by interior conversation with Him, there is required a union with Him who is "the brightness of his glory and the image of his substance, and upholding all things by the word of his power." Hence we see how wondrous is this contemplation by which Saint Augustine in his many writings leads souls to Divine Wisdom.

By the same mode of reasoning is the Wisdom of God to be found in the illumination of *natural philosophy,* which is concerned chiefly with the *formal causes* in *matter,* in the *soul,* and in the *Divine Wisdom.* These formal causes it is fitting to consider under three aspects: namely, as regards the *relation of proportion,* the *effect of causality,* and their *medium of union;* and in these three can be accordingly found the three (central ideas of the three senses of Holy Scripture) mentioned above.

Considering the formal causes according to their *relation of proportion*, we shall see therein the *Word Eternal* and the *Word Incarnate*. The *intellectual* and abstract causes are, as it were, midway between the *seminal* and the *ideal* causes. But *seminal* causes cannot exist in *matter* without the generation and production of form; neither can *intellectual* causes exist in the *soul* without the generation of the word in the mind. Therefore, *ideal* causes cannot exist *in God* without the generation of the Word from the Father in due proportion. Truly, this is a mark of dignity, and if it becomes the creature, how much more so the Creator. It was for this reason that Saint Augustine said the Son of God is the "art of the Father." Again, the natural tendency in matter is so ordained toward intellectual causes that the generation is in no way perfect unless the rational soul be united to the material body. By similar reasoning, therefore, we come to the conclusion that the highest and noblest perfection can exist in this world only if a nature in which there are the seminal causes, and a nature in which there are the intellectual causes, and a nature in which there are the ideal causes are simultaneously combined in the unity of one person, as was done in the Incarnation of the Son of God. Therefore all natural philosophy, by reason of the relation of proportion, predicates the Word of God begotten and become Incarnate so that He is the *Alpha* and the *Omega,* that is, He was begotten in the beginning and before all time but became Incarnate in the fullness of time.

Now if we think of these causes according to the *effect of causality,* we shall be considering the *pattern of human life,* since generation by seminal causes can take place in generative and corruptible matter only by the beneficent light of the heavenly bodies which are far removed from generation and corruption, that is, by the *sun,* the *moon,* and the *stars.* So too the soul can perform no living works unless it receive from the sun, that is, from Christ, the aid of His gratuitous light; unless it seek the protection of the moon, that is, of the Virgin Mary, Mother of Christ; and unless it imitate the example of the other saints. When all these concur, there is accomplished in the soul a living and perfect work; therefore the right order of living depends upon this threefold cooperation.

Moreover, if we consider these formal causes as regards their *medium of union,* we shall understand how *union of the soul with God* takes place, for the corporeal nature can be united to the soul only through the medium of moisture, (vital) spirit, and warmth—three conditions which dispose the body to receive life from the soul. So too we may understand that God gives life to the soul and is united to it only on the condition that it be *moistened* with tears of compunction and filial love, made *spiritual* by contempt of every earthly thing, and *be warmed* by desire for its heavenly home and its Beloved. Behold how in natural philosophy lies hidden the Wisdom of God.

In the same way is the light of *Sacred Scripture* to be found in the illumination of *moral philosophy.* Since moral philosophy is concerned principally with rectitude, it treats of general justice which Saint Anselm calls the "rectitude of the will." The term "right" has a threefold signification and accordingly, in the consideration of rectitude are revealed the three central ideas (of the senses of Sacred Scripture) previously mentioned. In one sense of the word, that is called "right," the middle of which is not out of line with its extreme points. If then God is perfect rectitude and that by His very nature since He is the Beginning and the End of all things, it follows that in God there must be an intermediary of *His own* nature so that there may be one Person who only produces, another who is only produced, but an intermediary who both produces and is produced. There is likewise need of an intermediary in the *going forth* and in the return of things: in the *going forth,* an intermediary which will be more on the part of the one producing; in the *return,* one which will be more on the part of the one returning. Therefore, as creatures went forth from God by the Word of God, so for a perfect return, it was necessary that the Mediator *between God* and man be not only God but also man so that He might lead men back to God.

In another sense, that is called "right" which is conformed to rule. Accordingly, in the consideration of rectitude there is seen the *rule of life.* For he indeed lives rightly who is guided by the regulations of the divine law, as is the case when the will of man accepts necessary *precepts,* salutary warnings, and *counsels* of perfection that he may thereby prove *the good* and *acceptable* and *perfect will of God.* And then is the rule of life right when no obliquity can be found therein.

In the third sense, that is called *"right"* the summit of which is raised upward, as for instance, we say that man has an upright posture. And in this sense, in the consideration of rectitude there is manifested the *union of the soul with God;* for since God is above, it necessarily follows that the apex of the mind itself must be raised aloft. And indeed this is what actually happens when man's *rational nature* assents to the First Truth for His own sake and above all things, when his *irascible nature* strives after the Highest Bounty, and when his *concupiscible nature* clings to the Greatest Good. He who thus keeps close to God *is one spirit with him.*

And so it is evident how the *manifold Wisdom of God,* which is clearly revealed in Sacred Scripture, lies hidden in all knowledge and in all nature. It is evident too how all divisions of knowledge are handmaids of theology, and it is for this reason that theology makes use of illustrations and terms pertaining to every branch of knowledge. It is likewise evident how wide is the illuminative way and how in everything which is perceived or known God Himself lies hidden within. And this is the fruit of all sciences, that in all, faith may be strengthened, *God may be honored,* character may be formed, and consolation may be derived from union of the Spouse with His beloved, a union which takes place through charity, to the attainment of which the whole purpose of Sacred Scripture, and consequently, every illumination descending from above, is directed—a charity without which all knowledge is vain—because no one comes to the Son except through the Holy Ghost who teaches us *all the truth, who is blessed forever. Amen.*

Review and Discussion Questions

1. Describe Bonaventure's third and fourth "lights."

2. Contemporary universities, we might say, excel in the "second light" (study of the works of nature). Those who promote the liberal arts sometimes seek to redress this balance by focusing exclusively on the "first light" (study of the works of man). Why, in Bonaventure's view, is neither sufficient?

3. Identify the four-fold sense of Scripture.

4. Chart the relation between the senses of Scripture, their ends, and the representative figures Bonaventure assigns to each.

❖ 14

ST. THOMAS AQUINAS (1225–74)

Summa Theologiae

> The truth about God such as reason could discover, would only be known by a few, and that after a long time, and with the admixture of many errors.

In this selection St. Thomas reflects on the place of theology within the family of the sciences. Every part of knowledge finds a home within the Thomistic university. In the coordination of knowledge, the theist scores decisive advantages over both the polytheist and the agnostic. Against polytheism, Christian wisdom shows how secondary causes can ultimately find their home in the one source of being, God. Evil and chaos are derivative, not ultimate observations. Goodness, beauty, and truth triumph. Man's aspiration for order is answered. Against the agnostic, Thomas provides a compelling alternative to numb unbelief. Science is no accident. Made in the image of the creator, the human mind is "hard-wired" to know. Creation comes from the Logos and will return to that same source.

Further Reading: Aidan Nichols, *An Introduction to Thomas Aquinas* (Grand Rapids, Mich.: Wm. B. Eerdmans, 2003); *Catechism of the Catholic Church* (New York: Doubleday, 1995), esp. paragraphs 26–197; G. K. Chesterton, *The Dumb Ox* (New York: Doubleday, 1956).

❖

Whether, besides philosophy, any further doctrine is required?

Objection 1: It seems that, besides philosophical science, we have no need of any further knowledge. For man should not seek to know what is above reason: "Seek not the things that are too high for thee" (Ecclus. 3:22). But whatever is not above reason is fully treated of in philosophical science. Therefore any other knowledge besides philosophical science is superfluous.

Objection 2: Further, knowledge can be concerned only with being, for nothing can be known, save what is true; and all that is, is true. But everything that is, is treated of in philosophical science—even God Himself; so that there is a part of philosophy called theology, or the divine science, as Aristotle has proved (*Metaph.* vi). Therefore, besides philosophical science, there is no need of any further knowledge.

On the contrary, It is written (2 Tim. 3:16): "All Scripture, inspired of God is profitable to teach, to reprove, to correct, to instruct in justice." Now Scripture, inspired of God, is no part of philosophical science, which has been built up by human reason. Therefore it is useful that besides philosophical science, there should be other knowledge, i.e. inspired of God.

I answer that, It was necessary for man's salvation that there should be a knowledge revealed by God besides philosophical science built up by human reason. Firstly, indeed, because man is directed to God, as to an end that surpasses the grasp of his reason: "The eye hath not seen, O God, besides Thee, what things Thou hast prepared for them that wait for Thee" (Is. 66:4). But the end must first be known by men who are to direct their thoughts and actions to the end. Hence it was necessary for the salvation of man that certain truths which exceed human reason should be made known to him by divine revelation. Even as regards those truths about God which human reason could have discovered, it was necessary that man should be taught by a divine revelation; because the truth about God such as reason could discover, would only be known by a few, and that after a long time, and with the admixture of many errors. Whereas man's whole salvation, which is in God, depends upon the knowledge of this truth. Therefore, in order that the salvation of men might be brought about more fitly and more surely, it was necessary that they should be taught divine truths by divine revelation. It was therefore necessary that besides philosophical science built up by reason, there should be a sacred science learned through revelation.

Reply to Objection 1: Although those things which are beyond man's knowledge may not be sought for by man through his reason, nevertheless, once they are revealed by God, they must be accepted by faith. Hence the sacred text continues, "For many things are shown to thee above the understanding of man" (Ecclus. 3:25). And in this, the sacred science consists.

Reply to Objection 2: Sciences are differentiated according to the various means through which knowledge is obtained. For the astronomer and the physicist both may prove the same conclusion: that the earth, for instance, is round: the astronomer by means of mathematics (i.e. abstracting from matter), but the physicist by means of matter itself. Hence there is no reason why those things which may be learned from philosophical science, so far as they can be known by natural reason, may not also be taught us by another science so far as they fall within revelation. Hence theology included in sacred doctrine differs in kind from that theology which is part of philosophy.

Review and Discussion Questions

1. Outline the various parts to the Thomistic "article." What function does each part fulfill?

2. What are the virtues and liabilities of this mode of presentation?

3. What is the strongest reason Thomas offers for *excluding* theology from among the sciences?

4. In your own words, summarize Thomas's positive reasons for including theology within a comprehensive curriculum.

BL. JOHN HENRY NEWMAN (1805–90)

The Idea of a University

> One of the special objects which a Catholic University would promote is that of the formation of a Catholic Literature in the English language.

In this critical section of Newman's *Idea*, he addresses the place of literature within the Catholic university. Literature is, on the whole, a reflection of the character of a people, a nation, a tongue. And, as Newman observes, the English tongue has been formed, quite irreversibly, by Protestants. Judged against the literature of other nations, Newman suggests, Catholics could do much worse; the speech shaped by Shakespeare, Johnson, Herbert and Donne, shares with Catholics the Bible and much of the culture of the Church. Along the way, Newman tells us of the proper uses and abuses of literature, and how we are to view its position within the constellation of the disciplines.

Further Reading: John Henry Newman, *Apologia Pro Vita Sua* (London: J. M. Dent and Sons, 1949); James Arthur and Guy Nicholls, *John Henry Newman* (London: Continuum, 2007); Avery Dulles, *John Henry Newman* (London: Continuum, 2009).

❖

English Catholic Literature

One of the special objects which a Catholic University would promote is that of the formation of a Catholic Literature in the English language. It is an object, however, which must be understood before it can be suitably prosecuted; and which will not be understood without some discussion and investigation. First ideas on the subject must almost necessarily be crude. The real state of the case, what is desirable, what is possible, has to be ascertained; and then what has to be done, and what is to be expected. We have seen in public matters, for half a year past, to what mistakes, and to what disappointments, the country has been exposed, from not having been able distinctly to put before it what was to be aimed at by its fleets and armies, what was practicable, what was probable, in operations of war: and so, too, in the field of literature, we are sure of falling into a parallel perplexity and dissatisfaction, if we start with a vague notion of doing something or other important by means of a Catholic University, without having the caution to examine what is feasible, and what is unnecessary or hopeless. Accordingly, it is natural I should wish to direct attention to this subject, even though it be too difficult to handle in any exact or complete way, and though my attempt must be left for others to bring into a more perfect shape, who are more fitted for the task.

Here I shall chiefly employ myself in investigating what the object is *not*.

In Its Relation to Religious Literature

When a "Catholic Literature in the English tongue" is spoken of as a *desideratum*, no reasonable person will mean by "Catholic works" much more than the "works of Catholics." The phrase does not mean a *religious* literature. "Religious Literature" indeed would mean much more than "the Literature of religious men;" it means over and above this, that the subject-matter of the Literature is religious; but by "Catholic Literature" is not to be understood a literature which treats exclusively or primarily of Catholic matters, of Catholic doctrine, controversy, history, persons, or politics; but it includes all subjects of literature whatever, treated as a Catholic would treat them, and as he only can treat them. Why it is important to have them treated by Catholics hardly need be explained here, though something will be incidentally said on the point as we proceed: meanwhile I am drawing attention to the distinction between the two phrases in order to avoid a serious misapprehension. For it is evident that, if by a Catholic Literature were meant nothing more or less than a religious literature, its writers would be mainly ecclesiastics; just as writers on Law are mainly lawyers, and writers on Medicine are mainly physicians or surgeons. And if this be so, a Catholic Literature is no object special to a University, unless a University is to be considered identical with a Seminary or a Theological School.

I am not denying that a University might prove of the greatest benefit even to our religious literature; doubtless it would, and in various ways; still it is concerned with Theology only as one great subject of thought, as the greatest indeed which can occupy the human mind, yet not as the adequate or direct scope of its institution. Yet I suppose it is not impossible for a literary layman to wince at the idea, and to shrink from the proposal, of taking part in a scheme for the formation of a Catholic Literature, under the apprehension that in some way or another he will be entangling himself in a semi-clerical occupation. It is not uncommon, on expressing an anticipation that the Professors of a Catholic University will promote a Catholic Literature, to have to encounter a vague notion that a lecturer or writer so employed must have something polemical about him, must moralize or preach, must (in Protestant language) *improve the occasion*, though his subject is not at all a religious one; in short, that he must do something else besides fairly and boldly go right on, and be a Catholic speaking as a Catholic spontaneously will speak, on the Classics, or Fine Arts, or Poetry, or whatever he has taken in hand. Men think that he cannot give a lecture on Comparative Anatomy without being bound to digress into the Argument from Final Causes; that he cannot recount the present geological theories without forcing them into an interpretation *seriatim* of the first two chapters of Genesis. Many, indeed, seem to go further still, and actually pronounce that, since our own University has been recommended by the Holy See, and is established by the Hierarchy, it cannot but be engaged in teaching religion and nothing else, and must and will have the discipline of a Seminary; which is about as sensible and logical a view of the matter as it would be to maintain that the Prime Minister *ipso facto* holds an ecclesiastical office, since he is always a Protestant; or that the members of the House of Commons must necessarily have been occupied in clerical duties, as long as they took an oath about Transubstantiation. Catholic Literature is not synonymous with Theology, nor does it supersede or interfere with the work of catechists, divines, preachers, or schoolmen.

I have been speaking of the authors of a literature, in their relation to the people and course of events to which they belong; but a prior consideration, at which I have already glanced, is their connection with the language itself, which has been their organ. If they are in great measure the creatures of their times, they are on the other hand in a far higher sense the creators of their language. It is indeed commonly called their mother tongue, but virtually it did not exist till they gave it life and form. All greater matters are carried on and perfected by a succession of individual minds; what is true in the history of thought and of action is true of language also. Certain masters of composition, as Shakespeare, Milton, and Pope, the writers of the Protestant Bible and Prayer Book, Hooker and Addison, Swift, Hume, and Goldsmith, have been the making of the English language; and as that language is a fact, so is the literature a fact, by which it is formed, and in which it lives. Men of great ability have taken it in hand, each in his own day, and have done for it what the master of a gymnasium does for the bodily frame. They have formed its limbs, and developed its strength; they have endowed it with vigour, exercised it in suppleness and dexterity, and taught it grace. They have made it rich, harmonious, various, and precise. They have furnished it with a variety of styles, which from their individuality may almost be called dialects, and are monuments both of the powers of the language and the genius of its cultivators.

How real a creation, how *sui generis*, is the style of Shakespeare, or of the Protestant Bible and Prayer Book, or of Swift, or of Pope, or of Gibbon, or of Johnson! Even were the subject-matter without meaning, though in truth the style cannot really be abstracted from the sense, still the style would, on that supposition, remain as perfect and original a work as Euclid's elements or a symphony of Beethoven. And, like music, it has seized upon the public mind; and the literature of England is no longer a mere letter, printed in books, and shut up in libraries, but it is a living voice, which has gone forth in its expressions and its sentiments into the world of men, which daily thrills upon our ears and syllables our thoughts, which speaks to us through our correspondents, and dictates when we put pen to paper. Whether we will or no, the phraseology and diction of Shakespeare, of the Protestant formularies, of Milton, of Pope, of Johnson's *Table Talk,* and of Walter Scott, have become a portion of the vernacular tongue, the household words, of which perhaps we little guess the origin, and the very idioms of our familiar conversation. The man in the comedy spoke prose without knowing it; and we Catholics, without consciousness and without offence, are ever repeating the half sentences of dissolute playwrights and heretical partisans and preachers. So tyrannous is the literature of a nation; it is too much for us. We cannot destroy or reverse it; we may confront and encounter it, but we cannot make it over again. It is a great work of man, when it is no work of God's.

I repeat, then, whatever we be able or unable to effect in the great problem which lies before us, any how we cannot undo the past. English Literature will ever *have been* Protestant. Swift and Addison, the most native and natural of our writers, Hooker and Milton, the most elaborate, never can become our co-religionists; and, though this is but the enunciation of a truism, it is not on that account an unprofitable enunciation.

I trust we are not the men to give up an undertaking because it is perplexed or arduous; and to do nothing because we cannot do everything. Much may be attempted, much attained, even granting English Literature is not Catholic. Something indeed may be said even in alleviation of the misfortune itself, on which I have been insisting; and with two remarks bearing upon this latter point I will bring this Section to an end.

1. First, then, it is to be considered that, whether we look to countries Christian or heathen, we find the state of literature there as little satisfactory as it is in these islands; so that, whatever are our difficulties here, they are not worse than those of Catholics all over the world. I would not indeed say a word to extenuate the calamity, under which we lie, of having a literature formed in Protestantism; still, other literatures have disadvantages of their own; and, though in such matters comparisons are impossible, I doubt whether we should be better pleased if our English Classics were tainted with licentiousness, or defaced by infidelity or scepticism. I conceive we should not much mend matters if we were to exchange literatures with the French, Italians, or Germans. About Germany, however, I will not speak; as to France, it has great and religious authors; its classical drama, even in comedy, compared with that of other literatures, is singularly unexceptionable; but who is there that holds a place among its writers so historical and important, who is so copious, so versatile, so brilliant, as that Voltaire who is an open scoffer at every thing sacred, venerable, or high-minded? Nor can Rousseau, though he has not the pretensions of Voltaire, be excluded from the classical writers of France. Again, the gifted Pascal, in the work on which his literary fame is mainly founded, does not approve himself to a Catholic judgment; and Descartes, the first of French philosophers, was too independent in his inquiries to be always correct in his conclusions. The witty Rabelais is said, by a recent critic, to show covertly in his former publications, and openly in his latter, his "dislike to the Church of Rome." La Fontaine was with difficulty brought, on his death-bed, to make public satisfaction for the scandal which he had done to religion by his immoral *Contes*, though at length he threw into the fire a piece which he had just finished for the stage. Montaigne, whose Essays "make an epoch in literature," by "their influence upon the tastes and opinions of Europe;" whose "school embraces a large proportion of French and English literature;" and of whose "brightness and felicity of genius there can be but one opinion," is disgraced, as the same writer tells us, by "a sceptical bias and great indifference of temperament;" and "has led the way" as an habitual offender, "to the indecency too characteristic of French literature."

Nor does Italy present a more encouraging picture. Ariosto, one of the few names, ancient or modern, who is allowed on all hands to occupy the first rank of Literature, is, I suppose, rightly arraigned by the author I have above quoted, of "coarse sensuality." Pulci, "by his sceptical insinuations, seems clearly to display an intention of exposing religion to contempt." Boccaccio, the first of Italian prose-writers, had in his old age touchingly to la-ment the corrupting tendency of his popular compositions; and Bellarmine has to vindicate him, Dante, and Petrarch, from the charge of virulent abuse of the Holy See. Dante certainly does not scruple to place in his *Inferno* a Pope, whom the Church has since canonized, and his work on *Monarchia* is on the Index. Another great Florentine, Macchiavel, is on the Index also; and Giannone, as great in political history at Naples as Macchiavel at Florence, is notorious for his disaffection to the interests of the Roman Pontiff.

These are but specimens of the general character of secular literature, whatever be the people to whom it belongs. One literature may be better than another, but bad will be the best, when weighed in the balance of truth and morality. It cannot be otherwise; human nature is in all ages and all countries the same; and its literature, therefore, will ever and everywhere be one and the same also. Man's work will savour of man; in his elements and powers excellent and admirable, but prone to disorder and excess, to error and to sin. Such too will be his literature; it will have the beauty and the fierceness, the sweetness and the rankness, of the natural man, and, with all its richness and greatness, will necessarily offend the senses of those who, in the Apostle's words, are really "exercised to discern between good and evil." "It is said of the holy Sturme," says an Oxford writer, "that, in passing a horde of unconverted Germans, as they were bathing and gambolling in the stream, he was so overpowered by the intolerable scent which arose from them that he nearly fainted away." National Literature is, in a parallel way, the untutored movements of the reason, imagination, passions, and affections of the natural man, the leapings and the friskings, the plungings and the snortings, the sportings and the buffoonings, the clumsy play and the aimless toil, of the noble, lawless savage of God's intellectual creation.

It is well that we should clearly apprehend a truth so simple and elementary as this, and not expect from the nature of man, or the literature of the world, what they never held out to us. Certainly, I did not know that the world was to be regarded as favourable to Christian faith or practice, or that it would be breaking any engagement with us, if it took a line divergent from our own. I have never fancied that we should have reasonable ground for surprise or complaint, though man's intellect *puris naturalibus* did prefer, of the two, liberty to truth, or though his heart cherished a leaning towards licence of thought and speech in comparison with restraint.

2. If we do but resign ourselves to facts, we shall soon be led on to the second reflection which I have promised—viz., that, not only are things not better abroad, but they might be worse at home. We have, it is true, a Protestant literature; but then it is neither atheistical nor immoral; and, in the

case of at least half a dozen of its highest and most influential departments, and of the most popular of its authors, it comes to us with very considerable alleviations. For instance, there surely is a call on us for thankfulness that the most illustrious amongst English writers has so little of a Protestant about him that Catholics have been able, without extravagance, to claim him as their own, and that enemies to our creed have allowed that he is only not a Catholic, because, and as far as, his times forbade it. It is an additional satisfaction to be able to boast that he offends in neither of those two respects, which reflect so seriously upon the reputation of great authors abroad. Whatever passages may be gleaned from his dramas disrespectful to ecclesiastical authority, still these are but passages; on the other hand, there is in Shakespeare neither contempt of religion nor scepticism, and he upholds the broad laws of moral and divine truth with the consistency and severity of an Æschylus, Sophocles, or Pindar. There is no mistaking in his works on which side lies the right; Satan is not made a hero, nor Cain a victim, but pride is pride, and vice is vice, and, whatever indulgence he may allow himself in light thoughts or unseemly words, yet his admiration is reserved for sanctity and truth. From the second chief fault of Literature, as indeed my last words imply, he is not so free; but, often as he may offend against modesty, he is clear of a worse charge, sensuality, and hardly a passage can be instanced in all that he has written to seduce the imagination or to excite the passions.

A rival to Shakespeare, if not in genius, at least in copiousness and variety, is found in Pope; and he was actually a Catholic, though personally an unsatisfactory one. His freedom indeed from Protestantism is but a poor compensation for a false theory of religion in one of his poems; but taking his works as a whole, we may surely acquit them of being dangerous to the reader, whether on the score of morals or of faith.

Again, the special title of moralist in English Literature is accorded by the public voice to Johnson, whose bias towards Catholicity is well known.

If we were to ask for a report of our philosophers, the investigation would not be so agreeable; for we have three of evil, and one of unsatisfactory repute. Locke is scarcely an honour to us in the standard of truth, grave and manly as he is; and Hobbes, Hume, and Bentham, in spite of their abilities, are simply a disgrace. Yet, even in this department, we find some compensation in the names of Clarke, Berkeley, Butler, and Reid, and in a name more famous than them all. Bacon was too intellectually great to hate or to condemn the Catholic faith; and he deserves by his writings to be called the most orthodox of Protestant philosophers.

Review and Discussion Questions

1. How does Newman distinguish Catholic literature from "religious literature"?

2. At one point Newman calls literature "tyrannous" over a nation. What does he mean by this?

3. Writing in the mid-nineteenth century, Newman claims "English Literature will ever *have been* Protestant." What evidence could be cited against his claim?

4. Given that English Literature (in Newman's view) is not and can never become Catholic, why does he nevertheless judge Catholics in English-speaking countries to live in a healthier cultural situation than Catholics in other countries?

❖ 16

JACQUES MARITAIN (1882–1973)

Education at the Crossroads

> … a young man will choose for himself and progress all the more rapidly and perfectly in vocational, scientific, or technical training in proportion as his education has been liberal and universal.

Elementary, liberal, and advanced study—according to this tripartite scheme the eminent French Catholic convert Jacques Maritain outlines both the structure and the rationale for a civilizing, liberal education. Though Maritain was deeply involved in the intellectual life of continental Europe (he helped draft the United Nation's 1948 *Universal Declaration of Human Rights* as a French delegate), in his later career he also taught in the United States. His recommendations draw inspiration from both the European liberal arts tradition and the American Great Books movement, which originated from the University of Chicago. Eschewing what he views as the plague of overspecialization, Mariatain proposes a curriculum which closely mirrors the natural mental and psychological development of the mind as it grows in its powers of observation and abstraction.

Further Reading: Jacques Maritain, *Degrees of Knowledge*, trans. Ralph McInerny (Notre Dame, Ind.: University of Notre Dame Press, 1999); Jacques Maritain, *An Introduction to Philosophy* (London: Continuum, 2005); Jude Dougherty, *Jacques Maritain: An Intellectual Profile* (Washington, D.C.: The Catholic University of America Press, 2003).

❖

In this third chapter I shall touch upon the three great stages of education: elementary education, the humanities, advanced studies. In reference to the second stage—the humanities—we shall have to discuss some problems concerning college and the curriculum; in reference to the third stage—advanced studies—I should like to outline the idea of a modern university, as the consummation of liberal education.

The Spheres of Knowledge

As to the principal stages in education, let us note that there are three great periods in education. I should like to designate them as the rudiments (or elementary education), the humanities (comprising both secondary and college education), and advanced studies (comprising graduate schools and higher specialized learning). And these periods correspond not only to three natural chronological periods in the growth of the youth but also to three naturally distinct and qualitatively determinate spheres of psychological development, and, accordingly, of knowledge.

The physical structure of the child is not that of the adult, shortened and abridged. The child is not a dwarf man. Nor is the adolescent. All this is much truer and much more crucial as regards the psychological than the physical structure of the youth. In the realm of physical training, of psychophysical conditioning, of animal and experimental psychology, contemporary education has understood more and more perfectly that a child of man is not just a diminutive man. It has not yet understood this in the spiritual realm of knowing: because, indeed, it is not interested in the psychology of spiritual activities. How, therefore, could I do anything but ignore that realm? The error is twofold. First we have forgotten that science and knowledge are not a self-sufficient set of notions, existing for their own sakes, abstracted and separate from man. Science and knowledge don't exist in books, they do exist in minds, they are vital and internal energies and must develop therefore according to the inner spiritual structure of the mind in which they have their being.

Secondly, we act as if the task of education were to infuse into the child or the adolescent, only abridging and concentrating it, the very science or knowledge of the adult—that is to say, of the philologist, the historian, the grammarian, the scientist, etc., the most specialized experts. So we try to cram young people with a chaos of summarized adult notions which have been either condensed, dogmatized, and textbookishly cut up or else made so easy that they are reduced to the vanishing point. As a result, we run the risk of producing either an instructed, bewildered intellectual dwarf, or an ignorant intellectual dwarf playing at dolls with our science. In a recent essay Professor Douglas Bush recalls "the classic anecdote of the young woman who was asked if she could teach English history. 'Oh yes,' she replied brightly, 'I've had it twice, once in clay and once in sand.'"

The knowledge to be given to youth *is not* the same as that of adults.... The universe of the adolescent is a transition state on the way to the universe of man. Judgment and intellectual strength are developing but are not yet really acquired. Such a mobile and anxious universe evolves under the rule of the natural impulses and tendencies of intelligence—an intelligence which is not yet matured and strengthened by those inner living energies, the sciences, arts, and wisdom, but which is sharp and fresh, eager to pass judgment on everything, and both trustful and exacting, and which craves intuitive sight. The knowledge which has to develop in the adolescent is knowledge appealing to the natural powers and gifts of the mind, knowledge as tending toward all things by the natural instinct of intelligence. The mental atmosphere for adolescence should be one of truth to be embraced. Truth is the inspiring force needed in the education of the youth—truth rather than erudition and self-consciousness—all-pervading truth rather than the objectively isolated truth at which each of the diverse sciences aims. Here we are confronted with a natural and instinctive impulse toward some all-embracing truth, which must be shaped little by little to critical reflection, but which I should like to compare primarily to the trend of the first thinkers of ancient Greece toward an undifferentiated world of science, wisdom, and poetry. Common sense and the spontaneous pervasiveness of natural insight and reasoning constitute the dynamic unity of the adolescent's universe of thought, before wisdom may achieve in man a stabler unity. Just as imagination was the mental heaven of childhood, so now ascending reason, natural reason with its freshness, boldness, and first sparkling ambitions, is the mental heaven of adolescence; it is with reasoning that adolescence happens to be intoxicated. Here is a natural impulse to be turned to account by education, both by stimulating and by disciplining reason....

Such are, to my mind, the considerations which should guide the teachers of youth in the most important and difficult part of their task, which consists in determining the mode in which the instruments of thought and the liberal arts are to be taught. The quality of the mode or style is of much greater moment than the quantity of things taught, it constitutes the very soul of teaching and preserves its unity and makes it alive and buoyant. If we seek to characterize the general objective of instruction at the stage of college education, we might say the objective is less the acquisition of science itself or art itself than the grasp of their meaning and the comprehension of the truth or beauty they yield. It is less a question of sharing in the very activity of the scientist or the poet than of nourishing oneself intellectually on the results of their achievement. Still less is it a question of developing one's own mental skill and taste in the fashion of the dilettante by gaining a superficial outlook on scientific or artistic procedures or the ways and means, the grammar, logic, methodology thereof. What I call the meaning of a science or art is contained in the specific truth or beauty it offers us. The objective of education is to see to it that the youth grasps this truth or beauty by the natural power and gifts of his mind and the natural intuitive energy of his reason backed up by his whole sensuous, imaginative, and emotional dynamism. In doing that a liberal education will cause his natural intelligence to follow in the footsteps of those intellectual virtues which are the eminent merit of the real scientist or artist. The practical condition for all that is to strive to penetrate as deeply as possible into the great achievements of the human mind rather than to tend toward material erudition and atomized memorization. So I should say that the youth is to learn and know music in order to understand the meaning of music rather than in order to become a composer. He must learn and know physics in order to understand the meaning of physics rather than to become a physicist. Thus college education can keep its necessary character of comprehensive universality and at the same time till and cultivate the whole mind, made available and alive, for the tasks of man. In a social order fitted to the common dignity of man, college education should be given to all,[1] so as to complete the preparation of the youth before he enters the state of manhood. To introduce specialization in this sphere is to do violence to the world of youth. As a matter of fact, a young man will choose his specialty for himself and progress all the more rapidly and perfectly in vocational, scientific, or technical training in proportion as his education has been liberal and universal. Youth has a right to education in the liberal arts, in order to be prepared for human work and for human leisure. But such education is killed by premature specialization.[2]

No doubt, a certain amount of specialization is to take place progressively, as the youth, leaving the public school and advancing into college education, gradually takes on the dimensions of a man. But this kind of specialization is merely that which the temperament, gifts, and inclinations of the youth himself spontaneously provide. Here we may observe that exacting from all pupils

The conclusion of all the preceding remarks implies a clear condemnation not only of the many pre-professional undergraduate courses which worm their way into college education but also of the elective system.[3]

If all this is true, what can we say now about the curriculum. In touching on this question my purpose is only to seek, from a philosophical point of view and with respect solely to the intrinsic requirements and suitabilities of the task of bringing up a man, what would be the main features of a normal college curriculum, for a Western youth of our day.

I advance the opinion, incidentally, that, in the general educational scheme, it would be advantageous to hurry the four years of college, so that the period of undergraduate studies would extend from sixteen to nineteen. Thus, after the years of secondary education, dealing primarily with national and foreign languages (which should be learned from early youth),[4] comparative grammar, history, natural history and the art of expression,[5] we would have the following for the four years of undergraduate school, during which the student enters and encompasses the universe of liberal arts : The year of *Mathematics and Poetry*, comprising: first, mathematics, and literature and poetry; second, logic; third, foreign languages, and the history of civilization.

The year of *Natural Sciences and Fine Arts*, comprising: first, physics and natural science; second, fine arts, mathematics, literature and poetry; third, history of the sciences.

The year of *Philosophy* comprising: first, philosophy, that is to say, metaphysics and philosophy of nature, theory of knowledge, psychology; second, physics and natural science; third, mathematics, literature and poetry, fine arts.

The year of *Ethical and Political Philosophy*, comprising: First, ethics, political and social philosophy; second, physics and natural science; third, mathematics, literature and poetry, fine arts, history of civilization and history of the sciences.[6]

I note that up to this year of ethical and political philosophy, morality, both personal and social, should have been the object of a particular teaching all through the period of the humanities. May I confess at this point that, although I believe in natural morality, I feel little trust in the educational efficacy of any merely rational moral teaching abstractly detached from its religious environment? Normally, the moral teaching of which I just spoke as contradistinguished from ethical and political philosophy, and which is to be given all through the period of the humanities, should, in my opinion, be embodied in religious training. What, however, is to be done about natural morality? Natural morality and the great ethical ideas conveyed by civilization should be taught during these years. They are the very treasure of classical humanism, they must be communicated to the youth, but not as a subject of special courses. They should be embodied in the humanities and liberal arts, especially as an integral part of the teaching of literature, poetry, fine arts, and history. This teaching should be permeated with the feeling for such values. The reading of Homer, Aeschylus, Sophocles, Herodotus, Thucydides, Demosthenes, Plutarch, Epictetus, Marcus Aurelius (better to read them carefully in translation than to learn their language and to read only bits), the reading of Virgil, Terence, Tacitus and Cicero, of Dante, Cervantes, Shakespeare, Pascal, Racine, Montesquieu, Gibbon, Goethe, Dostoevski, feeds the mind with the sense and knowledge of natural virtues, of honor and pity, of the dignity of man and of the spirit, the greatness of human destiny, the entanglements of good and evil, the *caritas humani generis*. Such reading, more than any course in natural ethics, conveys to the youth the moral experience of mankind.

Commenting upon our ideal curriculum, a few remarks may be offered. As I pointed out in the previous lecture, physics and natural science must be considered as one of the chief branches of liberal arts. They are mainly concerned with the mathematical reading of natural phenomena, and insure in this way the domination of the human spirit over the world of matter, not in terms of ontological causes but rather in terms of number and measurement. Thus they appear, so to speak, as a final realization of the Pythagorean and Platonist trends of thought in the very field of that world of experience and the becoming which Plato looked at as a shadow on the wall of the cave. Physics and natural science, if they are taught not only for the sake of practical applications but. essentially for the sake of knowledge, with reference to the specific epistemological approach they involve and in close connection with the history of the sciences and the history of civilization, provide man with a vision of the universe and an understanding of scientific truth and a sense of the sacred, exacting, unbending objectivity of the humblest truth, which play an essential part in the liberation of the mind and in liberal education. Physics should be taught and revered as a liberal art of the first rank, like poetry, and probably more important than even mathematics.

Our curriculum, besides, does not mention either Latin or Greek; in my opinion, they would represent chiefly a waste of time for the many destined to forget them; Latin, Greek, and Hebrew (or at least one of these three root languages of our civilization) should be learned later on—much more rapidly and fruitfully—by graduate students in languages, literature, history or philosophy. During the humanities, moreover, comparative grammar and philology[7] would provide the student with a most useful knowledge of the inner mechanisms of language. And foreign languages, studied not only for practical purposes but also in connection with the national language, would afford the required means of gaining mastery over the latter (particularly through exercises of translation).

Finally, as for literature and poetry, the direct reading and study of books written by great authors is the primary educational means; this point

The Feast of the Gods

has been clearly brought to light by the educators of St. John's College. Nothing can replace the "pure reading," as Charles Peguy put it, of a "pure text." Such reading is also essential in philosophy, and even, in some measure, in sciences. This nevertheless, it seems to me, is all the more profitable as the books in question are not too many in number and therefore may be seriously and lovingly scrutinized, and as they depend, I mean in part, on the free choice of the student.

Review and Discussion Questions

1. On what basis does Maritain designate three stages of education?

2. What does it mean to have a subject twice, "once in clay and once in sand"?

3. Maritain claims the college curriculum ought not present scientific or artistic objects "in the fashion of the dilettante." If not so, then how?

4. Maritain asserts, controversially, that the elective system in schools and colleges amounts to "a denial that there [is] content to education." How might a progressively minded educator respond?

5. Why does Maritain believe it is better to study ethics through Homer, Dante, and Dostoevsky than in a separate course in "Natural Ethics"?

❖ PART III

The Methods of Teaching

The School Walk

❖ 17

PLATO (427–347 BC)

Meno

O Socrates, I used to be told, before I knew you, that you were always doubting yourself and making others doubt; and now you are casting your spell
over me, and I am simply getting bewitched and enchanted, and am at my
wits' end.

Beyond aiding our own thinking about virtue, this early Platonic dialogue
introduces us to Socrates' distinctive pedagogy. Socrates distinguishes between two modes of enquiry. The first is antagonistic, pursued as between
combatants who trade arguments against each other's conclusions. The second, favored by Socrates, he calls dialectical. Dialectic is the mode of discussion proper among friends who seek the truth together. Truth is the final
object, sought, as he says, "in a milder strain." Instead of directly refuting
false claims (or those believed to be false), the Socratic teacher (and student) makes use of premises "which the person interrogated would be willing to admit." Though not the only mode of teaching, education, without
dialectic, can degenerate into indoctrination.

Further reading: Plato, *Symposium*, trans. A. Nehamas and P. Woodruff (Indianapolis, Ind.:
Hackett Publishing, 1989); *Song of Songs* in *The Holy Bible*, RSV: Second Catholic Edition (San
Francisco: Ignatius Press, 2006); John Cassian, *Conferences*, trans. Colm Luibheid in the Classics
of Western Spirituality Series (Mahwah, N.J.: Paulist Press, 1986).

❖

Meno. Can you tell me, Socrates, whether virtue is acquired by teaching or by practice; or if neither by teaching nor by practice, then whether it
comes to man by nature, or in what other way?

Socrates. O Meno, there was a time when the Thessalians were famous
among the other Hellenes only for their riches and their riding; but now, if
I am not mistaken, they are equally famous for their wisdom, especially at
Larisa, which is the native city of your friend Aristippus. And this is Gor-

gias' doing; for when he came there, the flower of the Aleuadae, among them your admirer Aristippus, and the other chiefs of the Thessalians, fell in love with his wisdom. And he has taught you the habit of answering questions in a grand and bold style, which becomes those who know, and is the style in which he himself answers all comers; and any Hellene who likes may ask him anything. How different is our lot! my dear Meno. Here at Athens there is a dearth of the commodity, and all wisdom seems to have emigrated from us to you. I am certain that if you were to ask any Athenian whether virtue was natural or acquired, he would laugh in your face, and say: "Stranger, you have far too good an opinion of me, if you think that I can answer your question. For I literally do not know what virtue is, and much less whether it is acquired by teaching or not." And I myself, Meno, living as I do in this region of poverty, am as poor as the rest of the world; and I confess with shame that I know literally nothing about virtue; and when I do not know the "quid" of anything how can I know the "quale"? How, if I knew nothing at all of Meno, could I tell if he was fair, or the opposite of fair; rich and noble, or the reverse of rich and noble? Do you think that I could?

Men. No, Indeed. But are you in earnest, Socrates, in saying that you do not know what virtue is? And am I to carry back this report of you to Thessaly?

Soc. Not only that, my dear boy, but you may say further that I have never known of any one else who did, in my judgment.

Men. Then you have never met Gorgias when he was at Athens?

Soc. Yes, I have.

Men. And did you not think that he knew?

Soc. I have not a good memory, Meno, and therefore I cannot now tell what I thought of him at the time. And I dare say that he did know, and that you know what he said: please, therefore, to remind me of what he said; or, if you would rather, tell me your own view; for I suspect that you and he think much alike.

Men. Very true.

Soc. Then as he is not here, never mind him, and do you tell me: By the gods, Meno, be generous, and tell me what you say that virtue is; for I shall be truly delighted to find that I have been mistaken, and that you and Gorgias do really have this knowledge; although I have been just saying that I have never found anybody who had.

Men. There will be no difficulty, Socrates, in answering your question. Let us take first the virtue of a man—he should know how to administer the state, and in the administration of it to benefit his friends and harm his enemies; and he must also be careful not to suffer harm himself. A woman's virtue, if you wish to know about that, may also be easily described: her duty is to order her house, and keep what is indoors, and obey her husband. Every age, every condition of life, young or old, male or female, bond or free, has a different virtue: there are virtues numberless, and no lack of definitions of them; for virtue is relative to the actions and ages of each of us in all that we do. And the same may be said of vice, Socrates.

Soc. How fortunate I am, Meno! When I ask you for one virtue, you present me with a swarm of them, which are in your keeping. Suppose that I carry on the figure of the swarm, and ask of you, What is the nature of the bee? and you answer that there are many kinds of bees, and I reply: But do bees differ as bees, because there are many and different kinds of them; or are they not rather to be distinguished by some other quality, as for example beauty, size, or shape? How would you answer me?

Men. I should answer that bees do not differ from one another, as bees.

Soc. And if I went on to say: That is what I desire to know, Meno; tell me what is the quality in which they do not differ, but are all alike;—would you be able to answer?

Men. I should.

Soc. And so of the virtues, however many and different they may be, they have all a common nature which makes them virtues; and on this he who would answer the question, "What is virtue?" would do well to have his eye fixed: Do you understand?

Men. I am beginning to understand; but I do not as yet take hold of the question as I could wish.

Soc. When you say, Meno, that there is one virtue of a man, another of a woman, another of a child, and so on, does this apply only to virtue, or would you say the same of health, and size, and strength? Or is the nature of health always the same, whether in man or woman?

Men. I should say that health is the same, both in man and woman.

Soc. And is not this true of size and strength? If a woman is strong, she will be strong by reason of the same form and of the same strength subsisting in her which there is in the man. I mean to say that strength, as strength, whether of man or woman, is the same. Is there any difference?

Men. I think not.

Soc. And will not virtue, as virtue, be the same, whether in a child or in a grown-up person, in a woman or in a man?

Men. I cannot help feeling, Socrates, that this case is different from the others.

Soc. But why? Were you not saying that the virtue of a man was to order a state, and the virtue of a woman was to order a house?

Men. I did say so.

Soc. And can either house or state or anything be well ordered without temperance and without justice?

Men. Certainly not.

Soc. Then they who order a state or a house temperately or justly order them with temperance and justice?

Men. Certainly.

Soc. Then both men and women, if they are to be good men and women, must have the same virtues of temperance and justice?

Men. True.

Soc. And can either a young man or an elder one be good, if they are intemperate and unjust?

Men. They cannot.

Soc. They must be temperate and just?

Men. Yes.

Soc. Then all men are good in the same way, and by participation in the same virtues?

Men. Such is the inference.

Soc. And they surely would not have been good in the same way, unless their virtue had been the same?

Men. They would not.

Soc. Then now that the sameness of all virtue has been proven, try and remember what you and Gorgias say that virtue is.

Men. Will you have one definition of them all?

Soc. That is what I am seeking.

Men. If you want to have one definition of them all, I know not what to say, but that virtue is the power of governing mankind.

Soc. And does this definition of virtue include all virtue? Is virtue the same in a child and in a slave, Meno? Can the child govern his father, or the slave his master; and would he who governed be any longer a slave?

Men. I think not, Socrates.

Soc. No, indeed; there would be small reason in that. Yet once more, fair friend; according to you, virtue is "the power of governing"; but do you not add "justly and not unjustly"?

Men. Yes, Socrates; I agree there; for justice is virtue.

Soc. Would you say "virtue," Meno, or "a virtue"?

Men. What do you mean?

Soc. I mean as I might say about anything; that a round, for example, is "a figure" and not simply "figure," and I should adopt this mode of speaking, because there are other figures.

Men. Quite right; and that is just what I am saying about virtue—that there are other virtues as well as justice.

Soc. What are they? Tell me the names of them, as I would tell you the names of the other figures if you asked me.

Men. Courage and temperance and wisdom and magnanimity are virtues; and there are many others.

Soc. Yes, Meno; and again we are in the same case: in searching after one virtue we have found many, though not in the same way as before; but we have been unable to find the common virtue which runs through them all.

Men. Why, Socrates, even now I am not able to follow you in the attempt to get at one common notion of virtue as of other things.

Soc. No wonder; but I will try to get nearer if I can, for you know that all things have a common notion. Suppose now that some one asked you the question which I asked before: Meno, he would say, what is figure? And if you answered "roundness," he would reply to you, in my way of speaking, by asking whether you would say that roundness is "figure" or "a figure"; and you would answer "a figure."

Men. Certainly.

Soc. And for this reason—that there are other figures?

Men. Yes.

Soc. And if he proceeded to ask, What other figures are there? you would have told him.

Men. I should.

Soc. And if he similarly asked what colour is, and you answered whiteness, and the questioner rejoined, Would you say that whiteness is colour or a colour? you would reply, A colour, because there are other colours as well.

Men. I should.

Soc. And if he had said, Tell me what they are?—you would have told him of other colours which are colours just as much as whiteness.

Men. Yes.

Soc. And suppose that he were to pursue the matter in my way, he would say: Ever and anon we are landed in particulars, but this is not what I want; tell me then, since you call them by a common name, and say that they are all figures, even when opposed to one another, what is that common nature which you designate as figure—which contains straight as well as round, and is no more one than the other—that would be your mode of speaking?

Men. Yes.

Soc. And in speaking thus, you do not mean to say that the round is round any more than straight, or the straight any more straight than round?

Men. Certainly not.

Soc. You only assert that the round figure is not more a figure than the straight, or the straight than the round?

Men. Very true.

Soc. To what then do we give the name of figure? Try and answer. Suppose that when a person asked you this question either about figure or colour, you were to reply, Man, I do not understand what you want, or know what you are saying; he would look rather astonished and say: Do you not understand that I am looking for the "simile in multis"? And then he might put the question in another form: Meno, he might say, what is that "simile in multis" which you call figure, and which includes not only round and straight figures, but all? Could you not answer that question, Meno? I wish that you would try; the attempt will be good practice with a view to the answer about virtue.

Men. I would rather that you should answer, Socrates.

Soc. Shall I indulge you?

Men. By all means.

Soc. And then you will tell me about virtue?

Men. I will.

Soc. Then I must do my best, for there is a prize to be won.

Men. Certainly.

Soc. Well, I will try and explain to you what figure is. What do you say to this answer?—Figure is the only thing which always follows colour. Will you be satisfied with it, as I am sure that I should be, if you would let me have a similar definition of virtue?

Men. But, Socrates, it is such a simple answer.

Soc. Why simple?

Men. Because, according to you, figure is that which always follows colour.

(**Soc.** Granted.)

Men. But if a person were to say that he does not know what colour is, any more than what figure is—what sort of answer would you have given him?

Soc. I should have told him the truth. And if he were a philosopher of the eristic and antagonistic sort, I should say to him: You have my answer, and if I am wrong, your business is to take up the argument and refute me.

But if we were friends, and were talking as you and I are now, I should reply in a milder strain and more in the dialectician's vein; that is to say, I should not only speak the truth, but I should make use of premisses which the person interrogated would be willing to admit. And this is the way in which I shall endeavour to approach you. You will acknowledge, will you not, that there is such a thing as an end, or termination, or extremity?—all which words use in the same sense, although I am aware that Prodicus might draw distinctions about them: but still you, I am sure, would speak of a thing as ended or terminated—that is all that I am saying—not anything very difficult.

Men. Yes, I should; and I believe that I understand your meaning.

Soc. And you would speak of a surface and also of a solid, as for example in geometry.

Men. Yes.

Soc. Well then, you are now in a condition to understand my definition of figure. I define figure to be that in which the solid ends; or, more concisely, the limit of solid.

Men. And now, Socrates, what is colour?

Soc. You are outrageous, Meno, in thus plaguing a poor old man to give you an answer, when you will not take the trouble of remembering what is Gorgias' definition of virtue.

Men. When you have told me what I ask, I will tell you, Socrates.

Soc. A man who was blindfolded has only to hear you talking, and he would know that you are a fair creature and have still many lovers.

Men. Why do you think so?

Soc. Why, because you always speak in imperatives: like all beauties when they are in their prime, you are tyrannical; and also, as I suspect, you have found out that I have weakness for the fair, and therefore to humour you I must answer.

Men. Please do.

Soc. Would you like me to answer you after the manner of Gorgias, which is familiar to you?

Men. I should like nothing better.

Soc. Do not he and you and Empedocles say that there are certain effluences of existence?

Men. Certainly.

Soc. And passages into which and through which the effluences pass?

Men. Exactly.

Soc. And some of the effluences fit into the passages, and some of them are too small or too large?

Men. True.

Soc. And there is such a thing as sight?

Men. Yes.

Soc. And now, as Pindar says, "read my meaning": colour is an effluence of form, commensurate with sight, and palpable to sense.

Men. That, Socrates, appears to me to be an admirable answer.

Soc. Why, yes, because it happens to be one which you have been in the habit of hearing: and your wit will have discovered, I suspect, that you may explain in the same way the nature of sound and smell, and of many other similar phenomena.

Men. Quite true.

Soc. The answer, Meno, was in the orthodox solemn vein, and therefore was more acceptable to you than the other answer about figure.

Men. Yes.

Soc. And yet, O son of Alexidemus, I cannot help thinking that the other was the better; and I am sure that you would be of the same opinion, if you would only stay and be initiated, and were not compelled, as you said yesterday, to go away before the mysteries.

Men. But I will stay, Socrates, if you will give me many such answers.

Soc. Well then, for my own sake as well as for yours, I will do my very best; but I am afraid that I shall not be able to give you very many as good: and now, in your turn, you are to fulfil your promise, and tell me what virtue is in the universal; and do not make a singular into a plural, as the facetious say of those who break a thing, but deliver virtue to me whole and sound, and not broken into a number of pieces: I have given you the pattern.

Men. Well then, Socrates, virtue, as I take it, is when he, who desires the honourable, is able to provide it for himself; so the poet says, and I say too: "Virtue is the desire of things honourable and the power of attaining them."

Soc. And does he who desires the honourable also desire the good?

Men. Certainly.

Soc. Then are there some who desire the evil and others who desire the good? Do not all men, my dear sir, desire good?

Men. I think not.

Soc. There are some who desire evil?

Men. Yes.

Soc. Do you mean that they think the evils which they desire, to be good; or do they know that they are evil and yet desire them?

Men. Both, I think.

Soc. And do you really imagine, Meno, that a man knows evils to be evils and desires them notwithstanding?

Men. Certainly I do.

Soc. And desire is of possession?

Men. Yes, of possession.

Soc. And does he think that the evils will do good to him who possesses them, or does he know that they will do him harm?

Men. There are some who think that the evils will do them good, and others who know that they will do them harm.

Soc. And, in your opinion, do those who think that they will do them good know that they are evils?

Men. Certainly not.

Soc. Is it not obvious that those who are ignorant of their nature do not desire them; but they desire what they suppose to be goods although they are really evils; and if they are mistaken and suppose the evils to be good they really desire goods?

Men. Yes, in that case.

Soc. Well, and do those who, as you say, desire evils, and think that evils are hurtful to the possessor of them, know that they will be hurt by them?

Men. They must know it.

Soc. And must they not suppose that those who are hurt are miserable in proportion to the hurt which is inflicted upon them?

Men. How can it be otherwise?

Soc. But are not the miserable ill-fated?

Men. Yes, indeed.

Soc. And does any one desire to be miserable and ill-fated?

Men. I should say not, Socrates.

Soc. But if there is no one who desires to be miserable, there is no one, Meno, who desires evil; for what is misery but the desire and possession of evil?

Men. That appears to be the truth, Socrates, and I admit that nobody desires evil.

Soc. And yet, were you not saying just now that virtue is the desire and power of attaining good?

Men. Yes, I did say so.

Soc. But if this be affirmed, then the desire of good is common to all, and one man is no better than another in that respect?

Men. True.

Soc. And if one man is not better than another in desiring good, he must be better in the power of attaining it?

Men. Exactly.

Soc. Then, according to your definition, virtue would appear to be the power of attaining good?

Men. I entirely approve, Socrates, of the manner in which you now view this matter.

Soc. Then let us see whether what you say is true from another point of view; for very likely you may be right: You affirm virtue to be the power of attaining goods?

Men. Yes.

Soc. And the goods which you mean are such as health and wealth and the possession of gold and silver, and having office and honour in the state—those are what you would call goods?

Men. Yes, I should include all those.

Soc. Then, according to Meno, who is the hereditary friend of the great king, virtue is the power of getting silver and gold; and would you add that they must be gained piously, justly, or do you deem this to be of no consequence? And is any mode of acquisition, even if unjust and dishonest, equally to be deemed virtue?

Men. Not virtue, Socrates, but vice.

Soc. Then justice or temperance or holiness, or some other part of virtue, as would appear, must accompany the acquisition, and without them the mere acquisition of good will not be virtue.

Men. Why, how can there be virtue without these?

Soc. And the non-acquisition of gold and silver in a dishonest manner for oneself or another, or in other words the want of them, may be equally virtue?

Men. True.

Soc. Then the acquisition of such goods is no more virtue than the non-acquisition and want of them, but whatever is accompanied by justice or honesty is virtue, and whatever is devoid of justice is vice.

Men. It cannot be otherwise, in my judgment.

Soc. And were we not saying just now that justice, temperance, and the like, were each of them a part of virtue?

Men. Yes.

Soc. And so, Meno, this is the way in which you mock me.

Men. Why do you say that, Socrates?

Soc. Why, because I asked you to deliver virtue into my hands whole and unbroken, and I gave you a pattern according to which you were to frame your answer; and you have forgotten already, and tell me that virtue is the power of attaining good justly, or with justice; and justice you acknowledge to be a part of virtue.

Men. Yes.

Soc. Then it follows from your own admissions, that virtue is doing what you do with a part of virtue; for justice and the like are said by you to be parts of virtue.

Men. What of that?

Soc. What of that! Why, did not I ask you to tell me the nature of virtue as a whole? And you are very far from telling me this; but declare every action to be virtue which is done with a part of virtue; as though you had told me and I must already know the whole of virtue, and this too when frittered away into little pieces. And, therefore, my dear I fear that I must begin again and repeat the same question: What is virtue? For otherwise, I can only say, that every action done with a part of virtue is virtue; what else is the meaning of saying that every action done with justice is virtue? Ought I not to ask the question over again; for can any one who does not know virtue know a part of virtue?

Men. No; I do not say that he can.

Soc. Do you remember how, in the example of figure, we rejected any answer given in terms which were as yet unexplained or unadmitted?

Men. Yes, Socrates; and we were quite right in doing so.

Soc. But then, my friend, do not suppose that we can explain to any one the nature of virtue as a whole through some unexplained portion of virtue, or anything at all in that fashion; we should only have to ask over again the old question, What is virtue? Am I not right?

Men. I believe that you are.

Soc. Then begin again, and answer me, What, according to you and your friend Gorgias, is the definition of virtue?

Men. O Socrates, I used to be told, before I knew you, that you were always doubting yourself and making others doubt; and now you are casting your spells over me, and I am simply getting bewitched and enchanted, and am at my wits' end. And if I may venture to make a jest upon you, you seem to me both in your appearance and in your power over others to be very like the flat torpedo fish, who torpifies those who come near him and touch him, as you have now torpified me, I think. For my soul and my tongue are really torpid, and I do not know how to answer you; and though I have been delivered of an infinite variety of speeches about virtue before now, and to many persons—and very good ones they were, as I thought—at this moment I cannot even say what virtue is. And I think that you are very wise in not voyaging and going away from home, for if you did in other places as you do in Athens, you would be cast into prison as a magician.

Soc. You are a rogue, Meno, and had all but caught me.

Men. What do you mean, Socrates?

Soc. I can tell why you made a simile about me.

Men. Why?

Soc. In order that I might make another simile about you. For I know that all pretty young gentlemen like to have pretty similes made about them—as well they may—but I shall not return the compliment. As to my being a torpedo, if the torpedo is torpid as well as the cause of torpidity in others, then indeed I am a torpedo, but not otherwise; for I perplex others, not because I am clear, but because I am utterly perplexed myself. And now I know not what virtue is, and you seem to be in the same case, although you did once perhaps know before you touched me. However, I have no objection to join with you in the enquiry.

Review and Discussion Questions

1. Characterize Socrates' method of discussion.

2. In Socrates' view, what is lacking in Meno's first definition (where he calls virtue "numberless")?

3. Socrates asks Meno to clarify whether justice is "virtue" or "a virtue." Why is this clarification necessary?

4. Describe a situation in which the Socratic method of teaching is useful and another in which it is not.

❖ 18

ST. AUGUSTINE (354–430)

On Christian Teaching

Who will dare to say that truth in the person of its defenders is to take its
stand unarmed against falsehood.

If you wish to speak and write well, read great books, and hear great speakers,
then imitate. Against the doctrine and practice of the schools of his time,
St. Augustine counseled a natural approach to speaking. He asserts that, although the rules for the acquisition of grammar and rhetoric matter (a truth
that has been forgotten by many), character matters more. The Christian
teacher must know his subject and judge his audience. If he is to teach, he
should instruct first by narrative; if he is to persuade, then he must use argument; to move, excite. Truth, not eloquence, remains the primary object of
the teacher; yet the maxim holds: truth unadorned remains truth ignored.

Further Reading: Boethius, *The Consolation of Philosophy*, trans. P. G. Walsh (Oxford: Clarendon
Press, 1999); F. L. Lukas, *Style* (London: Harriman House, 2012); Edward P. J. Corbett and R. J.
Connors, *Classical Rhetoric for the Modern Student* (Oxford: Oxford University Press, 1999).

❖

This Work Not Intended as a Treatise on Rhetoric

1. This work of mine, which is entitled *On Christian Doctrine*, was at
the commencement divided into two parts. For, after a preface, in which
I answered by anticipation those who were likely to take exception to the
work, I said, "There are two things on which all interpretation of Scripture
depends: the mode of ascertaining the proper meaning, and the mode of
making known the meaning when it is ascertained. I shall treat first of the
mode of ascertaining, next of the mode of making known, the meaning."
As, then, I have already said a great deal about the mode of ascertaining the
meaning, and have given three books to this one part of the subject, I shall
only say a few things about the mode of making known the meaning, in

order if possible to bring them all within the compass of one book, and so finish the whole work in four books.

2. In the first place, then, I wish by this preamble to put a stop to the expectations of readers who may think that I am about to lay down rules of rhetoric such as I have learnt, and taught too, in the secular schools, and to warn them that they need not look for any such from me. Not that I think such rules of no use, but that whatever use they have is to be learnt elsewhere; and if any good man should happen to have leisure for learning them, he is not to ask me to teach them either in this work or any other.

It Is Lawful for a Christian Teacher to Use the Art of Rhetoric

3. Now, the art of rhetoric being available for the enforcing either of truth or falsehood, who will dare to say that truth in the person of its defenders is to take its stand unarmed against falsehood? For example, that those who are trying to persuade men of what is false are to know how to introduce their subject, so as to put the hearer into a friendly, or attentive, or teachable frame of mind, while the defenders of the truth shall be ignorant of that art? That the former are to tell their falsehoods briefly, clearly, and plausibly, while the latter shall tell the truth in such a way that it is tedious to listen to, hard to understand, and, in fine, not easy to believe it? That the former are to oppose the truth and defend falsehood with sophistical arguments, while the latter shall be unable either to defend what is true, or to refute what is false? That the former, while imbuing the minds of their hearers with erroneous opinions, are by their power of speech to awe, to melt, to enliven, and to rouse them, while the latter shall in defense of the truth be sluggish, and frigid, and somnolent? Who is such a fool as to think this wisdom? Since, then, the faculty of eloquence is available for both sides, and is of very great service in the enforcing either of wrong or right, why do not good men study to engage it on the side of truth, when bad men use it to obtain the triumph of wicked and worthless causes, and to further injustice and error?

The Proper Age and the Proper Means for Acquiring Rhetorical Skill

4. But the theories and rules on this subject (to which, when you add a tongue thoroughly skilled by exercise and habit in the use of many words and many ornaments of speech, you have what is called eloquence or oratory) may be learnt apart from these writings of mine, if a suitable space of

time be set aside for the purpose at a fit and proper age. But only by those who can learn them quickly; for the masters of Roman eloquence themselves did not shrink from saying that anyone who cannot learn this art quickly can never thoroughly learn it at all.[1] Whether this be true or not, why need we inquire? For even if this art can occasionally be in the end mastered by men of slower intellect, I do not think it of so much importance as to wish men who have arrived at mature age to spend time in learning it. It is enough that boys should give attention to it; and even of these, not all who are to be fitted for usefulness in the Church, but only those who are not yet engaged in any occupation of more urgent necessity, or which ought evidently to take precedence of it. For men of quick intellect and glowing temperament find it easier to become eloquent by reading and listening to eloquent speakers than by following rules for eloquence. And even outside the canon, which to our great advantage is fixed in a place of secure authority, there is no want of ecclesiastical writings, in reading which a man of ability will acquire a tinge of the eloquence with which they are written, even though he does not aim at this, but is solely intent on the matters treated of; especially, of course, if in addition he practice himself in writing, or dictating, and at last also in speaking, the opinions he has formed on grounds of piety and faith. If, however, such ability be wanting, the rules of rhetoric are either not understood, or if, after great labor has been spent in enforcing them, they come to be in some small measure understood, they prove of no service. For even those who have learnt them, and who speak with fluency and elegance, cannot always think of them when they are speaking so as to speak in accordance with them, unless they are discussing the rules themselves. Indeed, I think there are scarcely any who can do both things—that is, speak well, and, in order to do this, think of the rules of speaking while they are speaking. For we must be careful that what we have got to say does not escape us whilst we are thinking about saying it according to the rules of art. Nevertheless, in the speeches of eloquent men, we find rules of eloquence carried out which the speakers did not think of as aids to eloquence at the time when they were speaking, whether they had ever learnt them, or whether they had never even met with them. For it is because they are eloquent that they exemplify these rules; it is not that they use them in order to be eloquent.

5. And, therefore, as infants cannot learn to speak except by learning words and phrases from those who do speak, why should not men become eloquent without being taught any art of speech, simply by reading and learning the speeches of eloquent men, and by imitating them as far as they

can? And what do we find from the examples themselves to be the case in this respect? We know numbers who, without acquaintance with rhetorical rules, are more eloquent than many who have learnt these; but we know no one who is eloquent without having read and listened to the speeches and debates of eloquent men. For even the art of grammar, which teaches correctness of speech, need not be learnt by boys, if they have the advantage of growing up and living among men who speak correctly. For without knowing the names of any of the faults, they will, from being accustomed to correct speech, lay hold upon whatever is faulty in the speech of anyone they listen to, and avoid it; just as city-bred men, even when illiterate, seize upon the faults of rustics.

6. It is the duty, then, of the interpreter and teacher of Holy Scripture, the defender of the true faith and the opponent of error, both to teach what is right and to refute what is wrong, and in the performance of this task to conciliate the hostile, to rouse the careless, and to tell the ignorant both what is occurring at present and what is probable in the future. But once that his hearers are friendly, attentive, and ready to learn, whether he has found them so, or has himself made them so, the remaining objects are to be carried out in whatever way the case requires. If the hearers need teaching, the matter treated of must be made fully known by means of narrative. On the other hand, to clear up points that are doubtful requires reasoning and the exhibition of proof. If, however, the hearers require to be roused rather than instructed, in order that they may be diligent to do what they already know, and to bring their feelings into harmony with the truths they admit, greater vigor of speech is needed. Here entreaties and reproaches, exhortations and upbraidings, and all the other means of rousing the emotions, are necessary.

7. And all the methods I have mentioned are constantly used by nearly everyone in cases where speech is the agency employed.

Wisdom of More Importance Than Eloquence to the Christian Teacher

But as some men employ these coarsely, inelegantly, and frigidly, while others use them with acuteness, elegance, and spirit, the work that I am speaking of ought to be undertaken by one who can argue and speak with wisdom, if not with eloquence, and with profit to his hearers, even though he profit them less than he would if he could speak with eloquence too. But we must beware of the man who abounds in eloquent nonsense and so much the more if the hearer is pleased with what is not worth listening to, and thinks that because the speaker is eloquent what he says must be true. And this opinion is held even by those who think that the art of rhetoric should be taught; for they confess that "though wisdom without eloquence is of little service to states, yet eloquence without wisdom is frequently a positive injury, and is of service never."[2] If, then, the men who teach the principles of eloquence have been forced by truth to confess this in the very books which treat of eloquence, though they were ignorant of the true, that is, the heavenly wisdom which comes down from the Father of Lights, how much more ought we to feel it who are the sons and the ministers of this higher wisdom! Now a man speaks with more or less wisdom just as he has made more or less progress in the knowledge of Scripture; I do not mean by reading them much and committing them to memory, but by understanding them aright and carefully searching into their meaning. For there are those who read and yet neglect them; they read to remember the words, but are careless about knowing the meaning. It is plain we must set far above these the men who are not so retentive of the words, but see with the eyes of the heart into the heart of Scripture. Better than either of these, however, is the man who, when he wishes, can repeat the words, and at the same time correctly apprehends their meaning.

8. Now it is especially necessary for the man who is bound to speak wisely, even though he cannot speak eloquently, to retain in memory the words of Scripture. For the more he discerns the poverty of his own speech, the more he ought to draw on the riches of Scripture, so that what he says in his own words he may prove by the words of Scripture; and he himself, though small and weak in his own words, may gain strength and power from the confirming testimony of great men. For his proof gives pleasure when he cannot please by his mode of speech. But if a man desire to speak not only with wisdom, but with eloquence also (and assuredly he will prove of greater service if he can do both), I would rather send him to read, and listen to, and exercise himself in imitating, eloquent men, than advise him to spend time with the teachers of rhetoric; especially if the men he reads and listens to are justly praised as having spoken, or as being accustomed to speak, not only with eloquence, but with wisdom also. For eloquent speakers are heard with pleasure; wise speakers with profit. And, therefore, Scripture does not say that the multitude of the eloquent, but "the multitude of the wise is the welfare of the world."[3] And as we must often swallow wholesome bitters, so we must always avoid unwholesome sweets. But what is better than wholesome sweetness or sweet wholesomeness? For the sweeter we try to make such things, the easier it is to make their wholesomeness serviceable. And so

there are writers of the Church who have expounded the Holy Scriptures, not only with wisdom, but with eloquence as well; and there is not more time for the reading of these than is sufficient for those who are studious and at leisure to exhaust them.

The Sacred Writers Unite Eloquence with Wisdom

9. Here, perhaps, someone inquires whether the authors whose divinely-inspired writings constitute the canon, which carries with it a most wholesome authority, are to be considered wise only, or eloquent as well. A question which to me, and to those who think with me, is very easily settled. For where I understand these writers, it seems to me not only that nothing can be wiser, but also that nothing can be more eloquent. And I venture to affirm that all who truly understand what these writers say, perceive at the same time that it could not have been properly said in any other way. For as there is a kind of eloquence that is more becoming in youth, and a kind that is more becoming in old age, and nothing can be called eloquence if it be not suitable to the person of the speaker, so there is a kind of eloquence that is becoming in men who justly claim the highest authority, and who are evidently inspired of God. With this eloquence they spoke; no other would have been suitable for them; and this itself would be unsuitable in any other, for it is in keeping with their character, while it mounts as far above that of others (not from empty inflation, but from solid merit) as it seems to fall below them. Where, however, I do not understand these writers, though their eloquence is then less apparent, I have no doubt but that it is of the same kind as that I do understand. The very obscurity, too, of these divine and wholesome words was a necessary element in eloquence of a kind that was designed to profit our understandings, not only by the discovery of truth, but also by the exercise of their powers.

10. I could, however, if I had time, show those men who cry up their own form of language as superior to that of our authors (not because of its majesty, but because of its inflation), that all those powers and beauties of eloquence which they make their boast, are to be found in the sacred writings which God in His goodness has provided to mould our characters, and to guide us from this world of wickedness to the blessed world above. But it is not the qualities which these writers have in common with the heathen orators and poets that give me such unspeakable delight in their eloquence; I am more struck with admiration at the way in which, by an eloquence peculiarly their own, they so use this eloquence of ours that it is not conspicuous either by its presence or its absence: for it did not become them ei-

ther to condemn it or to make an ostentatious display of it; and if they had shunned it, they would have done the former; if they had made it prominent, they might have appeared to be doing the latter. And in those passages where the learned do note its presence, the matters spoken of are such, that the words in which they are put seem not so much to be sought out by the speaker as spontaneously to suggest themselves; as if wisdom were walking out of its house—that is, the breast of the wise man, and eloquence, like an inseparable attendant, followed it without being called for.[4]

Review and Discussion Questions

1. Why should the young Christian learn rhetoric?

2. Describe the method of instruction Augustine proposes.

3. In what sense can Scripture teach even when it is obscure?

4. Give contemporary situations in which rhetoric is commonly employed.

❖ 19

ST. THOMAS AQUINAS (1225–74)
Summa Theologiae

Aristotle chose a middle course.

Aquinas's writings both exemplify and perfect the achievement of scholasticism. Attentive to Scripture and the Fathers, St. Thomas demonstrated how the most rigorous philosophic and scientific observations could find a place within an integrative *sacra doctrina*, or Christian wisdom. In a complementary text, his *Commentary on the Nicomachean Ethics* (paragraph 1211), Thomas observes that "the proper order of learning is that boys first be instructed in things pertaining to logic." This is because logic teaches the method of the whole of philosophy. Only much later in their course, after Mathematics and Natural Science, should the student—say at 18—begin to touch moral philosophy. The scientific study of Theology comes last, not because it is least important, but rather because its object (God) is most abstracted from matter and hence most difficult to reason about. The selection below tells us why this is so. Learning comes through a process Thomas calls "abstraction." Thomas's theory of knowledge derives largely, though not solely, from Aristotle. In addition, in the *Summa Theologiae* we find an analysis of the nature of truth according to Thomas's typical method: statement of question; statement of objections; an authoritative citation; a statement of his positive view; and finally, a reply to each of the objections.

Further Readings: V. Boland, *St. Thomas Aquinas*, Bloomsbury Library of Educational Thought (London: Bloomsbury Press, 2014); A. G. Sertillanges, O.P., *On the Intellectual Life: Its Sprit, Conditions, Methods*, trans. Mary Ryan (Washington, D.C.: The Catholic University of America Press, 1987; Jean Leclercq, O.S.B., *The Love of Learning and the Desire for God: A Study in the Monastic Culture* (New York: Fordham University Press, 1982).

❖

Whether intellectual knowledge is derived from sensible things?

Objection 1: It would seem that intellectual knowledge is not derived from sensible things. For Augustine says (*Eighty-Three Diverse Questions*, q. 9) that "we cannot expect to learn the fulness of truth from the senses of the body." This he proves in two ways. First, because "whatever the bodily senses reach, is continually being changed; and what is never the same cannot be perceived." Secondly, because "whatever we perceive by the body, even when not present to the senses, may be present to the imagination, as when we are asleep or angry: yet we cannot discern by the senses, whether what we perceive be the sensible object or the deceptive image thereof. Now nothing can be perceived which cannot be distinguished from its counterfeit." And so he concludes that we cannot expect to learn the truth from the senses. But intellectual knowledge apprehends the truth. Therefore intellectual knowledge cannot be conveyed by the senses.

Objection 2: Further, Augustine says (*Gen. ad lit.* xii, 16): "We must not think that the body can make any impression on the spirit, as though the spirit were to supply the place of matter in regard to the body's action; for that which acts is in every way more excellent than that which it acts on." Whence he concludes that "the body does not cause its image in the spirit, but the spirit causes it in itself." Therefore intellectual knowledge is not derived from sensible things.

Objection 3: Further, an effect does not surpass the power of its cause. But intellectual knowledge extends beyond sensible things: for we understand some things which cannot be perceived by the senses. Therefore intellectual knowledge is not derived from sensible things.

On the contrary, The Philosopher says (*Metaph.* i, 1; *Poster.* ii, 15) that the principle of knowledge is in the senses.

I answer that, On this point the philosophers held three opinions. For Democritus held that "all knowledge is caused by images issuing from the bodies we think of and entering into our souls," as Augustine says in his letter to Dioscorus (cxviii, 4). And Aristotle says (*De Somn. et Vigil.*) that Democritus held that knowledge is cause by a "discharge of images." And the reason for this opinion was that both Democritus and the other early philosophers did not distinguish between intellect and sense, as Aristotle relates (*De Anima* iii, 3). Consequently, since the sense is affected by the sensible, they thought that all our knowledge is affected by this mere impression brought about by sensible things. Which impression Democritus held to be caused by a discharge of images.

Plato, on the other hand, held that the intellect is distinct from the senses: and that it is an immaterial power not making use of a corporeal organ for its action. And since the incorporeal cannot be affected by the corporeal, he held that intellectual knowledge is not brought about by sensible things affecting the intellect, but by separate intelligible forms being participated by the intellect, as we have said above (cf. Q. 84 *articles* [4], 5). Moreover he held that sense is a power operating of itself. Consequently neither is sense, since it is a spiritual power, affected by the sensible: but the sensible organs are affected by the sensible, the result being that the soul is in a way roused to form within itself the species of the sensible. Augustine seems to touch on this opinion (*Gen. ad lit.* xii, 24) where he says that the "body feels not, but the soul through the body, which it makes use of as a kind of messenger, for reproducing within itself what is announced from without." Thus according to Plato, neither does intellectual knowledge proceed from sensible knowledge, nor sensible knowledge exclusively from sensible things; but these rouse the sensible soul to the sentient act, while the senses rouse the intellect to the act of understanding.

Aristotle chose a middle course. For with Plato he agreed that intellect and sense are different. But he held that the sense has not its proper operation without the cooperation of the body; so that to feel is not an act of the soul alone, but of the "composite." And he held the same in regard to all the operations of the sensitive part. Since, therefore, it is not unreasonable that the sensible objects which are outside the soul should produce some effect in the "composite," Aristotle agreed with Democritus in this, that the operations of the sensitive part are caused by the impression of the sensible on the sense: not by a discharge, as Democritus said, but by some kind of operation. For Democritus maintained that every operation is by way of a discharge of atoms, as we gather from *De Gener.* i, 8. But Aristotle held that the intellect has an operation which is independent of the body's cooperation. Now nothing corporeal can make an impression on the incorporeal. And therefore in order to cause the intellectual operation, according to Aristotle, the impression caused by the sensible does not suffice, but something more noble is required, for "the agent is more noble than the patient," as he says (*De Gener.* i, 5). Not, indeed, in the sense that the *intellectual* operation is effected in us by the mere impression of some superior beings, as Plato held; but that the higher and more noble agent which he calls the active *intellect*, of which we have spoken above (Q. 79, articles 3, 4), causes the phantasms received from the senses to be actually intelligible, by a process of abstraction.

According to this opinion, then, on the part of the phantasms, intellectual knowledge is caused by the senses. But since the phantasms cannot of themselves affect the passive intellect, and require to be made actually intelligible by the active intellect, it cannot be said that sensible knowledge is the total and perfect cause of intellectual knowledge, but rather that it is in a way the material cause.

Reply to Objection 1: Those words of Augustine mean that we must not expect the entire truth from the senses. For the light of the active intellect is needed, through which we achieve the unchangeable truth of changeable things, and discern things themselves from their likeness.

Reply to Objection 2: In this passage Augustine speaks not of intellectual but of imaginary knowledge. And since, according to the opinion of Plato, the imagination has an operation which belongs to the soul only, Augustine, in order to show that corporeal images are impressed on the imagination, not by bodies but by the soul, uses the same argument as Aristotle does in proving that the active intellect must be separate, namely, because "the agent is more noble than the patient." And without doubt, according to the above opinion, in the imagination there must needs be not only a passive but also an active power. But if we hold, according to the opinion of Aristotle, that the action of the imagination is an action of the "composite," there is no difficulty; because the sensible body is more noble than the organ of the animal, in so far as it is compared to it as a being in act to a being in potentiality; even as the object actually colored is compared to the pupil which is potentially colored. It may, however, be said, although the first impression of the imagination is through the agency of the sensible, since "fancy is movement produced in accordance with sensation" (*De Anima* iii, 3), that nevertheless there is in man an operation which by synthesis and analysis forms images of various things, even of things not perceived by the senses. And Augustine's words may be taken in this sense.

Reply to Objection 3: Sensitive knowledge is not the entire cause of intellectual knowledge. And therefore it is not strange that intellectual knowledge should extend further than sensitive knowledge.

Review and Discussion Questions

1. If the scientific study of theology should come last, why instruct boys and girls in the Catechism?

2. By what principles would Aquinas order the sequence of study?

3. If the "principle of knowledge is in the senses," how can we know an immaterial God?

4. How might a Thomist-inspired teacher approach the art of teaching differently from a Platonist-inspired teacher?

ERASMUS OF ROTTERDAM (1466–1536)

On the Method of Study, to Christianus of Lubeck

Avoid late and unseasonable studies, for they murder the wit.

Erasmus, along with Thomas More and John Colet, represents the finest of the sixteenth-century men of letters. Erasmus opposed what he viewed as the excessive emphasis on logic then prevalent among the schools. Through his labors Erasmus helped initiate a return to the Biblical and Patristic sources of the Catholic faith; in our time that return has been championed by the fathers of the Second Vatican Council. The recovery of original sources, both classical and Christian, is the hallmark of the best educational thinking in this period. In addition to returning to the sources of Christian civiliation, Erasmus, like other Church reformers, called for a return to evangelical simplicity and to moral fervor.

Further Reading: Thomas More, "Letter to the Masters at Oxford University[1518]," in *A Thomas More Source Book*, ed. G. B. Wegemer and S. W. Smith (Washington, D.C.: The Catholic University of America Press, 2004); Erasmus, *The Education of a Christian Prince*, ed. Lisa Jardine (Cambridge: Cambridge University Press, 1997); Johan Huizinga, *Erasmus and the Age of Reformation*, trans. F. Hopman (Mineola, N.Y.: Dover Publications, 2001).

❖

My special Friend *Christian*,

Making no doubt but that you have an ardent Desire of Literature, I thought you stood in no Need of Exhortation; but only a Guide to direct you in the Journey you have already enter'd upon: And that I look'd upon as my Duty to be, to you, the most nearly ally'd to me, and engaging; that is to say, to acquaint you with the Steps that I myself took, even from a Child: Which if you shall accept as heartily as I communicate, I trust I shall neither repent me of giving Directions, nor you of observing them.

Let it be your first Care to choose you a Master, who is a Man of Learning; for it cannot be, that one that is unlearned himself can render another learned. As soon as you have gotten such an one, endeavour all you can to engage him to treat you with the Affection of a Father, and yourself to act towards him with the Affection of a Son. And indeed, Reason ought to induce us to consider, that we owe more to those, from whom we receive the Way of living well, than to those to whom we owe our first Living in the World; and that a mutual Affection is of so great Moment to Learning, that it will be to no Purpose to have a Teacher, if he be not your Friend too. In the next Place, hear him attentively and assiduously. The Genius of Learners is often spoil'd by too much Contention. Assiduity holds out the longer, being moderate, and by daily Augmentations grows to a Heap larger than can be thought. There is nothing more pernicious than to be glutted with any Thing; and so likewise with Learning. And therefore an immoderate pressing on to Learning is sometimes to be relax'd; and Divertisements are to be intermix'd: But then they should be such as are becoming a Gentleman, and Student, and not much different from the Studies themselves. Nay, there ought to be a continual Pleasure in the very midst of Studies, that it may appear to us rather a Pastime than a Labour; for nothing will be of long Duration, that does not affect the Mind of the Doer with some Sort of Pleasure. It is the utmost Madness to learn that which must be unlearned again. Think that you ought to do the same by your Genius, that Physicians are wont to do in preserving the Stomach. Take Care that you don't oppress your Genius by Food, that is either noxious, or too much of it; both of them are equally offensive. Let alone *Ebrardus, Catholicon, Brachylogus,* and the rest of these Sort of Authors, all whose Names I neither can mention, nor is it worth while so to do, to others who take a Pleasure to learn Barbarism with an immense Labour. At the first it is no great Matter how much you Learn; but how well you learn it. And now take a Direction how you may not only learn well, but easily too; for the right Method of Art qualifies the Artist to perform his Work not only well and expeditiously, but easily too.

Divide the Day into Tasks, as we read *Pliny* the Second, and Pope *Pius* the Great did, Men worthy to be remember'd by all Men. In the first Part of it, which is the chief Thing of all, hear the Master interpret, not only attentively, but with a Sort of Greediness, not being content to follow him in his Dissertations with a slow Pace, but striving to out-strip him a little. Fix all his Sayings in your Memory, and commit the most material of them to Writing, the faithful Keeper of Words. And be sure to take Care not to rely upon them, as that ridiculous rich Man that *Seneca* speaks of did, who had form'd a Notion, that whatsoever of Literature any of his Servants had, was his own. By no Means have your Study furnish'd with learned Books, and be unlearned yourself. Don't suffer what you hear to slip out of your Memory, but recite it either with yourself, or to other Persons. Nor let this suffice you, but set apart some certain Time for Meditation; which one Thing as St. *Aurelius* writes does most notably conduce to assist both Wit and Memory. An Engagement and combating of Wits does in an extraordinary Manner both shew the Strength of Genius's, rouses them, and augments them. If you are in Doubt of any Thing, don't be asham'd to ask; or if you have committed an Error, to be corrected.

Avoid late and unseasonable Studies, for they murder Wit, and are very prejudicial to Health. The Muses love the Morning, and that is a fit Time for Study. After you have din'd, either divert yourself at some Exercise, or take a Walk, and discourse merrily, and Study between whiles. As for Diet, eat only as much as shall be sufficient to preserve Health, and not as much or more than the Appetite may crave. Before Supper, take a little Walk, and do the same after Supper. A little before you go to sleep read something that is exquisite, and worth remembring; and contemplate upon it till you fall asleep; and when you awake in the Morning, call yourself to an Account for it. Always keep this Sentence of *Pliny*'s in your Mind, *All that Time is lost that you don't bestow on Study.* Think upon this, that there is nothing more fleeting than Youth, which, when once it is past, can never be recall'd. But now I begin to be an Exhorter, when I promis'd to be a Director.

My sweet *Christian,* follow this Method, or a better, if you can; and so farewell.

Review and Discussion Questions

1. Why can't a bad man be a good teacher?

2. What does Erasmus mean: "At the first it is no great matter how much you learn; but how well you learn it"?

3. In the spirit of Erasmus's advice, sketch the sequence of a day's work that has been well regulated. What principles guide this order?

4. Given Erasmus's advice, what are two changes you could make to your own daily schedule?

❖ 21

MICHEL DE MONTAIGNE (1533–92)

Of the Education of Children

The charge of the tutor you shall provide for your son, upon the choice of
whom depends the whole success of his education, has several other great
and considerable parts and duties required in so important a trust.

In the midst of the blood and fire of the Reformation, and its Catholic response, stands Montaigne. Credited as the originator of the "essay"—neither
tract, nor treatise, but something highly personal, occasional, and in between—he is also sometimes claimed as a prototype of the modern sceptic.
Maybe; or maybe not. A faithful Catholic, he was cool to violent religious
controversies, but passionate about the observation and study of man. Here
we find Montaigne at the height of his powers, drawing distinctions, suggesting techniques, warning of the pitfalls that attend the art of education.
As he tells us, the liberal arts have as their final goal, flourishing. A parent's
greatest duty is the selection of a wise tutor. Through him, the child should
learn to seek things over words, to love virtue more than mere science, and
to master pleasure rather than be its servant.

Further Reading: Montaigne, *The Essays: A Selection*, trans. M. A. Screech (London: Penguin,
2004); Plutarch, *Plutarch's Lives*, Vols. I–II, trans. John Dryden (New York: The Modern Library
2001); *The Cambridge Companion to Montaigne*, ed. Ullrich Langer (Cambridge: Cambridge
University Press, 2005).

❖

To Madame Diane de Foix, Comtesse de Gurson
    … Now, madam, if I had any sufficiency in this subject, I could not pos-
sibly better employ it, than to present my best instructions to the little man
that threatens you shortly with a happy birth (for you are too generous to
begin otherwise than with a male); for, having had so great a hand in the
treaty of your marriage, I have a certain particular right and interest in the
greatness and prosperity of the issue that shall spring from it; beside that,

your having had the best of my services so long in possession, sufficiently obliges me to desire the honor and advantage of all wherein you shall be concerned. But, in truth, all I understand as to that particular is only this, that the greatest and most important difficulty of human science is the education of children. For as in agriculture, the husbandry that is to precede planting, as also planting itself, is certain, plain, and well known; but after that which is planted comes to life, there is a great deal more to be done, more art to be used, more care to be taken, and much more difficulty to cultivate and bring it to perfection so it is with men; it is no hard matter to get children; but after they are born, then begins the trouble, solicitude, and care rightly to train, principle, and bring them up. The symptoms of their inclinations in that tender age are so obscure, and the promises so uncertain and fallacious, that it is very hard to establish any solid judgment or conjecture upon them. Look at Cimon, for example, and Themistocles, and a thousand others, who very much deceived the expectation men had of them. Cubs of bears and puppies readily discover their natural inclination; but men, so soon as ever they are grownup, applying themselves to certain habits, engaging themselves in certain opinions, and conforming themselves to particular laws and customs, easily alter, or at least disguise, their true and real disposition; and yet it is hard to force the propension of nature. Whence it comes to pass, that for not having chosen the right course, we often take very great pains, and consume a good part of our time in training up children to things, for which, by their natural constitution, they are totally unfit. In this difficulty, nevertheless, I am clearly of opinion, that they ought to be eliminated in the best and most advantageous studies, without taking too much notice of, or being too superstitious in those light prognostics they give of themselves in their tender years, and to which Plato, in his *Republic*, gives, methinks, too much authority.

Madam, science is a very great ornament, and a thing of marvellous use, especially in persons raised to that degree of fortune in which you are. And, in truth, in persons of mean and low condition, it cannot perform its true and genuine office, being naturally more prompt to assist in the conduct of war, in the government of peoples, in negotiating the leagues and friendships of princes and foreign nations, than in forming a syllogism in logic, in pleading a process in law, or in prescribing a dose of pills in physic. Wherefore, madam, believing you will not omit this so necessary feature in the education of your children, who yourself have tasted its sweetness, and are of a learned extraction (for we yet have the writings of the ancient Counts of Foix, from whom my lord, your husband, and yourself, are both of you descended, and Monsieur de Candale, your uncle, every day obliges the world with others, which will extend the knowledge of this quality in your family for so many succeeding ages), I will, upon this occasion, presume to acquaint your ladyship with one particular fancy of my own, contrary to the common method, which is all I am able to contribute to your service in this affair.

The charge of the tutor you shall provide for your son, upon the choice of whom depends the whole success of his education, has several other great and considerable parts and duties required in so important a trust, besides that of which I am about to speak: these, however, I shall not mention, as being unable to add anything of moment to the common rules: and in this, wherein I take upon me to advise, he may follow it so far only as it shall appear advisable.

For a boy of quality then, who pretends to letters not upon the account of profit (for so mean an object is unworthy of the grace and favor of the Muses, and moreover, in it a man directs his service to and depends upon others), nor so much for outward ornament, as for his own proper and peculiar use, and to furnish and enrich himself within, having rather a desire to come out an accomplished cavalier than a mere scholar or learned man; for such a one, I say, I would, also, have his friends solicitous to find him out a tutor, who has rather a well-made than a well-filled head [Ed. note: "Tête bien faite," a celebrated French expression evidently coined by Montaigne.]—seeking, indeed, both the one and the other, but rather of the two to prefer manners and judgment to mere learning, and that this man should exercise his charge after a new method.

'Tis the custom of pedagogues to be eternally thundering in their pupil's ears, as they were pouring into a funnel, whilst the business of the pupil is only to repeat what the others have said: now I would have a tutor to correct this error, and, that at the very first, he should according to the capacity he has to deal with, put it to the test, permitting his pupil himself to taste things, and of himself to discern and choose them, sometimes opening the way to him, and sometimes leaving him to open it for himself; that is, I would not have him alone to invent and speak, but that he should also hear his pupil speak in turn. Socrates, and since him Arcesilaus, made first their scholars speak, and then they spoke to them—[Diogenes Laertius, iv. 36.]

Obest plerumque iis, qui discere volunt, auctoritas eorum, qui docent.

["The authority of those who teach, is very often an impediment to those who desire to learn."—Cicero, *De Natura Deor.*, i. 5.]

It is good to make him, like a young horse, trot before him, that he may judge of his going, and how much he is to abate of his own speed, to accommodate himself to the vigour and capacity of the other. For want of which due proportion we spoil all; which also to know how to adjust, and to keep within an exact and due measure, is one of the hardest things I know, and 'tis the effect of a high and well-tempered soul, to know how to condescend to such puerile motions and to govern and direct them. I walk firmer and more secure up hill than down.

Such as, according to our common way of teaching, undertake, with one and the same lesson, and the same measure of direction, to instruct several boys of differing and unequal capacities, are infinitely mistaken; and 'tis no wonder, if in a whole multitude of scholars, there are not found above two or three who bring away any good account of their time and discipline. Let the master not only examine him about the grammatical construction of the bare words of his lesson, but about the sense and let him judge of the profit he has made, not by the testimony of his memory, but by that of his life. Let him make him put what he has learned into a hundred several forms, and accommodate it to so many several subjects, to see if he yet rightly comprehends it, and has made it his own, taking instruction of his progress by the pedagogic institutions of Plato. 'Tis a sign of crudity and indigestion to disgorge what we eat in the same condition it was swallowed; the stomach has not performed its office unless it have altered the form and condition of what was committed to it to concoct. Our minds work only upon trust, when bound and compelled to follow the appetite of another's fancy, enslaved and captivated under the authority of another's instruction; we have been so subjected to the trammel, that we have no free, nor natural pace of our own; our own vigour and liberty are extinct and gone:

Nunquam tutelae suae fiunt.

["They are ever in wardship."—Seneca, *Ep.*, 33.]

I was privately carried at Pisa to see a very honest man, but so great an Aristotelian, that his most usual thesis was: "That the touchstone and square of all solid imagination, and of all truth, was an absolute conformity to Aristotle's doctrine; and that all besides was nothing but inanity and chimera; for that he had seen all, and said all." A position, that for having been a little too injuriously and broadly interpreted, brought him once and long kept him in great danger of the Inquisition at Rome.

Let him make him examine and thoroughly sift everything he reads, and lodge nothing in his fancy upon simple authority and upon trust. Aris-

totle's principles will then be no more principles to him, than those of Epicurus and the Stoics: let this diversity of opinions be propounded to, and
laid before him; he will himself choose, if he be able; if not, he will remain
in doubt.

> Che non men the saver, dubbiar m' aggrata.
>
> ["I love to doubt, as well as to know." —Dante, *Inferno*, xi. 93]

For, if he embrace the opinions of Xenophon and Plato, by his own reason,
they will no more be theirs, but become his own. Who follows another, follows nothing, finds nothing, nay, is inquisitive after nothing.

> Non sumus sub rege; sibi quisque se vindicet.
>
> ["We are under no king; let each vindicate himself." —Seneca, *Ep.*, 33]

Let him, at least, know that he knows. It will be necessary that he im-
bibe their knowledge, not that he be corrupted with their precepts; and no
matter if he forget where he had his learning, provided he know how to
apply it to his own use. Truth and reason are common to every one, and are
no more his who spake them first, than his who speaks them after: 'tis no
more according to Plato, than according to me, since both he and I equally
see and understand them. Bees cull their several sweets from this flower
and that blossom, here and there where they find them, but themselves afterwards make the honey, which is all and purely their own, and no more
thyme and marjoram: so the several fragments he borrows from others, he
will transform and shuffle together to compile a work that shall be absolutely his own; that is to say, his judgment: his instruction, labour and study,
tend to nothing else but to form that. He is not obliged to discover whence
he got the materials that have assisted him, but only to produce what he
has himself done with them. Men that live upon pillage and borrowing, expose their purchases and buildings to every one's view: but do not proclaim
how they came by the money. We do not see the fees and perquisites of a
gentleman of the long robe; but we see the alliances wherewith he fortifies
himself and his family, and the titles and honours he has obtained for him
and his. No man divulges his revenue; or, at least, which way it comes in but
everyone publishes his acquisitions. The advantages of our study are to become better and more wise. 'Tis, says Epicharmus, the understanding that
sees and hears, 'tis the understanding that improves everything, that orders
everything, and that acts, rules, and reigns: all other faculties are blind, and
deaf, and without soul. And certainly we render it timorous and servile, in
not allowing it the liberty and privilege to do anything of itself.

Whoever asked his pupil what he thought of grammar and rhetoric, or of such and such a sentence of Cicero? Our masters stick them, full feathered, in our memories, and there establish them like oracles, of which the letters and syllables are of the substance of the thing. To know by rote, is no knowledge, and signifies no more but only to retain what one has entrusted to our memory. That which a man rightly knows and understands, he is the free disposer of at his own full liberty, without any regard to the author from whence he had it, or fumbling over the leaves of his book. A mere bookish learning is a poor, paltry learning; it may serve for ornament, but there is yet no foundation for any superstructure to be built upon it, according to the opinion of Plato, who says, that constancy, faith, and sincerity, are the true philosophy, and the other sciences, that are directed to other ends; mere adulterate paint. I could wish that Paluel or Pompey, those two noted dancers of my time, could have taught us to cut capers, by only seeing them do it, without stirring from our places, as these men pretend to inform the understanding without ever setting it to work, or that we could learn to ride, handle a pike, touch a lute, or sing without the trouble of practice, as these attempt to make us judge and speak well, without exercising us in judging or speaking. Now in this initiation of our studies in their progress, whatsoever presents itself before us is book sufficient; a roguish trick of a page, a sottish mistake of a servant, a jest at the table, are so many new subjects.

And for this reason, conversation with men is of very great use and travel into foreign countries; not to bring back (as most of our young monsieurs do) an account only of how many paces Santa Rotonda—[the Pantheon of Agrippa]—is in circuit; or of the richness of Signora Livia's petticoats; or, as some others, how much Nero's face, in a statue in such an old ruin, is longer and broader than that made for him on some medal; but to be able chiefly to give an account of the humours, manners, customs, and laws of those nations where he has been, and that we may whet and sharpen our wits by rubbing them against those of others. I would that a boy should be sent abroad very young, and first, so as to kill two birds with one stone, into those neighbouring nations whose language is most differing from our own, and to which, if it be not formed betimes, the tongue will grow too stiff to bend.

And also 'tis the general opinion of all, that a child should not be brought up in his mother's lap. Mothers are too tender, and their natural affection is apt to make the most discreet of them all so overfond, that they can neither find in their hearts to give them due correction for the faults they may commit, nor suffer them to be inured to hardships and hazards, as they ought to be. They will not endure to see them return all dust and sweat from their exercise, to drink cold drink when they are hot, nor see them mount an unruly horse, nor take a foil in hand against a rude fencer, or so much as to discharge a carbine. And yet there is no remedy; whoever will breed a boy to be good for anything when he comes to be a man, must by no means spare him when young, and must very often transgress the rules of physic:

Vitamque sub dio, et trepidis agat
In rebus.
["Let him live in open air, and ever in movement about something."
—Horace, *Od.* ii., 3, 5.]

...

By what secret springs we move, and the reason of our various agitations and irresolutions: for, methinks the first doctrine with which one should season his understanding, ought to be that which regulates his manners and his sense; that teaches him to know himself, and how both well to dig and well to live. Amongst the liberal sciences, let us begin with that which makes us free; not that they do not all serve in some measure to the instruction and use of life, as all other things in some sort also do; but let us make choice of that which directly and professedly serves to that end. If we are once able to restrain the offices of human life within their just and natural limits, we shall find that most of the sciences in use are of no great use to us, and even in those that are, that there are many very unnecessary cavities and dilatations which we had better let alone, and, following Socrates' direction, limit the course of our studies to those things only where is a true and real utility:

Sapere aude;
Incipe; Qui recte vivendi prorogat horam,
Rusticus exspectat, dum defluat amnis; at ille
Labitur, et labetur in omne volubilis aevum.
["Dare to be wise; begin! he who defers the hour of living well is like the clown, waiting till the river shall have flowed out: but the river still flows, and will run on, with constant course, to ages without end."
—Horace, *Ep.*, i. 2.]

'Tis a great foolery to teach our children:

Quid moveant Pisces, animosaque signa Leonis,
Lotus et Hesperia quid Capricornus aqua,

["What influence Pisces have, or the sign of angry Leo, or Capricorn, washed by the Hesperian wave."—Propertius, iv. I, 89]

the knowledge of the stars and the motion of the eighth sphere before their own:

["What care I about the Pleiades or the stars of Taurus?"
—Anacreon, *Ode*, xvii. 10]

Anaximenes writing to Pythagoras, "To what purpose," said he, "should I trouble myself in searching out the secrets of the stars, having death or slavery continually before my eyes?" for the kings of Persia were at that time preparing to invade his country. Every one ought to say thus, "Being assaulted, as I am by ambition, avarice, temerity, superstition, and having within so many other enemies of life, shall I go ponder over the world's changes?"

After having taught him what will make him more wise and good, you may then entertain him with the elements of logic, physics, geometry, rhetoric, and the science which he shall then himself most incline to, his judgment being beforehand formed and fit to choose, he will quickly make his own. The way of instructing him ought to be sometimes by discourse, and sometimes by reading; sometimes his governor shall put the author himself, which he shall think most proper for him, into his hands, and sometimes only the marrow and substance of it; and if himself be not conversant enough in books to turn to all the fine discourses the books contain for his purpose, there may some man of learning be joined to him, that upon every occasion shall supply him with what he stands in need of, to furnish it to his pupil. And who can doubt but that this way of teaching is much more easy and natural than that of Gaza,—[Theodore Gaza, rector of the Academy of Ferrara]—in which the precepts are so intricate, and so harsh, and the words so vain, lean; and insignificant, that there is no hold to be taken of them, nothing that quickens and elevates the wit and fancy, whereas here the mind has what to feed upon and to digest. This fruit, therefore, is not only without comparison, much more fair and beautiful; but will also be much more early ripe.

...

Since philosophy is that which instructs us to live, and that infancy has there its lessons as well as other ages, why is it not communicated to children betimes?

Udum et molle lutum est; nunc, nunc properandus, et acri
Fingendus sine fine rota.

["The clay is moist and soft: now, now make haste, and form the
pitcher on the rapid wheel."—Persius, iii. 23]

They begin to teach us to live when we have almost done living. A hundred students have got the pox before they have come to read Aristotle's
lecture on temperance. Cicero said, that though he should live two men's
ages, he should never find leisure to study the lyric poets; and I find these
sophisters yet more deplorably unprofitable. The boy we would breed has
a great deal less time to spare; he owes but the first fifteen or sixteen years
of his life to education; the remainder is due to action. Let us, therefore,
employ that short time in necessary instruction. Away with the thorny
subtleties of dialectics; they are abuses, things by which our lives can never
be amended: take the plain philosophical discourses, learn how rightly to
choose, and then rightly to apply them; they are more easy to be understood
than one of Boccaccio's novels; a child from nurse is much more capable of
them, than of learning to read or to write. Philosophy has discourses proper
for childhood, as well as for the decrepit age of men.

I am of Plutarch's mind, that Aristotle did not so much trouble his
great disciple with the knack of forming syllogisms, or with the elements
of geometry; as with infusing into him good precepts concerning valour,
prowess, magnanimity, temperance, and the contempt of fear; and with this
ammunition, sent him, whilst yet a boy, with no more than thirty thousand
foot, four thousand horse, and but forty-two thousand crowns, to subjugate
the empire of the whole earth. For the other acts and sciences, he says, Alexander highly indeed commended their excellence and charm, and had them
in very great honour and esteem, but not ravished with them to that degree
as to be tempted to affect the practice of them in his own person:

Petite hinc, juvenesque senesque,
Finem ammo certum, miserisque viatica canis.

["Young men and old men, derive hence a certain end to the mind,
and stores for miserable grey hairs."—Persius, v. 64]

Epicurus, in the beginning of his letter to Meniceus,—[Diogenes Laertius, x. 122.]—says, "That neither the youngest should refuse to philosophise, nor the oldest grow weary of it." Who does otherwise, seems tacitly
to imply, that either the time of living happily is not yet come, or that it is
already past. And yet, for all that, I would not have this pupil of ours impris-

202 THE METHODS OF TEACHING

oned and made a slave to his book; nor would I have him given up to the morosity and melancholic humour of a sour ill-natured pedant.

I would not have his spirit cowed and subdued, by applying him to the rack, and tormenting him, as some do, fourteen or fifteen hours a day, and so make a pack-horse of him. Neither should I think it good, when, by reason of a solitary and melancholic complexion, he is discovered to be overmuch addicted to his book, to nourish that humour in him; for that renders him unfit for civil conversation, and diverts him from better employments. And how many have I seen in my time totally brutified by an immoderate thirst after knowledge? Carneades was so besotted with it, that he would not find time so much as to comb his head or to pare his nails. Neither would I have his generous manners spoiled and corrupted by the incivility and barbarism of those of another. The French wisdom was anciently turned into proverb: "Early, but of no continuance." And, in truth, we yet see, that nothing can be more ingenious and pleasing than the children of France; but they ordinarily deceive the hope and expectation that have been conceived of them; and grown up to be men, have nothing extraordinary or worth taking notice of: I have heard men of good understanding say, these colleges of ours to which we send our young people (and of which we have but too many) make them such animals as they are.

But to our little monsieur, a closet, a garden, the table, his bed, solitude, and company, morning and evening, all hours shall be the same, and all places to him a study; for philosophy, who, as the formatrix of judgment and manners, shall be his principal lesson, has that privilege to have a hand in everything. The orator Isocrates, being at a feast entreated to speak of his art, all the company were satisfied with and commended his answer: "It is not now a time," said he, "to do what I can do; and that which it is now time to do, I cannot do."—[Plutarch, *Symp.*, i. I.]—For to make orations and rhetorical disputes in a company met together to laugh and make good cheer, had been very unreasonable and improper, and as much might have been said of all the other sciences. But as to what concerns philosophy, that part of it at least that treats of man, and of his offices and duties, it has been the common opinion of all wise men, that, out of respect to the sweetness of her conversation, she is ever to be admitted in all sports and entertainments. And Plato, having invited her to his feast, we see after how gentle and obliging a manner, accommodated both to time and place, she entertained the company, though in a discourse of the highest and most important nature:

Aeque pauperibus prodest, locupletibus aeque;
Et, neglecta, aeque pueris senibusque nocebit.

["It profits poor and rich alike, but, neglected, equally hurts old and young."—Horace, *Ep.*, i. 25.]

By this method of instruction, my young pupil will be much more and better employed than his fellows of the college are. But as the steps we take in walking to and fro in a gallery, though three times as many, do not tire a man so much as those we employ in a formal journey, so our lesson, as it were accidentally occurring, without any set obligation of time or place, and falling naturally into every action, will insensibly insinuate itself. By which means our very exercises and recreations, running, wrestling, music, dancing, hunting, riding, and fencing, will prove to be a good part of our study. I would have his outward fashion and mien, and the disposition of his limbs, formed at the same time with his mind. 'Tis not a soul, 'tis not a body that we are training up, but a man, and we ought not to divide him. And, as Plato says, we are not to fashion one without the other, but make them draw together like two horses harnessed to a coach. By which saying of his, does he not seem to allow more time for, and to take more care of exercises for the body, and to hold that the mind, in a good proportion, does her business at the same time too?

As to the rest, this method of education ought to be carried on with a severe sweetness, quite contrary to the practice of our pedants, who, instead of tempting and alluring children to letters by apt and gentle ways, do in truth present nothing before them but rods and ferules, horror and cruelty. Away with this violence! away with this compulsion! than which, I certainly believe nothing more dulls and degenerates a well-descended nature. If you would have him apprehend shame and chastisement, do not harden him to them: inure him to heat and cold, to wind and sun, and to dangers that he ought to despise; wean him from all effeminacy and delicacy in clothes and lodging, eating and drinking; accustom him to everything, that he may not be a Sir Paris, a carpet-knight, but a sinewy, hardy, and vigorous young man. I have ever from a child to the age wherein I now am, been of this opinion, and am still constant to it. But amongst other things, the strict government of most of our colleges has evermore displeased me; peradventure, they might have erred less perniciously on the indulgent side. 'Tis a real house of correction of imprisoned youth. They are made debauched by being punished before they are so. Do but come in when they are about their lesson, and you shall hear nothing but the outcries of boys under execution, with the thundering noise of their pedagogues drunk with fury. A very pretty way this, to tempt these tender and timorous souls to love their book, with a furious countenance, and a rod in hand! A cursed and pernicious way of proceeding! Besides what Quintilian has very well observed, that this imperious authority is often attended by very dangerous consequences, and particularly our way of chastising. How much more decent would it be to see their classes strewed with green leaves and fine flowers, than with the bloody stumps of birch and willows? Were it left to my ordering, I should paint the school with the pictures of joy and gladness; Flora and the Graces, as the philosopher Speusippus did his. Where their profit is, let them there have their pleasure too. Such viands as are proper and wholesome for children, should be sweetened with sugar, and such as are dangerous to them, embittered with gall. 'Tis marvellous to see how solicitous Plato is in his Laws concerning the gaiety and diversion of the youth of his city, and how much and often he enlarges upon the races, sports, songs, leaps, and dances: of which, he says, that antiquity has given the ordering and patronage particularly to the gods themselves, to Apollo, Minerva, and the Muses. He insists long upon, and is very particular in, giving innumerable precepts for exercises; but as to the lettered sciences, says very little, and only seems particularly to recommend poetry upon the account of music.

All singularity in our manners and conditions is to be avoided, as inconsistent with civil society. Who would not be astonished at so strange a constitution as that of Demophoon, steward to Alexander the Great, who sweated in the shade and shivered in the sun? I have seen those who have run from the smell of a mellow apple with greater precipitation than from a harquebuss-shot; others afraid of a mouse; others vomit at the sight of cream; others ready to swoon at the making of a feather bed; Germanicus could neither endure the sight nor the crowing of a cock. I will not deny, but that there may, peradventure, be some occult cause and natural aversion in these cases; but, in my opinion, a man might conquer it, if he took it in time. Precept has in this wrought so effectually upon me, though not without some pains on my part, I confess, that beer excepted, my appetite accommodates itself indifferently to all sorts of diet. Young bodies are supple; one should, therefore, in that age bend and ply them to all fashions and customs: and provided a man can contain the appetite and the will within their due limits, let a young man, in God's name, be rendered fit for all nations and all companies, even to debauchery and excess, if need be; that is, where he shall do it out of complacency to the customs of the place. Let him be able to do everything, but love to do nothing but what is good. The philosophers themselves do not justify Callisthenes for forfeiting the favour of his master Alexander the Great, by refusing to pledge him a cup of wine. Let him laugh, play, wench with his prince: nay, I would have him, even in his debauches, too hard for the rest of the company, and to excel his companions in ability and vigour, and that he may not give over doing it, either through defect of power or knowledge how to do it, but for want of will.

Multum interest, utrum peccare aliquis nolit, an nesciat.

["There is a vast difference betwixt forbearing to sin, and not knowing how to sin."—Seneca, *Ep.*, 90]

I thought I passed a compliment upon a lord, as free from those excesses as any man in France, by asking him before a great deal of very good company, how many times in his life he had been drunk in Germany, in the time of his being there about his Majesty's affairs; which he also took as it was intended, and made answer, "Three times"; and withal told us the whole story of his debauches. I know some who, for want of this faculty, have found a great inconvenience in negotiating with that nation. I have often with great admiration reflected upon the wonderful constitution of Alcibiades, who so easily could transform himself to so various fashions without any prejudice to his health; one while outdoing the Persian pomp and luxury, and another, the Lacedaemonian austerity and frugality; as reformed in Sparta, as voluptuous in Ionia:

Omnis Aristippum decuit color, et status, et res.

["Every complexion of life, and station, and circumstance became
Aristippus."—Horace, *Ep.*, xvii. 23.]

I would have my pupil to be such an one,

Quem duplici panno patentia velat,
Mirabor, vitae via si conversa decebit,
Personamque feret non inconcinnus utramque.

["I should admire him who with patience bearing a patched garment, bears
well a changed fortune, acting both parts equally well."
—Horace *Ep.*, xvii. 25.]

These are my lessons, and he who puts them in practice shall reap more advantage than he who has had them read to him only, and so only knows them. If you see him, you hear him; if you hear him, you see him. God forbid, says one in Plato, that to philosophise were only to read a great many books, and to learn the arts.

Hanc amplissimam omnium artium bene vivendi disciplinam, vita magis quam literis,
persequuti sunt.

["They have proceeded to this discipline of living well, which of all arts is the greatest, by their lives, rather than by their reading."—Cicero, *Tusc. Quaes.*, iv. 3.]

... The first taste which I had for books came to me from the pleasure in reading the fables of Ovid's *Metamorphoses*; for, being about seven or eight years old, I gave up all other diversions to read them, both by reason that this was my own natural language, the easiest book that I was acquainted with, and for the subject, the most accommodated to the capacity of my age: for as for the *Lancelot of the Lake*, the *Amadis of Gaul*, the *Huon of Bordeaux*, and such farragos, by which children are most delighted with, I had never so much as heard their names, no more than I yet know what they contain; so exact was the discipline wherein I was brought up. But this was enough to make me neglect the other lessons that were prescribed me; and here it was infinitely to my advantage, to have to do with an understanding tutor, who very well knew discreetly to connive at this and other truantries of the same nature; for by this means I ran through Virgil's *Æneid,* and then Terence, and then Plautus, and then some Italian comedies, allured by the sweetness of the subject; whereas had he been so foolish as to have taken me off this diversion, I do really believe, I had brought away nothing from the college but a hatred of books, as almost all our young gentlemen do. But he carried himself very discreetly in that business, seeming to take no notice, and allowing me only such time as I could steal from my other regular studies, which whetted my appetite to devour those books. For the chief things my father expected from their endeavours to whom he had delivered me for education, were affability and good-humour; and, to say the truth, my manners had no other vice but sloth and want of metal. The fear was not that I should do ill, but that I should do nothing; nobody prognosticated that I should be wicked, but only useless; they foresaw idleness, but no malice; and I find it falls out accordingly: The complaints I hear of myself are these: "He is idle, cold in the offices of friendship and relation, and in those of the public, too particular, too disdainful." But the most injurious do not say, "Why has he taken such a thing? Why has he not paid such an one?" but, "Why does he part with nothing? Why does he not give?" And I should take it for a favour that men would expect from me no greater effects of supererogation than these. But they are unjust to exact from me what I do not owe, far more rigorously than they require from others that which they do owe. In condemning me to it, they efface the gratification of the action, and deprive me of the gratitude that would be my due for it; whereas the active well-doing ought to be of so much the greater value from my hands, by how much I have never been passive that way at all. I can the more freely dispose of my fortune the more it is mine, and of myself the more I am my own. Nevertheless, if I were good at setting out my own actions, I could, peradventure, very well repel these reproaches, and could give some to understand, that they are not so much offended, that I do not enough, as that I am able to do a great deal more than I do.

Yet for all this heavy disposition of mine, my mind, when retired into itself, was not altogether without strong movements, solid and clear judgments about those objects it could comprehend, and could also, without any helps, digest them; but, amongst other things, I do really believe, it had been totally impossible to have made it to submit by violence and force. Shall I here acquaint you with one faculty of my youth? I had great assurance of countenance, and flexibility of voice and gesture, in applying myself to any part I undertook to act: for before—

Alter ab undecimo tum me vix ceperat annus,

["I had just entered my twelfth year."—Virgil, *Bucol.*, 39.]

I played the chief parts in the Latin tragedies of Buchanan, Guerente, and Muret, that were presented in our College of Guienne with great dignity: now Andreas Goveanus, our principal, as in all other parts of his charge, was, without comparison, the best of that employment in France; and I was looked upon as one of the best actors. 'Tis an exercise that I do not disapprove in young people of condition; and I have since seen our princes, after the example of some of the ancients, in person handsomely and commendably perform these exercises; it was even allowed to persons of quality to make a profession of it in Greece.

Aristoni tragico actori rem aperit: huic et genus et fortuna honesta erant: nec ars, quia nihil tale apud Graecos pudori est, ea deformabat.

["He imparted this matter to Aristo the tragedian; a man of good family and fortune, which neither of them receive any blemish by that profession; nothing of this kind being reputed a disparagement in Greece."—Livy, xxiv. 24.]

Nay, I have always taxed those with impertinence who condemn these entertainments, and with injustice those who refuse to admit such comedians as are worth seeing into our good towns, and grudge the people that public diversion. Well-governed corporations take care to assemble their citizens, not only to the solemn duties of devotion, but also to sports and spectacles. They find society and friendship augmented by it; and besides, can there possibly be allowed a more orderly and regular diversion than what is performed m the sight of every one, and very often in the presence of the supreme magistrate himself? And I, for my part, should think it reasonable, that the prince should sometimes gratify his people at his own expense, out of paternal goodness and affection; and that in populous cities there should be theatres erected for such entertainments, if but to divert them from worse and private actions.

To return to my subject, there is nothing like alluring the appetite and affections; otherwise you make nothing but so many asses laden with books; by dint of the lash, you give them their pocketful of learning to keep; whereas, to do well you should not only lodge it with them, but make them espouse it.

Review and Discussion Questions

1. Why, precisely, ought the parents to invest care in the selection of a child's tutor?

2. What final purpose or goal of education does Montaigne identify?

3. Montaigne quotes extensively from classical authors. Given this habit of mind, what can you infer about Montaigne's approach to pedagogy?

4. Montaigne says the teacher should not produce "asses laden with books." How do you avoid this?

❖ 22

THE SOCIETY OF JESUS

Ratio Studiorum (1599)

[T]hese activities should be so handled and so varied in nature that in addition to their intrinsic value they may afford pleasure to the members and hold their interest.

As the old Jesuit saying goes, "Give me a boy till he's seven and I'll show you the man." Before you lies the text that educated Europe for more than two hundred years. Founded in 1534, the Jesuits quickly became the dominant arm of Catholic Europe's Counter-Reformation missionary and educational activity. Within less than a century, the Jesuits established some five hundred academies; during the seventeenth century, that number nearly doubled. Leading men, from Europe to Asia, were formed according to the template set out by the *Ratio Studiorum*. This most enduring of all teachers' manuals was constructed after wide consultations of both the most successful practices and the compelling theories that had been developed by medieval as well as renaissance educational philosophers. It is eminently practical. From suggestions on drills, to recitations, to the place of public lectures, to the distribution of awards, all is to be ordered with a view to instilling mental and moral discipline in a manner both efficient and pleasing. (It should be noted that "theologians and philosophers" refers not to professors but to aspiring pupils, and particularly those who might be headed to the priesthood. The "students of rhetoric and humanities" and the "students of the grammar classes," whose rules are given later in this selection, are the more junior students in the Studiorum.)

Further Reading: *The Ratio Studiorum: The Official Plan for Jesuit Education*, translation and commentary by Claude Pavur, S.J. (St. Louis: The Institute of Jesuit Sources, 2005); Vincent J. Duminuco, S.J., *The Jesuit "Ratio studiorum": 400th Anniversary Perspectives* (New York: Fordham University Press, 2000); Aldo Scaglione, *The Liberal Arts and the Jesuit College System* (Philadelphia: John Benjamins Publishing Company, 1986).

❖

Rules of the Academy of Theologians and Philosophers

1. The exercises of this academy are customarily of four kinds: daily repetitions of matter seen in class, disputations, academic lectures or the discussion of debatable questions, more formal disputations at which theses are defended in public.

2. Repetitions shall last for about an hour on all class days excepting the days of monthly disputations. They are to be held at the most convenient hours. During Lent, however, time must be left free at least twice a week for a sermon.

3. The different classes should hold repetitions separately, the students of theology forming one group, the philosophers forming three if there are that many professors. At the repetitions, one or two members of the academy should review the matter covered in class and one or two pose objections. For the repetitions in theology, the moderator of the academy should preside, or his assistant, or at least one of the more advanced theology students appointed by the rector of the college. For the students of philosophy, the presiding members in each group should generally be a Jesuit student of theology, likewise appointed by the rector of the college.

4. Disputations are to be scheduled once a week when there are only a few in the academy, twice a week when there are many members. They should be scheduled on the weekly holiday or on both the weekly holiday and on Sunday. One student, generally a philosopher, should defend a thesis for an hour on Sunday afternoon, while two object. On the recreation day, two or three are to defend theses for two hours, one a theology student, the others, students of philosophy, while as many or more will offer objections.

5. If only one student of theology defends, he will always include some theses in philosophy. A student of metaphysics will defend theses in physics and logic, and a student of physics will also defend theses in logic. Objectors against theologians should be theologians; against, philosophers, the first objector should be from the next higher class, and the second a member of the same class as the defendant.

6. If the teacher of the defendant attends the disputations, whether of philosophy or theology, he shall preside; otherwise the moderator of the academy or his assistant shall preside.

7. Lectures, too, may be given occasionally. A member of the academy will deliver from the chair a scholarly report that he has worked out on his own initiative or some original problem. He should present and establish arguments for both sides of the question and afterwards entertain counter-

arguments from one or more members. Lectures of this sort must first be shown to the moderator of the academy for his approval.

8. The president of the academy or some other member chosen by the moderator may at times hold a more formal disputation, at Christmas, for example, at Easter, Pentecost, or some other opportune time. The matter defended in such disputations should be some portion of philosophy or theology stated in the form of theses. The professor should preside.

9. These disputations should be conducted with a certain degree of ceremony. The defender should begin with a formal introduction and end with a similarly prepared conclusion, both of which should like all public utterances be checked and approved by the prefect. To make the event more notable, guests should be invited to attack the conclusions of the defendant, and others may be invited as auditors.

10. About a month prior to the opening of classes, the rector, if he wishes, may appoint a member of the Society or have the moderator appoint a member of the academy to give for fifteen days an introduction to or epitome of philosophy to those who are to begin their philosophical course.

11. Before any theses, whether for the more formal disputations or for the weekly disputations, are defended or posted, they must be looked over by the moderator of the academy and by the defendant's professor.

Rules of the Moderator of the Academy of Theologians and Philosophers

1. Besides the common directives laid down for all moderators in the rules of the academy, each moderator should see to it that in the daily repetitions the method of reviewing, proving, and discussing be identical with that used by members of the Society in repetitions at home. In public disputations, however, and in classroom defenses, the customary procedure is to be followed.

2. Accordingly, the moderator shall pay frequent visits to individual groups to see to it that they are functioning in a serious and proper manner, and that each individual is performing his part correctly. Let him give specific directions where such directions are needed.

3. It will be helpful to give more frequent practice to those who are preparing for their comprehensive examinations in philosophy and theology, or who will present a formal defense before the academy. He should also advise and direct them so that they may be the better prepared.

4. Should the rector of the college give him an assistant, he may divide his responsibility for his work with the academy in such a way that the as-

sistant will preside over the repetitions in theology and on alternate days, especially on holidays, take charge of the disputations. He may also use the services of the assistant to carry out other details connected with the everyday meetings and the more formal sessions of the academy.

Rules of the Academy of Students of Rhetoric and Humanities

1. The academy shall meet on Sunday or, where it is more convenient, on a recreation day, in a place assigned by the rector of the college.

2. The programs scheduled by the academy shall in general be as follows: the moderator, as he shall judge timely, may lecture on or throw open for discussion some suitable topic or passage from an author or he may explain some more challenging principles of oratory, as given by Aristotle, Cicero, or other rhetoricians, or he may rapidly read through an author and question the members of the academy on what he has read, or he may propose problems to be solved, and conduct other exercises of the sort.

3. Often, too, he should omit such exercises and have the members themselves deliver speeches or recite poems or give declamations, either from memory or ex tempore. With his approval, they may stage mock trials. They may deliver a lecture and answer questions on it proposed by two or more of the members. Again they may defend theses and offer objections to them in an oratorical rather than a dialectical style. They may compose symbols or mottoes or again epigrams or brief descriptions. They may compose and solve riddles, or have a drill in invention, each one either on the spur of the moment or after reflection suggesting sources of arguments on a proposed topic. Or as practice in style they may suit metaphors or sentence patterns to a suggested argument. They may write out the plot of dialogues or tragedies, or the plan of a poem. They may imitate a whole speech or poem of a famous orator or poet. They may propose a symbol of some sort and have each member contribute to its meaning. They may assign the various books of some author and have each member of the academy make a selection of thoughts and expressions from the book assigned to him. Finally, let them cultivate the gift of eloquent expression and whatever is associated with its practice.

4. It will be found worth while occasionally to have some of the better and more ambitious of these exercises or prelections, declamations, and defenses of theses presented, especially by the president of the academy, with a degree of external ceremony in the presence of a distinguished audience.

5. At times prizes may be awarded to those who do especially well in writing, reciting, or solving enigmas and puzzling problems.

6. More formal awards may be given to all the members of the academy once a year. The expense may be met by contributions or in whatever way the rector of the college thinks best.

7. At least once a year, some feast of the Blessed Virgin, designated by the rector of the college, should be celebrated with a great display of speeches, poems, verses, as well as symbols and mottoes, posted on the walls of the college.

Rules of the Academy of Students of the Grammar Classes

1. Generally the moderator will take some point of grammar which the members are later to study in class, or something from a graceful and pleasing writer, and give a prelection on it. He may hold a repetition or a drill on matter already explained in class.

2. One member should come each time prepared to open the meeting of the academy by answering questions on topics discussed at the last meeting. Three or more should propose difficulties or call on him to translate some sentences from the vernacular into Latin. Following the same procedure, the members should immediately review the prelection given by the moderator.

3. Frequent and spirited contest should be conducted. Sometimes the members will be tested on their literary style, sometimes on memory work, sometimes phrases will be expressed in a variety of ways, or some specimens of verse or precepts of Greek grammar may be discussed, or other similar exercises held at the discretion of the moderator.

4. Occasionally some of the members, or even all of them, should come prepared to recite from memory some short apothegm or to narrate some event.

5. Now and then members should be called upon to recite from the platform the prelections which their teacher gave them in class, adding a short introduction and, if it seems good, also some commentary.

6. It will be of advantage on occasion to have prelections given by members, and especially by the president of the academy, with a little greater solemnity and before a larger audience than usual. To this exercise may be added a contest between two or three of the members, and prizes may be awarded afterwards in private.

7. The moderator can exact some literary task in place of penalty, and he may read in public the names of those who have been slack or not well behaved.

8. Finally, these activities should be so handled and so varied in nature that in addition to their intrinsic value they may afford pleasure to the members and hold their interest. They will thus inspire a greater love of learning.

Review and Discussion Questions

1. List the techniques suggested in this manual (e.g., drills, disputations). What does each offer the student?

2. What good does "ceremony" add to an academic community?

3. What is one recommendation from the *Ratio Studiorum* that you might implement?

4. List the various functions that the *Ratio* assigns to the moderator and to the rector.

❖ 23

H. S. GERDIL (1718–1803)

The Anti-Emile

It is not necessary to describe the evils that premature liberty among young people is capable of causing.

In his advocacy of the "the natural man," Rousseau called for the abolition of parental authority over children. What rule they maintain is strictly a consequence of superior bodily strength. Children are to honor their father, as Rousseau claims "only as long as they need him to survive." Gerdil suggests such a view is madness. Not only does Rousseau's position wrongly describe the natural affection that binds children and parents; dismantling parental authority would damage the happiness of both children and the state. Hierarchy need not imply domination. Contra Rousseau, children are not born sinless; they need not only sustenance, but also moral correction. To abandon a boy or girl while their "reason is weak and their passions are violent" would, in Gerdil's Catholic view, not extend liberty, but exterminate it. Discipline is charity's eldest daughter.

Further Reading: Jean-Jacques Rousseau, *Emile*, trans. Allan Bloom (New York: Basic Books, 1979); Benedictine monks of Solesmes, *Papal Teachings: Education* (Boston: St. Paul Editions, 1960); Christopher Blum, ed., *Critics of the Enlightenment* (Wilmington, Del.: ISI Books, 2003).

❖

On the Importance of the Fear of God in the Moral Education of Children

The most appropriate and efficacious method of leading children to what is good and distancing them from evil is to inspire them with the fear of God. It will be in vain for Rousseau to say that the idea of God is too sublime for children. We are not speaking here of the speculative ideas that Simonides puzzled over, when he had asked of Hiero a day's time to explain to him what God was, the next day asked two, and afterwards four days, and

215

concluded with saying that the more he reflected on the question proposed to him by Hiero the more obscure and difficult he found it. A child knows that a house, a statue, a picture, or a piece of furniture did not make itself. He knows it, and let us point out to him whatever we choose, if he notices design and regularity in it, he will not fail to ask who made it. This disposition is natural to all children, and it may naturally open their minds to the knowledge of God. Let them be told that the world, which exhibits to their view so magnificent spectacle, did not make itself. In telling them this you tell them nothing new; they already knew that a house could not make itself. But who made the world? It is God, we shall answer. At the same time we will explain to them that God, who made the world, does not have a body like men, that we cannot see him with our eyes, that he knows everything and can do what he pleases. We shall further explain that he is good, that he created men to make them happy, that he is just, that he rewards the good and punishes the wicked. These truths are undoubtedly sublime, and we cannot wonder too much at the fact that they are nevertheless brought within the capacity of even the simplest souls. The reason for this fact is that the truths are necessary to the perfection and happiness of man. Hence we have the reason why they are found so conformable to the first reflective notions which develop in the mind of children and why they take hold with kind of homogeneity.

A child instructed in this manner, regardless of what Rousseau thinks, will be disposed to neither idolatry nor anthropomorphism. The greatest difficulty is to make him understand that God is not corporeal. The following is a method I have used successfully with some children. The child begins by asking: "God has no body? How can he have anything if he has no body?"

Teacher. Observe all the bodies you see. Isn't it true that all have some length and some breadth?
Child. This is true.
Teacher. Do you not see that they have a kind of figure, which is round, square, etc.?
Child. I see it.
Teacher. Do you not feel that they resist your hand when you touch and try to stir them?
Child. I feel it.
Teacher. Would you like to know in what manner God is not corporeal?
Child. Yes.
Teacher. You really have the will and the desire to know it.

Child. Yes.

Teacher. Assure me, then, that you have this will and this desire. I am still somewhat doubtful you have it.

Child. I assure you of it, believe me I have.

Teacher. You feel then this desire, this will?

Child. I do feel it.

Teacher. Strongly?

Child. Yes, strongly.

Teacher. Well, then, this desire which you so strongly feel in yourself, is it nothing or is it something?

Child. It is something.

Teacher. Come now, I tell you it is nothing.

Child. Nothing! If it was nothing, I should not feel it.

Teacher. Then this desire that you feel is something.

Child. Yes, without doubt.

Teacher. Tell me then is this desire as long and as broad as that table?

Child. O dear! It is neither long nor broad.

Teacher. Is it round or square?

Child. O dear!

Teacher. Is it yellow or green, as heavy as lead or as light as a feather?

Child. It is nothing of the sort.

Teacher. It is nothing, then.

Child. Pardon me, it certainly is something.

Teacher. It is then something that is neither long nor broad, neither yellow nor green, neither round nor square?

Child. Exactly.

Teacher. Your desire, then, is not a body like your hand, your hair, this mirror, this table, this fountain, nor like the air which may be felt when it is agitated.

Child. This is true.

Teacher. You conceive then that there are things that can be neither seen nor touched, and that nevertheless are something.

On the Authority of Fathers and the Obedience of Children

Rousseau limits the dependence of children to the need they have for their father, and he excludes every sentiment of obedience. This we have already seen. He adds in another place:

Command him nothing, whatever in the world it might be, absolutely nothing. Do not even allow him to imagine that you might pretend to have any authority over him. Let him know only that he is weak and you are strong, that by his condition and yours he is necessarily at your mercy. Let him know it, learn it, feel it. Let his haughty head at an early date feel the harsh yoke which nature imposes on man, the heavy yoke of necessity under which every finite being must bend. Let him see this necessity in things, never in the caprice of men. Let the bridle that restrains him be force and not authority.[1]

It is very strange that one should want to teach children not to depend on their father or on those who substitute in his place except because of the inevitable necessity of submitting to a superior power, which they cannot resist. Rousseau would have the child know that he is at the mercy of the strongest and that he must learn to be dependent; moreover, this dependence is to make him cognizant of the heavy yoke of necessity which nature imposes and accustoms him to bear. It seems to me that such a state of dependence is very sad and that it closely resembles that subordination of a slave to a despot, who is able to crush him at any instant. Even though every finite being bends, however unwillingly, to the yoke of domineering necessity, this submission does not prevent the heart from often rising up and murmuring at the burden that oppresses it. The submission of a son to his father should not be of this sort; nor is it at this school that he should learn to bear up under the unavoidable yoke of necessity. Every subordination founded exclusively on the superiority of an irresistible power serves only to inspire sentiments of fear, aversion, and a desire to free oneself. A child educated in accordance with such principles will only suffer with horror every human authority no matter what kind. He will bear the yoke to the extent he is unable to avoid it, but his heart will shudder at this hard necessity, and he will seek out every means to liberate himself from it. I ask whether, with such a disposition, it is possible for a child to become a good citizen in any part of the world he might find himself? I know that according to Rousseau's principles every human authority ought to be abolished. And it is perhaps the most original and novel idea that has been produced for many centuries. The discoveries of Newton, wonderful as they are, to some extent depended upon ancient theories, which contained their seeds. The abolition of all human authority, beginning with that of fathers over their children, is an idea for which Rousseau is indebted to no one. But while awaiting this great revolution in which all Europe will be divided into three or four hundred thousand cities where natural liberty will be so well maintained that by putting a man in prison one only obliges him to be free, it would seem one runs a great risk by educating children in principles that are so little consistent with the government of all the monarchies and all the republics that have so far existed and which will probably exist for a long time to come.

Let us consult nature and see if she has not arranged gentler ties to establish that dependence which children ought to have upon those who gave them life. Rousseau himself shows us the way. Children are susceptible of a natural affection toward their fathers and their mothers.

The child ought to love his mother before knowing that he ought to. If the voice of blood is not strengthened by habit and care, it is extinguished in the first years, and the heart dies, so to speak, before being born. Here we are, from the first steps, outside of nature.[2]

A child, badly treated by his mother, does not entrust himself to the first person who comes his way and tries to attract him with caresses; he returns to his mother, tries to soften her by his embraces, and finds comfort only on her breast. Children are susceptible of a parallel sentiment of affection toward their fathers.

Children have no difficulty conceiving that they belong to those who gave them life. They regard themselves as masters of the balls they have made with their own hands. This dominion which they assume over what belongs to them disposes them to recognize an analogous power over themselves in those to whom they belong.

Children know that their father and mother love them and that they only use their authority over them for their own good. They are aware that they are not in a position to procure for themselves the common necessities of life, that their parents voluntarily undertake this care upon themselves, and that they know better than themselves what is suitable for them.

We commonly find all these ideas in children of ten years of age. They are therefore capable of recognizing in their father and mother four kinds of power. (1) There is a power founded on a superiority of strength, but this is perhaps what they think of least. (2) There is a power founded on the fact of having given them life and by which they are charged with guiding them. It is the power they approve of and consider very differently than that of a robber who would carry off a child and keep him in his cavern. Children do not know how to express themselves on this subject in artful terms. But if they are questioned, one will see by their answers that they know very well a robber does wrong in seizing children who are not his own, but that a father has just reason for commanding those who belong to him. (3) Another power follows on the knowledge of what is to their advantage, and it requires on their part a subordination that will turn out to their own benefit. (4) There is a power that is tempered by love and requires on the child's part a return of affection and acknowledgment. Now the dependence founded on the motives we have described is nothing other than obedience and filial submission.

To these motives let us join the fear of God, a motive capable of acting powerfully in directing children toward the good. Let them be told that God rewards children who obey and punishes the disobedient; their still-fresh souls will open themselves spontaneously at the impression of these salutary maxims. Their nascent reason finds nothing in them to oppose. Depravity has not yet armed them against the force of truth. They do not know that it is the privilege of thinking beings to believe nothing of what vulgar people believe. It would therefore be difficult to find any children whose hearts would be closed to those beautiful sentiments that the Holy Spirit has put into the mouth of the wise man for their instruction:

Honor your father with all your heart, and forget not the sufferings of your mother. Remember that without them you would not have been at all, and do everything for them as they have done all for you. Listen, children, to the counsels of your father, and follow them that you may be saved. For God has made the father venerable to children, and has appointed over them the authority of the mother. He who fears the Lord will honor his father and mother, and will serve as his masters those who have given him life. Honor your father by actions, by words, by an unlimited patience, that he may bless you, and that his blessing may remain on you to the end. My son, comfort your father in his old age, and cause him no sorrow while he lives. How base is he who abandons his father, and how accursed of God is he who embitters the soul of his mother. [Sirach 3:1–17; 7:27–28]

This is not Rousseau's philosophy. But we must at least acknowledge that it is better suited for maintaining the peace, order, and harmony in families, for the formation of men, who from docile children become virtuous citizens, and by that means contribute to the happiness of humankind.

Can we say as much of Rousseau's principle that "no one, not even the father, has a right to command the child what is not for his good"?[3] The author of nature has charged fathers with raising their children, and in charging them with this responsibility, he has invested them with the authority necessary to carry out their duties. But has God, in imposing such a duty on fathers with respect to their children, imposed no duty at all on children with respect to their fathers? If it is just that the father should work for the sake of the child, is it not also just that the child should work for the sake of the father? Why therefore has not the father a right to command his son to do things, which though they may not be of any advantage to the son, may be profitable to the father? The abuse that one makes of a right does not always justify the privation of the right. A man acts wrongly who squanders his substance at gambling. Shall we say that on this account he has no right to make use of his property? A father ought not to command things absolutely useless. But while he limits himself to the administration of his family, the son is obliged to obey, as long as he can obey without sinning.

In short, it cannot be repeated too often that Rousseau's doctrine is by no means adapted to maintaining peace in families. Teach this lesson to a child, and he will set himself in judgment over all of his father's commands. He will want to know if that which is commanded of him would be of some good for him, and if, taken by some fancy, he were to find that what is commanded of him were of no good to him, then he will decide, trusting the word of Rousseau, that his father has no right to command him. He will disobey, or he will obey with an ill will, murmuring and champing against his father's authority. Can a lesson so dangerous in its consequences be true in its principle? Fathers and mothers who live in the sweet familial union, which Rousseau with so much reason recommends and which he paints so truly and in such charming colors, would, I believe, be quite aggrieved were their children taught that a father has no right to command his son to do any thing that will be of no advantage to him.

It is as a consequence of the same principle that Rousseau establishes the following maxim, which seems to require some correction: "The children remain bound to their father only as long as they need him to survive" (we shall see he should have added: "and to guide their conduct"). "As soon as this need ceases to exist, the natural bond is dissolved."[4]

A well-respected doctor in the Catholic schools, esteemed by Grotius and Leibnitz, despised by the elegant crowd who know him only by name sees this matter in quite a different light, but more consistently with the ends of nature, which is to say, with the designs of Providence. We find it where he deals with the stability of the conjugal bond. I shall only report what immediately relates to my subject. He first observes that in those animals where the female alone is sufficient for nourishing the young, as in the case of quadrupeds that nature has supplied with milk, the male does not remain with the female but immediately quits her. By contrast, in those species where the cooperation of the male is necessary to rear the young, the male does not separate himself from the female until their nurslings are in a condition to do without their assistance. This we see in birds, which nature has not furnished with a reservoir of milk for feeding their young ones. The father and mother go alternately in search of food for them, while one of them always remains in the nest to defend them and guard them from the cold. Now in the human species, the education of children requires, more than in any other, the cooperation of the father and mother. For children need not only nourishment with regard to the body, but instruction with regard to the spirit.

It is also useful to observe that other animals receive from nature an instinct, a kind of art and industry that quickly and invariably directs them to the pursuit of that which is necessary for their preservation and defense. Man alone has received no parallel instinct because reason is meant to serve him as a rule in his conduct. Now reason cannot properly guide him unless it is itself enlightened by prudence. This is why it is necessary that children remain a long time under the direction of their father and mother who, being instructed by experience, are in a position to share with them the insight they have acquired, in order to form their judgment and teach them as the occasion offers how to conduct themselves in life. This education is particularly necessary at the age in which the body is already grown strong and when the passions begin to have their play. At this age, reason is weak and the passions are violent; this is the time when young people most require restraint and correction. And this care falls particularly to the father, who has the greater maturity for instructing and that greater force for correcting.[5]

It must be that these ideas are consistent with nature and sound reason, for we see that the better ordered states preserve their customs and, as a consequence, their laws and their power, to the extent that the authority of fathers and the respect for elders, which follows from it, are maintained. It is not necessary to describe the evils that premature liberty of young people is capable of causing.

Review and Discussion Questions

1. Why does Rousseau think the idea of God is too sublime for children? Why does Gerdil reject this view?

2. In your own words, reconstruct Gerdil's technique for teaching a child that immaterial things exist.

3. Rousseau thinks a father has no right to rule over his child. According to Gerdil, how ought a father's "rule" to be understood and exercised?

4. Describe the pedagogical value of pleasure (promises) and pain (threats) in Gerdil's account.

MARIA MONTESSORI (1870–1952)

The Montessori Method

Now from the enjoyment of gross pleasures vicious habits often spring.

While we might object to Montessori's Hegelian, that is, progressive, view of history, her basic insight in this passage is sound: intellectual and cultural formation begins with the body. As a devout Catholic, Montessori understood the implications of the Incarnation for education. Children are not merely minds, but embodied souls, who learn first through their senses. An education that separates children from play, from experiment, from habitual familiarity with plants, animals and earth, is subhuman. Would Montessori allow children access to computers?

Further Reading: Angeline Stoll Lillard, *Montessori: The Science behind the Genius* (Oxford: Oxford University Press, 2008); Tim Seldin and Vanessa Davies, *How to Raise an Amazing Child the Montessori Way* (London: DK Adult, 2006); Charlotte Mason, *Toward a Philosophy of Education* (Radford, Va.: Wilder Publications, 2008).

❖

General Notes on the Education of the Senses

I do not claim to have brought to perfection the method of sense training as applied to young children. I do believe, however, that it opens a new field for psychological research, promising rich and valuable results.

Experimental psychology has so far devoted its attention to *perfecting the instruments by which the sensations are measured.* No one has attempted the *methodical* preparation *of the individual for the sensations.* It is my belief that the development of psychometry will owe more to the attention given to the preparation of the *individual* than to the perfecting of the *instrument.*

But putting aside this purely scientific side of the question, the *education of the senses* must be of the greatest *pedagogical* interest.

Our aim in education in general is two-fold, biological and social. From the biological side we wish to help the natural development of the individual, from the social standpoint it is our aim to prepare the individual for the environment. Under this last head technical education may be considered as having a place, since it teaches the individual to make use of his surroundings. The education of the senses is most important from both these points of view. The development of the senses indeed precedes that of superior intellectual activity and the child between three and seven years is in the period of formation.

We can, then, help the development of the senses while they are in this period. We may graduate and adapt the stimuli just as, for example, it is necessary to help the formation of language before it shall be completely developed.

All education of little children must be governed by this principle—to help the natural *psychic* and *physical development* of the child.

The other aim of education (that of adapting the individual to the environment) should be given more attention later on when the period of intense development is past.

These two phases of education are always interlaced, but one or the other has prevalence according to the age of the child. Now, the period of life between the ages of three and seven years covers a period of rapid physical development. It is the time for the formation of the sense activities as related to the intellect. The child in this age develops his senses. His attention is further attracted to the environment under the form of passive curiosity.

The stimuli, and not yet the reasons for things, attract his attention. This is, therefore, the time when we should methodically direct the sense stimuli, in such a way that the sensations which he receives shall develop in a rational way. This sense training will prepare the ordered foundation upon which he may build up a clear and strong mentality.

It is, besides all this, possible with the education of the senses to discover and eventually to correct defects which today pass unobserved in the school. Now the time comes when the defect manifests itself in an evident and irreparable inability to make use of the forces of life about him. (Such defects as deafness and near-sightedness.) This education, therefore, is physiological and prepares directly for intellectual education, perfecting the organs of sense, and the nerve-paths of projection and association.

But the other part of education, the adaptation of the individual to his environment, is indirectly touched. We prepare with our method the infancy of the *humanity of our time.* The men of the present civilisation are pre-eminently observers of their environment because they must utilise to the greatest possible extent all the riches of this environment. The art of today bases itself, as in the days of the Greeks, upon observation of the truth.

The progress of positive science is based upon its observations and all its discoveries and their applications, which in the last century have so transformed our civic environment, were made by following the same line—that is, they have come through observation. We must therefore prepare the new generation for this attitude, which has become necessary in our modern civilised life. It is an indispensable means—man must be so armed if he is to continue efficaciously the work of our progress.

We have seen the discovery of the Roentgen Rays born of observation. To the same methods are due the discovery of Hertzian waves, and vibrations of radium, and we await wonderful things from the Marconi telegraph. While there has been no period in which thought has gained so much from positive study as the present century, and this same century promises new light in the field of speculative philosophy and upon spiritual questions, the theories upon the matter have themselves led to most interesting metaphysical concepts. We may say that in preparing the method of observation, we have also prepared the way leading to spiritual discovery.

The education of the senses makes men observers, and not only accomplishes the general work of adaptation to the present epoch of civilisation, but also prepares them directly for practical life. We have had up to the present time, I believe, a most imperfect idea of what is necessary in the practical living of life. We have always started from ideas, and have *proceeded thence to motor activities*; thus, for example, the method of education has always been to teach intellectually, and then to have the child follow the principles he has been taught. In general, when we are teaching, we talk about the object which interests us, and then we try to lead the scholar, when he has understood, to perform some kind of work with the object itself; but often the scholar who has understood the idea finds great difficulty in the execution of the work which we give him, because we have left out of his education a factor of the utmost importance, namely, the perfecting of the senses. I may, perhaps, illustrate this statement with a few examples. We ask the cook to buy only "fresh fish." She understands the idea, and tries to follow it in her marketing, but, if the cook has not been trained to recognise through sight and smell the signs which indicate freshness in the fish, she will not know how to follow the order we have given her.

Such a lack will show itself much more plainly in culinary operations. A cook may be trained in book matters, and may know exactly the recipes and the length of time advised in her cook book; she may be able to perform all the manipulations necessary to give the desired appearance to the dishes, but when it is a question of deciding from the odor of the dish the exact moment of its being properly cooked, or with the eye, or the taste, the time at which she must put in some given condiment, then she will make a mistake if her senses have not been sufficiently prepared.

She can only gain such ability through long practice, and such practice on the part of the cook is nothing else than a *belated education* of the senses—an education which often can never be properly attained by the adult. This is one reason why it is so difficult to find good cooks.

Something of the same kind is true of the physician, the student of medicine who studies theoretically the character of the pulse, and sits down by the bed of the patient with the best will in the world to read the pulse, but, if his fingers do not know how to read the sensations his studies will have been in vain. Before he can become a doctor, he must gain a *capacity for discriminating between sense stimuli*.

The same may be said for the *pulsations* of the *heart*, which the student studies in theory, but which the ear can learn to distinguish only through practice.

We may say the same for all the delicate vibrations and movements, in the reading of which the hand of the physician is too often deficient. The thermometer is the more indispensable to the physician the more his sense of touch is unadapted and untrained in the gathering of the thermic stimuli. It is well understood that the physician may be learned, and most intelligent, without being a good practitioner, and that to make a good practitioner long practice is necessary. In reality, this *long practice* is nothing else than a tardy, and often inefficient, *exercise* of the senses. After he has assimilated the brilliant theories, the physician sees himself forced to the unpleasant labor of the semiography, that is, to making a record of the symptoms revealed by his observation of and experiments with the patients. He must do this if he is to receive from these theories any practical results.

Here, then, we have the beginner proceeding in a stereotyped way to tests of *palpation*, percussion, and auscultation, for the purpose of identifying the throbs, the resonance, the tones, the breathings, and the various sounds which *alone* can enable him to formulate a diagnosis. Hence the deep and unhappy discouragement of so many young physicians, and, above all, the loss of time; for it is often a question of lost years. Then, there is the immorality of allowing a man to follow a profession of so great responsibility, when, as is often the case, he is so unskilled and inaccurate in the taking of symptoms. The whole art of medicine is based upon an education of the senses; the schools, instead, *prepare* physicians through a study of the classics. All very well and good, but the splendid intellectual development of the physician falls, impotent, before the insufficiency of his senses.

One day, I heard a surgeon giving, to a number of poor mothers, a lesson on the recognition of the first deformities noticeable in little children from the disease of rickets. It was his hope to lead these mothers to bring to him their children who were suffering from this disease, while the disease was yet in the earliest stages, and when medical help might still be efficacious. The mothers understood the idea, but they did not know how to recognise these first signs of deformity, because they were lacking in the sensory education through which they might discriminate between signs deviating only slightly from the normal.

Therefore those lessons were useless. If we think of it for a minute, we will see that almost all the forms of adulteration in food stuffs are rendered possible by the torpor of the senses, which exists in the greater number of people. Fraudulent industry feeds upon the lack of sense education in the masses, as any kind of fraud is based upon the ignorance of the victim. We often see the purchaser throwing himself upon the honesty of the merchant, or putting his faith in the company, or the label upon the box. This is because purchasers are lacking in the capacity of judging directly for themselves. They do not know how to distinguish with their senses the different qualities of various substances. In fact, we may say that in many cases intelligence is rendered useless by lack of practice, and this practice is almost always sense education. Everyone knows in practical life the fundamental necessity of judging with exactness between various stimuli.

But very often sense education is most difficult for the adult, just as it is difficult for him to educate his hand when he wishes to become a pianist. It is necessary to begin the education of the senses in the formative period, if we wish to perfect this sense development with the education which is to follow. The education of the senses should be begun methodically in infancy, and should continue during the entire period of instruction which is to prepare the individual for life in society.

Æsthetic and moral education are closely related to this sensory education. Multiply the sensations, and develop the capacity of appreciating fine differences in stimuli and we *refine* the sensibility and multiply man's pleasures.

Beauty lies in harmony, not in contrast; and harmony is refinement;

therefore, there must be a fineness of the senses if we are to appreciate harmony. The æsthetic harmony of nature is lost upon him who has coarse senses. The world to him is narrow and barren. In life about us, there exist inexhaustible fonts of æsthetic enjoyment, before which men pass as insensible as the brutes seeking their enjoyment in those sensations which are crude and showy, since they are the only ones accessible to them.

Now, from the enjoyment of gross pleasures, vicious habits very often spring. Strong stimuli, indeed, do not render acute, but blunt the senses, so that they require stimuli more and more accentuated and more and more gross.

Onanism, so often found among normal children of the lower classes, alcoholism, fondness for watching sensual acts of adults—these things represent the enjoyment of those unfortunate ones whose intellectual pleasures are few, and whose senses are blunted and dulled. Such pleasures kill the man within the individual, and call to life the beast.

Indeed from the physiological point of view, the importance of the education of the senses is evident from an observation of the scheme of the diagrammatic arc which represents the functions of the nervous system. The external stimulus acts upon the organ of sense, and the impression is transmitted along the centripetal way to the nerve centre—the corresponding motor impulse is elaborated, and is transmitted along the centrifugal path to the organ of motion, provoking a movement. Although the arc represents diagrammatically the mechanism of reflex spinal actions, it may still be considered as a fundamental key explaining the phenomena of the more complex nervous mechanisms. Man, with the peripheral sensory system, gathers various stimuli from his environment. He puts himself thus in direct communication with his surroundings. The psychic life develops, therefore, in relation to the system of nerve centres; and human activity which is eminently social activity, manifests itself through acts of the individual—manual work, writing, spoken language, etc.—by means of the psychomotor organs.

Education should guide and perfect the development of the three periods, the two peripheral and the central; or, better still, since the process fundamentally reduces itself to the nerve centres, education should give to psychosensory exercises the same importance which it gives to psychomotor exercises.

Otherwise, we *isolate* man from his *environment*. Indeed, when with *intellectual culture* we believe ourselves to have completed education, we have but made thinkers, whose tendency will be to live without the world.

We have not made practical men. If, on the other hand, wishing through education to prepare for practical life, we limit ourselves to exercising the psychomotor phase, we lose sight of the chief end of education, which is to put man in direct communication with the external world.

Since *professional work* almost always requires man to *make use of his surroundings*, the technical schools are not forced to return to the very beginnings of education, sense exercises, in order to supply the great and universal lack.

Review and Discussion Questions

1. What does Montessori mean by the "education of the senses"?
2. Why is an education in the senses good for the individual child?
3. Why is an education in the senses good for civilization?
4. Montessori observes that base pleasures "kill the man within the individual, and call to life the beast." How can the teacher help reform the child's "beast"?

❖ 25

A. G. SERTILLANGES (1863–1948)

On the Intellectual Life

You must study yourself, consider what your life is, what it enables you to do, what it furthers or excludes, what of itself it suggests for the hours of intense activity.

"He who knows the value of time always has enough"; "Purchase your solitude; pay for your liberty by attentive thoughtfulness and kind acts of service"; "You cannot be charitable in every direction at once." Such is a sample of the wisdom contained in Fr. Sertillanges's classic guide to the intellectual life. True insight and scholarly excellence requires its own set of disciplines; devotion to education offers enormous rewards, but it demands sacrifice. In this selection the great Dominican reflects on the precious hours of morning and evening. For the Christian intellectual, all moments can be sanctified; study, too, can find its place within the well-ordered day.

Further reading: *The Wisdom of the Desert: Sayings from the Desert Fathers of the Fourth Century*, trans. Thomas Merton (New York: New Directions Books, 1960); Ralph McInerny, *The Very Rich Hours of Jacques Maritain: A Spiritual Life* (Notre Dame, Ind.: University of Notre Dame Press, 2011); James V. Schall, *The Order of Things* (San Francisco: Ignatius Press, 2007).

❖

Just as gentle and regular work can give harmony to the day, the unconscious work of night can bring peace and keep at bay wandering imaginations, crazy fancies that are exhausting or sinful, nightmares. If you take a child gently by the hand, his turbulence subsides.

We are in no way recommending excessive strain, nor any turning of night into day. No, you must sleep; sleep renews nature and is indispensable. But we are saying that night, as night, can itself work; that it "gives counsel"; that sleep, as sleep, is a serviceable craftsman; that rest, as rest, is an additional strength. It is entirely in accordance with their nature, and not by doing violence to their proper function, that we aim at using these helps. Rest is not death; it is life, and all life bears fruit. While you yourself can gather the fruit of sleep, do not leave it to the birds of night.

Mornings and Evenings

Hence the extreme importance, for the worker as well as for the religious man, of the mornings and evenings. One cannot prepare, supervise and end the hours of rest with an attentive spirit if those that immediately precede and follow are left to chance.

The morning is sacred; in the morning our soul, refreshed, looks out on life as from a turning-point from which we see it in one view. Our destiny lies outspread before us. We resume our task; this is the moment to accept it afresh, and to confirm, by an express act, our triple vocation as men, Christians, and intellectuals.

"Philip, remember that thou art a man": these words of the Macedonian slave to his master are spoken to us by the light of day, when falling on our eyes, it also awakens the lights of the soul; "a man" I say, not in a general sense, but specified in a precise instance, a man who stands here before God, a single, unique, personality; and, no matter how unimportant he is, alone capable of filling his own proper place.

Will not this man, emerging renewed and, as it were, reborn from the hours of unconsciousness, cast a rapid glance over his life as a whole, mark the point he has reached, map out the coming day, and so start out with springing step and clear mind on a new stage of his journey?

Such will be the combined effort of the first moment of waking, of morning prayer, of meditation, and, above all, of the Mass, if one has the possibility of hearing it or the happiness of saying it.

Waking must be a Sursum corda! To repeat a form of prayer at that moment is an excellent practice; to say it aloud is better; for, as psychologists know, our voice has an effect of self-suggestion on us and plays towards us the part of a double. That is a "slave" that we may not neglect; he has authority from us, he is us, and his voice reaches us with the strange domination of one who is at once the same and different.

Children are taught "to give their heart to God"; the intellectual, a child in that respect, must in addition give his heart to truth; he must remember that he is her servant, repudiate her enemies within himself, love her enemies without, so that they may return to her, and willingly accept the efforts that for the coming day truth asks of him.

Next comes prayer. Pere Gratry advises the intellectual to say Prime, which would have Compline for its pendant in the evening; and indeed there are no prayers more beautiful, more efficacious, more inspiring. The majority of liturgical prayers are masterpieces; but these are full and sweet like the rising and setting of a star. Try: you will never be able to say any other prayers. All true life is in them, all nature, and to prepare your work with them is like going out on a journey through a wide open door flooded with sunshine.

Whatever prayer he chooses, that of the intellectual should emphasize for a moment what is especially appropriate to himself, should extract its fruit and form from it the good resolution that will be kept by Christian work.

An act of faith in the lofty truths that are the foundation of knowledge; an act of hope that God will help us to light as well as to virtue; an act of love for Him who is infinitely lovable and for those whom our study aims at bringing near to Him; the Pater to ask for our bread and for the food of our intelligence; an Ave addressed to the Woman clothed with the sun, victorious over error as over evil. In these forms of words and in others, the intellectual finds his needs expressed, reminds himself of his task; and he can, without isolating his specialty from Christian life as a whole, profit by what is providentially deposited for him in the common treasure.

Meditation is so essential to the thinker that we need not urge it anew. We have recommended the spirit of prayer: where can it get more food than in these morning acts of contemplation in which the mind, rested, not yet caught up afresh in the cares of the day, borne and lifted up on the wings of prayer, rises with ease towards those founts of truth which study draws on laboriously?

If you can hear holy Mass, or say it, will its vastness and fullness not take possession of you? Will you not see from this other Calvary, from this Upper Room where the farewell Banquet is renewed the whole of humanity standing round you: that humanity with which you must not lose contact, that life lit up by the words of the Savior, that poverty succored by His riches which it is your task to succor along with Him, which you must enlighten and do your part to save while saving yourself?

The Mass really puts you into a state of eternity, into the spirit of the universal Church, and in the *Ite missa est* you are ready to see a mission, a sending out of your zeal to the destitution of the mad and ignorant earth.

The morning hours thus bedewed with prayer, freshened and vivified by the breezes of the spirit, cannot fail to be fruitful; you will begin them with faith; you will go through them with courage; the whole day will be spent in the radiance of the early light; evening will fall before the brightness is exhausted, as the year ends leaving some seed in the barns for the year to come.

Evening! How little, usually, people know about making it holy and quiet, about using it to prepare for really restorative sleep! How it is wasted, polluted, misdirected!

Let us not dwell on what men of pleasure make of it: their condition is alien to ours. But look at those serious people called workers: business men, industrialists, public officials, big merchants—I speak of them in the mass. When evening comes, they lay down the reins and throw off thought, giving their minds up to the dissipation which is supposed to refresh them, dining, smoking, playing cards, talking noisily, frequenting the theatres or the music halls, gaping at the cinema, and going to bed with minds "relaxed."

Yes, indeed, relaxed; but like a violin with all its strings completely slackened. What a labor next day to tune them all up again!

I know industrialists who find their relaxation in reading Pascal, Montaigne, Ronsard, Racine. Deep in a comfortable armchair well lit from behind, beside the fire, their family around them, quiet, or in the buzz of pleasant activity, they live awhile after having toiled all day. This is their moment; this is the moment of the man, when the specialist has done facing up with head and heart to innumerable difficulties.

An intellectual, if he does not need this mental compensation, needs the quietness even more. His evening should be a time of stillness, his supper a light refection, his play the simple task of setting the day's work in order and preparing the morrow's. He needs his Compline—this time I take the word figuratively—to complete and to inaugurate; for every completion of the continuous work which we postulate is a beginning as well as a terminal point. We close only to open again. Evening is the connecting medium between the daily sections which taken together make a life. In the morning we shall have forthwith to start living: we must get ready in the evening, and we must prepare the night which, after its fashion, and without our intervention links together the periods of our conscious toil.

In spite of the passionate and self-interested illusion of those who maintain that a part of man must be set aside for the life of pleasure, dissipation is not rest, it is exhaustion. Rest cannot be found in scattering one's energies. Rest means giving up all effort and withdrawing towards the fount of life; it means restoring our strength, not expending it foolishly.

I know indeed that to expend is sometimes to acquire: that is true of sport, of recreation, and we shall not merely tolerate, we shall demand, such active relaxation. But that is not the normal function of the evening. For the evening there is a double rest, spiritual and physical; rest in God and rest in mother nature. Now the first comes from prayer; the other, the rest of the body, precedes the more complete rest of the night and must lead up to it.

One should give oneself up in the evening to the quietly regular activities of which night breathing is the model. The wise thing is to let the easy bent of nature assert itself, to let habit take the place of initiative, to let keen activity give way to a simple familiar routine, in a word, to cease willing up to a point so that the renunciation of night may begin. And wisdom will appear in the ordering of this less intense life, of this peaceful semi-activity. The family will have a share in it; quiet conversation will set its seal on the union of souls; there will be an exchange of the day's impressions, of plans for the morrow; views and purposes will be strengthened; the passing of the day will have its consolations; harmony will reign; and the evening be a worthy eve of the festival that every new day should be for the Christian.

The sleeper often unconsciously takes up the position that he had long ago in his mother's womb. That is a symbol. Rest is a return to our origins: the origins of life, of strength, of inspiration; it is a retempering; that is signified by our withdrawal in the evening from the world and into ourselves. Now retempering cannot possibly be attained through fussy activity; it is rather like seeking a refuge, renewing the vigor of the human spirit by peaceful concentration; it is a restoration of organic life and of holy life in us by easing off happily, by prayer, silence, and sleep.

The Moments of Plenitude

We come at length, after speaking of the preparation, and the prolongation, and the profitable interruption of work, and of rest in view of work, to the work itself properly so-called, and the time devoted to studious concentration, to full effort. Accordingly, we shall give the name of full moments, moments of plenitude, to these culminating periods of the duration of our intellectual life.

The greater part of this treatise has no other object than to consider how to use that time: here we are speaking only of securing it, putting it on a stable basis, preserving it, guarding the "interior cell" against all that threatens to invade it.

Seeing that the moments of our life have very unequal values, and that for each of us the adjustment of these values obeys different laws, we cannot lay down any absolute rule; but we must insist on this one thing: you must study yourself, consider what your life is, what it enables you to do, what it furthers or excludes, what of itself it suggests for the hours of intense activity.

Will these be in the morning or in the evening, or partly in the morning and partly in the evening? You alone can decide, because you alone know your obligations and your character on which the mapping-out of your days depends.

When you have only a few free hours and can place them at will, morning seems to deserve the preference. Night has renewed your strength; prayer has given you wings; peace reigns all about you and the buzzing swarm of distractions has not begun. But for certain people there may be counterindications. If you sleep badly you may be upset and dull in the morning. Or solitude may be lacking, and then you must wait for the hours of isolation.

Whatever decision you have made, the chosen moments must be carefully secured, and you must take all personal precautions so as to use them to the fullest. You must see to it beforehand that nothing happens to crowd up, waste, shorten, or interfere with this precious time. You want it to be a time of plenitude; then shut remote preparation out of it; make all the necessary arrangements beforehand; know what you want to do and how you want to do it; gather your materials, your notes your books; avoid having to interrupt your work for trifles.

Further, in order to keep this time for your work and to keep it really free, rise punctually and promptly; breakfast lightly; avoid futile conversations, useless calls, limit your correspondence to what is strictly necessary; gag the newspapers! These rules, which we have given as a general safeguard for the life of study, apply most of all to its intense hours.

If you have so foreseen and settled everything, you can get straight at your work; you will be able to plunge deep into it, to get absorbed and to make progress; your attention will not be distracted, your effort scattered. Avoid half-work more than anything. Do not imitate those people who sit long at their desks but let their minds wander. It is better to shorten the time and use it intensely, to increase its value, which is all that counts.

Do something, or do nothing at all. Do ardently whatever you decide to do; do it with your might; and let the whole of your activity be a series of vigorous fresh starts. Half-work, which is half-rest, is good neither for rest nor for work.

Then invite inspiration. If the goddess does not always obey, she is always sensible of sincere effort. You must not strain yourself to excess, but you must find your direction, aim at your goal, and put out of your field of vision, like the marksman, everything else but the target. Renew the "spirit of prayer"; keep yourself in the state of eternity, your heart submissive to truth, your mind obeying its great laws, your imagination outspread like a wing, your whole being conscious of the silent stars above you, even by day, when they still shine faithfully. Beneath your feet, far below, will the sounds of life be; you will not notice them, you will hear only the music of the spheres which symbolizes in Scipio's Dream the harmony of the forces of creation.

Thus to open up one's being to truth, to withdraw from all else, and, if I may say so, to take a ticket for a different world, is true work. That is the kind of work of which we speak when we say that two hours daily are enough to yield a tangible worthwhile result. Evidently, they are not much; but they really suffice if all the conditions are fulfilled; and they are better than the fifteen hours a day that so many loud talkers boast of to the echoes.

Those fabulous figures have indeed been reached by certain people of abnormal capacity for work; they are instances of what might be called a lucky monstrosity, unless indeed that procedure be ruinous folly. Normal workers estimate at from two to six hours the time that can be steadily used with fruitful results. The principal question does not lie in the number of hours; but in their use and in the mind.

He who knows the value of time always has enough; not being able to lengthen it, he intensifies its value; and first of all he does nothing to shorten it. Time, like gold, has thickness; a solid medal, well struck and pure in line, has more value than the thin leaf from the gold-beater's hammer. Gold-beater, battage; the resemblance of the words is suggestive. [Battage, a collo-quial word for log-rolling, self-advertisement. The idea might be suggested in English by pairing the words gold-beater, drum-beating. (Tr. Note.)] Many people are the dupe of appearances, of vague and muddle-headed in-tentions, talk all the time and never work.

We must remark that the period of intensive work cannot be any more uniform than our intellectual life as a whole. Proportionally, it has the same phases; one gets into swing gradually, sometimes with great difficulty, one reaches one's maximum, and then grows tired. There is a complete cycle: fresh morning, burning midday, evening decline.

We must be the Josue of that evening, so that the battle which is always too short may be continued.

We shall have to speak later of the conditions of this careful economy of the work-time light; here I indicate only one: you must defend your soli-tude with a fierceness that makes no distinctions whatever. If you have du-ties, satisfy their demands at the normal time; if you have friends, arrange suitable meetings; if unwanted visitors come to disturb you, graciously shut the door on them.

The Artist's Garden

It is important, during the hours sacred to work, not only that you should not be disturbed, but that you should know you will not be disturbed; let perfect security on that score protect you, so that you can apply yourself intensely and fruitfully. You cannot take too many precautions about this. Keep a Cerberus at your door. Every demand on you from outside is a loss of inner power and may cost your mind some precious discovery: "when half-gods go, the gods arrive." [Ralph Waldo Emerson, *Poems*]

But note that this complete solitude, the only favorable atmosphere for work, need not be understood physically. Someone else's presence may double, instead of disturbing, your quietude. To have near you another worker equally ardent, a friend absorbed in some kindred thought or occupation, a chosen spirit who understands your work, joins in it, seconds your effort by silent affection and a keenness fired by your own—that is not a distraction, it is a help.

Sometimes in the public libraries you breathe in a sense of concentration; it is like an atmosphere bearing you up. You are invaded by a sort of religious impression; you dare not fall short of it, or let your mind wander. The more you are surrounded by these adorers of the True in spirit and in truth, the more you are alone with the True alone, and the easier and more delightful your contemplation becomes.

A young couple in the husband's study, where the wife's work-table or basket has its place, where love reigns in silence, its wings outstretched to the wind of inspiration and some noble dream, is another picture of work. In the oneness of the life entered on by Christian marriage, there is a place for oneness of thought and the stillness necessary for it. The more two sister souls are together, the more secure they are against the outside world.

Yet the fact remains that solitude, once understood and arranged for, must be obstinately defended. You must listen to no one, neither indiscreet friends, nor understanding relatives, nor chance comers, nor charity itself. You cannot be charitable in every direction at once. You belong to truth; serve her first. Except in certain clear and obvious cases, nothing should take precedence of your vocation.

The time of a thinker, when he really uses it, is in reality charity to all; only thus do we appreciate it properly. The man of truth belongs to the human race with truth itself; there is no risk of selfishness when one has isolated oneself jealously to serve this sublime and universal benefactor of mankind.

However, you must use your ingenuity to win the affectionate forgiveness of those from whom you turn away to work, and whom sometimes you hurt by doing so. Purchase your solitude; pay for your liberty by attentive thoughtfulness and kind acts of service. It is desirable that your retirement should be more advantageous to others that your companionship. In any case, let it be the least possible burden to them. Do your part, and let your relative independence be counterpoised by your absolute dependence when the time for your duties comes again.

Review and Discussion Questions

1. What in particular do morning and evening offer to the scholar?

2. What does Sertillanges mean when he claims: "dissipation is not rest"?

3. "You cannot be charitable in every direction at once." In your own words, give an account of how a Christian can also serve in an intellectual apostolate.

4. In light of this reading, what are two habits you might initiate?

❖ PART IV

On Renewal in Our Time

The Calling of the Apostles Peter and Andrew

❖ 26

LEO XIII (1810–1903)

On the Restoration of Christian Philosophy

… You should all furnish to studious youth a generous and copious supply of these purest of streams of wisdom flowing inexhaustibly from the precious fountainhead of the Angelic Doctor.

On the Restoration of Christian Philosophy is Leo XIII's answer to a world gone mad. Secularist polemic often presents the modern world as an age founded upon reason. That is not true. The modern world, insofar as it mirrors post-Christian philosophy, is based upon dramatic denials: Descartes denied the senses; Kant denied revelation; Nietzsche, truth. The great pope, who happens also to have founded modern Catholic social teaching (see *Rerum Novarum*), initiated through this document a worldwide renewal in Catholic education. As an antidote to skepticism and cynicism, Leo put forward Thomas. And, for a time, it worked. In answer to Leo III's call, universities, seminaries, and academies on every continent took up with zeal the study of Thomas. St. Thomas served as a bulwark against secularism up till the Second Vatican Council and inspired a new generation of philosophers (such as Etienne Gilson and Jacques Maritain) and a new generation of institutions (at Toronto, Ottawa, Notre Dame, Washington, Houston, and in Switzerland, France, Germany, Australia, and elsewhere.) And the tale of the modern Thomistic renewal has, of course, not yet reached its end.

Further Reading: G. K. Chesterton, *The Dumb Ox* (New York: Doubleday, 2001); Philip Gleason, *Contending with Modernity: Catholic Higher Education in the Twentieth Century* (Oxford: Oxford University Press, 1995); Wayne Hankey, "From Metaphysics to History, from Exodus to Neoplatonism, from Scholasticism to Pluaralism: The Fate of Gilsonian Thomism in English-Speaking North-America," *Dionysius* 16 (1998): 157–88.

❖

To the Patriarchs, Primates, Archbishops, and Bishops of the
Catholic World in Grace and Communion with the Apostolic See

The only-begotten Son of the Eternal Father, who came on earth to bring salvation and the light of divine wisdom to men, conferred a great and wonderful blessing on the world when, about to ascend again into heaven, He commanded the Apostles to go and teach all nations,[1] and left the Church which He had founded to be the common and supreme teacher of the peoples. For men whom the truth had set free were to be preserved by the truth; nor would the fruits of heavenly doctrines by which salvation comes to men have long remained had not the Lord Christ appointed an unfailing teaching authority to train the minds to faith. And the Church built upon the promises of its own divine Author, whose charity it imitated, so faithfully followed out His commands that its constant aim and chief wish was this: to teach religion and contend forever against errors. To this end assuredly have tended the incessant labors of individual bishops; to this end also the published laws and decrees of councils, and especially the constant watchfulness of the Roman Pontiffs, to whom, as successors of the blessed Peter in the primacy of the Apostles, belongs the right and office of teaching and confirming their brethren in the faith. Since, then, according to the warning of the apostle, the minds of Christ's faithful are apt to be deceived and the integrity of the faith to be corrupted among men by philosophy and vain deceit,[2] the supreme pastors of the Church have always thought it their duty to advance, by every means in their power, science truly so called, and at the same time to provide with special care that all studies should accord with the Catholic faith, especially philosophy, on which a right interpretation of the other sciences in great part depends. Indeed, venerable brethren, on this very subject among others, We briefly admonished you in Our first encyclical letter; but now, both by reason of the gravity of the subject and the condition of the time, we are again compelled to speak to you on the mode of taking up the study of philosophy which shall respond most fitly to the excellence of faith, and at the same time be consonant with the dignity of human science.

2. Whoso turns his attention to the bitter strifes of these days and seeks a reason for the troubles that vex public and private life must come to the conclusion that a fruitful cause of the evils which now afflict, as well as those which threaten, us lies in this: that false conclusions concerning divine and human things, which originated in the schools of philosophy, have now crept into all the orders of the State, and have been accepted by the common consent of the masses. For, since it is in the very nature of man to

follow the guide of reason in his actions, if his intellect sins at all his will soon follows; and thus it happens that false opinions, whose seat is in the understanding, influence human actions and pervert them. Whereas, on the other hand, if men be of sound mind and take their stand on true and solid principles, there will result a vast amount of benefits for the public and private good. We do not, indeed, attribute such force and authority to philosophy as to esteem it equal to the task of combating and rooting out all errors; for, when the Christian religion was first constituted, it came upon earth to restore it to its primeval dignity by the admirable light of faith, diffused "not by persuasive words of human wisdom, but in the manifestation of spirit and of power,"[3] so also at the present time we look above all things to the powerful help of Almighty God to bring back to a right understanding the minds of man and dispel the darkness of error.[4] But the natural helps with which the grace of the divine wisdom, strongly and sweetly disposing all things, has supplied the human race are neither to be despised nor neglected, chief among which is evidently the right use of philosophy. For, not in vain did God set the light of reason in the human mind; and so far is the super-added light of faith from extinguishing or lessening the power of the intelligence that it completes it rather, and by adding to its strength renders it capable of greater things.

3. Therefore, Divine Providence itself requires that, in calling back the people to the paths of faith and salvation, advantage should be taken of human science also—an approved and wise practice which history testifies was observed by the most illustrious Fathers of the Church. They, indeed, were wont neither to belittle nor undervalue the part that reason had to play, as is summed up by the great Augustine when he attributes to this science "that by which the most wholesome faith is begotten ... is nourished, defended, and made strong."[5]

4. In the first place, philosophy, if rightly made use of by the wise, in a certain way tends to smooth and fortify the road to true faith, and to prepare the souls of its disciples for the fit reception of revelation; for which reason it is well called by ancient writers sometimes a steppingstone to the Christian faith,[6] sometimes the prelude and help of Christianity,[7] sometimes the Gospel teacher.[8] And, assuredly, the God of all goodness, in all that pertains to divine things, has not only manifested by the light of faith those truths which human intelligence could not attain of itself, but others, also, not altogether unattainable by reason, that by the help of divine authority they may be made known to all at once and without any admixture of error. Hence it is that certain truths which were either divinely proposed for belief,

or were bound by the closest chains to the doctrine of faith, were discovered by pagan sages with nothing but their natural reason to guide them, were demonstrated and proved by becoming arguments. For, as the Apostle says, the invisible things of Him, from the creation of the world, are clearly seen, being understood by the things that are made: His eternal power also and divinity;[9] and the Gentiles who have not the Law show, nevertheless, the work of the Law written in their hearts.[10] But it is most fitting to turn these truths, which have been discovered by the pagan sages even, to the use and purposes of revealed doctrine, in order to show that both human wisdom and the very testimony of our adversaries serve to support the Christian faith—a method which is not of recent introduction, but of established use, and has often been adopted by the holy Fathers of the Church. What is more, those venerable men, the witnesses and guardians of religious traditions, recognize a certain form and figure of this in the action of the Hebrews, who, when about to depart out of Egypt, were commanded to take with them the gold and silver vessels and precious robes of the Egyptians, that by a change of use the things might be dedicated to the service of the true God which had formerly been the instruments of ignoble and superstitious rites. Gregory of NeoCaesarea[11] praises Origen expressly because, with singular dexterity, as one snatches weapons from the enemy, he turned to the defense of Christian wisdom and to the destruction of superstition many arguments drawn from the writings of the pagans. And both Gregory of Nazianzen[12] and Gregory of Nyssa[13] praise and commend a like mode of disputation in Basil the Great; while Jerome[14] especially commends it in Quadratus, a disciple of the Apostles, in Aristides, Justin, Irenaeus, and very many others. Augustine says: "Do we not see Cyprian, that mildest of doctors and most blessed of martyrs, going out of Egypt laden with gold and silver and vestments? And Lactantius, also and Victorinus, Optatus and Hilary? And, not to speak of the living, how many Greeks have done likewise?"[15] But if natural reason first sowed this rich field of doctrine before it was rendered fruitful by the power of Christ, it must assuredly become more prolific after the grace of the Saviour has renewed and added to the native faculties of the human mind. And who does not see that a plain and easy road is opened up to faith by such a method of philosophic study?

5. But the advantage to be derived from such a school of philosophy is not to be confined within these limits. The foolishness of those men who "by these good things that are seen could not understand Him, that is, neither by attending to the works could have acknowledged who was the workman,"[16] is gravely reproved in the words of Divine Wisdom. In the first

place, then, this great and noble fruit is gathered from human reason, that it demonstrates that God is; for the greatness of the beauty and of the creature the Creator of them may be seen so as to be known thereby.[17] Again, it shows God to excel in the height of all perfections, especially in infinite wisdom before which nothing lies hidden, and in absolute justice which no depraved affection could possibly shake; and that God, therefore, is not only true but truth itself, which can neither deceive nor be deceived. Whence it clearly follows that human reason finds the fullest faith and authority united in the word of God. In like manner, reason declares that the doctrine of the Gospel has even from its very beginning been made manifest by certain wonderful signs, the established proofs, as it were, of unshaken truth; and that all, therefore, who set faith in the Gospel do not believe rashly as though following cunningly devised fables,[18] but, by a most reasonable consent, subject their intelligence and judgment to an authority which is divine. And of no less importance is it that reason most clearly sets forth that the Church instituted by Christ (as laid down in the Vatican Council), on account of its wonderful spread, its marvellous sanctity, and its inexhaustible fecundity in all places, as well as of its Catholic unity and unshaken stability, is in itself a great and perpetual motive of belief and an irrefragable testimony of its own divine mission.[19]

6. Its solid foundations having been thus laid, a perpetual and varied service is further required of philosophy, in order that sacred theology may receive and assume the nature, form, and genius of a true science. For in this, the most noble of studies, it is of the greatest necessity to bind together, as it were, in one body the many and various parts of the heavenly doctrines, that, each being allotted to its own proper place and derived from its own proper principles, the whole may join together in a complete union; in order, in fine, that all and each part may be strengthened by its own and the others' invincible arguments. Nor is that more accurate or fuller knowledge of the things that are believed, and somewhat more lucid understanding, as far as it can go, of the very mysteries of faith which Augustine and the other fathers commended and strove to reach, and which the Vatican Council itself[20] declared to be most fruitful, to be passed over in silence or belittled. Those will certainly more fully and more easily attain that knowledge and understanding who to integrity of life and love of faith join a mind rounded and finished by philosophic studies, as the same Vatican Council teaches that the knowledge of such sacred dogmas ought to be sought as well from analogy of the things that are naturally known as from the connection of those mysteries one with another and with the final end of man.[21]

7. Lastly, the duty of religiously defending the truths divinely delivered, and of resisting those who dare oppose them, pertains to philosophic pursuits. Wherefore, it is the glory of philosophy to be esteemed as the bulwark of faith and the strong defense of religion. As Clement of Alexandria testifies, the doctrine of the Saviour is indeed perfect in itself and wanteth naught, since it is the power and wisdom of God. And the assistance of the Greek philosophy maketh not the truth more powerful; but, inasmuch as it weakens the contrary arguments of the sophists and repels the veiled attacks against the truth, it has been fitly called the hedge and fence of the vine.[22] For, as the enemies of the Catholic name, when about to attack religion, are in the habit of borrowing their weapons from the arguments of philosophers, so the defenders of sacred science draw many arguments from the store of philosophy which may serve to uphold revealed dogmas. Nor is the triumph of the Christian faith a small one in using human reason to repel powerfully and speedily the attacks of its adversaries by the hostile arms which human reason itself supplied. This species of religious strife St. Jerome, writing to Magnus, notices as having been adopted by the Apostle of the Gentiles himself; Paul, the leader of the Christian army and the invincible orator, battling for the cause of Christ, skillfully turns even a chance inscription into an argument for the faith; for he had learned from the true David to wrest the sword from the hands of the enemy and to cut off the head of the boastful Goliath with his own weapon.[23] Moreover, the Church herself not only urges, but even commands, Christian teachers to seek help from philosophy. For, the fifth Lateran Council, after it had decided that "every assertion contrary to the truth of revealed faith is altogether false, for the reason that it contradicts, however slightly, the truth,"[24] advises teachers of philosophy to pay close attention to the exposition of fallacious arguments; since, as Augustine testifies, "if reason is turned against the authority of sacred Scripture, no matter how specious it may seem, it errs in the likeness of truth; for true it cannot be."[25]

8. But in order that philosophy may be bound equal to the gathering of those precious fruits which we have indicated, it behooves it above all things never to turn aside from that path which the Fathers have entered upon from a venerable antiquity, and which the Vatican Council solemnly and authoritatively approved. As it is evident that very many truths of the supernatural order which are far beyond the reach of the keenest intellect must be accepted, human reason, conscious of its own infirmity, dare not affect to itself too great powers, nor deny those truths, nor measure them by its own standard, nor interpret them at will; but receive them, rather, with

a full and humble faith, and esteem it the highest honor to be allowed to wait upon heavenly doctrines like a handmaid and attendant, and by God's goodness attain to them in any way whatsoever. But in the case of such doctrines as the human intelligence may perceive, it is equally just that philosophy should make use of its own method, principles, and arguments—not, indeed, in such fashion as to seem rashly to withdraw from the divine authority. But, since it is established that those things which become known by revelation have the force of certain truth, and that those things which war against faith war equally against right reason, the Catholic philosopher will know that he violates at once faith and the laws of reason if he accepts any conclusion which he understands to be opposed to revealed doctrine.

9. We know that there are some who, in their overestimate of the human faculties, maintain that as soon as man's intellect becomes subject to divine authority it falls from its native dignity, and hampered by the yoke of this species of slavery, is much retarded and hindered in its progress toward the supreme truth and excellence. Such an idea is most false and deceptive, and its sole tendency is to induce foolish and ungrateful men wilfully to repudiate the most sublime truths, and reject the divine gift of faith, from which the fountains of all good things flow out upon civil society. For the human mind, being confined within certain limits, and those narrow enough, is exposed to many errors and is ignorant of many things; whereas the Christian faith, reposing on the authority of God, is the unfailing mistress of truth, whom whoso followeth he will be neither enmeshed in the snares of error nor tossed hither and thither on the waves of fluctuating opinion. Those, therefore, who to the study of philosophy unite obedience to the Christian faith, are philosophizing in the best possible way; for the splendor of the divine truths, received into the mind, helps the understanding, and not only detracts in nowise from its dignity, but adds greatly to its nobility, keenness, and stability. For surely that is a worthy and most useful exercise of reason when men give their minds to disproving those things which are repugnant to faith and proving the things which conform to faith. In the first case they cut the ground from under the feet of error and expose the viciousness of the arguments on which error rests; while in the second case they make themselves masters of weighty reasons for the sound demonstration of truth and the satisfactory instruction of any reasonable person. Whoever denies that such study and practice tend to add to the resources and expand the faculties of the mind must necessarily and absurdly hold that the mind gains nothing from discriminating between the true and the false. Justly, therefore, does the Vatican Council commemorate in these words the

great benefits which faith has conferred upon reason: Faith *frees* and saves reason *from error, and* endows it with *manifold* knowledge.[26] A wise man, therefore, would not accuse faith and look upon it as opposed to reason and natural truths, but would rather offer heartfelt thanks to God, and sincerely rejoice that, in the density of ignorance and in the flood-tide of error, holy faith, like a friendly star, shines down upon his path and points out to him the fair gate of truth beyond all danger of wandering.

. . .

17. Among the Scholastic Doctors, the chief and master of all towers Thomas Aquinas, who, as Cajetan observes, because "he most venerated the ancient doctors of the Church, in a certain way seems to have inherited the intellect of all."[27] The doctrines of those illustrious men, like the scattered members of a body, Thomas collected together and cemented, distributed in wonderful order, and so increased with important additions that he is rightly and deservedly esteemed the special bulwark and glory of the Catholic faith. With his spirit at once humble and swift, his memory ready and tenacious, his life spotless throughout, a lover of truth for its own sake, richly endowed with human and divine science, like the sun he heated the world with the warmth of his virtues and filled it with the splendor of his teaching. Philosophy has no part which he did not touch finely at once and thoroughly; on the laws of reasoning, on God and incorporeal substances, on man and other sensible things, on human actions and their principles, he reasoned in such a manner that in him there is wanting neither a full array of questions, nor an apt disposal of the various parts, nor the best method of proceeding, nor soundness of principles or strength of argument, nor clearness and elegance of style, nor a facility for explaining what is abstruse.

18. Moreover, the Angelic Doctor pushed his philosophic inquiry into the reasons and principles of things, which because they are most comprehensive and contain in their bosom, so to say, the seeds of almost infinite truths, were to be unfolded in good time by later masters and with a goodly yield. And as he also used this philosophic method in the refutation of error, he won this title to distinction for himself: that, single-handed, he victoriously combated the errors of former times, and supplied invincible arms to put those to rout which might in after-times spring up. Again, clearly distinguishing, as is fitting, reason from faith, while happily associating the one with the other, he both preserved the rights and had regard for the dignity of each; so much so, indeed, that reason, borne on the wings of Thomas to its human height, can scarcely rise higher, while faith could scarcely expect more or stronger aids from reason than those which she has already obtained through Thomas.

19. For these reasons most learned men, in former ages especially, of the highest repute in theology and philosophy, after mastering with infinite pains the immortal works of Thomas, gave themselves up not so much to be instructed in his angelic wisdom as to be nourished upon it. It is known that nearly all the founders and lawgivers of the religious orders commanded their members to study and religiously adhere to the teachings of St. Thomas, fearful least any of them should swerve even in the slightest degree from the footsteps of so great a man. To say nothing of the family of St. Dominic, which rightly claims this great teacher for its own glory, the statutes of the Benedictines, the Carmelites, the Augustinians, the Society of Jesus, and many others all testify that they are bound by this law.

20. And, here, how pleasantly one's thoughts fly back to those celebrated schools and universities which flourished of old in Europe—to Paris, Salamanca, Alcalá, to Douay, Toulouse, and Louvain, to Padua and Bologna, to Naples and Coimbra, and to many another! All know how the fame of these seats of learning grew with their years, and that their judgment, often asked in matters of grave moment, held great weight everywhere. And we know how in those great homes of human wisdom, as in his own kingdom, Thomas reigned supreme; and that the minds of all, of teachers as well as of taught, rested in wonderful harmony under the shield and authority of the Angelic Doctor.

21. But, furthermore, Our predecessors in the Roman pontificate have celebrated the wisdom of Thomas Aquinas by exceptional tributes of praise and the most ample testimonials. Clement VI in the bull *In Ordine;* Nicholas V in his brief to the friars of the Order of Preachers, 1451; Benedict XIII in the bull *Pretiosus,* and others bear witness that the universal Church borrows lustre from his admirable teaching; while St. Pius V declares in the bull *Mirabilis* that heresies, confounded and convicted by the same teaching, were dissipated, and the whole world daily freed from fatal errors; others, such as Clement XII in the bull *Verbo Dei,* affirm that most fruitful blessings have spread abroad from his writings over the whole Church, and that he is worthy of the honor which is bestowed on the greatest Doctors of the Church, on Gregory and Ambrose, Augustine and Jerome; while others have not hesitated to propose St. Thomas for the exemplar and master of the universities and great centers of learning whom they may follow with unfaltering feet. On which point the words of Blessed Urban V to the University of Toulouse are worthy of recall: "It is our will, which We hereby enjoin upon you, that ye follow the teaching of Blessed Thomas as the true and Catholic doctrine and that ye labor with all your force to profit by the

same."[28] Innocent XII, followed the example of Urban in the case of the University of Louvain, in the letter in the form of a brief addressed to that university on February 6, 1694, and Benedict XIV in the letter in the form of a brief addressed on August 26, 1752, to the Dionysian College in Granada; while to these judgments of great Pontiffs on Thomas Aquinas comes the crowning testimony of Innocent VI: "His teaching above that of others, the canonical writings alone excepted, enjoys such a precision of language, an order of matters, a truth of conclusions, that those who hold to it are never found swerving from the path of truth, and he who dare assail it will always be suspected of error."[29]

22. The ecumenical councils, also, where blossoms the flower of all earthly wisdom, have always been careful to hold Thomas Aquinas in singular honor. In the Councils of Lyons, Vienna, Florence, and the Vatican one might almost say that Thomas took part and presided over the deliberations and decrees of the Fathers, contending against the errors of the Greeks, of heretics and rationalists, with invincible force and with the happiest results. But the chief and special glory of Thomas, one which he has shared with none of the Catholic Doctors, is that the Fathers of Trent made it part of the order of conclave to lay upon the altar, together with sacred Scripture and the decrees of the supreme Pontiffs, the Summa of Thomas Aquinas, whence to seek counsel, reason, and inspiration.

23. A last triumph was reserved for this incomparable man—namely, to compel the homage, praise, and admiration of even the very enemies of the Catholic name. For it has come to light that there were not lacking among the leaders of heretical sects some who openly declared that, if the teaching of Thomas Aquinas were only taken away, they could easily battle with all Catholic teachers, gain the victory, and abolish the Church.[30] A vain hope, indeed, but no vain testimony.

24. Therefore, venerable brethren, as often as We contemplate the good, the force, and the singular advantages to be derived from his philosophic discipline which Our Fathers so dearly loved. We think it hazardous that its special honor should not always and everywhere remain, especially when it is established that daily experience, and the judgment of the greatest men, and, to crown all, the voice of the Church, have favored the Scholastic philosophy. Moreover, to the old teaching a novel system of philosophy has succeeded here and there, in which We fail to perceive those desirable and wholesome fruits which the Church and civil society itself would prefer. For it pleased the struggling innovators of the sixteenth century to philosophize without any respect for faith, the power of inventing in accordance with his

own pleasure and bent being asked and given in turn by each one. Hence, it was natural that systems of philosophy multiplied beyond measure, and conclusions differing and clashing one with another arose about those matters even which are the most important in human knowledge. From a mass of conclusions men often come to wavering and doubt; and who knows not how easily the mind slips from doubt to error? But, as men are apt to follow the lead given them, this new pursuit seems to have caught the souls of certain Catholic philosophers, who, throwing aside the patrimony of ancient wisdom, chose rather to build up a new edifice than to strengthen and complete the old by aid of the new—ill-advisedly, in sooth, and not without detriment to the sciences. For, a multiform system of this kind, which depends on the authority and choice of any professor, has a foundation open to change, and consequently gives us a philosophy not firm, and stable, and robust like that of old, but tottering and feeble. And if, perchance, it sometimes finds itself scarcely equal to sustain the shock of its foes, it should recognize that the cause and the blame lie in itself. In saying this We have no intention of discountenancing the learned and able men who bring their industry and erudition, and, what is more, the wealth of new discoveries, to the service of philosophy; for, of course, We understand that this tends to the development of learning. But one should be very careful lest all or his chief labor be exhausted in these pursuits and in mere erudition. And the same thing is true of sacred theology, which, indeed, may be assisted and illustrated by all kinds of erudition, though it is absolutely necessary to approach it in the grave manner of the Scholastics, in order that, the forces of revelation and reason being united in it, it may continue to be "the invincible bulwark of the faith."[31]

25. With wise forethought, therefore, not a few of the advocates of philosophic studies, when turning their minds recently to the practical reform of philosophy, aimed and aim at restoring the renowned teaching of Thomas Aquinas and winning it back to its ancient beauty.

26. We have learned with great joy that many members of your order, venerable brethren, have taken this plan to heart; and while We earnestly commend their efforts, We exhort them to hold fast to their purpose, and remind each and all of you that Our first and most cherished idea is that you should all furnish to studious youth a generous and copious supply of those purest streams of wisdom flowing inexhaustibly from the precious fountainhead of the Angelic Doctor.

27. Many are the reasons why We are so desirous of this. In the first place, then, since in the tempest that is on us the Christian faith is being

constantly assailed by the machinations and craft of a certain false wisdom, all youths, but especially those who are the growing hope of the Church, should be nourished on the strong and robust food of doctrine, that so, mighty in strength and armed at all points, they may become habituated to advance the cause of religion with force and judgment, "being ready always, according to the apostolic counsel, to satisfy every one that asketh you a reason of that hope which is in you,"[32] and that they may be able to exhort in sound doctrine and to convince the gainsayers.[33] Many of those who, with minds alienated from the faith, hate Catholic institutions, claim reason as their sole mistress and guide. Now, We think that, apart from the supernatural help of God, nothing is better calculated to heal those minds and to bring them into favor with the Catholic faith than the solid doctrine of the Fathers and the Scholastics, who so clearly and forcibly demonstrate the firm foundations of the faith, its divine origin, its certain truth, the arguments that sustain it, the benefits it has conferred on the human race, and its perfect accord with reason, in a manner to satisfy completely minds open to persuasion, however unwilling and repugnant.

28. Domestic and civil society even, which, as all see, is exposed to great danger from this plague of perverse opinions, would certainly enjoy a far more peaceful and secure existence if a more wholesome doctrine were taught in the universities and high schools—one more in conformity with the teaching of the Church, such as is contained in the works of Thomas Aquinas.

29. For, the teachings of Thomas on the true meaning of liberty, which at this time is running into license, on the divine origin of all authority, on laws and their force, on the paternal and just rule of princes, on obedience to the higher powers, on mutual charity one toward another—on all of these and kindred subjects—have very great and invincible force to overturn those principles of the new order which are well known to be dangerous to the peaceful order of things and to public safety. In short, all studies ought to find hope of advancement and promise of assistance in this restoration of philosophic discipline which We have proposed. The arts were wont to draw from philosophy, as from a wise mistress, sound judgment and right method, and from it, also, their spirit, as from the common fount of life. When philosophy stood stainless in honor and wise in judgment, then, as facts and constant experience showed, the liberal arts flourished as never before or since; but, neglected and almost blotted out, they lay prone, since philosophy began to lean to error and join hands with folly. Nor will the physical sciences themselves, which are now in such great repute, and by the renown of so many inventions draw such universal admiration to

themselves, suffer detriment, but find very great assistance in the restoration of the ancient philosophy. For, the investigation of facts and the contemplation of nature is not alone sufficient for their profitable exercise and advance; but, when facts have been established, it is necessary to rise and apply ourselves to the study of the nature of corporeal things, to inquire into the laws which govern them and the principles whence their order and varied unity and mutual attraction in diversity arise. To such investigations it is wonderful what force and light and aid the Scholastic philosophy, if judiciously taught, would bring.

30. And here it is well to note that our philosophy can only by the grossest injustice be accused of being opposed to the advance and development of natural science. For, when the Scholastics, following the opinion of the holy Fathers, always held in anthropology that the human intelligence is only led to the knowledge of things without body and matter by things sensible, they well understood that nothing was of greater use to the philosopher than diligently to search into the mysteries of nature and to be earnest and constant in the study of physical things. And this they confirmed by their own example; for St. Thomas, Blessed Albertus Magnus, and other leaders of the Scholastics were never so wholly rapt in the study of philosophy as not to give large attention to the knowledge of natural things; and, indeed, the number of their sayings and writings on these subjects, which recent professors approve of and admit to harmonize with truth, is by no means small. Moreover, in this very age many illustrious professors of the physical sciences openly testify that between certain and accepted conclusions of modern physics and the philosophic principles of the schools there is no conflict worthy of the name.

31. While, therefore, We hold that every word of wisdom, every useful thing by whomsoever discovered or planned, ought to be received with a willing and grateful mind, We exhort you, venerable brethren, in all earnestness to restore the golden wisdom of St. Thomas, and to spread it far and wide for the defense and beauty of the Catholic faith, for the good of society, and for the advantage of all the sciences. The wisdom of St. Thomas, We say; for if anything is taken up with too great subtlety by the Scholastic doctors, or too carelessly stated—if there be anything that ill agrees with the discoveries of a later age, or, in a word, improbable in whatever way— it does not enter Our mind to propose that for imitation to Our age. Let carefully selected teachers endeavor to implant the doctrine of Thomas Aquinas in the minds of students, and set forth clearly his solidity and excellence over others. Let the universities already founded or to be founded

by you illustrate and defend this doctrine, and use it for the refutation of prevailing errors. But, lest the false for the true or the corrupt for the pure be drunk in, be ye watchful that the doctrine of Thomas be drawn from his own fountains, or at least from those rivulets which, derived from the very fount, have thus far flowed, according to the established agreement of learned men, pure and clear; be careful to guard the minds of youth from those which are said to flow thence, but in reality are gathered from strange and unwholesome streams.

32. But well do We know that vain will be Our efforts unless, venerable brethren, He helps Our common cause who, in the words of divine Scripture, is called the God of all knowledge;[34] by which we are also admonished that "every best gift and every perfect gift is from above, coming down from the Father of lights",[35] and again: "If any of you want wisdom, let him ask of God, who giveth to all men abundantly, and upbraideth not: and it shall be given him."[36]

33. Therefore in this also let us follow the example of the Angelic Doctor, who never gave himself to reading or writing without first begging the blessing of God, who modestly confessed that whatever he knew he had acquired not so much by his own study and labor as by the divine gift; and therefore let us all, in humble and united prayer, beseech God to send forth the spirit of knowledge and of understanding to the children of the Church and open their senses for the understanding of wisdom. And that we may receive fuller fruits of the divine goodness, offer up to God the most efficacious patronage of the Blessed Virgin Mary, who is called the seat of wisdom; having at the same time as advocates St. Joseph, the most chaste spouse of the Virgin, and Peter and Paul, the chiefs of the Apostles, whose truth renewed the earth which had fallen under the impure blight of error, filling it with the light of heavenly wisdom.

34. In fine, relying on the divine assistance and confiding in your pastoral zeal, most lovingly We bestow on all of you, venerable brethren, on all the clergy and the flocks committed to your charge, the apostolic benediction as a pledge of heavenly gifts and a token of Our special esteem.

Given at St. Peter's, in Rome, the fourth day of August, 1879,
the second year of our pontificate.
Leo XIII

Review and Discussion Questions

1. For what reasons does Leo believe the Church's pastors bear "the duty to advance" philosophy?

2. What lesson does Leo draw from the Hebrew's theft of the Egyptian gold?

3. If "the doctrine of the savior is indeed perfect in itself" how can philosophy aid faith? And, what benefit does faith offer philosophy?

4. Name the reasons why Leo singles out Thomas as a guide?

5. In what ways would a renewal of Catholic teaching benefit the civil order?

6. Leo recommends the study of Thomas and the method of the scholastics. How ought a Catholic college approach the natural sciences?

G. K. CHESTERTON (1874–1936)

Orthodoxy

For the old humility made a man doubtful about his efforts, which might make him work harder. But the new humility makes a man doubtful about his aims, which will make him stop working altogether.

Himself much influenced by Pope Leo XIII, G. K. Chesterton is the wittiest of all twentieth-century Catholic apologists. Chesterton would not himself convert from Anglicanism until much later; but already in 1905 (at age 34), long before anyone had heard of "postmodernity," Chesterton had sifted the modern world and found it wanting. The root problem in our approach to learning and philosophy, so he claims, is not that modern agnostics are wicked. Rather, the problem is that for us sense has been severed from sensibility; our truth has become pitiless and our charity devoid of reason. Only a reunification of the old Christian virtues, argues Chesterton, would make possible the return to a practical philosophy of ethics and education that does not offend common sense.

Further Reading: G. K. Chesterton, "The Worship of Education" [1930] [sometimes reprinted "The Superstition of School"] in *The Collected Works of G. K. Chesterton*, ed. Lawrence Clipper, Vol. 35 (San Francisco: Ignatius Press, 1992), 295–99; Maisie Ward, *Gilbert Keith Chesterton* (Oxford: Sheed and Ward Books, 2006); John Haldane, "G. K. Chesterton on Education," in *Faithful Reason: Essays Catholic and Philosophical* (London: Routledge, 2004).

❖

The phrases of the street are not only forcible but subtle: for a figure of speech can often get into a crack too small for a definition. Phrases like "put out" or "off colour" might have been coined by Mr. Henry James in an agony of verbal precision. And there is no more subtle truth than that of the everyday phrase about a man having "his heart in the right place." It involves the idea of normal proportion; not only does a certain function exist, but it is rightly related to other functions. Indeed, the negation of this phrase would describe with peculiar accuracy the somewhat morbid mercy and perverse tenderness of the most representative moderns. If, for instance, I had to describe with fairness the character of Mr. Bernard Shaw, I could not express myself more exactly than by saying that he has a heroically large and generous heart; but not a heart in the right place. And this is so of the typical society of our time.

The modern world is not evil; in some ways the modern world is far too good. It is full of wild and wasted virtues. When a religious scheme is shattered (as Christianity was shattered at the Reformation), it is not merely the vices that are let loose. The vices are, indeed, let loose, and they wander and do damage. But the virtues are let loose also; and the virtues wander more wildly, and the virtues do more terrible damage. The modern world is full of the old Christian virtues gone mad. The virtues have gone mad because they have been isolated from each other and are wandering alone. Thus some scientists care for truth; and their truth is pitiless. Thus some humanitarians only care for pity; and their pity (I am sorry to say) is often untruthful. For example, Mr. Blatchford attacks Christianity because he is mad on one Christian virtue: the merely mystical and almost irrational virtue of charity. He has a strange idea that he will make it easier to forgive sins by saying that there are no sins to forgive. Mr. Blatchford is not only an early Christian, he is the only early Christian who ought really to have been eaten by lions. For in his case the pagan accusation is really true: his mercy would mean mere anarchy. He really is the enemy of the human race—because he is so human. As the other extreme, we may take the acrid realist, who has deliberately killed in himself all human pleasure in happy tales or in the healing of the heart. Torquemada tortured people physically for the sake of moral truth. Zola tortured people morally for the sake of physical truth. But in Torquemada's time there was at least a system that could to some extent make righteousness and peace kiss each other. Now they do not even bow. But a much stronger case than these two of truth and pity can be found in the remarkable case of the dislocation of humility.

It is only with one aspect of humility that we are here concerned. Humility was largely meant as a restraint upon the arrogance and infinity of the appetite of man. He was always outstripping his mercies with his own newly invented needs. His very power of enjoyment destroyed half his joys. By asking for pleasure, he lost the chief pleasure; for the chief pleasure is surprise. Hence it became evident that if a man would make his world large, he must be always making himself small. Even the haughty visions, the tall cities, and the toppling pinnacles are the creations of humility. Giants that tread down forests like grass are the creations of humility. Towers that vanish upwards above the loneliest star are the creations of humility. For towers are not tall unless we look up at them; and giants are not giants unless they are larger than we. All this gigantesque imagination, which is, perhaps, the mightiest of the pleasures of man, is at bottom entirely humble. It is impossible without humility to enjoy anything—even pride.

But what we suffer from to-day is humility in the wrong place. Modesty has moved from the organ of ambition. Modesty has settled upon the organ of conviction; where it was never meant to be. A man was meant to be doubtful about himself, but undoubting about the truth; this has been exactly reversed. Nowadays the part of a man that a man does assert is exactly the part he ought not to assert—himself. The part he doubts is exactly the part he ought not to doubt—the Divine Reason. Huxley preached a humility content to learn from Nature. But the new sceptic is so humble that he doubts if he can even learn. Thus we should be wrong if we had said hastily that there is no humility typical of our time. The truth is that there is a real humility typical of our time; but it so happens that it is practically a more poisonous humility than the wildest prostrations of the ascetic. The old humility was a spur that prevented a man from stopping; not a nail in his boot that prevented him from going on. For the old humility made a man doubtful about his efforts, which might make him work harder. But the new humility makes a man doubtful about his aims, which will make him stop working altogether.

At any street corner we may meet a man who utters the frantic and blasphemous statement that he may be wrong. Every day one comes across somebody who says that of course his view may not be the right one. Of course his view must be the right one, or it is not his view. We are on the road to producing a race of men too mentally modest to believe in the multiplication table. We are in danger of seeing philosophers who doubt the law of gravity as being a mere fancy of their own. Scoffers of old time were too proud to be convinced; but these are too humble to be convinced. The meek do inherit the earth; but the modern sceptics are too meek even to claim their inheritance. It is exactly this intellectual helplessness which is our second problem.

The last chapter has been concerned only with a fact of observation: that what peril of morbidity there is for man comes rather from his reason than his imagination. It was not meant to attack the authority of reason; rather it is the ultimate purpose to defend it. For it needs defence. The whole modern world is at war with reason; and the tower already reels.

The sages, it is often said, can see no answer to the riddle of religion. But the trouble with our sages is not that they cannot see the answer; it is that they cannot even see the riddle. They are like children so stupid as to notice nothing paradoxical in the playful assertion that a door is not a door. The modern latitudinarians speak, for instance, about authority in religion not only as if there were no reason in it, but as if there had never been any reason for it. Apart from seeing its philosophical basis, they cannot even see its historical cause. Religious authority has often, doubtless, been oppressive or unreasonable; just as every legal system (and especially our present one) has been callous and full of a cruel apathy. It is rational to attack the police; nay, it is glorious. But the modern critics of religious authority are like men who should attack the police without ever having heard of burglars. For there is a great and possible peril to the human mind: a peril as practical as burglary. Against it religious authority was reared, rightly or wrongly, as a barrier. And against it something certainly must be reared as a barrier, if our race is to avoid ruin.

That peril is that the human intellect is free to destroy itself. Just as one generation could prevent the very existence of the next generation, by all entering a monastery or jumping into the sea, so one set of thinkers can in some degree prevent further thinking by teaching the next generation that there is no validity in any human thought. It is idle to talk always of the alternative of reason and faith. Reason is itself a matter of faith. It is an act of faith to assert that our thoughts have any relation to reality at all. If you are merely a sceptic, you must sooner or later ask yourself the question, "Why should ANYTHING go right; even observation and deduction? Why should not good logic be as misleading as bad logic? They are both movements in the brain of a bewildered ape?" The young sceptic says, "I have a right to think for myself." But the old sceptic, the complete sceptic, says, "I have no right to think for myself. I have no right to think at all."

There is a thought that stops thought. That is the only thought that ought to be stopped. That is the ultimate evil against which all religious authority was aimed. It only appears at the end of decadent ages like our own: and already Mr. H. G. Wells has raised its ruinous banner; he has written a delicate piece of scepticism called "Doubts of the Instrument." In this he questions the brain itself, and endeavours to remove all reality from all his own assertions, past, present, and to come. But it was against this remote ruin that all the military systems in religion were originally ranked and ruled. The creeds and the crusades, the hierarchies and the horrible persecutions were not organized, as is ignorantly said, for the suppression of reason. They were organized for the difficult defence of reason. Man, by a blind instinct, knew that if once things were wildly questioned, reason could be questioned first. The authority of priests to absolve, the authority of popes to define the authority, even of inquisitors to terrify: these were all only dark defences erected round one central authority, more undemonstrable, more supernatural than all—the authority of a man to think. We know now that this is so; we have no excuse for not knowing it. For we can hear scepticism crashing through the old ring of authorities, and at the same moment we can see reason swaying upon her throne. In so far as religion is gone, reason is going. For they are both of the same primary and authoritative kind. They are both methods of proof which cannot themselves be proved. And in the act of destroying the idea of Divine authority we have largely destroyed the idea of that human authority by which we do a long-division sum. With a long and sustained tug we have attempted to pull the mitre off pontifical man; and his head has come off with it.

Lest this should be called loose assertion, it is perhaps desirable, though dull, to run rapidly through the chief modern fashions of thought which have this effect of stopping thought itself. Materialism and the view of everything as a personal illusion have some such effect; for if the mind is mechanical, thought cannot be very exciting, and if the cosmos is unreal, there is nothing to think about. But in these cases the effect is indirect and doubtful. In some cases it is direct and clear; notably in the case of what is generally called evolution.

Evolution is a good example of that modern intelligence which, if it destroys anything, destroys itself. Evolution is either an innocent scientific description of how certain earthly things came about; or, if it is anything more than this, it is an attack upon thought itself. If evolution destroys anything, it does not destroy religion but rationalism. If evolution simply means that a positive thing called an ape turned very slowly into a positive thing called a man, then it is stingless for the most orthodox; for a personal God might just as well do things slowly as quickly, especially if, like the Christian God, he were outside time. But if it means anything more, it means that there is no such thing as an ape to change, and no such thing as a man for him to change into. It means that there is no such thing as a thing. At best, there is only one thing, and that is a flux of everything and anything. This is an attack not upon the faith, but upon the mind; you cannot think if there are no things to think about. You cannot think if you are not separate from the subject of thought. Descartes said, "I think; therefore I am." The philosophic evolutionist reverses and negatives the epigram. He says, "I am not; therefore I cannot think."

Then there is the opposite attack on thought: that urged by Mr. H. G. Wells when he insists that every separate thing is "unique," and there are no categories at all. This also is merely destructive. Thinking means connecting things, and stops if they cannot be connected. It need hardly be said that this scepticism forbidding thought necessarily forbids speech; a man cannot open his mouth without contradicting it. Thus when Mr. Wells says (as he did somewhere), "All chairs are quite different," he utters not merely a misstatement, but a contradiction in terms. If all chairs were quite different, you could not call them "all chairs." Akin to these is the false theory of progress, which maintains that we alter the test instead of trying to pass the test. We often hear it said, for instance, "What is right in one age is wrong in another." This is quite reasonable, if it means that there is a fixed aim, and that certain methods attain at certain times and not at other times. If women, say, desire to be elegant, it may be that they are improved at one time by growing fatter and at another time by growing thinner. But you cannot say that they are improved by ceasing to wish to be elegant and beginning to wish to be oblong. If the standard changes, how can there be improvement, which implies a standard? Nietzsche started a nonsensical idea that men had once sought as good what we now call evil; if it were so, we could not talk of surpassing or even falling short of them. How can you overtake Jones if you walk in the other direction? You cannot discuss whether one people has succeeded more in being miserable than another succeeded in being happy. It would be like discussing whether Milton was more puritanical than a pig is fat.

It is true that a man (a silly man) might make change itself his object or ideal. But as an ideal, change itself becomes unchangeable. If the change-worshipper wishes to estimate his own progress, he must be sternly loyal to the ideal of change; he must not begin to flirt gaily with the ideal of monotony. Progress itself cannot progress. It is worth remark, in passing, that when Tennyson, in a wild and rather weak manner, welcomed the idea of infinite alteration in society, he instinctively took a metaphor which suggests an imprisoned tedium. He wrote: "Let the great world spin for ever down the ringing grooves of change." He thought of change itself as an unchangeable groove; and so it is. Change is about the narrowest and hardest groove that a man can get into.

The main point here, however, is that this idea of a fundamental alteration in the standard is one of the things that make thought about the past or future simply impossible. The theory of a complete change of standards in human history does not merely deprive us of the pleasure of honouring our fathers; it deprives us even of the more modern and aristocratic pleasure of despising them.

This bald summary of the thought-destroying forces of our time would not be complete without some reference to pragmatism; for though I have here used and should everywhere defend the pragmatist method as a preliminary guide to truth, there is an extreme application of it which involves the absence of all truth whatever. My meaning can be put shortly thus. I agree with the pragmatists that apparent objective truth is not the whole matter; that there is an authoritative need to believe the things that are necessary to the human mind. But I say that one of those necessities precisely is a belief in objective truth. The pragmatist tells a man to think what he must think and never mind the Absolute. But precisely one of the things that he must think is the Absolute. This philosophy, indeed, is a kind of verbal paradox. Pragmatism is a matter of human needs; and one of the first of human needs is to be something more than a pragmatist. Extreme pragmatism is just as inhuman as the determinism it so powerfully attacks. The determinist (who, to do him justice, does not pretend to be a human being) makes nonsense of the human sense of actual choice. The pragmatist, who professes to be specially human, makes nonsense of the human sense of actual fact.

To sum up our contention so far, we may say that the most characteristic current philosophies have not only a touch of mania, but a touch of suicidal mania. The mere questioner has knocked his head against the limits of human thought; and cracked it. This is what makes so futile the warnings of the orthodox and the boasts of the advanced about the dangerous boyhood of free thought. What we are looking at is not the boyhood of free thought; it is the old age and ultimate dissolution of free thought. It is vain for bishops and pious bigwigs to discuss what dreadful things will happen if wild scepticism runs its course. It has run its course. It is vain for eloquent atheists to talk of the great truths that will be revealed if once we see free thought begin. We have seen it end. It has no more questions to ask; it has questioned itself. You cannot call up any wilder vision than a city in which men ask themselves if they have any selves. You cannot fancy a more sceptical world than that in which men doubt if there is a world. It might certainly have reached its bankruptcy more quickly and cleanly if it had not been feebly hampered by the application of indefensible laws of blasphemy or by the absurd pretence that modern England is Christian. But it would have reached the bankruptcy anyhow. Militant atheists are still unjustly persecuted; but rather because they are an old minority than because they are a new one. Free thought has exhausted its own freedom. It is weary of its own success. If any eager freethinker now hails philosophic freedom as the dawn, he is only like the man in Mark Twain who came out wrapped in blankets to see the sun rise and was just in time to see it set. If any frightened curate still says that it will be awful if the darkness of free thought should spread, we can only answer him in the high and powerful words of Mr. Belloc, "Do not, I beseech you, be troubled about the increase of forces already in dissolution. You have mistaken the hour of the night: it is already morning." We have no more questions left to ask. We have looked for questions in the darkest corners and on the wildest peaks. We have found all the questions that can be found. It is time we gave up looking for questions and began looking for answers.

But one more word must be added. At the beginning of this preliminary negative sketch I said that our mental ruin has been wrought by wild reason, not by wild imagination. A man does not go mad because he makes a statue a mile high, but he may go mad by thinking it out in square inches. Now, one school of thinkers has seen this and jumped at it as a way of renewing the pagan health of the world. They see that reason destroys; but Will, they say, creates. The ultimate authority, they say, is in will, not in reason. The supreme point is not why a man demands a thing, but the fact that he does demand it. I have no space to trace or expound this philosophy of Will. It came, I suppose, through Nietzsche, who preached something that is called egoism. That, indeed, was simpleminded enough; for Nietzsche denied egoism simply by preaching it. To preach anything is to give it away. First, the egoist calls life a war without mercy, and then he takes the greatest possible trouble to drill his enemies in war. To preach egoism is to practise altruism. But however it began, the view is common enough in current literature. The main defence of these thinkers is that they are not thinkers; they are makers. They say that choice is itself the divine thing. Thus Mr. Bernard Shaw has attacked the old idea that men's acts are to be judged by the standard of the desire of happiness. He says that a man does not act for his happiness, but from his will. He does not say, "Jam will make me happy," but "I want jam." And in all this others follow him with yet greater enthusiasm. Mr. John Davidson, a remarkable poet, is so passionately excited about it that he is obliged to write prose. He publishes a short play with several long prefaces. This is natural enough in Mr. Shaw, for all his plays are prefaces: Mr. Shaw is (I suspect) the only man on earth who has never written any poetry. But that Mr. Davidson (who can write excellent poetry) should write instead laborious metaphysics in defence of this doctrine of will, does show that the doctrine of will has taken hold of men. Even Mr. H. G. Wells has half spoken in its language; saying that one should test acts not like a thinker, but like an artist, saying, "I FEEL this curve is right," or "that line SHALL go thus." They are all excited; and well they may be. For by this doctrine of the divine authority of will, they think they can break out of the doomed fortress of rationalism. They think they can escape.

But they cannot escape. This pure praise of volition ends in the same break up and blank as the mere pursuit of logic. Exactly as complete free thought involves the doubting of thought itself, so the acceptation of mere "willing" really paralyzes the will. Mr. Bernard Shaw has not perceived the real difference between the old utilitarian test of pleasure (clumsy, of course, and easily misstated) and that which he propounds. The real difference between the test of happiness and the test of will is simply that the test of happiness is a test and the other isn't. You can discuss whether a man's act in jumping over a cliff was directed towards happiness; you cannot discuss whether it was derived from will. Of course it was. You can praise an action by saying that it is calculated to bring pleasure or pain to discover truth or to save the soul. But you cannot praise an action because it shows will; for to say that is merely to say that it is an action. By this praise of will you cannot really choose one course as better than another. And yet choosing one course as better than another is the very definition of the will you are praising.

The worship of will is the negation of will. To admire mere choice is to refuse to choose. If Mr. Bernard Shaw comes up to me and says, "Will something," that is tantamount to saying, "I do not mind what you will," and that is tantamount to saying, "I have no will in the matter." You cannot admire will in general, because the essence of will is that it is particular. A brilliant anarchist like Mr. John Davidson feels an irritation against ordinary morality, and therefore he invokes will—will to anything. He only wants humanity to want something. But humanity does want something. It wants ordinary morality. He rebels against the law and tells us to will something or anything. But we have willed something. We have willed the law against which he rebels.

All the will-worshippers, from Nietzsche to Mr. Davidson, are really quite empty of volition. They cannot will, they can hardly wish. And if anyone wants a proof of this, it can be found quite easily. It can be found in this fact: that they always talk of will as something that expands and breaks out. But it is quite the opposite. Every act of will is an act of self-limitation. To desire action is to desire limitation. In that sense every act is an act of self-sacrifice. When you choose anything, you reject everything else. That objection, which men of this school used to make to the act of marriage, is really an objection to every act. Every act is an irrevocable selection and exclusion. Just as when you marry one woman you give up all the others, so when you take one course of action you give up all the other courses. If you become King of England, you give up the post of Beadle in Brompton. If you go to Rome, you sacrifice a rich suggestive life in Wimbledon. It is the existence of this negative or limiting side of will that makes most of the talk of the anarchic will-worshippers little better than nonsense. For instance, Mr. John Davidson tells us to have nothing to do with "Thou shalt not"; but it is surely obvious that "Thou shalt not" is only one of the necessary corollaries of "I will." "I will go to the Lord Mayor's Show, and thou shalt not stop me." Anarchism adjures us to be bold creative artists, and care for no laws or limits. But it is impossible to be an artist and not care for laws and limits. Art is limitation; the essence of every picture is the frame. If you draw a giraffe, you must draw him with a long neck. If, in your bold creative way, you hold yourself free to draw a giraffe with a short neck, you will really find that you are not free to draw a giraffe. The moment you step into the world of facts, you step into a world of limits. You can free things from alien or accidental laws, but not from the laws of their own nature. You may, if you like, free a tiger from his bars; but do not free him from his stripes. Do not free a camel of the burden of his hump: you may be freeing him from being a camel. Do not go about as a demagogue, encouraging triangles to break out of the prison of their three sides. If a triangle breaks out of its three sides, its life comes to a lamentable end. Somebody wrote a work called "The Loves of the Triangles"; I never read it, but I am sure that if triangles ever were loved, they were loved for being triangular. This is certainly the case with all artistic creation, which is in some ways the most decisive example of pure will. The artist loves his limitations: they constitute the THING he is doing. The painter is glad that the canvas is flat. The sculptor is glad that the clay is colourless.

Review and Discussion Questions

1. Chesterton claims "the modern world is not evil." What, then, is deficient in its approach to ethics?

2. On the matter of learning, Chesterton charges moderns with having the wrong sort of humility. What is the right sort?

3. What social harm does "the complete sceptic" inflict?

4. Moral relativists often claim that scepticism liberates. What—according to Chesterton—is constricting about the view that "moral standards always change"?

5. Why does Chesterton regard Nietzsche's view of the will as laughable?

❖ 28

RONALD KNOX (1888–1957)

On Christian Education

> We thought, perhaps, that in such an age of intellectual bewilderment He
> would send us a second St. Thomas, to solve our difficulties for us. He sent
> us, instead, Soeur Thérèse, to teach us that they were not the point.

Another twentieth-century Anglo-Catholic convert, Fr. Knox is perhaps best known for his translation of the English Bible (1955). A brilliant classicist and popular apologist—whose life is amiably recounted by Evelyn Waugh—his career focused, like Newman's, upon education. Also like Newman, Knox was an Oxford scholar, and he served as chaplain to the university's Catholic students between 1926 and 1939. Below he applies his gift of speech to the aid of London's Oratory school. He sets before his readers this puzzle: while intelligence is not necessary to sanctity, yet believers have always seen it fit to educate their young children carefully. If charity is the highest virtue, why do Christians invest lavishly in learning? As Knox argues, a child will be educated by someone. Believers must be simple, but not simplistic. In this age of unbelief, not tending to their formation is to condemn them to the world's deformation.

Further reading: Ronald Knox, *The Creed in Slow Motion* (Notre Dame, Ind.: Ave Maria Press, 2009); Evelyn Waugh, *Two Lives: Edmund Campion and Ronald Knox* (London: Continuum Press, 2005); Joseph Pearce, *Literary Converts: Spiritual Inspiration in an Age of Unbelief* (San Francisco: Ignatius Press, 2006).

❖

> Do not be boyish in your understanding, but be as children in respect of
> wickedness.
>
> CORINTHIANS 14.20

The Fathers of the Oratory have asked me to make an appeal this morning for their schools. And it might seem at first sight as if there could be no more appropriate day of the year for the launching of such an appeal as that.

We are commemorating, today, St. Teresa of Lisieux, the saint who found her vocation so young—found it so young that she never really managed to grow old, but lived through the short years of her maturity as the playmate of the Child Jesus, went to heaven with the eagerness of a schoolgirl just coming home for the holidays, preached to us, and preaches to us, the way of childhood as her own beautiful short cut to perfection. What could be more natural (we ask) than to plead, on such a festival, the cause of those generations of children who will derive benefit from the schools of this parish? What need is more likely to win alms from your charity, while such memories are still warm in your hearts, than the need of the very young?

At first sight, yes; but second thoughts bring with them a hesitation. That saint, who remained so childlike to the end, who clung so obstinately to the outlook of childhood, as the sovereign way of approaching Almighty God—would she really have been interested, or rather, is she really interested, in our schemes for educating children out of their childishness, and turning them into grown-up men and women? The gospel of her feast is the gospel in which our Lord warns us that we cannot enter the kingdom of heaven except as children; the collect of her feast, alone I think of all the prayers in the Church's liturgy, asks that we may follow the example of her simplicity—the simplicity of a child. What is the use of encouraging children to grow older, if the grand lesson of life is, after all, to learn to be as young as they?

Don't think that I am raising a mere debating point. It is, I think, intensely significant that the Church should have discovered, in these last years, a fresh jewel in the crown our Lord wears; discovered it, not because it was never there before, but because we never saw the glint of it till it was mirrored for us in the life of Soeur Thérèse. It was, and is, an over-educated age that needs to sit at the feet of an under-educated saint. We must go to her for lessons in simplicity, because our own brains are tired out and distracted by the multiplicity of the world in which we live; its clashing interests, its jarring battle-cries, its irreconcilable philosophies. We have got to learn that the way to God for this or that soul is not through comparing and contrasting all these rival claims upon our intellectual adhesion, making a synthesis of them and reducing them to a theology. The way to God lies in turning our backs on these images, shutting our ears to these interruptions, and adhering to him by a simple, personal approach, by cultivating a sense of that intimacy by which he mikes himself immediately present to the Christian soul. We thought, perhaps, that in such an age of intellectual bewilderment he would send us a second St. Thomas, to solve our difficulties for us. He sent us, instead, Soeur Thérèse, to teach us that they were not the point.

If you come to think of it, there is this curious paradox running through the whole history of Christian piety—that holy people have always despised the intellect, and yet they have been the first and the greatest educators of the world.

From the earliest times, the Church would never countenance the idea that getting to heaven had anything to do with passing examination papers. It was part of the heretical tendency which she noticed in the Alexandrines, Clement and Origen, that they set too much store by theology. We are all familiar with that in the *Imitation of Christ*. "I would rather feel compunction, (says its author) than know how to defend compunction. If you knew all the Bible by heart, and all the sayings of the philosophers, what would it all profit you, without the love of God? ... When the day of judgment comes, we shall not be asked what we have read, but what we have done, not how well we have spoken, but how devoutly we have lived," and so on. And yet as I say the saints have always been educators, from St Benedict to St John Bosco; to be sure, their main design was to train souls for heaven, but their method of doing it, again and again, has been to collect all the ragged boys they could find and educate them. Teach them the catechism, yes, but teach them the three R's as well.

Even St. Philip, who loved above all things to be a fool for Christ's sake, and told us that the whole of perfection lay in mortifying the intellect, would have boys running about the place and distracting him, because he saw that was the best way of keeping them out of mischief. And now his spiritual descendants, the Fathers of the Oratory, whose prime duty it is to preach the Gospel in such a way that it can be understood by simple and unlettered people, come to you hat in hand and ask you to contribute to a fund for making the children of their neighbourhood less simple and less unlettered. How are we to get to the bottom of it?

Well, I have tried to solve that difficulty beforehand by using the words which I took as my text. St. Paul says that we are not to be boys in our understanding; it is in respect of malice that we are to be as little children. He does not want us to arrest our mental development at the age of twelve, that will do no good; we are to arrest our development in wickedness at about the age of six. And, you know, St. Paul was not a man who overvalued the intellect. He was a university man, and learned in the Jewish law; and he did once, at Athens, try to preach a severely intellectual sermon, to what he thought was rather a high-brow audience—but it was not a great success.

When he went on to Corinth, immediately afterwards, he came to them, as he says, not preaching the words of human wisdom, but Christ the power of God and the wisdom of God. The love of Christ, he tells us, is to bring our intellects into captivity; there are not many wise, not many mighty, that take a high place in the kingdom of heaven. Yet, in writing to these same Corinthians, he is careful to claim that there is something to be said for cultivating our mental powers. He wants us to be like children, but in saying that he means that we are to be innocent, not that we are to be ignorant; in understanding we must be men.

Why does he say that? Why is it that he wants Christians, after all, to be intelligent Christians? I think there is an obvious answer, which applies perhaps even more strongly in our day than it did in his. Christian children must be educated into Christian men and women, because it would be impossible, in the ordinary circumstances of our human life, to arrest their mental development altogether. If we don't educate our children someone else will. In our day, of course, the someone else is the State; and the State, we can be quite certain, will make a hash of it, even if it does try and teach our children to be Christians; why, even when it tries to educate them so as to be loyal citizens, the State makes a hash of it. And even if the State didn't step in, our children would get educated all right, I mean, our children would get educated all wrong, so long as they had learned to read. The cinemas would educate them, the cheap newspapers would educate them, the advertisement hoardings would educate them. We go about, nowadays, being educated all the time, whether we want it or not; if we shut our eyes to get away from the thing, the wireless or the gramophone comes and shouts into our ears, educating us still. And what an education! So much fine talking, so many unimpeachable sentiments about honesty is the best policy and kindness to animals and the League of Nations; but no word of God, no word of sin, no word of the Sacraments—nothing that will help man to attain the supernatural end which is the true end of his being. If our children are to hear about that, it is from us that they must hear it.

And notice this—the appeals which are being made to your charity nowadays on behalf of Catholic schools are not so much appeals on behalf of the very simple, for fear they should not be educated at all. They are made, mostly, owing to recent movements in legislation, on behalf of those rather brighter boys and girls who deserve, in view of the talents they show and the opportunities which open out before them, to receive a finer, a more complete education than the rest. And these are the people who in a sense matter most of all; for it is these who, as their minds open to fresh avenues of knowledge, will come up more than the rest against the spirit of our age, be more exposed to its false doctrines. If we had only the children of the very poor to care about, it wouldn't matter so much; they couldn't learn much even if they tried. And if we had only the children of the very rich to care about, it wouldn't matter so much; they wouldn't try to learn much even if they could. But it is the children who have brains, who mean to get on and to better their position, who are in most danger of drifting away, culpably, from their religion. And it is to save these, above all, that the Oratory Fathers are appealing to you.

Well, you won't expect a report and balance sheet as the peroration of a sermon. It is enough to say that the Central Schools have already cost over thirty thousand pounds; that the Community itself, lest the parish should be unduly burdened, found more than twelve thousand pounds of that money, and that the debt still stands at over nine thousand. And now, owing to the new regulations which the Board of Education is bringing into force, it will be necessary to find another seven thousand five hundred to meet the new requirements; which means that well over fifteen thousand has got to come from somewhere. Some of it is in your pocket now; is in your handbag now. Nobody loves to give money for educational purposes, because nobody believes that he or she was educated as well as they might have been. But it is not to provide mere book-learning for our Catholic children that this appeal is made. It is made, so that the children who are going to be educated whatever happens may be educated with a chance of learning that love of God, that intelligent devotion to the things of God, which will make it possible for them to adjust their religious ideas to their whole mental environment; which will foster, please God, amidst all that multiplicity which the needs of the modern life demand, that spirit of simplicity which comes, and comes only, from living close to him. May the Child Jesus, and the Blessed Mother from whom he learned his first lessons at Nazareth, move your hearts to charity for the glory of God and the preservation, in these perplexing times, of our holy faith.

Review and Discussion Questions

1. What initial objection to the idea of Christian education does Knox raise?

2. In your own words, rephrase Knox's counsel that "we are to be innocent, not ... ignorant."

3. What negative conduits of cultural formation does Knox cite?

4. What makes Knox's final appeal for support for Catholic education effective?

❖ 29

C. S. LEWIS (1898–1963)

Learning in War-Time

Good philosophy must exist, if for no other reason, because bad philosophy needs to be answered.

The old Barbarians wielded swords and clubs. The new ones, too, may carry guns, but they are just as likely to work in labs with computers. A moving encomium to liberal learning delivered on the eve of World War II, Lewis's sermon is a tribute to the enduring value of culture in a time of incivility. Western civilization has tottered on the brink of collapse before. As our age enters its own dark night, we can be confident, Lewis counsels, that the only lasting drama is the conflict of the soul. As long as we draw breath, as long as the Lord grants day, Christians must work to carry the candle of learning—not merely of technique—and of goodness.

Further Reading: C. S. Lewis, *The Abolition of Man* (New York: HarperOne, 2001); R. L. Green and Walter Hooper, *C. S. Lewis: A Biography* (London: Harvest Books, 1994); Humphrey Carpenter, *The Inklings* (London: HarperCollins, 2006).

❖

A University is a society for the pursuit of learning. As students, you will be expected to make yourselves, or to start making yourselves, in to what the Middle Ages called clerks: into philosophers, scientists, scholars, critics, or historians. And at first sight this seems to be an odd thing to do during a great war. What is the use of beginning a task which we have so little chance of finishing? Or, even if we ourselves should happen not to be interrupted by death or military service,why should we—indeed how can we—continue to take an interest in these placid occupations when the lives of our friends and the liberties of Europe are in the balance? Is it not like fiddling while Rome burns?

Now it seems to me that we shall not be able to answer these questions until we have put them by the side of certain other questions which every

Christian ought to have asked himself in peace-time. I spoke just now of fiddling while Rome burns. But to a Christian the true tragedy of Nero must be not that he fiddles while the city was on fire but that he fiddles on the brink of hell. You must forgive me for the crude monosyllable. I know that many wiser and better Christians than I in these days do not like to mention heaven and hell even in a pulpit. I know, too, that nearly all the references to this subject in the New Testament come from a single source. But then that source is Our Lord Himself. People will tell you it is St. Paul, but that is untrue. These overwhelming doctrines are dominical. They are not really removable from the teaching of Christ or of His Church.

If we do not believe them, our presence in this church is great tom-foolery. If we do, we must sometime overcome our spiritual prudery and mention them. The moment we do so we can see that every Christian who comes to a university must at all times face a question compared with which the questions raised by the war are relatively unimportant. He must ask himself how it is right, or even psychologically possible, for creatures who are every moment advancing either to heaven or to hell, to spend any fraction of the little time allowed them in this world on such comparative trivialities as literature or art, mathematics or biology. If human culture can stand up to that, it can stand up to anything. To admit that we can retain our interest in learning under the shadow of these eternal issues, but not under the shadow of a European war, would be to admit that our ears are closed to the voice of reason.…

Under the aegis of His Church, and in the most Christian ages, learning and the arts flourish. The solution of this paradox is, of course, well known to you. "Whether ye eat or drink or whatsoever ye do, do all to the glory of God." All our merely natural activities will be accepted, if they are offered to God, even the humblest: and all of them, even the noblest, will be sinful if they are not.…

We are now in a position to answer the view that human culture is an inexcusable frivolity on the part of creatures loaded with such awful re-sponsibilities as we. I reject at once an idea which lingers in the mind of some modern people that cultural activities are in their own right spiritual and meritorious—as though scholars and poets were intrinsically more pleasing to God than scavengers and bootblacks. I think it was Matthew Arnold who first used the English word spiritual in the sense of the German geistlich, and so inaugurated this most dangerous and most anti-Christian error. Let us clear it forever from our minds. The work of a Beethoven, and the work of a charwoman, become spiritual on precisely the same condition, that of being offered to God, of being done humbly "as to the Lord." This does not, of course, mean that it is for anyone a mere toss-up whether he should sweep rooms or compose symphonies. A mole must dig to the glory of God and a cock must crow. We are members of one body, but differentiated members, each with his own vocation. A man's upbringing, his talents, his circumstances are usually a tolerable index of his vocation. If our parents have sent us to Oxford, if our country allows us to remain there, this is prima facie evidence that the life which we, at any rate, can best lead to the glory of God at present is the learned life.

By leading that life to the glory of God I do not, of course, mean any attempt to make our intellectual inquiries work out to edifying conclusions. That would be, as Bacon says, to offer to the author of truth the unclean sacrifice of a lie. I mean the pursuit of knowledge and beauty, in a sense, for their own sake, but in a sense which does not exclude their being for God's sake. An appetite for these things exists in the human mind, and God makes no appetite in vain. We can therefore pursue knowledge as such, and beauty, as such, in the sure confidence that by so doing we are either advancing to the vision of God ourselves or indirectly helping others to do so. Humility, no less than the appetite, encourages us to concentrate simply on the knowledge or the beauty, not too much concerning ourselves with their ultimate relevance to the vision of God. That relevance may not be intended for us but for our betters—for men who come after and find the spiritual significance of what we dug out in blind and humble obedience to our vocation. This is the teleological argument that the existence of the impulse and the faculty prove that they must have a proper function in God's scheme—the argument by which Thomas Aquinas proves that sexuality would have existed even without the Fall. The soundness of the argument, as regards culture, is proved by experience. The intellectual life is not the only road to God, nor the safest, but we find it to be a road, and it may be the appointed road for us. Of course it will be so only so long as we keep the impulse pure and disinterested. That is the great difficulty. As the author of the *Theologia Germanicai* says, we may come to love knowledge—our knowing—more than the thing known: to delight not in the exercise of our talents but in the fact that they are ours, or even in the reputation they bring us. Every success in the scholar's life increases this danger. If it becomes irresistible, he must give up his scholarly work. The time for plucking the right eye has arrived.

That is the essential nature of the learned life as I see it. But it has indirect values which are especially important today. If all the world were Christian, it might not matter if all the world were uneducated. But, as it is, a cultural life will exist outside the Church whether it exists inside or not. To be ignorant and simple now—not to be able to meet the enemies on their own ground—would be to throw down our weapons, and to betray our uneducated brethren who have, under God, no defense but us against the intellectual attacks of the heathen. Good philosophy must exist, if for no other reason, because bad philosophy needs to be answered. The cool intellect must work not only against cool intellect on the other side, but against the muddy heathen mysticisms which deny intellect altogether.

Most of all, perhaps we need intimate knowledge of the past. Not that the past has any magic about it, but because we cannot study the future, and yet need something to set against the present, to remind us that periods and that much which seems certain to the uneducated is merely temporary fashion. A man who has lived in many a place is not likely to be deceived by the local errors of his native village: the scholar has lived in many times and is therefore in some degree immune from the great cataract of nonsense that pours from the press and the microphone of his own age.

The learned life then is, for some, a duty. At the moment it looks as if it were your duty. I am well aware that there may seem to be an almost comic discrepancy between the high issues we have been considering and the immediate task you may be set down to, such as Anglo-Saxon sound laws or chemical formulae. But there is a similar shock awaiting us in every vocation—a young priest finds himself involved in choir treats and a young subaltern in accounting for pots of jam. It is well that it should be so. It weeds out the vain, windy people and keeps in those who are both humble and tough. On that kind of difficulty we need waste no sympathy.

But the peculiar difficulty imposed on you by the war is another matter: and of it I would again repeat, what I have been saying in one form or another ever since I started—do not let your nerves and emotions lead you into thinking your present predicament more abnormal than it really is. Perhaps it may be useful to mention the three mental exercises which may serve as defenses against the three enemies which war raises up against the scholar. The first enemy is excitement—the tendency to think and feel about the war when we had intended to think about our work. The best defense is a recognition that in this, as in everything else, the war has not really raised up a new enemy but only aggravated an old one. There are always plenty of rivals to our work. We are always falling in love or quarreling, looking for jobs or fearing to lose them, getting ill and recovering, following public affairs. If we let ourselves, we shall always be waiting for some distraction or other to end before we can really get down to our work. The only people who achieve much are those who want knowledge so badly that they seek it while the conditions are still unfavorable. Favorable conditions never come. There are, of course, moments when the pressure of the excitement is so great that any superhuman self-control could not resist it. They come both in war and peace. We must do the best we can.

The second enemy is frustration—the feeling that we shall not have time to finish. If I say to you that no one has time to finish, that the longest human life leaves a man, in any branch of learning, a beginner, I shall seem to you to be saying something quite academic and theoretical. You would be surprised if you knew how soon one begins to feel the shortness of the tether: of how many things, even in middle life, we have to say "No time for that," "Too late now," and "Not for me." But Nature herself forbids you to share that experience. A more Christian attitude, which can be attained at any age, is that of leaving futurity in God's hands. We may as well, for God will certainly retain it whether we leave it to Him or not. Never, in peace or war, commit your virtue or your happiness to the future. Happy work is best done by the man who takes his long-term plans somewhat lightly and works from moment to moment "as to the Lord." It is only our daily bread that we are encouraged to ask for. The present is the only time in which any duty can be done or any grace received.

The third enemy is fear. War threatens us with death and pain. No man—and specially no Christian who remembers Gethsemane—need try to attain a stoic indifference about these things: but we can guard against the illusions of the imagination. We think of the streets of Warsaw and contrast the deaths there suffered with an abstraction called Life. But there is no question of death or life for any of us; only a question of this death or of that—of a machine gun bullet now or a cancer forty years later. What does war do to death? It certainly does not make it more frequent; 100 percent of us die, and the percentage cannot be increased. It puts several deaths earlier; but I hardly suppose that that is what we fear. Certainly when the moment comes, it will make little difference how many years we have behind us. Does it increase our chance of a painful death? I doubt it. As far as I can find out, what we call natural death is usually preceded by suffering; and a battlefield is one of the very few places where one has a reasonable prospect of dying with no pain at all. Does it decrease our chances of dying at peace with God? I cannot believe it. If active service does not persuade a man to prepare for death, what conceivable concatenation of circumstance would? Yet war does do something to death. It forces us to remember it. The only reason why the cancer at sixty or the paralysis at seventy-five do not bother us is that we forget them. War makes death real to us: and that would have been regarded as one of its blessings by most of the great Christians of the past. They thought it good for us to be always aware of our mortality. I am inclined to think they were right.

All the animal life in us, all schemes of happiness that centered in this world, were always doomed to a final frustration. In ordinary times only a wise man can realize it. Now the stupidest of us know. We see unmistakably the sort of universe in which we have all along been living, and must come to terms with it. If we had foolish un-Christian hopes about human culture, they are now shattered. If we thought we were building up a heaven on earth, if we looked for something that would turn the present world from a place of pilgrimage into a permanent city satisfying the soul of man, we are disillusioned, and not a moment too soon. But if we thought that for some souls, and at some times, the life of learning, humbly offered to God, was, in its own small way, one of the appointed approaches to the Divine reality and the Divine beauty which we hope to enjoy hereafter, we can think so still.

Review and Discussion Questions

1. Lewis raises the objection that studying during war-time is no better than "fiddling while Rome burns." How does he answer it?

2. In Lewis's view is it better to be a scholar or a house-cleaner (char-woman)?

3. In what sense does Lewis agree, and disagree, with the assertion of Matthew Arnold (who offered an earlier, though less theologically inspired, defense of liberal education) that truth should be pursued "for its own sake"?

4. At what point ought a scholar to give up his work?

5. Lewis's sermon was delivered before a gathering largely composed of young Christian students. What three enemies does he warn will work against them and their God-assigned vocation?

DOROTHY SAYERS (1893–1957)

The Lost Tools of Learning

> For the tools of learning are the same, in any and every subject; and the person who knows how to use them will, at any age, get the mastery of a new subject in half the time and with a quarter of the effort expended by the person who has not the tools at his command.

Playwright, apologist, and translator of the *Divine Comedy*, Dorothy Sayers was a member of the Inklings and mother of the Lord Peter Wimsey detective stories. Do we wonder about the lowering standards of schools? Do we worry about losing our children to the internet? Do we wince at the spoiled grammar of newspaper editorials? Sayers makes a plea for the recovery of the classical tools of learning. What is not needed is more time in school. Nor is money the main fix. What is needed is a better grasp of the fundamentals, and a return "back" to the trivium of the Middle Ages. What Miss Sayers proposes is a progressive retrogression. Is she a reactionary? Perhaps. But while we cannot reverse the revolutions of the earth, men can and ought, as Miss Sayers argues, go "back" whenever a misstep has been taken.

Further Reading: Sr. Miriam Joseph, C.S.C., *The Trivium: The Liberal Arts of Logic, Grammar, and Rhetoric*, ed. Marguerite McGlinn (Philadelphia: Paul Dry Books, 2002); Jeffry C. Davis and Philip G. Ryken, eds., *Liberal Arts for the Christian Life* (Wheaton, Ill.: Crossway Books, 2012); David L. Wagner, ed., *The Seven Liberal Arts in the Middle Ages* (Bloomington: Indiana University Press, 1986).

❖

That I, whose experience of teaching is extremely limited, should presume to discuss education is a matter, surely, that calls for no apology. It is a kind of behavior to which the present climate of opinion is wholly favorable. Bishops air their opinions about economics; biologists, about metaphysics; inorganic chemists, about theology; the most irrelevant people are appointed to highly technical ministries; and plain, blunt men write to the papers to say that Epstein and Picasso do not know how to draw. Up to a certain point, and provided the criticisms are made with a reasonable modesty, these activities are commendable. Too much specialization is not a good thing. There is also one excellent reason why the veriest amateur may feel entitled to have an opinion about education. For if we are not all professional teachers, we have all, at some time or another, been taught. Even if we learnt nothing—perhaps in particular if we learnt nothing—our contribution to the discussion may have a potential value.

However, it is in the highest degree improbable that the reforms I propose will ever be carried into effect. Neither the parents, nor the training colleges, nor the examination boards, nor the boards of governors, nor the ministries of education, would countenance them for a moment. For they amount to this: that if we are to produce a society of educated people, fitted to preserve their intellectual freedom amid the complex pressures of our modern society, we must turn back the wheel of progress some four or five hundred years, to the point at which education began to lose sight of its true object, towards the end of the Middle Ages.

Before you dismiss me with the appropriate phrase—reactionary, romantic, mediaevalist, laudator temporis acti (praiser of times past), or whatever tag comes first to hand—I will ask you to consider one or two miscellaneous questions that hang about at the back, perhaps, of all our minds, and occasionally pop out to worry us.

When we think about the remarkably early age at which the young men went up to university in, let us say, Tudor times, and thereafter were held fit to assume responsibility for the conduct of their own affairs, are we altogether comfortable about that artificial prolongation of intellectual childhood and adolescence into the years of physical maturity which is so marked in our own day? To postpone the acceptance of responsibility to a late date brings with it a number of psychological complications which, while they may interest the psychiatrist, are scarcely beneficial either to the individual or to society. The stock argument in favor of postponing the school-leaving age and prolonging the period of education generally is there is now so much more to learn than there was in the Middle Ages. This is partly true, but not wholly. The modern boy and girl are certainly taught more subjects—but does that always mean that they actually know more?

Has it ever struck you as odd, or unfortunate, that today, when the proportion of literacy throughout Western Europe is higher than it has ever been, people should have become susceptible to the influence of advertisement and mass propaganda to an extent hitherto unheard of and unimagined? Do you put this down to the mere mechanical fact that the press and the radio and so on have made propaganda much easier to distribute over a wide area? Or do you sometimes have an uneasy suspicion that the product of modern educational methods is less good than he or she might be at disentangling fact from opinion and the proven from the plausible?

Have you ever, in listening to a debate among adult and presumably responsible people, been fretted by the extraordinary inability of the average debater to speak to the question, or to meet and refute the arguments of speakers on the other side? Or have you ever pondered upon the extremely high incidence of irrelevant matter which crops up at committee meetings, and upon the very great rarity of persons capable of acting as chairmen of committees? And when you think of this, and think that most of our public affairs are settled by debates and committees, have you ever felt a certain sinking of the heart?

Have you ever followed a discussion in the newspapers or elsewhere and noticed how frequently writers fail to define the terms they use? Or how often, if one man does define his terms, another will assume in his reply that he was using the terms in precisely the opposite sense to that in which he has already defined them? Have you ever been faintly troubled by the amount of slipshod syntax going about? And, if so, are you troubled because it is inelegant or because it may lead to dangerous misunderstanding?

Do you ever find that young people, when they have left school, not only forget most of what they have learnt (that is only to be expected), but forget also, or betray that they have never really known, how to tackle a new subject for themselves? Are you often bothered by coming across grown-up men and women who seem unable to distinguish between a book that is sound, scholarly, and properly documented, and one that is, to any trained eye, very conspicuously none of these things? Or who cannot handle a library catalogue? Or who, when faced with a book of reference, betray a curious inability to extract from it the passages relevant to the particular question which interests them?

Do you often come across people for whom, all their lives, a "subject" remains a "subject," divided by watertight bulkheads from all other "subjects," so that they experience very great difficulty in making an immediate mental connection between let us say, algebra and detective fiction, sewage disposal and the price of salmon—or, more generally, between such spheres of knowledge as philosophy and economics, or chemistry and art?

Are you occasionally perturbed by the things written by adult men and women for adult men and women to read? We find a well-known biologist writing in a weekly paper to the effect that: "It is an argument against the existence of a Creator" (I think he put it more strongly; but since I have, most unfortunately, mislaid the reference, I will put his claim at its lowest)—"an argument against the existence of a Creator that the same kind of variations which are produced by natural selection can be produced at will by stock breeders." One might feel tempted to say that it is rather an argument for the existence of a Creator. Actually, of course, it is neither; all it proves is that the same material causes (recombination of the chromosomes, by crossbreeding, and so forth) are sufficient to account for all observed variations—just as the various combinations of the same dozen tones are materially sufficient to account for Beethoven's Moonlight Sonata and the noise the cat makes by walking on the keys. But the cat's performance neither proves nor disproves the existence of Beethoven; and all that is proved by the biologist's argument is that he was unable to distinguish between a material and a final cause.

Here is a sentence from no less academic a source than a front-page article in the *Times Literary Supplement:* "The Frenchman, Alfred Epinas, pointed out that certain species (e.g., ants and wasps) can only face the horrors of life and death in association." I do not know what the Frenchman actually did say; what the Englishman says he said is patently meaningless. We cannot know whether life holds any horror for the ant, nor in what sense the isolated wasp which you kill upon the window-pane can be said to "face" or not to "face" the horrors of death. The subject of the article is mass behavior in man; and the human motives have been unobtrusively transferred from the main proposition to the supporting instance. Thus the argument, in effect, assumes what it set out to prove—a fact which would become immediately apparent if it were presented in a formal syllogism. This is only a small and haphazard example of a vice which pervades whole books—particularly books written by men of science on metaphysical subjects.

Another quotation from the same issue of the *TLS* comes in fittingly here to wind up this random collection of disquieting thoughts—this time from a review of Sir Richard Livingstone's "Some Tasks for Education": "More than once the reader is reminded of the value of an intensive study of at least one subject, so as to learn 'the meaning of knowledge' and what precision and persistence is needed to attain it. Yet there is elsewhere full recognition of the distressing fact that a man may be master in one field and show no better judgement than his neighbor anywhere else; he remembers what he has learnt, but forgets altogether how he learned it."

I would draw your attention particularly to that last sentence, which offers an explanation of what the writer rightly calls the "distressing fact" that the intellectual skills bestowed upon us by our education are not readily transferable to subjects other than those in which we acquired them: "he remembers what he has learnt, but forgets altogether how he learned it."

Is not the great defect of our education today—a defect traceable through all the disquieting symptoms of trouble that I have mentioned—that although we often succeed in teaching our pupils "subjects," we fail lamentably on the whole in teaching them how to think: they learn everything, except the art of learning. It is as though we had taught a child, mechanically and by rule of thumb, to play "The Harmonious Blacksmith" upon the piano, but had never taught him the scale or how to read music; so that, having memorized "The Harmonious Blacksmith," he still had not the faintest notion how to proceed from that to tackle "The Last Rose of Summer." Why do I say, "as though"? In certain of the arts and crafts, we sometimes do precisely this—requiring a child to "express himself" in paint before we teach him how to handle the colors and the brush. There is a school of thought which believes this to be the right way to set about the job. But observe: it is not the way in which a trained craftsman will go about to teach himself a new medium. He, having learned by experience the best way to economize labor and take the thing by the right end, will start off by doodling about on an odd piece of material, in order to "give himself the feel of the tool."

Let us now look at the mediaeval scheme of education—the syllabus of the Schools. It does not matter, for the moment, whether it was devised for small children or for older students, or how long people were supposed to take over it. What matters is the light it throws upon what the men of the Middle Ages supposed to be the object and the right order of the educative process.

The syllabus was divided into two parts: the Trivium and Quadrivium. The second part—the Quadrivium—consisted of "subjects," and need not for the moment concern us. The interesting thing for us is the composition of the Trivium, which preceded the Quadrivium and was the preliminary discipline for it. It consisted of three parts: Grammar, Dialectic, and Rhetoric, in that order.

Now the first thing we notice is that two at any rate of these "subjects" are not what we should call "subjects" at all: they are only methods of dealing with subjects. Grammar, indeed, is a "subject" in the sense that it does mean definitely learning a language—at that period it meant learning Latin. But language itself is simply the medium in which thought is expressed. The whole of the Trivium was, in fact, intended to teach the pupil the proper use of the tools of learning, before he began to apply them to "subjects" at all. First, he learned a language; not just how to order a meal in a foreign language, but the structure of a language, and hence of language itself—what it was, how it was put together, and how it worked. Secondly, he learned how to use language; how to define his terms and make accurate statements; how to construct an argument and how to detect fallacies in argument. Dialectic, that is to say, embraced Logic and Disputation. Thirdly, he learned to express himself in language—how to say what he had to say elegantly and persuasively.

At the end of his course, he was required to compose a thesis upon some theme set by his masters or chosen by himself, and afterwards to defend his thesis against the criticism of the faculty. By this time, he would have learned—or woe betide him— not merely to write an essay on paper, but to speak audibly and intelligibly from a platform, and to use his wits quickly when heckled. There would also be questions, cogent and shrewd, from those who had already run the gauntlet of debate.

It is, of course, quite true that bits and pieces of the mediaeval tradition still linger, or have been revived, in the ordinary school syllabus of today. Some knowledge of grammar is still required when learning a foreign language—perhaps I should say, "is again required," for during my own lifetime, we passed through a phase when the teaching of declensions and conjugations was considered rather reprehensible, and it was considered better to pick these things up as we went along. School debating societies flourish; essays are written; the necessity for "self-expression" is stressed, and perhaps even over-stressed. But these activities are cultivated more or less in detachment, as belonging to the special subjects in which they are pigeon-holed rather than as forming one coherent scheme of mental training to which all "subjects" stand in a subordinate relation. "Grammar" belongs especially to the "subject" of foreign languages, and essay-writing to the "subject" called "English"; while Dialectic has become almost entirely divorced from the rest of the curriculum, and is frequently practiced unsystematically and out of school hours as a separate exercise, only very loosely related to the main business of learning. Taken by and large, the great difference of emphasis between the two conceptions holds good: modern education concentrates on "teaching subjects," leaving the method of thinking, arguing, and expressing one's conclusions to be picked up by the scholar as he goes along, mediaeval education concentrated on first forging and learning to handle the tools of learning, using whatever subject came handy as a piece of material on which to doodle until the use of the tool became second nature.

"Subjects" of some kind there must be, of course. One cannot learn the theory of grammar without learning an actual language, or learn to argue and orate without speaking about something in particular. The debating subjects of the Middle Ages were drawn largely from theology, or from the ethics and history of antiquity. Often, indeed, they became stereotyped, especially towards the end of the period, and the far-fetched and wire-drawn absurdities of Scholastic argument fretted Milton and provide food for merriment even to this day. Whether they were in themselves any more hackneyed and trivial then the usual subjects set nowadays for "essay writing" I should not like to say: we may ourselves grow a little weary of "A Day in My Holidays" and all the rest of it. But most of the merriment is misplaced, because the aim and object of the debating thesis has by now been lost sight of.

A glib speaker in the Brains Trust once entertained his audience (and reduced the late Charles Williams to helpless rage) by asserting that in the Middle Ages it was a matter of faith to know how many archangels could dance on the point of a needle. I need not say, I hope, that it never was a "matter of faith"; it was simply a debating exercise, whose set subject was the nature of angelic substance: were angels material, and if so, did they occupy space? The answer usually adjudged correct is, I believe, that angels are pure intelligences; not material, but limited, so that they may have location in space but not extension. An analogy might be drawn from human thought, which is similarly non-material and similarly limited. Thus, if your thought is concentrated upon one thing—say, the point of a needle—it is located there in the sense that it is not elsewhere; but although it is "there," it occupies no space there, and there is nothing to prevent an infinite number of different people's thoughts being concentrated upon the same needle-point at the same time. The proper subject of the argument is thus seen to be the distinction between location and extension in space; the matter on which the argument is exercised happens to be the nature of angels (although, as we have seen, it might equally well have been something else); the practical lesson to be drawn from the argument is not to use words like "there" in a loose and unscientific way, without specifying whether you mean "located there" or "occupying space there."

Scorn in plenty has been poured out upon the mediaeval passion for hair-splitting; but when we look at the shameless abuse made, in print and on the platform, of controversial expressions with shifting and ambiguous connotations, we may feel it in our hearts to wish that every reader and hearer had been so defensively armored by his education as to be able to cry: "Distinguo."

For we let our young men and women go out unarmed, in a day when armor was never so necessary. By teaching them all to read, we have left them at the mercy of the printed word. By the invention of the film and the radio, we have made certain that no aversion to reading shall secure them from the incessant battery of words, words, words. They do not know what the words mean; they do not know how to ward them off or blunt their edge or fling them back; they are a prey to words in their emotions instead of being the masters of them in their intellects. We who were scandalized in 1940 when men were sent to fight armored tanks with rifles, are not scandalized when young men and women are sent into the world to fight massed propaganda with a smattering of "subjects"; and when whole classes and whole nations become hypnotized by the arts of the spell binder, we have the impudence to be astonished. We dole out lip-service to the importance of education—lip-service and, just occasionally, a little grant of money; we postpone the school-leaving age, and plan to build bigger and better schools; the teachers slave conscientiously in and out of school hours; and yet, as I believe, all this devoted effort is largely frustrated, because we have lost the tools of learning, and in their absence can only make a botched and piecemeal job of it.

What, then, are we to do? We cannot go back to the Middle Ages. That is a cry to which we have become accustomed. We cannot go back—or can we? Distinguo. I should like every term in that proposition defined. Does "go back" mean a retrogression in time, or the revision of an error? The first is clearly impossible per se; the second is a thing which wise men do every day. "Cannot"—does this mean that our behavior is determined irreversibly, or merely that such an action would be very difficult in view of the opposition it would provoke? Obviously the twentieth century is not and cannot be the fourteenth; but if "the Middle Ages" is, in this context, simply a picturesque phrase denoting a particular educational theory, there seems to be no a priori reason why we should not "go back" to it—with modifications—as we have already "gone back" with modifications, to, let us say, the idea of playing Shakespeare's plays as he wrote them, and not in the "modernized" versions of Cibber and Garrick, which once seemed to be the latest thing in theatrical progress.

Let us amuse ourselves by imagining that such progressive retrogression is possible. Let us make a clean sweep of all educational authorities, and furnish ourselves with a nice little school of boys and girls whom we may experimentally equip for the intellectual conflict along lines chosen by ourselves. We will endow them with exceptionally docile parents; we will staff our school with teachers who are themselves perfectly familiar with the aims and methods of the Trivium; we will have our building and staff large enough to allow our classes to be small enough for adequate handling; and we will postulate a Board of Examiners willing and qualified to test the products we turn out. Thus prepared, we will attempt to sketch out a syllabus—a modern Trivium "with modifications" and we will see where we get to.

But first: what age shall the children be? Well, if one is to educate them on novel lines, it will be better that they should have nothing to unlearn; besides, one cannot begin a good thing too early, and the Trivium is by its nature not learning, but a preparation for learning. We will, therefore, "catch 'em young," requiring of our pupils only that they shall be able to read, write, and cipher.

My views about child psychology are, I admit, neither orthodox nor enlightened. Looking back upon myself (since I am the child I know best and the only child I can pretend to know from inside) I recognize three states of development. These, in a rough-and-ready fashion, I will call the Poll-Parrot, the Pert, and the Poetic—the latter coinciding, approximately, with the onset of puberty. The Poll-Parrot stage is the one in which learning by heart is easy and, on the whole, pleasurable; whereas reasoning is difficult and, on the whole, little relished. At this age, one readily memorizes the shapes and appearances of things; one likes to recite the number-plates of cars; one rejoices in the chanting of rhymes and the rumble and thunder of unintelligible polysyllables; one enjoys the mere accumulation of things. The Pert age, which follows upon this (and, naturally, overlaps it to some extent), is characterized by contradicting, answering back, liking to "catch people out" (especially one's elders); and by the propounding of conundrums. Its nuisance-value is extremely high. It usually sets in about the Fourth Form. The Poetic age is popularly known as the "difficult" age. It is self-centered; it yearns to express itself; it rather specializes in being misunderstood; it is restless and tries to achieve independence; and, with good luck and good guidance, it should show the beginnings of creativeness; a reaching out towards a synthesis of what it already knows, and a deliberate eagerness to know and do some one thing in preference to all others. Now it seems to me that the layout of the Trivium adapts itself with a singular appropriateness to these three ages: Grammar to the Poll-Parrot, Dialectic to the Pert, and Rhetoric to the Poetic age.

Let us begin, then, with Grammar. This, in practice, means the grammar of some language in particular; and it must be an inflected language. The grammatical structure of an uninflected language is far too analytical to be tackled by any one without previous practice in Dialectic. Moreover, the inflected languages interpret the uninflected, whereas the uninflected are of little use in interpreting the inflected. I will say at once, quite firmly, that the best grounding for education is the Latin grammar. I say this, not because Latin is traditional and mediaeval, but simply because even a rudimentary knowledge of Latin cuts down the labor and pains of learning almost any other subject by at least fifty percent. It is the key to the vocabulary and structure of all the Teutonic languages, as well as to the technical vocabulary of all the sciences and to the literature of the entire Mediterranean civilization, together with all its historical documents.

Those whose pedantic preference for a living language persuades them to deprive their pupils of all these advantages might substitute Russian, whose grammar is still more primitive. Russian is, of course, helpful with the other Slav dialects. There is something also to be said for Classical Greek. But my own choice is Latin. Having thus pleased the Classicists among you, I will proceed to horrify them by adding that I do not think it either wise or necessary to cramp the ordinary pupil upon the Procrustean bed of the Augustan Age, with its highly elaborate and artificial verse forms and oratory. Post-classical and mediaeval Latin, which was a living language right down to the end of the Renaissance, is easier and in some ways livelier; a study of it helps to dispel the widespread notion that learning and literature came to a full stop when Christ was born and only woke up again at the Dissolution of the Monasteries.

Latin should be begun as early as possible—at a time when inflected speech seems no more astonishing than any other phenomenon in an astonishing world; and when the chanting of "Amo, amas, amat" is as ritually agreeable to the feelings as the chanting of "eeny, meeny, miney, moe."

During this age we must, of course, exercise the mind on other things besides Latin grammar. Observation and memory are the faculties most lively at this period; and if we are to learn a contemporary foreign language we should begin now, before the facial and mental muscles become rebellious to strange intonations. Spoken French or German can be practiced alongside the grammatical discipline of the Latin.

In English, meanwhile, verse and prose can be learned by heart, and the pupil's memory should be stored with stories of every kind—classical myth, European legend, and so forth. I do not think that the classical stories and masterpieces of ancient literature should be made the vile bodies on which to practice the techniques of Grammar—that was a fault of mediaeval education which we need not perpetuate. The stories can be enjoyed and remembered in English, and related to their origin at a subsequent stage. Recitation aloud should be practiced, individually or in chorus; for we must not forget that we are laying the groundwork for Disputation and Rhetoric.

The grammar of History should consist, I think, of dates, events, anecdotes, and personalities. A set of dates to which one can peg all later historical knowledge is of enormous help later on in establishing the perspective of history. It does not greatly matter which dates: those of the Kings of England will do very nicely, provided that they are accompanied by pictures of costumes, architecture, and other everyday things, so that the mere mention of a date calls up a very strong visual presentment of the whole period.

Geography will similarly be presented in its factual aspect, with maps, natural features, and visual presentment of customs, costumes, flora, fauna, and so on; and I believe myself that the discredited and old-fashioned memorizing of a few capitol cities, rivers, mountain ranges, etc., does no harm. Stamp collecting may be encouraged.

Science, in the Poll-Parrot period, arranges itself naturally and easily around collections—the identifying and naming of specimens and, in general, the kind of thing that used to be called "natural philosophy." To know the name and properties of things is, at this age, a satisfaction in itself; to recognize a devil's coach-horse at sight, and assure one's foolish elders, that, in spite of its appearance, it does not sting; to be able to pick out Cassiopeia and the Pleiades, and perhaps even to know who Cassiopeia and the Pleiades were; to be aware that a whale is not a fish, and a bat not a bird—all these things give a pleasant sensation of superiority; while to know a ring snake from an adder or a poisonous from an edible toadstool is a kind of knowledge that also has practical value.

The grammar of Mathematics begins, of course, with the multiplication table, which, if not learnt now, will never be learnt with pleasure; and with the recognition of geometrical shapes and the grouping of numbers. These exercises lead naturally to the doing of simple sums in arithmetic. More complicated mathematical processes may, and perhaps should, be postponed, for the reasons which will presently appear.

So far (except, of course, for the Latin), our curriculum contains nothing that departs very far from common practice. The difference will be felt rather in the attitude of the teachers, who must look upon all these activities less as "subjects" in themselves than as a gathering-together of material for use in the next part of the Trivium. What that material is, is only of secondary importance; but it is as well that anything and everything which can be usefully committed to memory should be memorized at this period, whether it is immediately intelligible or not. The modern tendency is to try and force rational explanations on a child's mind at too early an age. Intelligent questions, spontaneously asked, should, of course, receive an immediate and rational answer; but it is a great mistake to suppose that a child cannot readily enjoy and remember things that are beyond his power to analyze—particularly if those things have a strong imaginative appeal (as, for example, "Kubla Kahn"), an attractive jingle (like some of the memory-rhymes for Latin genders), or an abundance of rich, resounding polysyllables (like the Quicunque vult).

This reminds me of the grammar of Theology. I shall add it to the curriculum, because theology is the mistress-science without which the whole educational structure will necessarily lack its final synthesis. Those who disagree about this will remain content to leave their pupil's education still full of loose ends. This will matter rather less than it might, since by the time that the tools of learning have been forged the student will be able to tackle theology for himself, and will probably insist upon doing so and making sense of it. Still, it is as well to have this matter also handy and ready for the reason to work upon. At the grammatical age, therefore, we should become acquainted with the story of God and Man in outline—i.e., the Old and New testaments presented as parts of a single narrative of Creation, Rebellion, and Redemption—and also with the Creed, the Lord's Prayer, and the Ten Commandments. At this early stage, it does not matter nearly so much that these things should be fully understood as that they should be known and remembered.

It is difficult to say at what age, precisely, we should pass from the first to the second part of the Trivium. Generally speaking, the answer is: so soon as the pupil shows himself disposed to pertness and interminable argument. For as, in the first part, the master faculties are Observation and Memory, so, in the second, the master faculty is the Discursive Reason. In the first, the exercise to which the rest of the material was, as it were, keyed, was the Latin grammar; in the second, the key exercise will be Formal Logic. It is here that our curriculum shows its first sharp divergence from modern standards. The disrepute into which Formal Logic has fallen is entirely unjustified; and its neglect is the root cause of nearly all those disquieting symptoms which we have noted in the modern intellectual constitution. Logic has been discredited, partly because we have come to suppose that we are conditioned almost entirely by the intuitive and the unconscious. There is no time to argue whether this is true; I will simply observe that to neglect the proper training of the reason is the best possible way to make it true. Another cause for the disfavor into which Logic has fallen is the belief that it is entirely based upon universal assumptions that are either unprovable or tautological. This is not true. Not all universal propositions are of this kind. But even if they were, it would make no difference, since every syllogism whose major premise is in the form "All A is B" can be recast in hypothetical form. Logic is the art of arguing correctly: "If A, then B." The method is not invalidated by the hypothetical nature of A. Indeed, the practical utility of Formal Logic today lies not so much in the establishment of positive conclusions as in the prompt detection and exposure of invalid inference.

Let us now quickly review our material and see how it is to be related to Dialectic. On the Language side, we shall now have our vocabulary and morphology at our fingertips; henceforward we can concentrate on syntax and analysis (i.e., the logical construction of speech) and the history of language (i.e., how we came to arrange our speech as we do in order to convey our thoughts).

Our Reading will proceed from narrative and lyric to essays, argument and criticism, and the pupil will learn to try his own hand at writing this kind of thing. Many lessons—on whatever subject—will take the form of debates; and the place of individual or choral recitation will be taken by dramatic performances, with special attention to plays in which an argument is stated in dramatic form.

Mathematics—algebra, geometry, and the more advanced kinds of arithmetic—will now enter into the syllabus and take its place as what it really is: not a separate "subject" but a sub-department of Logic. It is neither more nor less than the rule of the syllogism in its particular application to number and measurement, and should be taught as such, instead of being, for some, a dark mystery, and, for others, a special revelation, neither illuminating nor illuminated by any other part of knowledge.

History, aided by a simple system of ethics derived from the grammar of theology, will provide much suitable material for discussion: Was the behavior of this statesman justified? What was the effect of such an enactment? What are the arguments for and against this or that form of government? We shall thus get an introduction to constitutional history—a subject meaningless to the young child, but of absorbing interest to those who are prepared to argue and debate. Theology itself will furnish material for argument about conduct and morals; and should have its scope extended by a simplified course of dogmatic theology (i.e., the rational structure of Christian thought), clarifying the relations between the dogma and the ethics, and lending itself to that application of ethical principles in particular instances which is properly called casuistry. Geography and the Sciences will likewise provide material for Dialectic.

But above all, we must not neglect the material which is so abundant in the pupils' own daily life.

There is a delightful passage in Leslie Paul's "The Living Hedge" which tells how a number of small boys enjoyed themselves for days arguing about an extraordinary shower of rain which had fallen in their town—a shower so localized that it left one half of the main street wet and the other dry. Could one, they argued, properly say that it had rained that day on or over the town or only in the town? How many drops of water were required to constitute rain? And so on. Argument about this led on to a host of similar problems about rest and motion, sleep and waking, est and non est, and the infinitesimal division of time. The whole passage is an admirable example of the spontaneous development of the ratiocinative faculty and the natural and proper thirst of the awakening reason for the definition of terms and exactness of statement. All events are food for such an appetite.

An umpire's decision; the degree to which one may transgress the spirit of a regulation without being trapped by the letter: on such questions as these, children are born casuists, and their natural propensity only needs to be developed and trained—and especially, brought into an intelligible relationship with the events in the grown-up world. The newspapers are full of good material for such exercises: legal decisions, on the one hand, in cases where the cause at issue is not too abstruse; on the other, fallacious reasoning and muddleheaded arguments, with which the correspondence columns of certain papers one could name are abundantly stocked.

Wherever the matter for Dialectic is found, it is, of course, highly important that attention should be focused upon the beauty and economy of a fine demonstration or a well-turned argument, lest veneration should wholly die. Criticism must not be merely destructive; though at the same time both teacher and pupils must be ready to detect fallacy, slipshod reasoning, ambiguity, irrelevance, and redundancy, and to pounce upon them like rats. This is the moment when precis-writing may be usefully undertaken; together with such exercises as the writing of an essay, and the reduction of it, when written, by 25 or 50 percent.

It will, doubtless, be objected that to encourage young persons at the Pert age to browbeat, correct, and argue with their elders will render them perfectly intolerable. My answer is that children of that age are intolerable anyhow; and that their natural argumentativeness may just as well be canalized to good purpose as allowed to run away into the sands. It may, indeed, be rather less obtrusive at home if it is disciplined in school; and anyhow, elders who have abandoned the wholesome principle that children should be seen and not heard have no one to blame but themselves.

Once again, the contents of the syllabus at this stage may be anything you like. The "subjects" supply material; but they are all to be regarded as mere grist for the mental mill to work upon. The pupils should be encouraged to go and forage for their own information, and so guided towards the proper use of libraries and books for reference, and shown how to tell which sources are authoritative and which are not.

Towards the close of this stage, the pupils will probably be beginning to discover for themselves that their knowledge and experience are insufficient, and that their trained intelligences need a great deal more material to chew upon. The imagination—usually dormant during the Pert age—will reawaken, and prompt them to suspect the limitations of logic and reason. This means that they are passing into the Poetic age and are ready to embark on the study of Rhetoric. The doors of the storehouse of knowledge should now be thrown open for them to browse about as they will. The things once learned by rote will be seen in new contexts; the things once coldly analyzed can now be brought together to form a new synthesis; here and there a sudden insight will bring about that most exciting of all discoveries: the realization that truism is true.

It is difficult to map out any general syllabus for the study of Rhetoric: a certain freedom is demanded. In literature, appreciation should be again allowed to take the lead over destructive criticism; and self-expression in writing can go forward, with its tools now sharpened to cut clean and observe proportion. Any child who already shows a disposition to specialize should be given his head: for, when the use of the tools has been well and truly learned, it is available for any study whatever. It would be well, I think, that each pupil should learn to do one, or two, subjects really well, while taking a few classes in subsidiary subjects so as to keep his mind open to the inter-relations of all knowledge. Indeed, at this stage, our difficulty will be to keep "subjects" apart; for Dialectic will have shown all branches of learning to be inter-related, so Rhetoric will tend to show that all knowledge is one. To show this, and show why it is so, is pre-eminently the task of the mistress science. But whether theology is studied or not, we should at least insist that children who seem inclined to specialize on the mathematical and scientific side should be obliged to attend some lessons in the humanities and vice versa. At this stage, also, the Latin grammar, having done its work, may be dropped for those who prefer to carry on their language studies on the modern side; while those who are likely never to have any great use or aptitude for mathematics might also be allowed to rest, more or less, upon their oars. Generally speaking, whatsoever is mere apparatus may now be allowed to fall into the background, while the trained mind is gradually prepared for specialization in the "subjects" which, when the Trivium is completed, it should be perfectly will equipped to tackle on its own. The final synthesis of the Trivium—the presentation and public defense of the thesis—should be restored in some form; perhaps as a kind of "leaving examination" during the last term at school.

The scope of Rhetoric depends also on whether the pupil is to be turned out into the world at the age of 16 or whether he is to proceed to the university. Since, really, Rhetoric should be taken at about 14, the first category of pupil should study Grammar from about 9 to 11, and Dialectic from 12 to 14; his last two school years would then be devoted to Rhetoric, which, in this case, would be of a fairly specialized and vocational kind, suiting him to enter immediately upon some practical career. A pupil of the second category would finish his Dialectical course in his preparatory school, and take Rhetoric during his first two years at his public school. At 16, he would be ready to start upon those "subjects" which are proposed for his later study at the university: and this part of his education will correspond to the mediaeval Quadrivium. What this amounts to is that the ordinary pupil, whose formal education ends at 16, will take the Trivium only; whereas scholars will take both the Trivium and the Quadrivium.

Is the Trivium, then, a sufficient education for life? Properly taught, I believe that it should be. At the end of the Dialectic, the children will probably seem to be far behind their coevals brought up on old-fashioned "modern" methods, so far as detailed knowledge of specific subjects is concerned. But after the age of 14 they should be able to overhaul the others hand over fist. Indeed, I am not at all sure that a pupil thoroughly proficient in the Trivium would not be fit to proceed immediately to the university at the age of 16, thus proving himself the equal of his mediaeval counterpart, whose precocity astonished us at the beginning of this discussion. This, to be sure, would make hay of the English public-school system, and disconcert the universities very much. It would, for example, make quite a different thing of the Oxford and Cambridge boat race.

But I am not here to consider the feelings of academic bodies: I am concerned only with the proper training of the mind to encounter and deal with the formidable mass of undigested problems presented to it by the modern world. For the tools of learning are the same, in any and every subject; and the person who knows how to use them will, at any age, get the mastery of a new subject in half the time and with a quarter of the effort expended by the person who has not the tools at his command. To learn six subjects without remembering how they were learnt does nothing to ease the approach to a seventh; to have learnt and remembered the art of learning makes the approach to every subject an open door.

Before concluding these necessarily very sketchy suggestions, I ought to say why I think it necessary, in these days, to go back to a discipline which we had discarded. The truth is that for the last three hundred years or so we have been living upon our educational capital. The post-Renaissance world, bewildered and excited by the profusion of new "subjects" offered to it, broke away from the old discipline (which had, indeed, become sadly dull and stereotyped in its practical application) and imagined that henceforward it could, as it were, disport itself happily in its new and extended Quadrivium without passing through the Trivium. But the Scholastic tradition, though broken and maimed, still lingered in the public schools and universities: Milton, however much he protested against it, was formed by it—the debate of the Fallen Angels and the disputation of Abdiel with Satan have the tool-marks of the Schools upon them, and might, incidentally, profitably figure as set passages for our Dialectical studies. Right down to the nineteenth century, our public affairs were mostly managed, and our books and journals were for the most part written, by people brought up in homes, and trained in places, where that tradition was still alive in the memory and almost in the blood. Just so, many people today who are atheist or agnostic in religion, are governed in their conduct by a code of Christian ethics which is so rooted that it never occurs to them to question it.

But one cannot live on capital forever. However firmly a tradition is rooted, if it is never watered, though it dies hard, yet in the end it dies. And today a great number—perhaps the majority—of the men and women who handle our affairs, write our books and our newspapers, carry out our research, present our plays and our films, speak from our platforms and pulpits—yes, and who educate our young people—have never, even in a lingering traditional memory, undergone the Scholastic discipline. Less and less do the children who come to be educated bring any of that tradition with them. We have lost the tools of learning—the axe and the wedge, the hammer and the saw, the chisel and the plane—that were so adaptable to all tasks. Instead of them, we have merely a set of complicated jigs, each of which will do but one task and no more, and in using which eye and hand receive no training, so that no man ever sees the work as a whole or "looks to the end of the work."

What use is it to pile task on task and prolong the days of labor, if at the close the chief object is left unattained? It is not the fault of the teachers— they work only too hard already. The combined folly of a civilization that has forgotten its own roots is forcing them to shore up the tottering weight of an educational structure that is built upon sand. They are doing for their pupils the work which the pupils themselves ought to do. For the sole true end of education is simply this: to teach men how to learn for themselves; and whatever instruction fails to do this is effort spent in vain.

Review and Discussion Questions

1. What is Sayers's thesis?

2. How does she dispose of the claim of the atheistic biologist? (It might be helpful here to look back to our first selection from Aristotle, and his discussion of the four causes.)

3. On what basis are the two parts of the medieval liberal arts curriculum divided?

4. What does each of the liberal arts contribute to a student's grasp of the whole of knowledge?

5. Imagine a school board or principal accepted Sayers's proposal. What would a typical week of study look like for a 12-year-old boy or girl?

❖ 31

CHRISTOPHER DAWSON (1889–1970)

Crisis in Western Education

> What is needed, so it seems to me, is a study of Christian culture as a social
> reality ... for this would provide a background or framework that would
> integrate the liberal studies which at present are apt to disintegrate into un-
> related specialisms.

English convert and Harvard academic, Christopher Dawson is widely regarded as the finest Catholic historian of the twentieth century. His numerous essays and books contributed to the Catholic literary renewal of the
decades preceding the Second Vatican Council (1962–65). In this selection
Dawson outlines a practical solution to the homelessness of the Western
mind. Already in 1961 he observed the surge of hyper-specialization in our
universities, and the subsequent loss of a coherent cultural memory among
our youth. His proposal: the study of Christian culture. At this late hour
a return to Plato, Aristotle, and Dante may save some, but as J. S. Bach
grates on ears accustomed to Hip Hop, so a direct encounter with the great
works of literature and philosophy is not likely win over young minds until they have been taught, by habit and example, to love such works. This
is what a course in Christian culture can offer. Western man must repair
his memory before he can recover his wits. The "Catholic Studies Movement" across Canadian and American universities is one fruit of Dawson's
proposal.

Further Reading: Christopher Dawson, *Christianity and European Culture: Selections from the
Work of Christopher Dawson*, ed. G. J. Russello (Washington, D.C.: The Catholic University of
America Press, 1998); Bradley J. Birzer, *Sanctifying the World: The Augustinian Life and Mind
of Christopher Dawson* (Front Royal, Va.: Christendom Press, 2007); Allan Bloom, *The Closing
of the American Mind* (New York: Basic Books, 1987).

❖

The Case for the Study of Christian Culture

At first sight it may seem surprising that there is any need for the discussion of Christian culture study, at least among Catholic educationalists, for one would have expected that the whole question would have been thrashed out years ago and there was no longer room for any difference of opinion. But as a matter of fact this is far from being the case, and the more one looks into the subject, the more one is struck by the vagueness and uncertainty of educated opinion in this matter and the lack of any accepted doctrine or educational policy.

No doubt the situation in all the English-speaking countries differs essentially from that of Catholic Europe, where the Church has either preserved a privileged position in educational matters or, more frequently, has been forced to resist the hostile pressure of an anti-clerical or "laicist" regime. The Catholics of the English-speaking countries, in England as well as in America and in Australia, have not had the need to face the continental type of political anti-clericalism, but on the other hand, they have no privileged position and no publicly established educational institutions of their own. They have had to build their whole educational system from the bottom upwards with their own scanty resources. And so the main problem of Catholic education in the English-speaking countries has been the problem of the primary school—how to secure the necessary minimum of religious instruction for their children. The urgency of this issue has relegated all the problems of higher education to the second place. Catholics have felt that if they can save the schools, the universities can look after themselves. And in fact they have done so, up to a point. Catholics have managed to adapt themselves fairly successfully to the English and American systems of higher education. Nevertheless it has been a question of adaptation to an external system, and there has been little opportunity to decide what the nature of higher education should be or to create their own curriculum of studies.

All this is comparatively simple. But it is much more difficult to explain the situation in the past, when the Church dominated the whole educational system—schools, colleges and universities—and determined the whole course of higher studies. Surely one would have expected that the study of Christian culture would have formed the basis for the higher studies and that the foundations of an educational tradition would have been laid which would have dominated Christian education ever since. But what actually happened was that for centuries higher education has been so identified with the study of one particular historic culture—that of ancient

Greece and Rome—that there was no room left for anything else. Even the study of our own particular national culture, including both history and literature, did not obtain full recognition until the nineteenth century, while the concept of Christian culture as an object of study has never been recognized at all.

The great obstacle to this study has not been religious or secularist prejudices but strictly cultural. It had its origins in the idealization of classical antiquity by the humanist scholars and artists of the fifteenth and sixteenth centuries. And it followed from this conception that the period that intervened between the fall of Rome and the Renaissance offered the historian, as Voltaire says, "the barren prospect of a thousand years of stupidity and barbarism." They were "middle ages" in the original sense of the word—that is, a kind of cultural vacuum between two ages of cultural achievement which (to continue the same quotation) "vindicate the greatness of the human spirit."

This view, which necessarily ignores the achievements and even the existence of Christian culture, was passed on almost unchanged from the Renaissance to the eighteenth-century Enlightenment and from the latter to the modern secularist ideologies. And though today every instructed person recognizes that it is based on a completely erroneous view of history and very largely on a sheer ignorance of history, it still continues to exert an immense influence, both consciously and unconsciously, on modern education and on our attitude to the past.

It is therefore necessary for educators to make a positive effort to exorcise the ghost of this ancient error and to give the study of Christian culture the place it deserves in modern education. We cannot leave this to the medievalists alone, for they are to some extent themselves tied to the error by the limitations of their specialism. Christian culture is not the same thing as medieval culture. It existed before the Middle Ages began and it continued to exist after they had ended. We cannot understand medieval culture unless we study its foundations in the age of the Fathers and the Christian Empire, and we cannot understand the classical vernacular literatures of post-Renaissance Europe unless we study their roots in medieval culture. Even the Renaissance itself, as Conrad Burdach and E. R. Curtius have shown, is not intelligible unless it is studied as part of a movement which had its origins deep in the Middle Ages.

Moreover, it seems that the time is ripe for a new approach to the subject, since our educational system—and not in one country alone, but throughout the Western world—is passing through a period of rapid and fundamental change. The old domination of classical humanism has passed away, and nothing has taken its place except the scientific specialisms which do not provide a complete intellectual education, and rather tend to disintegrate into technologies. Every educator recognizes that this is unsatisfactory. A scientific specialist or a technologist is not an educated person. He tends to become merely an instrument of the industrialist or the bureaucrat, a worker ant in an insect society, and the same is true of the literary specialist, though his social function is less obvious.

But even the totalitarians do not accept this solution; on the contrary, they insist most strongly on the importance of the cultural element in education whether their ideal of culture is nationalist and racial, as with the Nazis, or cosmopolitan and proletarian, as with the Communists. No doubt from our point of view this totalitarian culture means the forcible indoctrination of scientist and worker alike with the same narrow party ideology, but at least it does provide a simple remedy for the disintegrating effects of modern specialization and gives the whole educational system a unifying purpose.

Heaven forbid that we should try to solve our educational problems in this way by imposing a compulsory political ideology on the teacher and the scientist! But we cannot avoid this evil by sitting back and allowing higher education to degenerate into a chaos of competing specialisms without any guidance for the student except the urgent practical necessity of finding a job and making a living as soon as his education is finished. This combination of utilitarianism and specialism is not only fatal to the idea of a liberal education, it is also one of the main causes of the intellectual disintegration of modern Western culture under the aggressive threat of totalitarian nationalism and Communism.

Some cultural education is necessary if Western culture is to survive, but we can no longer rely exclusively on the traditional discipline of classical humanism, though this is the source of all that was best in the tradition of Western liberalism and Western science. For we cannot ignore the realities of the situation—the progressive decline of the great tradition of Western humanism, the dwindling number of classical scholars and the development of a vast nation-wide system of professional education which has nothing in common with the old classical culture.

Nevertheless the decline of classical studies does not necessarily involve the decline of liberal education itself. In America the liberal arts college still maintains its prestige and American educationalists have continued to advocate the ideals of liberal education. But there is still no general agreement on how the lost unity of humanist education can be recovered. The liberal arts college itself tends to disintegrate under the growing number of subjects until it becomes an amorphous collection of alternative courses. It is to remedy this state of things that American educationalists have introduced or proposed a general integrative study of our culture which would provide a common intellectual background for the students of the liberal arts.

The problem for Catholics is a somewhat different one. They have never altogether lost sight of the medieval ideal of an order and hierarchy of knowledge and the integration of studies from above by a higher spiritual principle. In other words Catholics have a common theology and a common philosophy—the unitive disciplines which the modern secular system of higher education lacks. Yet in spite of this enormous advantage it cannot be claimed that the Catholic university has solved the problem of modern higher education or that it stands out as a brilliant exception from the educational chaos of the rest of the world. For the Catholic liberal arts college suffers from very much the same weaknesses as the secular ones.

It is losing ground externally in relation to the other schools within the university, and internally it is becoming disintegrated by the multiplicities of different studies and courses. And the reason for this is that Catholic education has suffered no less—perhaps even more—than secular education from the decline of classical studies and the loss of the old humanist culture. This was the keystone of the whole educational structure, and when it was removed the higher studies of theology and philosophy became separated from the world of specialist and vocational studies which inevitably absorb the greater part of the time and money and personnel of the modern university.

It is therefore of vital importance to maintain the key position of the liberal arts college in the university and to save the liberal arts course from further disintegration. And it is with these ends in view that I have made my suggestions for the study of Christian culture as a means of integration and unity. Its function would be very similar to that of the general courses in contemporary civilization, Western civilization, or American culture which are actually in operation in some of the non-Catholic universities. Indeed it is the same thing adapted to the needs of Catholic higher studies. For if we study Western culture in the light of Catholic theology and philosophy, we are in fact studying Christian culture or one aspect of it. I believe that the study of Christian culture is the missing link which it is essential to supply if the tradition of Western education and Western culture is to survive, for it is only through this study that we can understand how Western culture came to exist and what are the essential values for which it stands.

I see no reason to suppose, as some have argued, that such a study would have a narrowing and cramping effect on the mind of the student. On the contrary, it is eminently a liberal and liberalizing study, since it shows us how to relate our own contemporary social experience to the wider perspectives of universal history. For, after all, Christian culture is nothing to be ashamed of. It is no narrow sectarian tradition. It is one of the four great historic civilizations on which the modern world is founded. If modern education fails to communicate some understanding of this great tradition, it has failed in one of its most essential tasks. For the educated person cannot play his full part in modern life unless he has a clear sense of the nature and achievements of Christian culture: how Western civilization became Christian and how far it is Christian today and in what ways it has ceased to be Christian: in short, a knowledge of our Christian roots and of the abiding Christian elements in Western culture.

When I speak of Western culture I am not using the word in the limited sense in which it was used by Matthew Arnold and the humanists, who were concerned only with the highest level of cultivated intelligence, but in the sense of the anthropologists and social historians, who have widened it out to cover the whole pattern of human life and thought in a living society. In this sense of the word, a culture is a definite historical unity, but as Dr. Toynbee explains so clearly in the Introduction to his *Study of History*, it has a much wider expansion in space and time than any purely political unit, and it alone constitutes an intelligible field of historical study, since no part of it can be properly understood except in relation to the whole.

Behind the existing unity of Western culture, we have the older unity of Christian culture which is the historic basis of our civilization. For more than a thousand years from the conversion of the Roman Empire down to the Reformation the peoples of Europe were fully conscious of their membership in the great Christian society and accepted the Christian faith and the Christian moral law as the ultimate bond of social unity and the spiritual basis of their way of life. Even after the unity of Christendom had been broken by the Reformation, the tradition of Christian culture still survived in the culture and institutions of the different European peoples, and in some cases exists even in the midst of our secularized culture, as we see so strikingly in the English monarch's coronation rite.

Consequently anyone who wishes to understand our own culture as it exists today cannot dispense with the study of Christian culture, whether he is a Christian or not. Indeed in some ways this study is more necessary for the secularist than for the Christian, because he lacks that ideological key to the understanding of the past which every Christian ought to possess.

The subject is a vast one which could occupy the lifetime of an advanced scholar. But the same may be said of the study of Western civilization in the secular universities, or indeed of the study of classical culture in the past. Nevertheless it can also provide the ordinary student who is going out into the world to earn his living in professional life with a glimpse of the intellectual and spiritual riches to which he is heir and to which he can return in later years for light and refreshment.

If the college or university can only inspire its students with a sense of the value of this inheritance and a desire to know more about it, it will have taken the first and most essential step. No doubt higher education is not unaware of this need and has made some attempt to satisfy it both in the liberal arts college and in the graduate school. But it has done so hitherto in a somewhat haphazard and piecemeal fashion. The student can study any number of subjects which have a bearing on the subject of Christian culture or form part of it; but none of these will give him any comprehensive view of the whole. What is needed, so it seems to me, is a study of Christian culture as a social reality—its origins, development and achievements—for this would provide a background or framework that would integrate the liberal studies which at present are apt to disintegrate into unrelated specialisms.

This kind of program is not simply a study of the Christian classics; nor is it primarily a literary study. It is a cultural study in the sociological and historical sense, and it would devote more attention to the social institutions and. the moral values of Christian culture than to its literary and artistic achievements. Christian culture has indeed flowered again and again in literature and art, and these successive flowerings are well worthy of our study. But obviously it is out of the question to make the average arts student study all of them. Such a proposal, which one critic of Christian culture study assumes to be my intention, is to misunderstand the nature of the problem. What we need is not an encyclopedic knowledge of all the products of Christian culture, but a study of the culture process itself from its spiritual and theological roots, through its organic historical growth to its cultural fruits. It is this organic relation between theology, history and culture which provides the integrative principle in Catholic higher education, and the only one that is capable of taking the place of the old classical humanism which is disappearing or has already disappeared.

Moreover, if we desire to promote religious and intellectual understanding among the different religious groups within American society, surely the best way to do this is to understand and appreciate our own culture in all its depth and breadth. Without this full cultural awareness it is impossible either to interpret one's culture to others or to understand the problems of intercultural relations, problems which are of such incalculable importance for the future of the modern world.

I do not deny that there are great practical obstacles in the way of this study. The secularist is naturally afraid that it might be used as an instrument of religious propaganda, and he is consequently anxious to minimize the importance of the Christian element in our culture and exaggerate the gulf between modern civilization and the Christian culture of the past.

The Christian, on the other hand, is often afraid lest the historical study of Christian culture should lead to an identification of Christianity with a culture and a social system which belong to the dead past. But for the Christian the past can never be dead, as it often seems to the secularist, since we believe the past and the present are united in the one Body of the Church and that the Christians of the past are still present as witnesses and helpers in the life of the Church today.

No doubt it would be an error to apply this principle to the particular forms of Christian culture which are conditioned by material factors and limited by the change of historical circumstances. But as there is an organic relation between the Christian faith and the Christian life, so also there is a relation between Christian life and Christian culture. The relation between faith and life is completely realized only in the life of the saint. But there has never been a temporal society of saints, and the attempt to create one, as in Puritan England or Massachusetts, represents a sectarian perversion of Christian culture. Nevertheless it is the very nature of the Christian faith and the Christian life to penetrate and change the social environment in which they exist, and there is no aspect of human life which is closed to this leavening and transforming process. Thus Christian culture is the periphery of the circle which has its center in the Incarnation and the faith of the Church and the lives of the saints.

All this is to be seen in history. Christianity did actually come into the historical world and did actually transform the societies with which it came into contact: first, the Hellenistic-Oriental society of the Eastern Roman Empire, and secondly, the Latin and barbarian societies of Western Europe. From this two new cultures were born—the Byzantine culture of the East and Western Christendom, both of which, in spite of their ultimate separation, share a large number of common characteristics.

Both of these cultures have now been secularized, but the process of secularization is so recent and even incomplete that it is absolutely impossible to understand them in their secularized form unless we have studied their Christian past.

Unfortunately it is nobody's business to study or to teach this subject, and it is extremely difficult under existing conditions for anyone to acquire the necessary knowledge, even if he can spare the time and energy to do so. Nevertheless the very reasons which make the study of the subject so difficult are also reasons in its favor from the educational point of view. They are due to the fact that it is an integrative subject involving the co-operation of a number of different specialized studies, in the same way as the study of *litterae humaniores* in the Greats School at Oxford involves the co-operation of philosophers and historians as well as philologists and literary critics. A curriculum in Christian culture would thus embrace a co-operative study of Christian philosophy, Christian literature and Christian history.

What are the principles upon which such a study should be based? We must recognize that Christian culture can be studied in two ways: externally, as an objective historical study of Christendom as one of the four great world civilizations on which the modem world is founded; and from within, as the study of the history of the Christian people—a study of the ways in which Christianity has expressed itself in human thought and life and institutions through the ages.

The first is necessary for every historian, since it is an essential aspect of the study of world civilization. The second is necessary to the Christian, since it deals with his own spiritual history and with the successive stages of Christian life and thought.

For educational purposes, both these studies should be combined. The student should be given a general knowledge of the external development of Christian civilization from the beginning to the present day, and this should be accompanied by a more detailed study of Christian life and thought and institutions during some one particular period.

The development of Christian culture has passed through six successive phases or periods, each with its distinctive form of culture:

1. Primitive Christianity, from the first to the beginning of the fourth century. This is the age which saw the birth of the Church: the subterranean expansion of the Christian way of life beneath the surface of a pagan civilization and the development of an autonomous Christian society widely distributed through the great cities of the Roman Empire, above all in the Eastern Mediterranean.

2. Patristic Christianity, from the fourth to the sixth centuries: the age

of the conversion of the Roman-Hellenistic world and the establishment of Christian-Roman or Byzantine culture.

3. The Formation of Western Christendom, from the sixth to the eleventh centuries: the age of the conversion of Northern Europe and the formation of Western Christendom through the gradual permeation of the barbarian cultures—Celtic, Germanic, and Slavonic—by Christian influence. At the same time a large part of the old Christian world was lost by the rise of Islam and the development of a new non-Christian culture there.

4. Medieval Christendom, from the eleventh to the fifteenth centuries. This is the age in which Western Christian culture attained full development and cultural consciousness and created new social institutions and new forms of artistic and literary expression.

5. Divided Christendom, from the sixteenth to the eighteenth centuries: the age of the development of the national European cultures. In spite of the internal religious strife which characterized the period, it was also an age of expansion, so that Christian culture gradually came to incorporate the whole of the New World. It also saw a great, though unsuccessful, effort to spread Christianity from Europe to India, China and Japan.

6. Secularized Christendom, from the eighteenth century to the present. During this period Western culture achieved a position of world hegemony, but at the same time it ceased to be Christian, and the old institutional framework of Christian culture was swept away by revolutionary movements. Nevertheless Christianity survived and Western culture still retains considerable traces of its Christian origins. Moreover the world expansion of Western culture has been accompanied by a new expansion of Christian missionary influence, especially in Africa and Australia.

Each of these periods has its own specific character, which can be studied in art and philosophy, in literature and in social institutions. Most important and characteristic of all are the successive forms of the religious life itself which have manifested themselves in each of the different periods.

This study covers much the same ground chronologically as the general courses in the history of Western civilization, but it has an internal principle of organic unity which they do not possess, and every period and every aspect of a particular period has an organic relation to the whole. It is especially valuable as a co-ordinating study which will help us to understand the resemblances and differences of the different national and regional cultures by explaining the common factors that have influenced them all. Institutions that are common to the whole of Christendom such as monasticism and the university, or even constitutional monarchy and the representative system of government, are none of them entirely explicable within the framework of national history, within which they are usually studied. They can only be understood as parts of a common international heritage of Christian culture. In the same way the spiritual archetypes which formed the character and inspired the life of Western man are of Christian origin, and however imperfectly they were realized in practice, it is impossible to understand his pattern of behavior unless we take account of them.

We study political ideas in relation to history, although we know that the majority of men are never governed by purely ideological motives. How much more then should we study the religious element in culture, for this affected the majority of men from the cradle to the grave and has been a continuous influence on Western culture for more than twelve centuries. It was not studied in the past, because men took it for granted like the air they breathed. But now that our civilization is becoming predominantly and increasingly secular, it is necessary to make an express study of it, if we are to understand our past and the nature of the culture that we have inherited.

Review and Discussion Questions

1. In Dawson's view, what obstacles do American and European Catholics, respectively, face?

2. Dawson claims that it is "of vital importance ... to save the liberal arts course from further disintegration." By what steps did he try to lead the reader to this conclusion?

3. Dawson proposes the study of Christian culture as the "missing link" that could help graft students back into the tradition of Western education. What would a study of "Christian culture" entail?

4. Instead of a call to return to the New Testament, *The Republic*, *The Divine Comedy*, and other great books, Dawson recommends we turn attention to the "social institutions and the moral values of Christian culture." In his view, why aren't the great books good enough?

❖ 32

ST. JOHN XXIII (1881–1963)

On the Study of Latin

> Finally, the Church has a dignity far surpassing that of every merely human
> society, for it was founded by Christ the Lord. It is altogether fitting, there-
> fore, that the language it uses should be noble, majestic, and non-vernacular.

The Holy Father here offers three reasons to study Latin: it stabilizes, it elevates, and it unites. Latin stabilizes the community of the present by putting
us in contact with the community of the past; as the gateway to the liturgy,
Latin elevates our sentiments; finally, the Church's common tongue unites
believers not only across time but also across space—drawing us into a more
perfect communion with men from every nation. In this document, promulgated just weeks prior to the opening of the Second Vatican Council,
John XXIII gives a vigorous defense for the study and promotion of Latin
among Christians worldwide. John XXIII never witnessed the disintegration of the scholastic curriculum within seminaries and Catholic colleges
that followed his Council. Whatever he might have thought of the coming
theological pluralism, good Pope John certainly would have deplored the
lowering of intellectual standards among the clergy.

Further Reading: Frederic Wheelock, *Wheelock's Latin*, Seventh Edition (New York: Harper
Collins Publishers, 2011); John F. Collins, *A Primer of Ecclesiastical Latin* (Washington, D.C.:
The Catholic University of America Press, 1985); Ralph McInerny, *Let's Read Latin* (Notre
Dame, Ind.: Dumb Ox Books, 1995).

❖

The wisdom of the ancient world, enshrined in Greek and Roman literature, and the truly memorable teaching of ancient peoples, served, surely,
to herald the dawn of the Gospel which God's Son, "the judge and teacher
of grace and truth, the light and guide of the human race,"[1] proclaimed on
earth. Such was the view of the Church Fathers and Doctors. In these outstanding literary monuments of antiquity, they recognized man's spiritual

preparation for the supernatural riches which Jesus Christ communicated to mankind "to give history its fulfilment."[2] Thus the inauguration of Christianity did not mean the obliteration of man's past achievements. Nothing was lost that was in any way true, just, noble and beautiful.

The Church has ever held the literary evidences of this wisdom in the highest esteem. She values especially the Greek and Latin languages in which wisdom itself is cloaked, as it were, in a vesture of gold. She has likewise welcomed the use of other venerable languages, which flourished in the East. For these too have had no little influence on the progress of humanity and civilization. By their use in sacred liturgies and in versions of Holy Scripture, they have remained in force in certain regions even to the present day, bearing constant witness to the living voice of antiquity.

But amid this variety of languages a primary place must surely be given to that language which had its origins in *Latium*, and later proved so admirable a means for the spreading of Christianity throughout the West. And since in God's special Providence this language united so many nations together under the authority of the Roman Empire—and that for so many centuries—it also became the rightful language of the Apostolic See.[3] Preserved for posterity, it proved to be a bond of unity for the Christian peoples of Europe.

Of its very nature Latin is most suitable for promoting every form of culture among peoples. It gives rise to no jealousies. It does not favor any one nation, but presents itself with equal impartiality to all and is equally acceptable to all. Nor must we overlook the characteristic nobility of Latin formal structure. Its "concise, varied and harmonious style, full of majesty and dignity"[4] makes for singular clarity and impressiveness of expression.

For these reasons the Apostolic See has always been at pains to preserve Latin, deeming it worthy of being used in the exercise of her teaching authority "as the splendid vesture of her heavenly doctrine and sacred laws."[5] She further requires her sacred ministers to use it, for by so doing they are the better able, wherever they may be, to acquaint themselves with the mind of the Holy See on any matter, and communicate the more easily with Rome and with one another.

Thus the "knowledge and use of this language," so intimately bound up with the Church's life, "is important not so much on cultural or literary grounds, as for religious reasons."[6] These are the words of Our Predecessor Pius XI, who conducted a scientific inquiry into this whole subject, and indicated three qualities of the Latin language which harmonize to a remarkable degree with the Church's nature. "For the Church, precisely because it embraces all nations and is destined to endure to the end of time ... of its very nature requires a language which is universal, immutable, and non-vernacular."[7]

Since "every Church must assemble round the Roman Church,"[8] and since the Supreme Pontiffs have "true episcopal power, ordinary and immediate, over each and every Church and each and every Pastor, as well as over the faithful"[9] of every rite and language, it seems particularly desirable that the instrument of mutual communication be uniform and universal, especially between the Apostolic See and the Churches which use the same Latin rite. When, therefore, the Roman Pontiffs wish to instruct the Catholic world, or when the Congregations of the Roman Curia handle matters or draw up decrees which concern the whole body of the faithful, they invariably make use of Latin, for this is a maternal voice acceptable to countless nations.

Furthermore, the Church's language must be not only universal but also immutable. Modern languages are liable to change, and no single one of them is superior to the others in authority. Thus if the truths of the Catholic Church were entrusted to an unspecified number of them, the meaning of these truths, varied as they are, would not be manifested to everyone with sufficient clarity and precision. There would, moreover, be no language which could serve as a common and constant norm by which to gauge the exact meaning of other renderings.

But Latin is indeed such a language. It is set and unchanging. it has long since ceased to be affected by those alterations in the meaning of words which are the normal result of daily, popular use. Certain Latin words, it is true, acquired new meanings as Christian teaching developed and needed to be explained and defended, but these new meanings have long since become accepted and firmly established.

Finally, the Catholic Church has a dignity far surpassing that of every merely human society, for it was founded by Christ the Lord. It is altogether fitting, therefore, that the language it uses should be noble, majestic, and non-vernacular.

In addition, the Latin language "can be called truly catholic."[10] It has been consecrated through constant use by the Apostolic See, the mother and teacher of all Churches, and must be esteemed "a treasure ... of incomparable worth."[11] It is a general passport to the proper understanding of the Christian writers of antiquity and the documents of the Church's teaching.[12] It is also a most effective bond, binding the Church of today with that of the past and of the future in wonderful continuity.

There can be no doubt as to the formative and educational value either of the language of the Romans or of great literature generally. It is a most effective training for the pliant minds of youth. It exercises, matures and perfects the principal faculties of mind and spirit. It sharpens the wits and gives keenness of judgment. It helps the young mind to grasp things accurately and develop a true sense of values. It is also a means for teaching highly intelligent thought and speech.

It will be quite clear from these considerations why the Roman Pontiffs have so often extolled the excellence and importance of Latin, and why they have prescribed its study and use by the secular and regular clergy, forecasting the dangers that would result from its neglect.

And We also, impelled by the weightiest of reasons—the same as those which prompted Our Predecessors and provincial synods[13]—are fully determined to restore this language to its position of honor, and to do all We can to promote its study and use. The employment of Latin has recently been contested in many quarters, and many are asking what the mind of the Apostolic See is in this matter. We have therefore decided to issue the timely directives contained in this document, so as to ensure that the ancient and uninterrupted use of Latin be maintained and, where necessary, restored.

We believe that We made Our own views on this subject sufficiently clear when We said to a number of eminent Latin scholars:

It is a matter of regret that so many people, unaccountably dazzled by the marvelous progress of science, are taking it upon themselves to oust or restrict the study of Latin and other kindred subjects.... Yet, in spite of the urgent need for science, Our own view is that the very contrary policy should be followed. The greatest impression is made on the mind by those things which correspond more closely to man's nature and dignity. And therefore the greatest zeal should be shown in the acquisition of whatever educates and ennobles the mind. Otherwise poor mortal creatures may well become like the machines they build—cold, hard, and devoid of love.[14]

With the foregoing considerations in mind, to which We have given careful thought, We now, in the full consciousness of Our Office and in virtue of Our authority, decree and command the following:

1. Bishops and superiors-general of religious orders shall take pains to ensure that in their seminaries and in their schools where adolescents are trained for the priesthood, all shall studiously observe the Apostolic See's decision in this matter and obey these Our prescriptions most carefully.

2. In the exercise of their paternal care they shall be on their guard lest anyone under their jurisdiction, eager for revolutionary changes, writes

against the use of Latin in the teaching of the higher sacred studies or in the Liturgy, or through prejudice makes light of the Holy See's will in this regard or interprets it falsely.

3. As is laid down in Canon Law (can. 1364) or commanded by Our Predecessors, before Church students begin their ecclesiastical studies proper they shall be given a sufficiently lengthy course of instruction in Latin by highly competent masters, following a method designed to teach them the language with the utmost accuracy. "And that too for this reason: lest later on, when they begin their major studies ... they are unable by reason of their ignorance of the language to gain a full understanding of the doctrines or take part in those scholastic disputations which constitute so excellent an intellectual training for young men in the defense of the faith."[15]

We wish the same rule to apply to those whom God calls to the priesthood at a more advanced age, and whose classical studies have either been neglected or conducted too superficially. No one is to be admitted to the study of philosophy or theology except he be thoroughly grounded in this language and capable of using it.

4. Wherever the study of Latin has suffered partial eclipse through the assimilation of the academic program to that which obtains in State public schools, with the result that the instruction given is no longer so thorough and well-grounded as formerly, there the traditional method of teaching this language shall be completely restored. Such is Our will, and there should be no doubt in anyone's mind about the necessity of keeping a strict watch over the course of studies followed by Church students; and that not only as regards the number and kinds of subjects they study, but also as regards the length of time devoted to the teaching of these subjects.

Should circumstances of time and place demand the addition of other subjects to the curriculum besides the usual ones, then either the course of studies must be lengthened, or these additional subjects must be condensed or their study relegated to another time.

5. In accordance with numerous previous instructions, the major sacred sciences shall be taught in Latin, which, as we know from many centuries of use, "must be considered most suitable for explaining with the utmost facility and clarity the most difficult and profound ideas and concepts."[16] For apart from the fact that it has long since been enriched with a vocabulary of appropriate and unequivocal terms, best calculated to safeguard the integrity of the Catholic faith, it also serves in no slight measure to prune away useless verbiage.

Hence professors of these sciences in universities or seminaries are required to speak Latin and to make use of textbooks written in Latin. If ignorance of Latin makes it difficult for some to obey these instructions, they shall gradually be replaced by professors who are suited to this task. Any difficulties that may be advanced by students or professors must be overcome by the patient insistence of the bishops or religious superiors, and the good will of the professors.

6. Since Latin is the Church's living language, it must be adequate to daily increasing linguistic requirements. It must be furnished with new words that are apt and suitable for expressing modern things, words that will be uniform and universal in their application and constructed in conformity with the genius of the ancient Latin tongue. Such was the method followed by the sacred Fathers and the best writers among the scholastics.

To this end, therefore, We commission the Sacred Congregation of Seminaries and Universities to set up a Latin Academy staffed by an international body of Latin and Greek professors. The principal aim of this Academy—like the national academies founded to promote their respective languages—will be to superintend the proper development of Latin, augmenting the Latin lexicon where necessary with words which conform to the particular character and color of the language.

It will also conduct schools for the study of Latin of every era, particularly the Christian one. The aim of these schools will be to impart a fuller understanding of Latin and the ability to use it and to write it with proper elegance. They will exist for those who are destined to teach Latin in seminaries and ecclesiastical colleges, or to write decrees and judgments or conduct correspondence in the ministries of the Holy See, diocesan curias, and the offices of religious orders.

7. Latin is closely allied to Greek both in formal structure and in the importance of its extant writings. Hence—as Our Predecessors have frequently ordained—future ministers of the altar must be instructed in Greek in the lower and middle schools. Thus when they come to study the higher sciences—and especially if they are aiming for a degree in Sacred Scripture or theology—they will be enabled to follow the Greek sources of scholastic philosophy and understand them correctly; and not only these, but also the original texts of Sacred Scripture, the Liturgy, and the sacred Fathers.[17]

8. We further commission the Sacred Congregation of Seminaries and Universities to prepare a syllabus for the teaching of Latin which all shall faithfully observe. The syllabus will be designed to give those who follow it an adequate understanding of the language and its use. Episcopal boards may indeed rearrange this syllabus if circumstances warrant, but they must

never curtail it or alter its nature. Ordinaries may not take it upon themselves to put their own proposals into effect until these have been examined and approved by the Sacred Congregation.

Finally, in virtue of Our apostolic authority, We will and command that all the decisions, decrees, proclamations and recommendations of this Our Constitution remain firmly established and ratified, notwithstanding anything to the contrary, however worthy of special note.

> *Given at Rome, at Saint Peter's, on the feast of Saint Peter's Throne on the 22nd day of February in the year 1962, the fourth of our pontificate.*

Review and Discussion Questions

1. In John XXIII's view, how does Latin stabilize the Christian community?

2. In what senses does Latin "elevate"?

3. What objection does St. John consider against the study of Latin (and why does he dismiss it)?

4. Name one of the pope's practical suggestions that you think is likely to be deemed "impractical" by others.

❖ 33

JOHN SENIOR (1923–99)

The Restoration of Christian Culture

The seminal ideas of Plato, Aristotle, St. Augustine, St. Thomas, only properly grow in an imaginative ground saturated with fables, fairy tales, stories,
rhymes, romances, adventures of Grimm, Stevenson, Dickens, Scott, Dumas
and the rest.

Great books without good books? John Senior thinks not. In this dazzling
selection, Senior argues for the revival of habits of mind that are the pre-
cursors to greatness. What has been neglected in the contemporary revival
of the great books tradition, he observes, is not so much the great books;
what is missing is precisely everything else, upon which the books depend.
Catholic culture is a web of practices, not merely a stack of articles. To restore faith you must repair culture. And the reading of "the thousand good
books" is a first step along the long road back. During the 1970s, Senior
taught at the University of Kansas's long-ago suppressed "Integrated Humanities Program," where, it is reported, he was instrumental in some two
hundred conversions to Catholicism.

Further Reading: John Senior, *The Death of Christian Culture* (New Rochelle, N.Y.: Arlington
House Publishers, 1978); Dennis B. Quinn, ed., *The Integration of Knowledge: Discourses on Education* [with essays by Adler, Nelick, Quinn, and Senior] (Lawrence: The Integrated Humanities
Program, University of Kansas, 1979); James S. Taylor, *Poetic Knowledge: The Recovery of Education* (Albany: State University of New York Press, 1998).

❖

Well, it is simply so. Catholics have accepted some of the worst distortions of their Faith in the order of music, art and literature without a shiver
of discontent because they never really heard the "Tantum Ergo" or the "Ave
Maris Stella"—not for lack of faith, but because there had never been ordinary music in the home to have created the habit of good sound and sense.

And as for reading in the home; it isn't done at all. The Great Books movement of the last generation didn't so much fail as fizzle, and not because of any defect in the books; they are the "best that has been thought and said," in Matthew Arnold's famous phrase; but like champagne in cracked bottles, the books went flat in minds which lacked the habit of reading. To change the figure, the seeds grew but the cultural soil had been depleted; the seminal ideas of Plato, Aristotle, St. Augustine, St. Thomas, only properly grow in an imaginative ground saturated with fables, fairy tales, stories, rhymes, romances, adventures—the thousand good books of Grimm, Andersen, Stevenson, Dickens, Scott, Dumas and the rest. Western tradition, taking all that was the best of the Greco-Roman world into itself, has given us a culture in which the Faith properly grows; and since the conversion of Constantine that culture has become Christian. It is the seedbed of intelligence and will, the ground for all studies in the arts and sciences, including theology, without which they are inhumane and destructive. The brutal athlete and the aesthetic fop suffer vices opposed to the virtues of what Newman called the "gentleman." Anyone working in any art or science, whether "pure" or "practical," will discover he has made a quantum leap when he gets even a small amount of cultural ground under him; he will grow like an undernourished plant suddenly fertilized and watered.

And the right point of view is that of the amateur, the ordinary person who enjoys what he reads, not expert in critical, historical or textual techniques which destroy what they analyze and are as inimical to culture as sex-clinics to marriage or scientific agriculture to farming. Whatever you do, don't poison the wells and salt the fields with dictionaries, encyclopedias, atlases, study-guides, critical editions, notes, biographical and historical appendices—all of that is the science of literature-it is a misapplication of scientific method to subject matter outside its competence. We want what Robert Louis Stevenson called "a child's garden," something simple, direct, enjoyable, unreflective, uncritical, spontaneous, free, romantic, if you will, with the full understanding that such experience is not sufficient for salvation as the Romantic School thought, nor sufficient for science and philosophy, but indispensable as the cultural soil of moral, intellectual and spiritual growth. And so instead of an argument, I propose a reading of the thousand good books.

Because sight is the first of the senses and especially powerful in the earliest years, it is important to secure editions illustrated by artists working in the cultural tradition we are restoring, both as introduction to art and as part of the imaginative experience of the book. This is not to disparage all contemporary artists any more than the tradition itself denies experiment;

quite the contrary, one of the fruits of such reading should be the encouragement of good writing and drawing by the reader. A standard is not a straitjacket but a teacher of norms and a model for imitation. Book illustration reached its classical perfection in the hundred years before World War I in the work of "Phiz," Gordon Browne, the Brock brothers, Beatrix Potter, Sir John Tenniel, Arthur Rackham, Howard Pyle, N. C. Wyeth, Randolph Caldecott, Walter Crane, Kate Greenaway, George Cruickshank, Leslie Brooke and many others. The rule of thumb is to find an old edition in a secondhand shop or at least facsimiles which, though not as sharp in line or true in color, are available at more moderate prices.

For English-speaking Catholics there is a difficulty which would take a whole treatise to deal with adequately: English literature is substantially Protestant. It is all well and good to quote St. Paul that "whatever is true is from the Holy Ghost" and argue that this literature, whether Protestant, Jewish or Infidel, so long as it is true, is Catholic despite the persuasion of its authors. All well and good provided that literature were abstract science; a matter of two and two are four. But literature by definition is that paradoxical thing the "concrete universal," imitating men in action in their actual affective and moral and spiritual struggles. And so Catholics have to live with a difficulty. The thousand good books which are the indispensable soil of the understanding of the Catholic Faith and indirectly requisite to the Kingdom of Heaven, are not Catholic but Protestant.

The recognition of this has led some well-meaning Catholic teachers to the recommendation of texts and reading lists of strictly Catholic authors, which can only be done by supplying large amounts of Latin, French, Italian and other foreign authors in translation along with those very few Englishmen who happened to be Catholic and alas, though by no means bad, are all second-rate. No matter how you do it, the attempt is hopeless. First, we are English-speaking people. Our language is English and if we are to learn it, we must absorb its own peculiar genius. If we are to have English Catholic authors or even readers, they must be schooled in the English language as it is, and not in even the best work of translators who are not men of genius, no matter how great the works they are translating. Dorothy Sayers, for example, is a fine Christian lady, I am told, and the Italian Catholic Dante is one of only three candidates for the title of greatest poet who ever lived; but Dorothy Sayers' translation of the *Divine Comedy* is something of a comedy in another sense and not even remotely in a class of excellence with the Puritan Latin Secretary to the arch-heretic and murderer of Catholic Ireland, John Milton, or even with the atheist Irish sympathizer Shelley, whom Miss Sayers imitates in attempting—disastrously—Dante's *terza rima*. English literature is not an option; it is a fact. And it is Protestant; we are at once blest and stuck with it—blest because it is the finest literature in the world, and stuck because it cannot ever be done again.

Catholic parents and teachers must read and reread Cardinal Newman's long, balanced, incomparable essay on the whole subject, "Catholic Literature in the English Tongue," in his *Idea of a University*.

The upshot of the difficulty is that the heart, indeed, the very delicate viscera, the physical constitution and emotional dispositions as well as the imaginations, of children will be formed by authors who are off the Catholic center and some very far off; and yet, not to read them is not to develop these essential aptitudes and faculties.

Having stated the facts first as a difficulty, I hasten to add that it is a difficulty we can live with and flourish under. First of all, insofar as the literature is Protestant, it is Biblical and Christian; the existence of God, the Divinity of Christ, the necessity of prayer and obedience to the commandments is its very strong stuff for the most part and there is little anywhere in direct violation of the Catholic Faith, though there is some overt, sometimes crude, sometimes true, accusation. Since Protestantism stands in between its Catholic and Jewish antecedents in a kind of Hebraic Christianity, at least in its Calvinist tendencies, its popular literature has been both anti-Catholic and anti-Jewish. Charles Kingsley's *Westward Ho!*, one of the best boys' books, is filled with outrageous lies about the Jesuits; and both Shakespeare and Dickens, with Shylock and Fagin, have exploited and exaggerated the avarice of the Jews. But what Chesterton said of *Westward Ho!*—"It's a lie, but a healthy one"—could be said of *A Merchant of Venice* and *Oliver Twist*. It is the unhealthy pharisaical Catholic and Jew who resent the caricatures of themselves. The health and excellence of caricature always consists in its accidental prevarication of essential truths. The fact is that Jesuits have sometimes been a scandal, despite the glorious Company of their saints; and Jews have been conspicuous usurers, pornographers and Communists, despite their large courage in the face of unjust persecution and the smaller company of converted saints. Good Catholics and Jews can laugh and weep at once at the truth in these cartoons, just as a temperate Irishman—if you can find one—would laugh and weep at the stage Irish drunk, or an honest Italian, at *The Godfather*.

One of the most famous and best of geniuses in the list of classical children's books is not an English Protestant but some kind of French Catholic. By the time you finish *The Three Musketeers* it is clear enough that sin is punished. Aramis, who had played his part in satirizing religious vocations early on in the novel, actually becomes a monk at last—albeit in a sequel, though not a very good one! There is one lurid scene in which D'Artagnan, the golden boy and best of heroes, commits explicit and rather preposterous adultery under sensational conditions with the most fatal femme fatale in literature; but both participants suffer the consequences, she a horrid death and he a harrowing education. Perhaps *The Three Musketeers* is best reserved for the older end of the adolescent spectrum, around sixteen; but taken all in all, it is an adolescent book and the paradigm of dashing derring-do, and it is good—I mean morally good. Like it or not, the kind of adventure you get in Alexandre Dumas is there in literature as the Rocky Mountains are there in geography. You might have got to California quicker if they weren't, but getting there was "half the fun" in the one case; and the chivalry, intrigue and romance is all the fun in the other.

The worst failure in English classical literature is indirect, that is its omissions—the conspicuous absence of Our Blessed Mother and the Blessed Sacrament and, following from the loss of these principal mysteries, all the rich accidentals of Catholic life, the veneration of saints and relics, the use of medals, scapulars, holy water, Rosaries. When these are present, which is rare, it is usually, alas, to disparage them as superstition—though not always; for example, there is the tender scene in *Little Women* where the French servant explains the Rosary to the incredulous but amazed and edified little Amy. But no doubt about it, the omissions are a great disappointment and must be compensated for by daily use of these instruments and by a rich Catholic, and especially Latin, liturgical life. From the cultural point of view, which I must insist is not a minor or accidental thing but indispensable to the ordinary means of salvation, and prescinding from all the complex canonical and theological disputes about its validity and liceity—whatever defense can be made of it on pastoral and other grounds—from the cultural point of view, the new Catholic Mass established in the United States has been a disaster and I must give public witness to my private petitions, with all due respect to the authorities, that its great predecessor—the most refined and brilliant work of art in the history of the world, the heart and soul and most powerful determinant factor in Western Civilization, seedbed of saints—be restored. Catholic children brought up on the best English literature must at the same time be immersed in the traditional Catholic practices like Rosaries, Benedictions, Stations of the Cross. And when there is explicit disparagement of anything Catholic in the literature, the parent and teacher must censor it—not with the scissors, which is impossible because these things are too intimately connected with the context—but by explanations. For younger children the parent or sister who reads the stories aloud can correct misunderstandings tastefully in quiet conversation, using the errors themselves as occasions to teach the truth—sometimes the truth that Catholics have not lived up to their Faith. For the school child teachers can use distortions and caricatures as a stimulus for further reading; Kingsley's violence to the Jesuits, for example, can be an occasion for a child to read the lives of St. Isaac Jogues and his companions and other missionary saints. For the adolescent and youth, his own strength in the Faith should be sufficient; anti-Catholic texts should provide a kind of test of his understanding, and teachers can conduct colloquia to bring the questions out.

But I have belabored the point too long. In the hundreds of thousands of pages of the thousand books, the number of passages calling for such correction are very few. The chief difficulty, as it is of modern culture in general, is the lack of those ordinary Catholic accidentals determinant to Faith; and these must be restored in the Church and at home. Actually, since we are English-speaking people, living in a non-Catholic subculture, it is good for a Catholic child to grow up with an imaginative grasp of the hostile environment—short, of course, of anything pornographic, ironic and sly, and there is none of that in the classic children's literature; all in a common sense way are "good," artistically, morally and spiritually, though they are not complete.

Perhaps there is a need for just one further caution on adolescent reading: Here you are dealing with a time of life which is by definition dangerous. "Adolescent" comes from a Latin word meaning "to burn," and it is certainly a burning age. The literature of adolescence, say, Shakespeare's *Romeo and Juliet*, sometimes overheats an excitable imagination; those star-crossed lovers fall desperately and hotly in love, and it may well be that the reading of certain of its best passages could lead young people into sin, like the wretched souls in Dante's *Inferno* who blame their eternal damnation on the reading of an Arthurian romance. "A galeotto was that book," Francesca says—galeotto is an Italian word for pimp. There is no question that adolescent reading must be accompanied by strict, serious, complete dogmatic and moral teaching and by a strong, active, vigorous gymnastics program. But a severe warning is in order for Catholic parents who, the more conservative they are in their Faith, tend toward a Jansenism in their discipline of children. When a child hits twelve, he is ready for the adolescent experience, and that means the explosions of physical aptitudes and the emotional responses to them—the call to dangerous adventures and to experiments in romance. There IS a certain kind of parent who wants to bind a child's soul the way the Chinese are said to have bound their little girls' feet to keep them dainty. There are Catholic families who proudly send their eighteen-year-olds up to college carefully bound and wrapped at the emotional and spiritual age of twelve—good little boys and girls in cute dresses and panty-waists who never get into trouble or into knowledge and love. The Kingdom of Heaven is the knowledge and love of God, and we learn to bear the living flames of that love only through suffering the paler heats of human desire; and adolescence is as necessary to the normal development of the body and soul as the Faith itself. Faith presupposes nature and cannot be efficacious in its atrophy. There is little point in keeping children out of Hell if you don't afford them the means of getting into Heaven.

So give them solid catechetics, strong preaching, good example, healthy exercise, supervision in a general and determinant way but not in each par-ticular and by all means permitting them the freedom of the good, dan-gerous books as well as the dangerous games such as football or mountain climbing. Given the state of man, some will break their necks and sin; but in good Catholic families with common sense, the falls should be few and the bodies and souls recoverable. The positive power of the literature and the games is so good and great that we must thank God English literature and sport have been so richly blessed, though we sometimes, as we shouldn't, grudge the genius of those marvelously gifted Protestants, some of them even terrible Protestants like John Milton!

Fortunately, for the most part, the majority of the authors are sympa-thetic to the Faith and some like Shakespeare, may even have been in pec-tor Catholic. Dickens had a visionary dream he took very seriously of the Virgin Mary who instructed him to write more warmly of Catholics, which he did in one of his greatest novels, *Barnaby Rudge*. Despite the revisionist historians, the past is past and cannot be changed. If you dispense with the classics, you lose the culture—and whatever the culture is, it is ours, still in its roots and in its truth, goodness, and beauty, Catholic.

To conclude not so much with a proof of anything as an exhortation to experiment: Read, preferably aloud, the good English books from Mother Goose to the works of Jane Austen. There really is no need for reading lists; the surest sign of a classic is that everyone knows its name. And sing some songs from the golden treasury around the piano every night. Music really is the food of love, and music in the wide sense is a specific sign of the civi-lized human species. Steeped in the ordinary pot of the Christian imagination, we shall have learned to listen to that language by absorption, that mysterious music the Bridegroom speaks; and we shall begin to love one another as he loves us; we shall see at last the Star of Hope which "flames in the forehead of the morning sky" at the end of this dark night. We shall see, because we love—*Ubi amor ibi oculus*—though not without her help: *Rosa Mystica, Turris Davidica, Domus Aurea, Stella Matutina* ... Morning Star.

Review and Discussion Questions

1. Explain Senior's charge: "like Champagne in cracked bottles, the books went flat...."

2. In Senior's view, how can students gain contact again with "a culture in which the Faith properly grows"?

3. What particular difficulty must English-speaking Catholics overcome?

4. "There is little point in keeping children out of Hell if you don't afford them the means of getting into Heaven." Assuming the truth of this counsel, what implications for education follow?

❖ 34

ST. JOHN PAUL II (1920-2005)

On the Role of the Christian Family

The right of parents to choose an education in conformity with their religious faith must be absolutely guaranteed.

In his magisterial essay *The Role of the Christian Family in the Modern World*, John Paul II did for the family what Pope Leo XIII did for workers. The Holy Father presents a sweeping view of the nature, task, and enemies of the family. Traditional Catholic teaching, such as the family's irreducible role as the glue of society, is reaffirmed; most encouragingly, the Pope articulates for parents the dignity of their vocation as teachers. Though the task of education can be shared, it cannot be abrogated. Mom and Dad, not the state, are the kids' first teachers. Since what is given first to a child often remains longest, parents must see to it that no foreign authority dislodge this natural and God-assigned duty.

Further Reading: John Paul II, *Evangelium Vitae* (On the Gospel of Life) (Vatican: Libreria Editrice Vaticana,1995); Vatican Council II, *Gaudium et Spes* (The Church in the Modern World) in *Vatican Council II: Volume 1, The Conciliar and Post Conciliar Documents,* Revised Edition, ed. Austin Flannery, O.P. (Northport, N.Y.: Costello Publishing Co., 1996); Pontifical Council for Justice and Peace, *Compendium of the Social Doctrine of the Church* (Vatican: Libreria Editrice Vaticana, 2006).

❖

The Situation of the Family in the World Today

6. The situation in which the family finds itself presents positive and negative aspects: the first are a sign of the salvation of Christ operating in the world; the second, a sign of the refusal that man gives to the love of God.

On the one hand, in fact, there is a more lively awareness of personal freedom and greater attention to the quality of interpersonal relationships in marriage, to promoting the dignity of women, to responsible procreation, to the education of children. There is also an awareness of the need for the development of interfamily relationships, for reciprocal spiritual and material assistance, the rediscovery of the ecclesial mission proper to the family and its responsibility for the building of a more just society. On the other hand, however, signs are not lacking of a disturbing degradation of some fundamental values: a mistaken theoretical and practical concept of the independence of the spouses in relation to each other; serious misconceptions regarding the relationship of authority between parents and children; the concrete difficulties that the family itself experiences in the transmission of values; the growing number of divorces; the scourge of abortion; the ever more frequent recourse to sterilization; the appearance of a truly contraceptive mentality.

At the root of these negative phenomena there frequently lies a corruption of the idea and the experience of freedom, conceived not as a capacity for realizing the truth of God's plan for marriage and the family, but as an autonomous power of self-affirmation, often against others, for one's own selfish well-being.

Worthy of our attention also is the fact that, in the countries of the so-called Third World, families often lack both the means necessary for survival, such as food, work, housing and medicine, and the most elementary freedoms. In the richer countries, on the contrary, excessive prosperity and the consumer mentality, paradoxically joined to a certain anguish and uncertainty about the future, deprive married couples of the generosity and courage needed for raising up new human life: thus life is often perceived not as a blessing, but as a danger from which to defend oneself.

The historical situation in which the family lives therefore appears as an interplay of light and darkness.

This shows that history is not simply a fixed progression towards what is better, but rather an event of freedom, and even a struggle between freedoms that are in mutual conflict, that is, according to the well-known expression of St. Augustine, a conflict between two loves: the love of God to the point of disregarding self, and the love of self to the point of disregarding God.[1]

It follows that only an education for love rooted in faith can lead to the capacity of interpreting "the signs of the times," which are the historical expression of this twofold love.

The Influence of Circumstances on the Consciences of the Faithful

7. Living in such a world, under the pressures coming above all from the mass media, the faithful do not always remain immune from the obscur-

ing of certain fundamental values, nor set themselves up as the critical conscience of family culture and as active agents in the building of an authentic family humanism.

Among the more troubling signs of this phenomenon, the Synod Fathers stressed the following, in particular: the spread of divorce and of recourse to a new union, even on the part of the faithful; the acceptance of purely civil marriage in contradiction to the vocation of the baptized to "be married in the Lord," the celebration of the marriage sacrament without living faith, but for other motives; the rejection of the moral norms that guide and promote the human and Christian exercise of sexuality in marriage.

Our Age Needs Wisdom

8. The whole Church is obliged to a deep reflection and commitment, so that the new culture now emerging may be evangelized in depth, true values acknowledged, the rights of men and women defended, and justice promoted in the very structures of society. In this way the "new humanism" will not distract people from their relationship with God, but will lead them to it more fully.

Science and its technical applications offer new and immense possibilities in the construction of such a humanism. Still, as a consequence of political choices that decide the direction of research and its applications, science is often used against its original purpose, which is the advancement of the human person.

It becomes necessary, therefore, on the part of all, to recover an awareness of the primacy of moral values, which are the values of the human person as such. The great task that has to be faced today for the renewal of society is that of recapturing the ultimate meaning of life and its fundamental values. Only an awareness of the primacy of these values enables man to use the immense possibilities given him by science in such a way as to bring about the true advancement of the human person in his or her whole truth, in his or her freedom and dignity. Science is called to ally itself with wisdom.

The following words of the Second Vatican Council can therefore be applied to the problems of the family: "Our era needs such wisdom more than bygone ages if the discoveries made by man are to be further humanized. For the future of the world stands in peril unless wiser people are forthcoming."[2]

The education of the moral conscience, which makes every human being capable of judging and of discerning the proper ways to achieve self-realization according to his or her original truth, thus becomes a pressing requirement that cannot be renounced.

Modern culture must be led to a more profoundly restored covenant with divine Wisdom. Every man is given a share of such Wisdom through the creating action of God. And it is only in faithfulness to this covenant that the families of today will be in a position to influence positively the building of a more just and fraternal world.

The Right and Duty of Parents Regarding Education

36. The task of giving education is rooted in the primary vocation of married couples to participate in God's creative activity: by begetting in love and for love a new person who has within himself or herself the vocation to growth and development, parents by that very fact take on the task of helping that person effectively to live a fully human life. As the Second Vatican Council recalled, "since parents have conferred life on their children, they have a most solemn obligation to educate their offspring. Hence, parents must be acknowledged as the first and foremost educators of their children. Their role as educators is so decisive that scarcely anything can compensate for their failure in it. For it devolves on parents to create a family atmosphere so animated with love and reverence for God and others that a well-rounded personal and social development will be fostered among the children. Hence, the family is the first school of those social virtues which every society needs."[3]

The right and duty of parents to give education is essential, since it is connected with the transmission of human life; it is original and primary with regard to the educational role of others, on account of the uniqueness of the loving relationship between parents and children; and it is irreplaceable and inalienable, and therefore incapable of being entirely delegated to others or usurped by others.

In addition to these characteristics, it cannot be forgotten that the most basic element, so basic that it qualifies the educational role of parents, is parental love, which finds fulfillment in the task of education as it completes and perfects its service of life: as well as being a source, the parents' love is also the animating principle and therefore the norm inspiring and guiding all concrete educational activity, enriching it with the values of kindness, constancy, goodness, service, disinterestedness and self-sacrifice that are the most precious fruit of love.

Educating in the Essential Values of Human Life

37. Even amid the difficulties of the work of education, difficulties which are often greater today, parents must trustingly and courageously train their children in the essential values of human life. Children must grow up with a correct attitude of freedom with regard to material goods, by adopting a simple and austere life style and being fully convinced that "man is more precious for what he is than for what he has."[4]

In a society shaken and split by tensions and conflicts caused by the violent clash of various kinds of individualism and selfishness, children must be enriched not only with a sense of true justice, which alone leads to respect for the personal dignity of each individual, but also and more powerfully by a sense of true love, understood as sincere solicitude and disinterested service with regard to others, especially the poorest and those in most need. The family is the first and fundamental school of social living: as a community of love, it finds in self-giving the law that guides it and makes it grow. The self-giving that inspires the love of husband and wife for each other is the model and norm for the self-giving that must be practiced in the relationships between brothers and sisters and the different generations living together in the family. And the communion and sharing that are part of everyday life in the home at times of joy and at times of difficulty are the most concrete and effective pedagogy for the active, responsible and fruitful inclusion of the children in the wider horizon of society.

Education in love as self-giving is also the indispensable premise for parents called to give their children a clear and delicate sex education. Faced with a culture that largely reduces human sexuality to the level of something common place, since it interprets and lives it in a reductive and impoverished way by linking it solely with the body and with selfish pleasure, the educational service of parents must aim firmly at a training in the area of sex that is truly and fully personal: for sexuality is an enrichment of the whole person—body, emotions and soul—and it manifests its inmost meaning in leading the person to the gift of self in love.

Sex education, which is a basic right and duty of parents, must always be carried out under their attentive guidance, whether at home or in educational centers chosen and controlled by them. In this regard, the Church reaffirms the law of subsidiarity, which the school is bound to observe when it cooperates in sex education, by entering into the same spirit that animates the parents.

In this context education for chastity is absolutely essential, for it is a virtue that develops a person's authentic maturity and makes him or her capable of respecting and fostering the "nuptial meaning" of the body. Indeed Christian parents, discerning the signs of God's call, will devote special attention and care to education in virginity or celibacy as the supreme form of that self-giving that constitutes the very meaning of human sexuality.

In view of the close links between the sexual dimension of the person and his or her ethical values, education must bring the children to a knowledge of and respect for the moral norms as the necessary and highly valuable guarantee for responsible personal growth in human sexuality.

For this reason the Church is firmly opposed to an often widespread form of imparting sex information dissociated from moral principles. That would merely be an introduction to the experience of pleasure and a stimulus leading to the loss of serenity—while still in the years of innocence—by opening the way to vice.

The Mission to Educate and the Sacrament of Marriage

38. For Christian parents the mission to educate, a mission rooted, as we have said, in their participation in God's creating activity, has a new specific source in the sacrament of marriage, which consecrates them for the strictly Christian education of their children: that is to say, it calls upon them to share in the very authority and love of God the Father and Christ the Shepherd, and in the motherly love of the Church, and it enriches them with wisdom, counsel, fortitude and all the other gifts of the Holy Spirit in order to help the children in their growth as human beings and as Christians.

The sacrament of marriage gives to the educational role the dignity and vocation of being really and truly a "ministry" of the Church at the service of the building up of her members. So great and splendid is the educational ministry of Christian parents that Saint Thomas has no hesitation in comparing it with the ministry of priests: "Some only propagate and guard spiritual life by a spiritual ministry: this is the role of the sacrament of Orders; others do this for both corporal and spiritual life, and this is brought about by the sacrament of marriage, by which a man and a woman join in order to beget offspring and bring them up to worship God."[5]

A vivid and attentive awareness of the mission that they have received with the sacrament of marriage will help Christian parents to place themselves at the service of their children's education with great serenity and trustfulness, and also with a sense of responsibility before God, who calls them and gives them the mission of building up the Church in their children. Thus in the case of baptized people, the family, called together by word and sacrament as the Church of the home, is both teacher and mother, the same as the worldwide Church.

First Experience of the Church

39. The mission to educate demands that Christian parents should present to their children all the topics that are necessary for the gradual maturing of their personality from a Christian and ecclesial point of view. They will therefore follow the educational lines mentioned above, taking care to show their children the depths of significance to which the faith and love of Jesus Christ can lead. Furthermore, their awareness that the Lord is entrusting to them the growth of a child of God, a brother or sister of Christ, a temple of the Holy Spirit, a member of the Church, will support Christian parents in their task of strengthening the gift of divine grace in their children's souls.

The Second Vatican Council describes the content of Christian education as follows: "Such an education does not merely strive to foster maturity ... in the human person. Rather, its principal aims are these: that as baptized persons are gradually introduced into a knowledge of the mystery of salvation, they may daily grow more conscious of the gift of faith which they have received; that they may learn to adore God the Father in spirit and in truth (cf. Jn. 4:23), especially through liturgical worship; that they may be trained to conduct their personal life in true righteousness and holiness, according to their new nature (Eph. 4:22–24), and thus grow to maturity, to the stature of the fullness of Christ (cf. Eph. 4:13), and devote themselves to the upbuilding of the Mystical Body. Moreover, aware of their calling, they should grow accustomed to giving witness to the hope that is in them (cf. 1 Pt. 3:15), and to promoting the Christian transformation of the world."[6]

The Synod too, taking up and developing the indications of the Council, presented the educational mission of the Christian family as a true ministry through which the Gospel is transmitted and radiated, so that family life itself becomes an itinerary of faith and in some way a Christian initiation and a school of following Christ. Within a family that is aware of this gift, as Paul VI wrote, "all the members evangelize and are evangelized."[7]

By virtue of their ministry of educating, parents are, through the witness of their lives, the first heralds of the Gospel for their children. Furthermore, by praying with their children, by reading the word of God with them and by introducing them deeply through Christian initiation into the Body of Christ-both the Eucharistic and the ecclesial Body—they become fully parents, in that they are begetters not only of bodily life but also of the life that through the Spirit's renewal flows from the Cross and Resurrection of Christ.

In order that Christian parents may worthily carry out their ministry of educating, the Synod Fathers expressed the hope that a suitable catechism for families would be prepared, one that would be clear, brief and easily assimilated by all. The Episcopal Conferences were warmly invited to contribute to producing this catechism.

Relations with Other Educating Agents

40. The family is the primary but not the only and exclusive educating community. Man's community aspect itself—both civil and ecclesial—demands and leads to a broader and more articulated activity resulting from well-ordered collaboration between the various agents of education. All these agents are necessary, even though each can and should play its part in accordance with the special competence and contribution proper to itself.[8]

The educational role of the Christian family therefore has a very important place in organic pastoral work. This involves a new form of cooperation between parents and Christian communities, and between the various educational groups and pastors. In this sense, the renewal of the Catholic school must give special attention both to the parents of the pupils and to the formation of a perfect educating community.

The right of parents to choose an education in conformity with their religious faith must be absolutely guaranteed.

The State and the Church have the obligation to give families all possible aid to enable them to perform their educational role properly. Therefore both the Church and the State must create and foster the institutions and activities that families justly demand, and the aid must be in proportion to the families' needs. However, those in society who are in charge of schools must never forget that the parents have been appointed by God Himself as the first and principal educators of their children and that their right is completely inalienable.

But corresponding to their right, parents have a serious duty to commit themselves totally to a cordial and active relationship with the teachers and the school authorities.

If ideologies opposed to the Christian faith are taught in the schools, the family must join with other families, if possible through family associations, and with all its strength and with wisdom help the young not to depart from the faith. In this case the family needs special assistance from pastors of souls, who must never forget that parents have the inviolable right to entrust their children to the ecclesial community.

...

Family Prayer

59. The Church prays for the Christian family and educates the family to live in generous accord with the priestly gift and role received from Christ the High Priest. In effect, the baptismal priesthood of the faithful, exercised in the sacrament of marriage, constitutes the basis of a priestly vocation and mission for the spouses and family by which their daily lives are transformed into "spiritual sacrifices acceptable to God through Jesus Christ."[9] This transformation is achieved not only by celebrating the Eucharist and the other sacraments and through offering themselves to the glory of God, but also through a life of prayer, through prayerful dialogue with the Father, through Jesus Christ, in the Holy Spirit.

Family prayer has its own characteristic qualities. It is prayer offered in common, husband and wife together, parents and children together. Communion in prayer is both a consequence of and a requirement for the communion bestowed by the sacraments of Baptism and Matrimony. The words with which the Lord Jesus promises His presence can be applied to the members of the Christian family in a special way: "Again I say to you, if two of you agree on earth about anything they ask, it will be done for them by my Father in heaven. For where two or three are gathered in my name, there am I in the midst of them."[10]

Family prayer has for its very own object family life itself, which in all its varying circumstances is seen as a call from God and lived as a filial response to His call. Joys and sorrows, hopes and disappointments, births and birthday celebrations, wedding anniversaries of the parents, departures, separations and homecomings, important and far-reaching decisions, the death of those who are dear, etc.—all of these mark God's loving intervention in the family's history. They should be seen as suitable moments for thanksgiving, for petition, for trusting abandonment of the family into the hands of their common Father in heaven. The dignity and responsibility of the Christian family as the domestic Church can be achieved only with God's unceasing aid, which will surely be granted if it is humbly and trustingly petitioned in prayer.

Educators in Prayer

60. By reason of their dignity and mission, Christian parents have the specific responsibility of educating their children in prayer, introducing them to gradual discovery of the mystery of God and to personal dialogue with Him: "It is particularly in the Christian family, enriched by the grace and the office of the sacrament of Matrimony, that from the earliest years

children should be taught, according to the faith received in Baptism, to have a knowledge of God, to worship Him and to love their neighbor."[11]

The concrete example and living witness of parents is fundamental and irreplaceable in educating their children to pray. Only by praying together with their children can a father and mother—exercising their royal priesthood—penetrate the innermost depths of their children's hearts and leave an impression that the future events in their lives will not be able to efface. Let us again listen to the appeal made by Paul VI to parents: "Mothers, do you teach your children the Christian prayers? Do you prepare them, in conjunction with the priests, for the sacraments that they receive when they are young: Confession, Communion and Confirmation? Do you encourage them when they are sick to think of Christ suffering to invoke the aid of the Blessed Virgin and the saints Do you say the family rosary together? And you, fathers, do you pray with your children, with the whole domestic community, at least sometimes? Your example of honesty in thought and action, joined to some common prayer, is a lesson for life, an act of worship of singular value. In this way you bring peace to your homes: Pax huic domui. Remember, it is thus that you build up the Church."[12]

Liturgical Prayer and Private Prayer

61. There exists a deep and vital bond between the prayer of the Church and the prayer of the individual faithful, as has been clearly reaffirmed by the Second Vatican Council.[13] An important purpose of the prayer of the domestic Church is to serve as the natural introduction for the children to the liturgical prayer of the whole Church, both in the sense of preparing for it and of extending it into personal, family and social life. Hence the need for gradual participation by all the members of the Christian family in the celebration of the Eucharist, especially on Sundays and feast days, and of the other sacraments, particularly the sacraments of Christian initiation of the children. The directives of the Council opened up a new possibility for the Christian family when it listed the family among those groups to whom it recommends the recitation of the Divine Office in common.[14] Likewise, the Christian family will strive to celebrate at home, and in a way suited to the members, the times and feasts of the liturgical year.

As preparation for the worship celebrated in church, and as its prolongation in the home, the Christian family makes use of private prayer, which presents a great variety of forms. While this variety testifies to the extraordinary richness with which the Spirit vivifies Christian prayer, it serves also to meet the various needs and life situations of those who turn to the Lord in prayer. Apart from morning and evening prayers, certain forms of prayer are to be expressly encouraged, following the indications of the Synod Fathers, such as reading and meditating on the word of God, preparation for the reception of the sacraments, devotion and consecration to the Sacred Heart of Jesus, the various forms of veneration of the Blessed Virgin Mary, grace before and after meals, and observance of popular devotions.

While respecting the freedom of the children of God, the Church has always proposed certain practices of piety to the faithful with particular solicitude and insistence. Among these should be mentioned the recitation of the rosary: "We now desire, as a continuation of the thought of our predecessors, to recommend strongly the recitation of the family rosary.... There is no doubt that ... the rosary should be considered as one of the best and most efficacious prayers in common that the Christian family is invited to recite. We like to think, and sincerely hope, that when the family gathering becomes a time of prayer the rosary is a frequent and favored manner of praying."[15] In this way authentic devotion to Mary, which finds expression in sincere love and generous imitation of the Blessed Virgin's interior spiritual attitude, constitutes a special instrument for nourishing loving communion in the family and for developing conjugal and family spirituality. For she who is the Mother of Christ and of the Church is in a special way the Mother of Christian families, of domestic Churches.

Prayer and Life

62. It should never be forgotten that prayer constitutes an essential part of Christian life, understood in its fullness and centrality. Indeed, prayer is an important part of our very humanity: it is "the first expression of man's inner truth, the first condition for authentic freedom of spirit."[16]

Far from being a form of escapism from everyday commitments, prayer constitutes the strongest incentive for the Christian family to assume and comply fully with all its responsibilities as the primary and fundamental cell of human society. Thus the Christian family's actual participation in the Church's life and mission is in direct proportion to the fidelity and intensity of the prayer with which it is united with the fruitful vine that is Christ the Lord.[17]

The fruitfulness of the Christian family in its specific service to human advancement, which of itself cannot but lead to the transformation of the world, derives from its living union with Christ, nourished by Liturgy, by self-oblation and by prayer.[18]

Review and Discussion Questions

1. John Paul II opens with a conspectus of the challenges that confront the modern family. In brief form, recapitulate his list.

2. How does the pope defend the assertion that the task of education is "rooted in the primary vocation of married couples"?

3. For what reasons do some argue that the primary duty to educate a child rests not with the parents but with the state?

4. John Paul II exhorts parents to educate children in a love that is "self-giving." What is he meaning to exclude?

5. What does John Paul II suggest is the "greatest help that parents can give their children" as educators?

❖ 35

LAURA M. BERQUIST

Designing Your Own Classical Curriculum

Natural history, the study of animals and plants, makes students aware of the workings of nature, which prepares them for a philosophical study of nature.

Wife, mother, homeschooling parent, author, speaker, conference organizer, Laura Berquist is a leader within the international homeschooling movement. In the United States, roughly the same number of students learn at home as in Catholic schools. No longer a marginal phenomenon, on average, homeschooled children dramatically outperform public school students in academic and social achievement. And the movement continues to grow (increasing at a rate of about seven percent per annum). Drawing from her own experience as a student, mother, and teacher, Berquist sounds a plea for moderation in the curriculum. Help students to follow an argument before you turn them over to logic. Teach rhetoric only after they have memorized the Gettysburg Address—and other speeches like it. Let them have a feeling for the joys and sorrows of romance before you introduce them to Anna Karenina. The mind, like any muscle, needs to prepare before heavy lifting.

Further reading: Susan Wise Bauer and Jessie Wise, *The Well-Trained Mind: A Guide to Classical Education at Home* (New York: W. W. Norton, 2009); Laura Berquist, *The Harp and Laurel Wreath: Poetry and Dictation for the Classical Curriculum* (San Francisco: Ignatius Press, 1999); Mitchell Kalpakgian, *The Lost Arts of Modern Civilization* (Long Prairie, Minn.: Neumann Press, 2009).

❖

This book is primarily about resources to use in constructing a curriculum suitable for your child and your family. I would like to propose briefly some suggestions about what not to use.

When I was thirteen I read Tolstoy's *Anna Karenina*. That is, I read the words. I thought I had read the story, but I did not realize until ten years later that reading the words is not necessarily the same as reading the story.

I was too young to understand Anna, because I did not have the experience required to read the book profitably. I knew it was about an adulterous woman, but I did not see the full gravity of Anna's sin and the kind of consequences that are only to be expected in such a situation.

In college I read *War and Peace*, also by Tolstoy, and thought I was in a position to compare these two works. After all, I said to myself, I had read them both. Then I went back to *Anna Karenina* and found a work that had a richness I had completely missed. It was not about the external actions of a sinful woman but about the internal and gradual corruption of a soul and about possible alternative behaviors, embodied in other characters.

Reading that book when I was thirteen was a mistake on my part. I should have been reading other books, more suitable to my age, that would have prepared and disposed me to read Anna well later on. Further, I thought for ten years that I had read one of the "great" books, when I had completely missed the point. Fortunately, I read it again, but not before I had made some very foolish comparisons between this book and *War and Peace*.

In Ecclesiastes we read, "For everything there is a season, and a time for every matter under heaven" (Qo 3:1). This experience is something I try to keep in mind when planning the curriculum of my children. There is a right time for thinking about subjects and a right way to think about them at a given time. This right time depends on more than the ability to perform the action. The student may be able to read the words, but understanding comes with maturity, and maturity comes from experience and a reflection on experience that requires a certain amount of time.

There is often a temptation, when planning a curriculum, to include material that is too difficult. We want to see the students moving on to the next stage of development. We want them to excel, and we do not want them to miss out on the "classics". But when we include difficult material before the students are ready to do it, they will not do it well they may or may not realize that the material is too hard for them, but the chances are good that they will not enjoy it. They are also apt to make the mistake that I made and think that they have understood something when they have not. This is not necessarily a question of intelligence. It is a question of maturity.

One might think, for example, that reading Plato's Dialogues at length in early adolescence would whet the appetite for more in subsequent years when one is actually ready to do philosophy. Unfortunately, my experience is that doing difficult material of this kind before a student is ready to think about it in the right way tends to make him less likely to do it well, or at all, later on. Partly, this is because he thinks he has already done it, and partly it is because the work does not engage his interest until it speaks to an experience the student has had himself.

The questions raised in Plato's *Meno* are really interesting to someone who has considered the nature of learning. Or even for someone who has not yet thought about it but who has had experiences of different types of learning and can reflect on how learning takes place. Reading the *Meno* too early does not dispose a student to read it well later; he is inclined to think it is uninteresting or silly. Or he may like it, but he will not yet have given much thought to how virtue is taught, and thus he will not bring to a consideration of the dialogue the essential ingredient. If you want your student to read the *Meno* intelligently, at the right time of life, you would be better advised to have him read lots of history, with examples of virtuous fathers and their offspring. Plutarch's *Lives* would be fine, if you want to use classical literature, but William Thomas Walsh's books would also do well. It is the acquaintance with history and wondering why virtuous fathers often do not have virtuous children that is advantageous.

I live in a college community, one where the great books of Western civilization are read as a matter of course. Such books are taken seriously, and the general opinion is that one's education is not complete without an acquaintance with them. Yet, the considered view among many of those who deal on a daily basis with college students is that the best students are not those who come to the college already having read the books included in the program. Rather, for the most part, the best students are those who have read history, literature and natural history and who have done basic astronomy, as well as Latin or another inflected language. A reasonable study of these disciplines will make the harder courses easy when the time comes.

These studies are better preparation for the difficult considerations appropriate to college students than attempts to do the college material itself would be. The study of history expands the experience of young people vicariously, and great literature presents truths about reality that they would not be apt to see themselves. Natural history, the study of animals and plants, makes students aware of the workings of nature, which prepares them for a philosophical study of nature. These are the types of materials that we should include in our curriculum, because they equip the student to do more difficult studies by helping him acquire experience and by encouraging reflection on that experience.

We should also allow time for reflection, time for the young to wonder about reality and to investigate their areas of interest. A curriculum can be too difficult because it does not allow the student enough time really to think, as well as by its use of material that is not proportioned to his abilities.

One might ask, then, what happens to the classical curriculum this book is supposed to consider? How can one have a classical curriculum without reading the classics? The answer is that one cannot have a classical curriculum in the fullest and most perfect sense until one has students who are capable of the kind of abstract thinking required for a study of the subjects of the Trivium: grammar, logic, rhetoric; and the Quadrivium: arithmetic, geometry, music and astronomy. To do these subjects fully, one needs to be able to read Martin of Denmark and Thomas of Erfert on speculative grammar, Aristotle on the *Prior* and *Posterior Analytics* and *Rhetoric*, Euclid's *Elements*, Plato's *Timaeus* and Ptolemy's *Almagest*. Further, these studies are ordered to philosophy and *Anima*, *Ethics* and *Metaphysics*, St. Augustine's *City of God*, the *Summa Theologiae* of St. Thomas Aquinas and various other treatises.

These are hard subjects, really exciting, but abstract. Even more than *Anna Karenina*, they require preparation: experience, maturity and disposing formation.

It is the disposing formation that occupies our attention as homeschooling parents. This formation, because it is a preparation for classical education, can in an extended sense be said to be classical education. It is not classical education in the fullest sense, but it may still be truly called classical, both because it leads to such an education and because it employs the method of such an education. It is this beginning of a classical education that we should keep in mind as we design our children's course of studies.

There is a beginning to the study of grammar that involves learning the vocabulary and forms of language and parsing sentences. Memory and observation characterize this stage of formation, which distinguishes the student up to sixth grade. The freshman in college who studies speculative grammar is employing those same powers, but in an abstract consideration. He will be better off for having worked on grammar earlier in the way that was commensurate with his talents at that time.

Similarly, there is a beginning to the study of logic that involves simply becoming familiar with intellectual argument. As I mentioned earlier, students at this stage of formation should work on recognizing the argument present in the material they use in their studies. Making outlines of the discussion in the text or even highlighting the topic sentence in every paragraph of a speech or essay will draw the student's attention explicitly to the progression of the author's thought. He will see whether the conclusion drawn follows from the premises given. Such exercises are a natural preparation for formal logic.

The science of rhetoric begins with an ability to assemble thoughts and ideas and present them well. This requires attention to the power of language, and that requires a certain experience of good and bad rhetoric. The study of poetry (not poetry in translation) and the reading of various authors who intend to convince their audience of a particular position are very helpful in seeing why what Aristotle says in the *Rhetoric* is true.

This is the classical curriculum for children as Dorothy Sayers envisions it in her landmark essay, "The Lost Tools of Learning." Such an education is about formation rather than information and depends more on the method used with the texts than on which particular texts are used. One still looks for good texts, and some texts are better than others, both in themselves and for a particular child. There are a number of subjects that should be addressed in every curriculum, primarily those subjects mentioned above. Every curriculum should include the truths of the faith at each stage of development. Chances are good that your student will not like all these disciplines equally, but he should nonetheless develop the different powers of the soul. All of this having been said, it is still true that the formation of this education comes chiefly from the method employed in the study of the subjects.

This formation develops habits of thought that make it possible to use information rightly. A consideration of what kind of logical study is appropriate for the seventh- to ninth-grade student will illustrate the difference between the two modes of "classical education". Students in these years are ready to think about argument. They can see that this premise either does or does not follow from that one. But it is a mistake to assume that this means they are ready for the abstract considerations required for formal logic. Before they start thinking about whether the universal affirmative converts universally they should· have followed arguments in which that relationship is illustrated.

The junior high and high school student who has looked at and thought about a number of intellectual arguments will be in a stronger position to study formal logic when the time comes. Picking a speech from a period in history that is of interest, outlining it, laying the outline aside for a few days and then using it to reproduce the speech helps the student think about the argument present in the speech. Jumbling the order of the outline and then later trying to reduce the confusion to the best possible sequence also enables him to think about what comes first and why.

After a number of such exercises, the student can write a paper defending a controversial position, using the techniques he has learned by his close examination of various speeches. Further, his attention can be directed to the argument present in whatever materials he is using for his school subjects. Does this follow from that? Where is this said? Is there an implication here? What are the four major sentences in this four-paragraph essay? Asking these kinds of questions in every subject is the way to form the intelligence. The subjects provide material for that formation, and discussion and analysis form the heart of the curriculum.

Such a preparation will make the theoretical treatment of logic in Aristotle, or even in a textbook about formal logic, much more intelligible and therefore more fruitful for the student. For a parent designing a classical curriculum, it is better to concentrate on exercises like those mentioned above than to buy a textbook about teaching logic to your children.

If you do this, you will both prepare your children to think about the harder and more abstract subjects when they are ready to do so, and you will be helping them develop the habits of thought that enable them to think well about any subject they choose when they want to know more about it. They will have the "tools of learning" and can go on to study the Trivium and the Quadrivium, or any other area of interest, in its fullness.

The goal of the high school curriculum is to help the student express himself elegantly and persuasively. Doing this requires practice; in terms of writing it means writing and rewriting, cutting down, rephrasing and rewriting again. It also means encouraging discussion, where the student tries to present a sequenced position about his understanding of a text. What the subject matter of the papers is or what the discussion centers on may vary from student to student. Your curriculum may reflect your interests and those of your students, but the method is essential and should remain the same for all students of this age.

My point is that we should not think that a classical curriculum for older students, a curriculum that prepares them for thinking about high and noble things, depends on doing Greek and Roman classical texts exclusively, or even predominantly. Nor is it helpful to assign excessively difficult texts. In fact, such texts may be detrimental to intellectual development, and all really difficult texts should be chosen carefully for their suitability and used in moderation, leaving plenty of time for reflection.

A friend who taught swimming to small children found that at a certain age the children would begin to retain what they had learned from one summer to the next and could build on the previously acquired skills. Before that point, they would have to start over each summer, getting used to the water and learning to float anew. She finally began to say to the parents who asked her to teach swimming to their very young children, "I'll be happy to accept your money and play with your children, but if it is learning to swim that you have in mind, I advise you to wait for a few years."

Patience is a virtue that is employed in many ways in the raising of children, including the development of their curriculum. The tools of learning are acquired by concentrating, at each stage, on the areas of development that are appropriate to that stage. It is not essential to use ancient authors to have this kind of a classical curriculum. What is essential is that the children do what is appropriate at each stage of learning. They should memorize at the grammatical stage. This strengthens and makes docile their imagination so that in the next stage of learning, the logical, they will have the help of a trained imagination in following and constructing arguments. In turn, it is essential to this education that when the children are capable of grasping and marshaling arguments, they should practice doing so. If they do, then the last stage, the rhetorical, can be given to articulating those arguments elegantly, in the service of the truly noble. This formation will give them the tools of learning, a formation that may be truly called classical and that will dispose them to a formal study of the highest and best subjects at the proper time.

Review and Discussion Questions

1. Why shouldn't teens read *Anna Karenina*?

2. When Berquist speaks of "disposing formation," to what does she refer?

3. How do the aims of college education differ from the aims of high-school education?

4. How does Berquist defend the claim that a classical curriculum need not rely heavily upon "Greek and Roman classical texts"?

MICHAEL D. O'BRIEN

A Landscape with Dragons

The undermining of a child's perceptions in forms that are apparently harmless may be the most destructive [attack] of all.

Parents will find few better guides to children's literature than Michael O'Brien. A talented author and painter, a husband and father, O'Brien has devoted his life to the study of imaginative literature and here offers principles to help guide our sifting between the good, the bad, and the mediocre. O'Brien traces the shift in recent fantasy stories away from their Christian origins—and their traditional celebration of the conquest of good over evil, virtue over sloth, beauty over sentimentality—toward a more Gnostic vision of the cosmos.

Further Reading: Stratford Caldecott, *Beauty in the Word: Rethinking the Foundations of Education* (Tacoma, Wash.: Angelico Press, 2012); Mitchell Kalpakgian, *Mysteries of Life in Children's Literature* (Long Prairie, Minn.: Neumann Press, 2000); Jacob and Wilhelm Grimm, *Grimm's Complete Fairy Tales* (San Diego, Calif.: Canterbury Classics, 2011).

❖

It is important to recall at this point that during the second century there were several "Christian Gnostic" sects that attempted to reconcile Christianity and paganism and did so by incorporating many praiseworthy elements from the true faith. Similarly, Luke [Skywalker, of Star Wars] and company act according to an admirable moral code, but we must ask ourselves on what moral foundation this code is based, and what its source is. There is no mention of a transcendent God or any attempt to define the source of "the Force." And why is the use of psychic power considered acceptable? A major theme throughout the series is that good can be fostered by the use of these supernatural powers, which in our world are exclusively allied with evil forces. Moreover, the key figures in the overthrow of the malevolent empire are the Jedi masters, the enlightened elite, the initiates, the possessors of secret knowledge. Is this not Gnosticism?

At the very least these issues should suggest a close appraisal of the series by parents, especially since the films were revised and re-released in 1997, and a new generation of young people is being influenced by them. The most pressing question that should be asked is, which kind of distortion will do the more damage: blatant falsehood or falsehood mixed with the truths that we hunger for?

Vigilance, Paranoia, and Uncle Walt

No assessment of the situation should overlook the influence of Walt Disney Productions. Its unequalled accomplishments in the field of animation and in drama for children have made it a keystone in the culture of the West. Walt Disney became a kind of secular saint, a patron of childhood, the archangel of the young imagination. Some of this reputation was merited. Who among us has not been delighted and, indeed, formed by the films released in the early years of production, modern retellings of classic fairy stories such as *Sleeping Beauty*, *Pinocchio*, and *Snow White*. In these and other films, evil is portrayed as evil, and virtue as a moral struggle fraught with trial and error. Telling lies makes your nose grow long; indulging in vice turns you into a donkey; sorcery is a device of the enemy used against the good; witches are deadly. There are even moments that approach evangelization. In *Fantasia*, for example, "The Sorcerer's Apprentice" segment is a warning about dabbling in occult powers. In the final segment, "Night on Bald Mountain," the devil is shown in all his malice, seducing and raging, but defeated by the prayers of the saints. As the pilgrims process toward the dawn, they are accompanied by the strains of Schubert's "Ave Maria." Although there are parts of this film too frightening for small children, its final word is holiness.

Upon that reputation many parents learned to say, "Oh, it's by Disney. It must be okay!" But even in the early years of the Disney studios, the trends of modernity were present. As our culture continued to follow that tendency, films continued to diverge from the traditional Christian worldview. *Snow White* and *Pinocchio* are perhaps the most pure interpretations of the original fairy tales, because the changes by Disney were of degree, not of kind. Much of the editing had to do with putting violence and other grotesque scenes off-screen (such as the demise of the wicked queen), because reading a story and seeing it are two different experiences, especially for children.

By the time *Cinderella* hit the theaters, the changes were more substantial. For example, Cinderella's stepsisters (in the Grimm version) were as beautiful as she, but vain and selfish. And the prince (in both the Grimm and Perrault versions) sees Cinderella in rags and ashes and still decides to love her, before she is transformed back into the beauty of the ball. These elements are changed in the Disney version, with the result that Cinderella wins the prince's hand, not primarily because of her virtue, but because she is the prettiest gal in town. Some prince!

Walt Disney died in 1966. During the late 1960s and 1970s the studio's approach gradually changed. Its fantasy and science fiction films began to show symptoms of the spreading moral confusion in that genre. "Bad guys" were at times presented as complex souls, inviting pity if not sympathy. "Good guys" were a little more tarnished than they once had been and, indeed, were frequently portrayed as foolish simpletons. A strain of "realism" had entered children's films—sadly so, because a child's hunger for literature (visual or printed) is his quest for a "more real world." He needs to know what is truly heroic in simple, memorable terms. He needs to see the hidden foundations of his world before the complexities and the nuances of the modern mind come flooding in to overwhelm his perceptions. The creators of the new classics had failed to grasp this timeless role of the fairy tale. Or, if they had grasped it, they arbitrarily decided it was time to change it. What began as a hairline crack began to grow into a chasm.

The Watcher in the Woods is a tale of beings from another dimension, séances, ESP, and channeling (spirits speaking through a human medium), a story that dramatically influences the young audience to believe that occult powers, though sometimes frightening, can bring great good for mankind. *Bedknobs and Broomsticks*, a comedy about a "good" witch, softens ancient fears about witchcraft. *Pete's Dragon* is the tale of a cute, friendly dragon who becomes a pal to the young hero and helps to defeat the "bad guys." In another time and place such films would probably be fairly harmless. Their impact must be understood in the context of the much larger movement that is inverting the symbol-life that grew from the Judeo-Christian revelation. This is more than just a haphazard development, more than just a gradual fading of right discernment in the wake of a declining Christian culture.

This is an anti-culture pouring in to take its place. Some of it is full-frontal attack, but much of it is subtler and pleasurably packaged. Still more of it seems apparently harmless. But the undermining of a child's perceptions in forms that are apparently harmless may be the most destructive of all.

By the 1990s, old fairy tales such as *Aladdin, Beauty and the Beast*, and *The Little Mermaid* were being remade by Walt Disney Productions in an effort to capture the imagination (and the market potential) of a new generation. *The Little Mermaid* represents an even greater break from the original intention of fairy stories than earlier retellings such as *Cinderella*. The mermaid's father is shown to be an unreasonable patriarchist and she justifiably rebellious. In order to obtain her desire (marriage to a landbased human prince), she swims away from home and makes a pact with an evil Sea Witch, who turns her into a human for three days, long enough to make the prince kiss her. If she can entice him to do so, she will remain a human forever and marry him. So far, the film is close to Hans Christian Andersen's original fairy story. But a radical departure is to be found in the way the plot resolves itself. Despite the disasters the little mermaid causes, only other people suffer the consequences of the wrong she has done, and in the end she gets everything she wants. Charming as she is, she is really a selfish brat whose only abiding impulse is a shallow romantic passion. In the original Andersen tale, the little mermaid faces some difficult moral decisions and decides for the good, choosing in the end to sacrifice her own desires so that the prince will remain happily married to his human bride. As a result of her self-denial, she is taken up into the sky among the "children of the air," the benign spirits who do good in the world.

"In three hundred years we shall float like this into the Kingdom of God!" one of them cries. "But we may get there sooner!" whispers one of the daughters of the air. "Unseen, we fly into houses where there are children, and for every day that we find a good child who gives its parents joy ... God shortens the time of [our] probation."

Obviously there has been some heavy-handed editing in the film version, a trivialization of the characters, stripping the tale of moral content and references to God, with a net result that the meaning of the story is seriously distorted, even reversed. In a culture dominated by consumerism and pragmatism, it would seem that the best message modern producers are capable of is this: In the "real" world the "healthy ego" goes after what it wants. You can even play with evil and get away with it, maybe even be rewarded for your daring by hooking the handsomest guy in the land, winning for yourself your own palace, your own kingdom, and happiness on your own terms.

Harmless? I do not think so.

Aladdin especially represents the kind of films that are apparently harmless. To criticize it in the present climate is extremely difficult, because so many people in Christian circles have simply accepted it as "family enter-tainment." But *Aladdin* begs some closer examination.

The animated version is adapted from the *Arabian Nights*, a fairy tale that originated in Persia and reflects the beliefs of its Muslim author. According to the original tale, a magician hires a poor Chinese boy named Aladdin to go into an underground cave in search of a magic lamp that contains untold power. Aladdin is not merely poor, he is lazy. Through neglect of his duties, he failed to learn a trade from his father before he died and now is vulnerable to temptation. When he finds the lamp, Aladdin refuses to give it up and is locked in the cave. When he accidentally rubs the lamp, a jinn (spirit) of the lamp materializes. In the Islamic religion the jinni are demonic spirits, intelligent, fiery beings of the air, who can take on many forms, including human and animal. Some jinni are better characters than others, but they are considered on the whole to be tricksters. According to Arabian mythology, they were created out of flame, while men and angels were created out of clay and light. Whoever controls a jinn is master of tre-mendous power, for the jinn is his slave. Aladdin, helped by such a spirit, marries the Sultan's daughter, and thejinn builds them a fabulous palace. But the wicked magician tricks them out of the lamp and transports the palace to Africa. Aladdin chases them there, regains the lamp in a heroic struggle, and restores the palace to China.

In the Disney remake, Aladdin is now a young hustler who speaks American urban slang in an Arabian marketplace. He is a likeable teenage thief who is poor through no fault of his own. He wants to make it big. When he meets the Sultan's daughter, who is fleeing the boring confine-ment of her palace, and rescues her through wit and "street-smarts," the ro-mance begins. The film strives to remain true to some of the original plot, but in the characterization one sees evidence of the new consciousness. The film's genie is a comedian of epic proportions, changing his roles at light-ning speed, so that the audience barely has time to laugh before the next sophisticated entertainment industry joke is trotted out. He becomes Ed Sullivan, the Marx Brothers, a dragon, a homosexual, female belly dancers, Pinocchio, and on and on. It is a brilliant and fascinating display. He is ca-pable of colossal powers, and he is, wonder of wonders, Aladdin's slave. An intoxicating recipe for capturing a child's imagination.

This is a charming film. It contains some very fine scenes and deserves some praise for an attempt at morality. The genie, for example, admonishes the young master that there are limits to the wishes he can grant: no killing, no making someone fall in love with you, no bringing anyone back from the dead. Aladdin is really a "good thief," who robs from the comfortable and gives to the poor. He is called a "street-rat" by his enemies, yet he feels within himself aspirations to something better, something great. He is kind and generous to hungry, abandoned children; he defies the arrogant and the rich, and he is very, very brave. He is only waiting for an opportunity to show what sterling stuff he is made of. It is possible that this film may even have a good effect on the many urban children who live close to that level of poverty and desperation. By providing an attractive role model of a young person determined to overcome adversity, it may do much good in the world. There are even moments when spiritual insight is clear and true—when, for example, at the climax of the tale the magician takes on his true form, that of a gigantic serpent. And yet, there is something on the subliminal level, some undefinable warp in the presentation that leaves the discerning viewer uneasy.

Most obvious, perhaps, is the feeling of sensuality that dominates the plot. It is a romance, of course, and it must be understood that a large number of old literary fairy tales were also romances. But this is modern romance, complete with stirring music and visual impact. Aladdin and the Princess are both scantily clad throughout the entire performance, and, like so many characters in Disney animation, they appear to be bursting with hormones. There is a kiss that is more than a chaste peck. Nothing aggressively wrong, really. Nothing obscene, but all so thoroughly modern. At the very least, one should question the effect this stirring of the passions will have on the many children who flock to see the latest Disney cartoon. The cartoon, by its very nature, says "primarily for children." But this is, in fact, an adolescent romance, with some good old cartoon effects thrown in to keep the little ones' attention and some sly innuendo to keep the adults chuckling.

The handling of the supernatural element is, I believe, a more serious defect. To put it simply, the jinn is a demon. But such a charming demon. Funny and sad, clever and loyal (as long as you're his master), harmless, helpful, and endlessly entertaining.

Just the kind of guardian spirit a child might long for. Does this film implant a longing to conjure up such a spirit?

The film's key flaw is its presentation of the structure of reality. It is an utterly delightful advertisement for the concept of "the light side of the Force and the dark side of the Force," and as such it is a kind of cartoon Star Wars. Like Luke Skywalker, Aladdin is a young hero pitched against impossible odds, but the similarities do not end there. Luke becomes strong enough to battle his foes only by going down into a cave in a mysterious swamp and facing there "the dark side" of himself. Then, by developing supernatural powers, he is enabled to go forth to defeat the evil in the world. Similarly, Aladdin first seeks to obtain the lamp by going down into the jaws of a lionlike beast that rises up out of the desert and speaks with a ghastly, terrifying voice. The lamp of spiritual power resides in a cave in the belly of the beast, and Aladdin takes it from him. Here is a clear message to the young who aspire to greater things: If you want to improve your lot in life, spiritual power is an even better possession than material powers such as wealth or physical force. It could be argued that Luke does not enlist the aid of demonic beings, nor does he cooperate with supernatural forces for selfish purposes. Indeed, he is a shining idealist. But this argument presumes that developing occult powers does not place one in contact with such evil beings—a very shaky presumption to say the least. At best there is an ambiguity in Luke's cooperation with "the Force" that leaves ample room for the young to absorb Gnostic messages.

What is communicated about the nature of spiritual power in Aladdin? Leave aside for the moment the question of the hero being helped by a "good demon" to overcome a bad one. Leave aside also the problem of telling the young that they should ignore their natural terrors of the supernatural in order to succeed in their quests. Leave aside, moreover, the subtle inference that light and darkness, good and evil, are merely reverse sides of the same cosmic coin. There are subtler messages in the film. For example, a theme running throughout is that Aladdin is "worthy" to master such power, though we never learn what constitutes his worthiness. The viewer assumes that it is his bravado, cunning, and basically good heart. In reality, none of us is worthy of powers that properly belong to God alone. None of us is worthy of restoration to Paradise. Salvation is God's gift to mankind by the merits of his death on the Cross. Even so, we have not yet reached our one true home. We have all sinned and fallen short of the glory of God, and in this world no one is capable of wielding evil supernatural powers without being corrupted by them. It is modern man's ignorance of this principle that is now getting the world into a great deal of trouble. A powerful falsehood is implanted in the young by heroes who are given knowledge of good and evil, given power over good and evil, who play with evil but are never corrupted by it.

Beauty and the Beast handles the problem differently, but the end result is the same—the taming of the child's instinctive reaction to the image of the horrible. The Beast is portrayed as a devil-like being. He is not merely deformed or grotesque, as he is in the written fable. In the film his voice is unearthly and horrifying; he is sinister in appearance, his face a hideous mimicry of medieval gargoyles, his body a hybrid abomination of lion, bull, bear, and demon. His castle is full of diabolical statues. Of course, the central themes are as true and timeless as ever: Love sees beneath the surface appearance to the interior reality of the person; and love breaks the spell that evil casts over a life.

Yet here too there are disturbing messages: A "good witch" casts the spell in order to improve the Beast's character, implying that good ends come from evil means. But no truly good person does harm in order to bring about a good. While it is true that good can come out of evil situations, it is only because God's love is greater than evil. God's primary intention is that we always choose the good. In the original fairy tale, the spell is cast by an evil sorcerer, and the good conclusion to the plot is brought about in spite of him.

The Disney Beast really has a heart of gold. By contrast, handsome Gaston, the "normal" man, proves to be the real villain. He is a despicable parody of masculinity, a stupid, vain macho-man, who wishes to marry the heroine and chain her to the ennui of dull village life. The Beauty in the original tale embraces the virtues of hard work and the simple country life that result from her father's misfortune. The Disney Beauty pines for something "better." There is a feminist message here, made even stronger by the absence of any positive male role models. Even her father is a buffoon, though loveable. This gross characterization of "patriarchy" would not be complete without a nasty swipe at the Church, and sure enough, Gaston has primed a clown-like priest to marry them. (The depiction of ministers of religion as either corrupt or ridiculous is practically unrelieved in contemporary films-Disney films are especially odious in this respect.)

To return for a moment to the question of beauty: A principle acknowledged in all cultures (except those in a terminal phase of self-destruction) is that physical beauty in creation is a living metaphor of spiritual beauty. The ideal always points to something higher than itself, to some ultimate good. In culture this principle is enfleshed, made visible. If at times spiritual beauty is present in unbeautiful fictional characters or situations, this only serves to underline the point that the physical is not an end in itself. In Disney's *Pocahontas* we find this principle inverted. Dazzling the viewer's eyes with superb scenes that are more like impressionistic paintings than solid narrative, stirring the emotions with haunting music and the supercharged atmosphere of sexual desire, its creators are really about a much bigger project than cranking out yet another tale of boy-meets-girl. Beauty is now harnessed to the task of promoting environmentalism and eco-spirituality. The real romance here is the mystique of pantheism, a portrayal of the earth as alive, animated with spirits (for example, a witchlike tree-spirit gives advice to Pocahontas about the nature of courtship). The earth and the flesh no longer point to something higher than themselves; they are ends in themselves. The "noble savage" understands this; the white, male, European Christian does not. And as usual, Disney portrays masculinity in its worst possible light (excepting only the hero, Smith, who is sensitive and confused). The other European males are rapacious predators, thoughtless builders, dominators, polluters, and killers; and those who are not any of the foregoing are complete nincompoops. It is all so predictable, all so very "consciousness-raising." What child does not take away from the film the impression that, in order to solve his problems, industrial-technological man need only reclaim the lost innocence of this pre-Columbian Eden?

I did not view Disney's *The Hunchback of Notre Dame* in a theater but watched the video release at home. The effect of the full-screen experience must have been overwhelming for audiences, because the visual effects in the video version were very impressive, clearly among Disney's most brilliant achievements in animation. However, I was disturbed by themes that have now become habitual with this studio. Within the first ten minutes of the story, a self-righteous Catholic moralist rides into the plot on horseback and chases a poor gypsy mother, who runs barefoot through the streets of Paris, carrying her baby in her arms, in a desperate attempt to reach the sanctuary of Notre Dame cathedral. She stumbles on the steps of the church and dies. The moralist picks up the baby, discovers that he is deformed, a "monster," and decides to dispose of him by dropping him down a well, all the while muttering pious imprecations against this "spawn of the devil." So far, not a great portrait of Catholicism. In the only redeeming moment in the film, a priest rushes out of the cathedral, sees the dead woman, and warns the moralist that his immortal soul is in danger. To amend for his sin, he must agree to be the legal guardian of the baby. The moralist agrees, on the condition that the monster be raised in secret in Notre Dame.

In the next scene the baby is now a young man, Quasimodo, a badly deformed hunchback who lives in isolation in the tower of the cathedral. He is the bell ringer, a sweet soul, humble, good, and creative, content to make art and little toys and to observe from his lonely height the life of the people of Paris. His solitude is broken only by the occasional visits of the moralist, who takes delight in reminding Quasimodo that he is a worthless monster who survives only because of his (the moralist's) "kindness." Is there anyone in the audience who has missed the point: The moralist is the ultimate hypocrite, the real monster. Quasimodo's only other friends are three gargoyles, charming, humorous little demons who are reminiscent of the Three Stooges.

They encourage him to believe in love, to believe in himself, to have courage. In one interesting short scene, the gargoyles mock a carving of the Pope. Later in the film there is a scene depicting the churchgoers praying below in the cathedral. Without exception they pray for wealth, power, and gratification of their desires—a portrait of Catholics as utterly selfish, shallow people.

A sensual young gypsy woman flees into the cathedral to escape the moralist (who is also a judge). Safe inside, she prays for divine assistance in a vague, agnostic fashion. In stark contrast to the prayers of the Catholics, there is nothing selfish in her prayer. She merely asks for justice for her people. As the music swells, she turns away from the altar, still singing her "prayer," strolling in the opposite direction of the Catholics who are approaching the altar. Her supplication dissolves into a romantic musing that is more sentiment than insight into the nature of real mercy and justice. Disney's point is clear: Traditional Christianity is weak, blind, and selfish; "real Christianity" is sociological and "politically correct."

The romantic element, a mutual attraction between the gypsy woman and a young soldier, is simply a rehash of the screen romances that have become a necessary ingredient in Disney animated films. Lots of body language, lots of enticing flesh, a garish portrayal of the tormented moralist's secret lusts, a contrasting depiction of the beautiful young couple's sexual desire as pure and natural, and a sensual screen kiss that is inappropriate for young viewers (as it is in *Aladdin*, *The Little Mermaid*, and other Disney films). Perhaps we should ask ourselves if viewing such intimate moments between man and woman is ever appropriate, even for adults. Is voyeurism, in any form, good for the soul?

The Hunchback of Notre Dame concludes with a frenzied climax in which the forces of love and courage are pitted against the ignorance of the medieval Church. Quasimodo has overcome the lie of his worthlessness through the counsel of his gargoyles and is now strong enough to defy the moralist. He rescues the gypsy girl, who is about to be burned for witchcraft, and flees with her to the bell-tower. There the moralist tracks them down (after first pushing aside the ineffectual priest who tries to stop him) and attempts to kill them. As one might expect, he comes to a bad end. The gypsy and the soldier are reunited, and Quasimodo makes do with platonic love. All's well that ends well.

Based on Victor Hugo's novel of the same title (published in 1831), the film retains much of the plot and characterization and even manages to communicate some truths. But the reality-shift evidenced in the modern version is a serious violation of the larger architecture of truth. The truths are mixed with untruths, and because of the sensory impact of the film medium, it is that much more difficult for an audience to discern rightly between the two. This is especially damaging to children, who because of their age are in a state of formation that is largely impressionistic. Moreover, most modern people do not know their history and do not possess the tools of real thought and thus are vulnerable to manipulation of their feelings. Young and old, we are becoming a race of impressionists.

Rather than thinking with ideas, we "think" in free-form layers of images loosely connected by emotions. There would be little harm in this if the sources of these images were honest. But few sources in culture and entertainment are completely honest these days. And even if the mind were well stocked with the best of images (a very rare state), it is still not equipped to meet the spiritual and ideological confusion of our times. The problem is much deeper than a lack of literacy, because even the mental imagery created by the printed word can be merely a chain of misleading impressions, however well articulated they may be. The real problem is religious illiteracy, by which I mean the lack of an objective standard against which we can measure our subjective readings of sensation and experience. Without this objective standard, one's personal gnosis will inevitably push aside the objective truth and subordinate it to a lesser position, when it does not banish it altogether. That is why a modern maker of culture who feels strongly that Catholicism is bad for people has no qualms about rewriting history or creating anti-Catholic propaganda and will use all the powers of the modern media to do so. One wonders what Disney studios would do with Hugo's *Les Misérables* (published in 1862), an expressly Christian story in which two central characters, the bishop and Jean Valjean, are heroic Catholics fighting for truth, mercy, and justice in the face of the icy malice of the secular humanists, against the background of the French Revolution. Would the scriptwriters and executives sanitize and politically correct these characters by deCatholicizing them? It would be interesting to observe the contortions necessary for such a transformation. Perhaps they would do what Hollywood did to Dominique Lapierre's wonderful book, *The City of Joy*. The central character in that true story, a Christ-like young priest who chose to live among the most abject of Calcutta's poor, is entirely replaced in the film version by a handsome young American doctor (who was a secondary character in the book). In the Hollywood rewrite, the doctor is idealistic but amoral, and he is in the throes of an identity crisis. Uncertain at first if he is merely a technician of the body, slowly awakening to the possibility that he might become a minister to the whole person, in the end he chooses the latter. Following the gnostic pattern, he becomes the knower as healer, the scientist as priest. It is a well-made film, containing some good insights and moving scenes, but by displacing the priest of Christ, it loses an important part of the original story's "soul," cheating us of the real meaning of the events on which it is based.

Where Catholicism is not simply weeded out of the culture, it is usually attacked, though the attacks tend to be swift cheap-shots. Take, for instance, Steven Spielberg's smash hit, *Jurassic Park*.

Again, there is much to recommend this film, such as the questions it raises about science and morality, especially the issue of genetic engineering. In the struggle between people and dinosaurs there is plenty of human heroism, and the dinosaurs are even presented as classic reptiles—no taming or befriending here. So far so good. On the level of symbolism, however, we are stunned with an image of the reptile as practically omnipotent. The Tyrannosaurus Rex is power incarnate, and its smaller cousin, the Velociraptor, is not only fiercely powerful, it is intelligent and capable of learning.

There is a telling scene in which the most despicable character in the film, a sleazy lawyer, is riding in a car with two young children. When a dinosaur approaches the car to destroy it, the lawyer abandons the children to their fate and flees into an outdoor toilet cubicle. The T-Rex blows away the flimsy structure, exposing the lawyer, who is seated on the "john," quivering uncontrollably and whining the words of the Hail Mary. The T-Rex picks him up in its jaws, crunches hard, and gulps him down its throat. In the theater where I saw the film, the audience cheered.

Where Is It All Leading?

At this point, the reader may be saying to himself, "What you describe may be true. I've seen evidence of it, and I've struggled to understand it. I've tried to pick my way through the flood of things coming at my children, but I'm not having much success. I'm uneasy about the new culture, but I don't seem to have the skills to argue with it."

I think most conscientious parents feel this way. We know something is not right, but we don't quite know how to assess it.

We worry that our children might be affected adversely by it, but at the same time we don't want to overreact. The image of the "witch-hunt" haunts us (a fear that is strongly reinforced by the new culture), but we are equally concerned about the need to protect our children from being indoctrinated into paganism. What, then, are we to do?

Our first step must be in the direction of finding a few helpful categories, a standard against which we can measure examples of the new culture. I have found it useful to divide the field of children's culture into roughly four main categories:

1. Material that is entirely good.
2. Material that is fundamentally good but disordered in some details.
3. Material that appears good on the surface but is fundamentally disordered.
4. Material that is blatantly evil, rotten to the core.

I will return to these categories in the next chapter's assessment of children's literature, where I hope to develop them in greater detail. I introduce them here to make a different point. Two generations ago the culture of the Western world was composed of material that, with few exceptions, was either entirely good (1) or fundamentally good but disordered in some details (2). About forty years ago there began a culture-shift that steadily gathered momentum, a massive influx of material that appeared good on the surface but was fundamentally disordered (3). It became the new majority. During this period entirely good material became the minority, and at the same time more material that was diabolically evil began to appear (4). There is a pattern here. And it raises the question: Where is it all leading?

I think it highly unlikely that we will ever see a popular culture that is wholly dominated by the blatantly diabolical, but I do believe that unless we recognize what is happening, we may soon be living in a culture that is totally dominated by the fundamentally disordered and in which the diabolical is respected as an alternative worldview and becomes more influential than the entirely good. Indeed, we may be very close to that condition. I can think of half a dozen recent films that deliberately reverse the meaning of Christian symbols and elevate the diabolical to the status of a saving mythology.

The 1996 film *Dragon Heart*, for example, is the tale of a tenth century kingdom that suffers under a tyrannical king. When the king is killed in a peasant uprising, his son inherits the crown but is himself wounded when he is accidentally impaled on a spike. His heart is pierced, and he is beyond all hope of recovery. The queen takes her son into an underground cave that is the lair of a dragon. She kneels before the dragon, calls him "Lord," and begs him to save the prince's life. The dragon removes half of his own heart and inserts it into the gaping wound of the prince's chest, then heals the wound with a touch of his claw.

The queen says to her son, "He [the dragon] will save you." And to the dragon she says, "He [the prince] will grow in your grace." The prince recovers and grows to manhood, the dragon's heart beating within him.

The prince becomes totally evil, a tyrant like his father, and the viewer is led to believe that, in this detail at least, traditional symbolism is at work— the heart of a dragon will make a man into a dragon. Not so, for later we learn that the prince's own evil nature has overshadowed the dragon's good heart. When the dragon reappears in the plot and becomes the central character, we begin to learn that he is not the terrifying monster we think him to be. He dabbles in the role the superstitious peasants have assigned to him (the traditional concept of dragon), but he never really does any harm, except to dragon slayers, and then only when they attack him without provocation. Through his growing friendship with a reformed dragon slayer, we gradually come to see the dragon's true character. He is wise, noble, ethical, and witty. He merely plays upon the irrational fears of the humans regarding dragons because he knows that they are not yet ready to understand the higher wisdom, a vision known only to dragons and their enlightened human initiates. It is corrupt human nature, we are told, that has deformed man's understanding of dragons.

The dragon and his knight-friend assist the peasants in an uprising against the evil prince. Even a Catholic priest is enlisted in the battle. This character is yet another Hollywood buffoon priest, who in his best moments is a silly, poetic dreamer and at worst a confused and shallow remnant of a dishonored Christian myth. Over and over again, we are shown the ineffectiveness of Christianity against evil and the effective power of The People when they ally themselves with the dragon. The priest sees the choice, abandons his cross, and takes up a bow and arrow, firing two shafts into the head and groin of a practice dummy. In a final battle, he overcomes his Christian scruples and begins to shoot at enemy soldiers, quoting Scripture humorously (even the words of Jesus) every time he shoots. An arrow in a soldier's buttock elicits the priest's sly comment, "Turn the other cheek, brother!" When he aims at the evil prince, he murmurs, "Thou shalt not kill! Thou shalt not kill!" then proceeds to disobey the divine commandment. The arrow goes straight into the prince's heart, but he does not fall.

He pulls the arrow from his heart and smiles. Neither Christian myth nor Christian might can stop this kind of evil!

Here we begin to understand the objectives that the scriptwriter has subtly hatched from the very beginning of the film. The prince cannot die because a dragon's heart beats within him, even though he, not the dragon, has corrupted that heart. The evil prince will die only when the dragon dies. Knowing this, the dragon willingly sacrifices his own life in order to end the reign of evil, receiving a spear thrust into his heart. At this point we see the real purpose of the film—the presentation of the dragon as a Christ-figure!

Shortly before this decisive climax, the dragon describes in mystical tones his version of the history of the universe: "Long ago, when man was young and the dragon already old, the wisest of our race took pity on man. He gathered together all the dragons, who vowed to watch over man always. And at the moment of his death, the night became alive with those stars (pointing to the constellation Draco), and thus was born the dragon's heaven." He explains that he had shared his heart with the dying young prince in order to "reunite man and dragon and to ensure my place among my ancient brothers of the sky."

In the final moments of the film, after the dragon's death, he is assumed into the heavens amidst heart-throbbing music and star bursts and becomes part of the constellation Draco. The crowd of humans watch the spectacle, their faces filled with religious awe. A voice-over narrator says that in the years following "Draco's sacrifice" a time of justice and brotherhood came upon the world, "golden years warmed by an unworldly light. And when things became most difficult, Draco's star shone more brightly for all of us who knew where to look."

Few members of the audience would know that, according to the lore of witchcraft and Satanism, the constellation Draco is the original home of Satan and is reverenced in their rituals. Here is a warning about where Gnosticism can lead. What begins as one's insistence on the right to decide the meaning of good and evil leads inevitably to spiritual blindness. Step by step we are led from the wholly good to flawed personal interpretations of good; then, as the will is weakened and the mind darkened, we suffer more serious damage to the foundation itself and arrive finally, if we should lose all reason, at some manifestation of the diabolical.

When this process is promulgated with the genius of modern cinematic technology, packaged in the trappings of art and mysticism, our peril increases exponentially. My wife and I have known devout, intelligent, Christian parents who allowed their young children to watch *Dragon Heart* because they thought it was "just mythology." This is an understandable naivete, but it is also a symptom of our state of unpreparedness. The evil in corrupt mythology is never rendered harmless simply because it is encapsulated in a literary genre, as if sealed in a watertight compartment. Indeed, there are few things as infectious as mythology. We would be sadly mistaken if we assumed that the cultural invasion is mainly a conflict of abstract ideas. It is a major front in the battle for the soul of modern man, and as such it necessarily entails elements of spiritual combat. For this reason parents must ask God for the gifts of wisdom, discernment, and vigilance during these times. We must also plead for extraordinary graces and intercede continuously for our children. The invasion reaches into very young minds, relaxing children's instinctive aversion to what is truly frightening. It begins there, but we must understand that it will not end there, for its logical end is a culture that exalts the diabolical. There are a growing number of signs that this process is well under way.

In most toy shops, for example, one can find a number of soft, cuddly dragons and other monsters to befriend. There are several new children's books about lovable dragons who are not evil, merely misunderstood. In one such book, given as a Christmas present to our children by a well-meaning friend, we found six illustrations that attempted to tame the diabolical by dressing it in ingratiating costumes. The illustrator exercised a certain genius that made his work well nigh irresistible. One of the images portrayed a horrible, grotesque being at the foot of a child's bed. The accompanying story told how the child, instead of driving it away, befriended it, and together they lived happily ever after. The demonic being had become the child's guardian. One wonders what has become of guardian angels! Such works seek to help children integrate "the dark side" into their natures, to reconcile good and evil within, and, as our friend expressed it, to "embrace their shadows."

In *Lilith*, a classical fantasy by the nineteenth-century Christian writer George MacDonald, the voice of Eve calls this darkness "the mortal foe of my children." In one passage a character describes the coming of "The Shadow": "He was nothing but blackness. We were frightened the moment we saw him, but we did not run away, we stood and watched him. He came on us as if he would run over us. But before he reached us he began to spread and spread, and grew bigger and bigger, till at last he was so big that he went out of our sight, and we saw him no more, and then he was upon us." It is when they can no longer see him that his power over them is at its height. They then describe how the shadow temporarily possessed them and bent their personalities in the direction of hatred. He is thrown off by love welling up within their hearts.

The German writer Goethe, in his great classic work *Faust*, uses a different approach to depict the seduction of mankind. At one point the devil says:

> Humanity's most lofty power,
> Reason and knowledge pray despise!
> But let the Spirit of all lies
> With works of dazzling magic blind you,
> Then absolutely mine, I'll have and bind you!

In children's culture a growing fascination with the supernatural is hastening the breakdown of the Christian vision of the spiritual world and the moral order of the universe. Reason and a holy knowledge are despised, while intoxicating signs and wonders increase.

Review and Discussion Questions

1. What is the error of Gnosticism?

2. Trace the shift over the years—in O'Brien's narrative of the events—in Disney's portrayal of Good and Evil.

3. In O'Brien's view, what is corrupting in Disney's telling of *The Hunchback of Notre Dame*?

4. Why not depict "friendly" dragons?

❖ 37

ARCHBISHOP J. MICHAEL MILLER, CSB

The Holy See's Teaching on Catholic Schools

> Catholic educators should have a sound understanding of the human person
> that addresses the requirements of both the natural and the supernatural
> perfection of the children entrusted to their care.

Drawing upon post-conciliar documents, the former Secretary of the Congregation for Catholic Education offers a bird's-eye view of magisterial
teaching on education. Beyond prudential advice (as in, hire "practicing
Catholics who are committed to the Church"), Miller highlights a number
of striking claims, such as: that all teaching is done "in the name of parents"; that a "state monopoly of education" contravenes natural justice; that
schools ought to be beautiful and "express physically and visibly the external signs of Catholic culture"; and finally, against relativism, that Catholic
educators must instill in students the confident conviction that "human beings can grasp the truth of things." The archbishop concludes with a provocative proposal. Just as state schools must pass accreditation exams to ensure funding, so Catholic schools ought—he avers—to prove their fidelity
to the Church, or else publicly receive a failing grade.

Further Reading: *Gravissimum Educationis* (Declaration on Christian Education) in *Vatican
Council II: Volume 1, The Conciliar and Post Conciliar Documents, Revised Edition*, ed. Austin
Flannery, O.P. (Northport, N.Y.: Costello Publishing Co., 1996); Curtis L. Hancock, *Recovering
a Catholic Philosophy of Elementary Education* (Mount Pocono, Penn.: Newman House Press,
2005); Jason Boffetti, *All Schools Are Public Schools: A Case for State Aid to Private Education and
Homeschooling Parents* (Washington, D.C.: Faith and Reason Institute, 2001).

❖

I. The Current Situation of America's Catholic Schools

Certainly there is much to applaud in the American Catholic school
system that currently enrolls almost 2.5 million students in its primary and

secondary schools. By any measure this is an outstanding testimony to the vigor of Catholic life in the United States.

Even so, we cannot hide the fact that the number of students in Catholic schools continues to decline. The peak was reached in 1965 when 5.5 million students were enrolled in Catholic elementary and high schools. In 1930, there were more Catholic elementary schools (7,225), with 2.5 million students, than in 2004 (6,574),with 1.78 million students. Moreover in the same seventy-five-year period, the Catholic population tripled: from 20.2 million in 1930 to over 66 million in 2004.

Since 1990, more than 400 new Catholic schools have opened in the United States. But during that period there has been a net loss of more than 760 Catholic schools. Most of the decline has been concentrated in urban, inner city, and rural areas.[1]

Clearly the Church in America is facing a serious challenge in serving her children and young people, one that cannot be swept under the rug or dismissed as the inevitable result of an increasingly secularized society.

In the past forty years, not only in the United States but also in most of the developed world, religious vocations have plummeted. In 1965, there were 180,000 religious sisters in the United States; today there are fewer than 75,000, of whom more than 50 percent are over seventy years of age. Moreover, in 1965 there were 3.95 sisters for every 1,000 Catholics; in 2002, there was 1.16.[2]

Since Vatican II, Catholic elementary and secondary schools have shown a steady decline in the number of religious and priests who are administrators and teachers, and an increase in the number of laypersons who fill those positions.[3] Today religious women constitute less than 4 percent of the full-time professional staff of Catholic schools, while 95 percent of the teachers are laypersons.

For generations religious women provided the backbone of the parochial school system in the United States, contributing to its establishment and allowing it to flourish by their generous and sacrificial apostolate. In its documents, the Holy See frequently extols the specific contribution made by religious to the Church's educational apostolate:

> Because of their special consecration, their particular experience of the gifts of the Spirit, their constant listening to the word of God, their practice of discernment, their rich heritage of pedagogical traditions built up since their establishment of their Institute, and their profound grasp of spiritual truth [cf. Eph. 2:17], consecrated persons are able to be especially effective in educational activities and to offer a specific contribution to the work of other educators.[4]

Undoubtedly, for years, the presence of religious in most parochial and secondary schools served as a built-in guarantee of their Catholic identity, which parents and pastors took for granted. And the vast network of schools established did indeed provide a sound religious and academic education, especially for Catholic immigrant children. The shift to lay leadership in Catholic schools, which has followed from the dearth of religious, presents its own set of challenges.

In no way do I wish to suggest that the laity are somehow second-best as Catholic educators. Still, theirs is a new responsibility and presents a new opportunity for the Church, one full of promise and hope. They, too, have a "supernatural vocation"[5] as educators.

To be effective bearers of the Church's educational tradition however, laypersons who teach in Catholic schools need a "religious formation that is equal to their general, cultural, and most especially, professional formation."[6] It is up to the ecclesial community to see to it that such formation is required of and made available to all Catholic-school educators, those already in the system and those preparing to enter it. In this regard, Catholic universities have a special responsibility to assist Catholic schools by providing teacher training courses and programs serving this constituency.

Some Catholic teachers bring to their educational apostolate the charism of a particular religious institute, with all that it involves in terms of a specific spirituality and approach to pedagogy. This is highly commendable. But more important than handing on elements of a particular charism to certain members of the laity is safeguarding and promoting schools' Catholic ethos. We cannot forget that a school is *first* Catholic before it can be molded according to the specific charism of a religious institute.

In light of the teaching of the Second Vatican Ecumenical Council that "lay people have their own proper competence in the building up of the Church,"[7] I believe that men and women, precisely as members of the lay faithful, have their own charism of teaching, independent of the charism of a particular religious congregation.

In the not-too-distant future, individual religious communities might die out or might flourish once again—we do not know. What we do know, however, is that the Church herself will survive; and she must have schools that are recognizably Catholic.

I. Shared Responsibilities

Parental Rights and Subsidiarity

The Church's clear teaching, constantly reiterated by the Holy See, affirms that parents are the first educators of their children. Parents have the original, primary and inalienable right to educate their offspring in conformity with the family's moral and religious convictions.[8] They are educators because they are parents. At the same time, the vast majority of parents share their educational responsibilities with other individuals and institutions, primarily the school.

Elementary education is, then, "an extension of parental education; it is extended and cooperative home schooling."[9] In a true sense schools are extensions of the home. Parents—and not schools either of the state or the Church—have the primary moral responsibility of educating children to adulthood. Like a good Mother, the Church offers help to families by establishing Catholic schools that ensure the integral formation of their children.[10]

In keeping with a baic tenet of Catholic social doctrine, the principle of subsidiarity must always govern relations among families, the Church, and the state. As Pope John Paul II wrote in his 1994 *Letter to Families*:

> Subsidiarity thus complements paternal and maternal love and confirms its fundamental nature, inasmuch as all other participants in the process of education are only able to carry out their responsibilities in the name of the parents, with their consent and, to a certain degree, with their authorization.[11]

For subsidiarity to be effective, families must enjoy true liberty deciding how their children are to be educated. This means that "in principle, a state monopoly of education is not permissible, and that only a pluralism of school systems will respect the fundamental right and the freedom of individuals—although the exercise of this right may be conditioned by a multiplicity of factors, according to the social realities of each country."[12] Thus, the Catholic Church upholds "the principle of a plurality of school systems in order to safeguard her objectives."[13]

Right to Government Financial Assistance

A pressing problem for Catholic schools in the United States is the lack of government financial assistance. The Church's teaching authority has frequently addressed the rights of parents to such help in fulfilling their obligation to educate their children. At Vatican II, the Fathers declared that "the public power, which has the obligation to protect and defend the rights of citizens, must see to it, in its concern for distributive justice, that public subsidies are paid out in such a way that parents are truly free to choose according to their conscience the schools they want for their children."[14]

The *Compendium of the Social Doctrine of the Church* (2005) states laconically that "the refusal to provide public economic support to non-public schools that need assistance and that render a service to civil society is to be considered an injustice."[15] Furthermore, the state is obliged to provide such public subsidies because of the enormous contribution that Catholic schools make to society by serving the common good.[16]

Most countries with substantial Christian majorities accept this obligation in justice: Australia, Belgium, Canada, England, France, Germany, Ireland, the Netherlands, Spain, and Scotland, to name a few. Their governments give Catholic schools financial assistance, some up to 100 percent. Italy, Mexico, China, Cuba, North Korea, and the United States are exceptions in withholding assistance.

For many families, especially those in the working and middle classes, the financial burden of providing Catholic education for their children is sizeable and often too great. Since 1990, the average tuition in elementary and secondary Catholic schools has more than doubled. In 2004, it stood at $2,432 for elementary schools and $5,870 for secondary schools.

As the American bishops recently stated, there is no other way to address this question of cost than "to advocate for parental school choice and personal and corporate tax credits."[17] To advocate for some kind of government funding for Catholic education, as long as no unacceptable strings are attached, is the responsibility not just of parents of school-age children, but of all Catholics in their pursuit of justice. Too often Catholic Americans fail to appreciate that they have a *right* to subsidies for their schools because these institutions provide a service to society. In no way would such assistance compromise the constitutional separation of Church and state. Rather, it guarantees the fundamental right of parents to choose a school for their children.

Where the government bears its fair share of the financial burden, Catholic schools can flourish. Take the example of Melbourne, Australia. Melbourne is about the size of Houston; both cities have about four million inhabitants and more than one million Catholics. To serve its Catholic children, Melbourne has 256 elementary schools in its archdiocese and sixty-five secondary schools, compared with the Houston Archdiocese's fifty-two elementary and nine high schools. Why the difference? No doubt the answer lies in the generous public funding made available to Melbourne's Catholic schools.

Without some kind of government assistance or at least tax relief, it is difficult to see how Catholic education can remain affordable and accessible, especially to the increasing numbers of immigrant children, primarily Hispanics. Within less than a generation, Hispanics will constitute more than 50 percent of American Catholics and an even higher proportion of our Catholic children.

All Catholic children, not just those whose families have the financial means, have a right to a Catholic education. Vatican documents stress that the Church's preferential option for the poor means that she offers her education ministry in the first place to "those who are poor in the goods of this world."[18] The Holy see supports the concern of the American bishops to provide for the poor and those who might be underprepared for high academic achievement: the Catholic school "is a school for all, with special attention to those who are weakest."[19] Guaranteeing this "for all" will require a new politics of educational funding in the United States.

III. Five Essential Marks of Catholic Schools

Papal interventions and Roman documents repeatedly emphasize that certain characteristics must be present for a school to be considered authentically Catholic. Like the marks of the Church proclaimed in the Creed— one, holy, catholic, and apostolic—so, too, does the Holy See identify the principal features of a school as *Catholic:* a Catholic school should be inspired by a supernatural vision, founded on Christian anthropology, animated by communion and community, imbued with a Catholic worldview throughout its curriculum, and sustained by gospel witness. These benchmarks help to answer the critical question: *Is this a Catholic school according to the mind of the Church?*

Pope John Paul II reminded a group of American bishops during their 2004 *ad limina* visit:

It is of utmost importance, therefore, that the Church's institutions be genuinely Catholic: Catholic in their self-understanding and Catholic in their identity.[20]

It is precisely because of its Catholic identity, which is anything but sectarian, that a school derives the originality that enables it to be a genuine instrument of the Church's evangelizing mission.[21] Michael Guerra, former president of the National Catholic Educational Association put the challenge succinctly: "The first and most important task for Catholic schools is to maintain and continually strengthen their Catholic identity."[22]

The five elements that necessarily belong to a school's Catholic identity are the principles propose by the Holy See that justify the Church's heavy investment in schooling. Moreover, they are measurable benchmarks, forming the backbone and inspiring the mission of every Catholic school.

Let us now look at each of the marks that give a school a Catholic identity.

1. Inspired by a Supernatural Vision

The Church sees education as a process that, in light of man's transcendent destiny, forms the whole child and seeks to fix his or her eyes on heaven.[23] The specific purpose of a Catholic education is the formation of boys and girls who will be good citizens of this world, loving God and neighbor and enriching society with the leaven of the gospel, and who will also be citizens of the world to come, thus fulfilling their destiny to become saints.[24]

In a speech addressed to American Catholic educators in New Orleans, Pope John Paul II presented them with

the pressing challenge of clearly identifying the aims of Catholic education, and applying proper methods in Catholic elementary and secondary education.... It is the challenge of fully understanding the educational enterprise, of properly evaluating its content, and of transmitting the full truth concerning the human person, created in God's image and called to life in Christ through the Holy Spirit.[25]

An emphasis on the inalienable dignity of the human person—above all on his or her spiritual dimension—is especially necessary today. Unfortunately, far too many in government, business, the media, and even the educational establishment perceive education to be merely an instrument for the acquisition of information that will improve the chances of worldly success and a more comfortable standard of living. Such an impoverished vision of education is not Catholic.

If Catholic educators, parents, and others who dedicate themselves to this apostolate fail to keep in mind a high supernatural vision, all their talk about Catholic schools will be no more than "a gong booming or a cymbal clashing" (1 Cor. 13:1).

2. Founded on a Christian Anthropology

Emphasis on the supernatural destiny of students, on their holiness, brings with it a profound appreciation of the need to perfect children in all their dimensions as images of God (cf. Gen 1:26–27). Catholic theology teaches that grace builds on nature. Because of this complementarity of the natural and supernatural, Catholic educators should have a sound understanding of the human person that addresses the requirements of both natural and supernatural perfection of the children entrusted to their care.[26]

Repeatedly the Holy See's documents emphasize the need for an educational philosophy built on a correct understanding of who the human person is. How do they describe such an anthropological vision?

In *Lay Catholics in Schools: Witnesses to Faith* the Vatican proposes a response:

In today's pluralistic world, the Catholic educator must consciously inspire his or her activity with the Christian concept of the person, in communion with the Magisterium of the Church. It is a concept which includes a defense of human rights, but also attributes to the human person the dignity of a child of God; it attributes the fullest liberty, freed from sin itself by Christ, the most exalted destiny, which is the definitive and total possession of God himself, through love. It establishes the strictest possible relationship of solidarity among all persons; through mutual love and an ecclesial community. It calls for the fullest development of all that is human, because we have been made masters of the world by its Creator. Finally, it proposes Christ, Incarnate Son of God and perfect Man, as both model and means; to imitate him, is, for all men and women, the inexhaustible source of personal and communal perfection.[27]

All this says nothing more than the words from *the Pastoral Constitution on the Church in the Modern World, so frequently* quoted by Pope John Paul II: "It is only in the mystery of the Word made flesh that the mystery of man truly becomes clear."[28]

A Catholic school, therefore, cannot be a factory for the learning of various skills and competencies designed to fill the echelons of business and industry. Nor is it for "clients" and "consumers" in a competitive marketplace that values academic achievement. Education is not a commodity, even if Catholic schools equip their graduates with enviable skills. Rather, "the Catholic school sets out to be a school for the human person and of human persons."[29]

The Holy See's documents insist that, to be worthy of its name, a Catholic school must be founded on Jesus Christ the Redeemer. It is he who, through his Incarnation, is united with each student. Christ is not an afterthought or an add-on to Catholic educational philosophy; he is the center and fulcrum of the entire enterprise, the light enlightening every boy and girl who comes into a Catholic school (cf. Jn 1:9). In its document *The Catholic School*, the Sacred Congregation for Catholic Education states:

The Catholic school is committed thus to the development of the whole man, since in Christ, the perfect man, all human values find their fulfilment and unity. Herein lies the specifically Catholic character of the school. Its duty to cultivate human values in their own legitimate right in accordance with its particular mission to serve all men has its origin in the figure of Christ. He is the one who ennobles man, gives meaning to human life, and is the model which the Catholic school offers to its pupils.[30]

The gospel of Jesus Christ and his very person are to inspire and guide the Catholic school in its every dimension of its life and activity—its philosophy of education, its curriculum, community life, its selection of teachers, and even its physical environment.

Christ is *the* Teacher in Catholic schools. Nevertheless, this conviction, in its very simplicity, can sometimes be overlooked. Catholic schools have the task of being the living and provocative memory of Christ. All too many Catholic schools fall into the trap of a secular academic success culture, putting their Christological focus and its accompanying understanding of the human person in second place. Christ is "fitted in" rather than being the school's vital principle.

As John Paul II wrote in his 1979 Message to the National Catholic Educational Association, "Catholic education is above all a question of communicating Christ, of helping to form Christ in the lives of others."[31] Authentic Catholic educators recognize Christ and his understanding of the human person as the measure of a school's catholicity. He is "the foundation of the whole educational enterprise in a Catholic school,"[32] and the principles of his gospel are its guiding educational norms:

In a Catholic school, everyone should be aware of the living presence of Jesus the "Master" who, today as always, is with us in our journey through life as the one genuine "Teacher," the perfect Man in whom all human values find their fullest perfection. The inspiration of Jesus must be translated from the ideal into the real. The gospel spirit should be evident in a Christian way of thought and life which permeates all facets of the educational climate.[33]

3. Animated by Communion and Community

A third mark of catholicity is the emphasis on the school as a community—a community of persons and, even more to the point, "a genuine community of faith."[34] Such an emphasis proposes an alternative model for Catholic schools to that of an individualistic society. This communal dimension is rooted both in the social nature of the human person and the reality the Church as a "the home and the school of communion."[35] That the Catholic school is an educational *community* "is one of the most enriching developments for the contemporary school."[36] The Congregation's *Religious Dimension of Education in a Catholic School* sums up this new emphasis:

The declaration *Gravissimum Educationis* notes an important advance in the way a Catholic school is thought of: the transition from the school as an institution to the school as a community. This community dimension is, perhaps, one result of the new awareness of the Church's nature as developed by the Council. In the Council texts, the community dimension is primarily a theological concept rather than a sociological category.[37]

The Holy See describes the school as a community in four areas: the teamwork among all those involved; the cooperation between educators and bishops; the interaction of students with teachers; and the school's physical environment.

Teamwork   Elementary schools "should try to create a community school climate that reproduces, as far as possible, the warm and intimate atmosphere of family life. Those responsible for these schools will, therefore, do everything they can to promote a common spirit of trust and spontaneity."[38] This means that educators should develop a willingness to collaborate among themselves. Teachers, both religious and lay, together with parents and school board members, are to work as a team for the school's common good.[39] Their communion fosters appreciation of the various charisms and vocations that build up a genuine school community and strengthen scholastic solidarity.[40] Educators, administrators, parents, and bishops guide the school to make choices that promote "overcoming individualistic self-promotion, solidarity instead of competition, assisting the weak instead of marginalization, responsible participation instead of indifference."[41]

The Holy See is, moreover, ever mindful of ensuring the appropriate involvement of parents in Catholic schools:

Close cooperation with the family is especially important when treating sensitive issues such as religious, moral, or sexual education, orientation toward a profession, or a choice of one's vocation in life. It is not a question of convenience, but a partnership based on faith.[42]

Now, more than in the past, teachers and administrators must often encourage parental participation in the school's mission and life. Such a partnership is directed not just toward dealing with academic problems but also toward planning and evaluating the effectiveness of the school's mission.

Even though consecrated men and women are now few in the schools, the witness of their collaboration with the laity enriches the ecclesial value of educational communities. As "experts in communion" because of their experience in community life, religious foster those "human and spiritual bonds that promote the mutual exchange of gifts" with all others involved in the school.[43] In the words of a recent Vatican document:

Consecrated persons are thus leaven that is able to create relations of increasingly deep communion that are themselves educational. They promote solidarity, mutual enhancement, and joint responsibility in the educational plan, and, above all, they give an explicit Christian testimony.[44]

Cooperation between Educators and Bishops   The catholicity of American schools also depends largely on the bonds of ecclesial communion between bishops and Catholic educators. They are to help one another in carrying out the task to which they are mutually committed. Personal relationships marked by mutual trust, close cooperation, and continuing dialogue are required for a genuine spirit of communion.

First, trust. This goes beyond the personal relationships of those involved. These might or might not be marked by warmth and friendship, depending on the concrete situation. The more profound foundation for such trust is shared adherence to the person of Jesus Christ. Trust is fostered by listening to one another, by respecting the different gifts of each, and by recognizing one another's specific responsibilities. With trust comes dialogue. Both bishops and educators, whether singly or in associations, should avail themselves of open, sincere, and regular dialogue in their joint efforts on behalf of Catholic schools.

Educators and ecclesial authorities should cooperate closely in fostering a school's catholicity. Such collaboration is not only an ideal but also a time-honored ecclesial practice in the United States. A spirituality of communion should be the guiding principle of Catholic education. Without this spiritual path, all external structures of cooperation serve very little purpose; they would be mere mechanisms without a soul.[45]

Catholic educators recognize that the bishop's pastoral leadership is pivotal in supporting the establishment and ensuring the catholicity of the schools in his pastoral care. Indeed, "only the bishop can set the tone, ensure the priority, and effectively present the importance of the cause to the Catholic people."[46] His responsibility for Catholic schools derives from the *munus docendi*, the office of teaching, he received at ordination.[47] As the Code of Canon Law states, "Pastors of souls have the duty of making all possible arrangements so that all the faithful may avail themselves of a Catholic education."[48]

With regard to Catholic schools, episcopal responsibility is twofold. First, the bishop must integrate schools into his diocese's pastoral program; and, second, he must oversee the teaching within them. As John Paul II straightforwardly affirmed, "Bishops need to support and enhance the work of Catholic schools."[49]

The bishop must see to it that the education in his schools is based on the principles of Catholic doctrine. This vigilance includes even schools established or directed by members of religious institutes.[50] The bishop's particular responsibilities include ensuring that teachers are sound in their doctrine and outstanding in their integrity of life.[51] It is he who must judge whether the children in the Catholic schools in his diocese are receiving the fullness of the Church's faith in their catechetical and religious formation.

It is important that the bishop be involved in Catholic schools not only by exercising veto power—whether over texts, curricula, or teachers—but also by taking an active role in fostering the specifically Catholic ethos of schools under his jurisdiction. In an *ad limina* address to a group of American bishops in June 2004, Pope John Paul II summed up this point: "The Church's presence in elementary and secondary education must ... be the object of your special attention as shepherds of the People of God."[52] In particular, pastors should set in place "specific programs of formation" that will enable the laity to take on responsibilities for teaching in Catholic schools.[53]

Interaction of Students with Teachers   The Catholic philosophy of education has always paid special attention to the interpersonal relations in the school community, especially those between teachers and students. This concern ensures that the student is seen as a person whose intellectual growth is harmonized with spiritual, religious, emotional, and social growth.[54] Because, as St. John Bosco said, "education is a thing of the heart,"[55] authentic formation of young people requires the personalized accompanying of a teacher. "During childhood and adolescence a student needs to experience personal relations with outstanding educators, and what is taught has greater influence on the student's formation when placed in a context of personal involvement, genuine reciprocity, coherence of attitudes, lifestyle and day to day behavior."[56] Direct and personal contact between teachers and students is a hallmark of the Catholic school. A learning atmosphere which encourages the befriending of students is far removed from the caricature of the remote disciplinarian so cherished by the media.

In measured terms the Congregation's document *Lay Catholics in Schools: Witnesses to Faith* describes the student-teaching relationship:

A personal relationship is always a dialogue rather than a monologue, and the teacher must be convinced that the enrichment in the relationship is mutual. But the mission must never be lost sight of: the educator can never forget that students need a companion and guide during their period of growth; they need help from others in order to overcome doubts and disorientation. Also, rapport with the students ought to be a prudent combination of familiarity and distance; and this must be adapted to the need of each individual student. Familiarity will make a personal relationship easier, but a certain distance is also needed.[57]

Catholic schools, then, safeguard the priority of the person, both student and teacher. They foster the proper friendship between them, since "an authentic formative process can only be initiated through a personal relationship."[58]

Physical Environment   A school's physical environment is also an integral element that embodies the genuine community values of the Catholic tradition. Since the school is rightly considered an extension of the home, it ought to have "some of the amenities which can create a pleasant and family atmosphere."[59] This includes an adequate physical plant and equipment.

It is especially important that this "school-home" be immediately recognizable as Catholic:

From the first moment that a student sets foot in a Catholic school, he or she ought to have the impression of entering a new environment, one illumined by the light of faith, and having its own unique characteristics.[60]

The Incarnation, which emphasizes the *bodily* coming of God's Son into the world, leaves its seal on every aspect of Christian life. The very fact of the Incarnation tells us that the created world is the means God chose to communicate his life to us. What is human and visible can bear the divine.

If Catholic schools are to be true to their identity, they will suffuse their environment with a delight in the sacramental. Therefore they should express physically and visibly the external signs of Catholic culture through images, symbols, icons and other objects of traditional devotion. A chapel, classroom crucifixes and statues, liturgical celebrations, and other sacramental reminders of Catholic life, including good art that is not explicitly religious in its subject matter, should be evident. All these signs embody the community ethos of Catholicism.

Prayer should be a normal part of the school day, so that students learn to pray in times of sorrow and joy, of disappointment and celebration, of difficulty and success. Such prayer teaches students that they belong to the communion of saints, a community that knows no bounds. The sacraments of the Eucharist and Reconciliation in particular should mark the rhythm of a Catholic school's life. Mass should be celebrated regularly, with the students and teachers participating appropriately. Traditional Catholic devotions should also have their place: praying the Rosary, decorating May altars, singing hymns, reading from the Bible, recounting the lives of the saints, and celebrating the Church's liturgical year. The sacramental vitality of the Catholic faith is expressed in these and similar acts of religion that belong to everyday ecclesial life and should be evident in every school.

4. Imbued with a Catholic Worldview throughout Its Curriculum

A fourth distinctive characteristic of Catholic schools is that the "spirit of Catholicism" should permeate the entire curriculum.

Catholic education is "intentionally directed to the growth of the whole person."[61] An integral education aims to develop gradually every capability of every student: his or her intellectual, physical, psychological, moral, and religious capacities. Vatican documents speak of an education that responds to all the needs of the human person:

> The integral formation of the human person, which is the purpose of education, includes the development of all the human faculties of the students, together with preparation for professional life, formation of ethical and social awareness, becoming aware of the transcendental, and religious education. Every school, and every educator in the school, ought to be striving "to form strong and responsible individuals, who are capable of making free and correct choices," thus preparing young people "to open themselves more and more to reality, and to form in themselves a clear idea of the meaning of life" [*The Catholic School*, 31].[62]

To be integral or complete, Catholic schooling must be constantly inspired and guided by the Gospel. As we have seen, the Catholic school would betray its purpose if it failed to found itself on the person of Christ and his teaching: "It derives all the energy necessary for its educational work from him."[63]

Because of the gospel's vital and guiding role in a Catholic school, one might be tempted to think that the school's distinctiveness lies only in the quality of its religious instruction, catechesis, and pastoral activities. Nothing is further from the position of the Holy See. Rather, the Catholic school must embody its genuine catholicity even apart from such programs and projects. It is Catholic because it undertakes to educate the whole child, addressing the requirements of his or her natural and supernatural perfection. It is Catholic because it provides an education in the intellectual and moral virtues. It is Catholic because it prepares for a fully human life at the service of others and for the life of the world to come. All instruction, therefore, must be authentically Catholic in content and methodology across the entire program of studies.

Catholicism is a "comprehensive way of life"[64] that should animate every aspect of its activities and its curriculum. Although Vatican documents on education do not cover lesson planning, the order of teaching the various subjects, or the relative merit of different pedagogical methods, the Holy See does provide guidelines meant to inspire the content of the curriculum. If a Catholic school is to deliver on its promise to provide students with an integral education, it must foster love for wisdom and truth, and must integrate faith, culture, and life.

Love for Wisdom and Passion for Truth   In an age of information overload, Catholic schools must be especially attentive in their instruction to strike the delicate balance between human experience and understanding. Catholic educators do not want our students to say, "We had the experience but missed the meaning."[65]

Knowledge and understanding are far more than the accumulation of information. Again T. S. Eliot puts it just right: "Where is the wisdom we have lost in knowledge? Where is the knowledge we have lost in information?"[66] Catholic schools do far more than convey information to passive students. They aspire to teach love for wisdom, habituating each student "to desire learning so much that he or she will delight in becoming a self-learner."[67]

Intrinsically related to the search for wisdom is another idea frequently repeated in Vatican teaching: the confidence that the human mind, however limited its powers, can come to a knowledge of truth. This conviction about the nature of truth is too important for Catholics to be confused about. Unlike skeptics and relativists, Catholic educators share a specific belief about truth: that, to a limited but real extent, it can be attained and communicated to others. Catholic schools take up the daunting task of freeing boys and girls from the insidious consequences of what Pope Benedict XVI has called the "dictatorship of relativism"[68]—a dictatorship that cripples all genuine education. Catholic teachers are to cultivate in themselves and develop in others a passion for truth that defeats moral and cultural relativism. They are to educate "in the truth."

In an *ad limina* address to a group of American bishops, Pope John Paul II pinpointed the importance of having a correct grasp of truth if the Church's educational efforts are to bear fruit:

The greatest challenge to Catholic education in the United States today, and the greatest contribution that authentically Catholic education can make to American culture, is to restore to that culture the conviction that human beings can grasp the truth of things, and in grasping that truth can know their duties to God, to themselves and their neighbors. In meeting that challenge, the Catholic educator will hear an echo of Christ's words: "If you continue in my word, you are truly my disciples, and you will know the truth, and the truth will make you free" (Jn 8:32). The contemporary world urgently needs the service of educational institutions which uphold and teach that truth is "that fundamental value without which freedom, justice and human dignity are extinguished" [*Veritatis Splendor*, 4].[69]

Closely following papal teaching, the Holy See's documents on schools insist that education is about truth—both in its natural and supernatural dimensions:

The school considers human knowledge as a truth to be discovered. In the measure in which subjects are taught by someone who knowingly and without restraint seeks the truth, they are to that extent Christian. Discovery and awareness of truth leads man to the discovery of Truth itself.[70]

While Catholic schools conform to government-mandated curricula, they implement their programs with an overall religious orientation. Such a perspective includes criteria such as "confidence in our ability to attain truth, at least in a limited way—a confidence based not on feeling but on faith ... [and] the ability to make judgments about what is true and what is false."[71] Unwavering commitment to truth is at home in an authentically Catholic school.

Faith, Culture, and Life   A second principle that derives from communicating a Catholic worldview to children is the notion that they should learn to transform culture in light of the gospel. Schools prepare students to relate the Catholic faith to their particular culture and to live that faith in practice.

In *The Catholic School on the Threshold of the Third Millennium*, the Congregation for Catholic Education commented:

From the nature of the Catholic school also stems one of the most significant elements of its educational project: the synthesis of culture and faith. The endeavor to interweave reason and faith, which has become the heart of individual subjects, makes for unity, articulation and coordination, bringing forth within what is learned in a school a Christian vision of the world, of life, of culture, and of history.[72]

Schools form students within their own culture, teaching them an appreciation of its positive elements and fostering a more profound integration of the gospel in their particular situation. Faith and culture are intimately related, and students should be led, in ways suitable to the level of their intellectual development, to grasp the importance of this relationship. "We must always remember that, while faith is not to be identified with any one culture and is independent of all cultures, it must inspire every culture."[73]

Furthermore, young Catholics, in a way appropriate to their age, must also learn to make judgments based on religious and moral truths. They should be led to be critical and evaluative. It is the Catholic faith that provides young people with the essential principles for critique an evaluation.[74]

The educational philosophy that guides Catholic schools also seeks to ensure that they are places where "faith, culture, and life are brought into harmony."[75] Central to the Catholic school is its mission of holiness, of saint-making. Mindful of redemption in Christ, the Catholic school aims to form in its pupils those particular virtues that will enable them to live a new life in Christ and help them to play their part in serving society and the Church. It strives to develop virtue "by the integration of culture with faith and of faith with living."[76] The Congregation for Catholic Education has written that "the Catholic school tries to create within its walls a climate in which the pupil's faith will gradually mature and enable him to assume the responsibility placed on him by Baptism."[77]

A primary way of helping Catholic students become more committed to their faith is by providing solid religious instruction. To be sure, "education in the faith is a part of the finality of a Catholic school."[78] For young Catholics, such instruction embraces both teaching the truths of the faith and fostering its practice.[79] Still, we must always take special care to avoid the error that a Catholic school's distinctiveness rests solely on the shoulders of its religious-education program. Such a position would foster the misunderstanding that faith and life can be divorced, that religion is a merely private affair without doctrinal content or moral obligations.

5. Sustained by Gospel Witness

A final indicator of a school's authentic catholicity is the vital witness of tis teachers and administrators. With them lies the primary responsibility for creating a Christian school climate, as individuals and as a community.[80] Indeed, "it depends chiefly on them whether the Catholic school achieves its purpose."[81] Consequently the Holy See's documents pay a great deal of attention to the vocation of teachers and their participation in the Church's evangelizing mission. Theirs is a supernatural calling and not simply the exercise of a profession.[82] "The nobility of the task to which teachers are called demands that, in imitation of Christ, the only Teacher, they reveal the Christian message not only by word but also by every gesture of their behavior."[83]

More than a master who teaches, a Catholic educator is a person who gives testimony by his or her life. Shortly after his election, Pope Benedict XVI spoke about the kind of witness required of all teachers of the faith, including those in Catholic schools:

> The central figure in the work of educating ... is specifically the form of witness.... The witness never refers to himself but to something, or rather, to Someone greater than he, whom he has encountered and whose dependable goodness he has sampled. Thus, every educator and witness finds an unequaled model in Jesus Christ, the Father's great witness, who said nothing about himself but spoke as the Father had taught him [cf. John 8:28].[84]

Hiring Committed Catholics   To fulfill their responsibility of speaking about the Father, educators in Catholic schools, with very few exceptions, should be practicing Catholics who are committed to the Church and living her sacramental life. Despite the difficulties sometimes involved, those responsible for hiring teachers must see to it that these criteria are met. When addressing Catholic-school principals in the *National Directory for Catechesis* (2005), the American bishops give unequivocal direction: "Recruit teachers who are practicing Catholics, who can understand and accept the teachings of the Catholic Church and the moral demands of the gospel, and who can contribute to the achievement of the school's Catholic identity and apostolic goals."[85] Elsewhere the bishops also affirmed, "While some situations might entail compelling reasons for members of another faith tradition to teach in a Catholic school, as much as possible, all teachers in a Catholic school should be practicing Catholics."[86]

When such a policy is ignored, it is inevitable that children will absorb, even if they are not explicitly taught, a soft indifferentism that will sustain neither their practice of the faith nor their ability to imbue society with Christian values. Principals, pastors, school-board members, parents, and bishops share in the serious duty of hiring teachers who meet the standards of doctrine and integrity of life essential to a flourishing Catholic school.

The Holy See shares the solicitude of the American bishops about employing teachers with a clear understanding of and commitment to Catholic education. A primary way to foster a school's catholicity is by carefully hiring men and women who enthusiastically endorse its distinctive ethos, for Catholic education is strengthened by witnesses to the gospel.

Transparent Witness of Life   As well as fostering a Catholic worldview across the curriculum, even in so-called secular subjects, "if students in Catholic schools are to gain a genuine experience of the Church, the example of teachers and others responsible for their formation is crucial: the witness of adults in the school community is a vital part of the school's identity."[87]

Children will pick up far more by the example of their educators than by masterful pedagogical techniques, especially in the practice of Christian virtues. In the words of Pope Benedict XVI:

The central figure in the work of educating, and especially in education in the faith, which is the summit of the person's formation and is his or her most appropriate horizon, is specifically the form of witness. This witness becomes a proper reference point to the extent that the person can account for the hope that nourishes his life [cf. 1 Pet.3:15] and is personally involved in the truth that he proposes.[88]

The prophetic words of Pope Paul VI ring as true today as they did more than thirty years ago: "Modern man listens more willingly to witnesses than to teachers, and if he does listen to teachers, it is because they are witnesses."[89] What educators do and how they act are more significant than what they say—inside and outside the classroom. This is how the Church evangelizes. "The more completely an educator can give concrete witness to the model of the ideal person [Christ] that is being presented to the students, the more this ideal will be believed and imitated."[90]

Hypocrisy turns off today's students. While their demands are high, perhaps sometimes even unreasonably so, if teachers fail to model fidelity to the truth and virtuous behavior, then even the best of curricula cannot successfully embody a Catholic school's distinctive ethos. For example, if teachers and administrators demonstrate the individualistic and competitive ethic that now marks so much public education, they will fail to inspire students with the values of solidarity and community, even if they praise those values verbally. The same can be said about a failure to give clear witness to the Church's teaching on the sanctity of marriage and the inviolability of human life.

Catholic educators are expected to be models for their students by bearing transparent witness to Christ and to the beauty of the gospel. If boys and girls are to experience the splendor of the Church, the Christian example of teachers and others responsible for their formation is indispensable, and no effort should be spared in guaranteeing the presence of such witness in every Catholic school.

Conclusion

The Holy See, through papal interventions and the documents of the Congregation for Catholic Education, recognizes the priceless treasure of Catholic schools as an indispensable instrument of evangelization. Ensuring their genuinely Catholic identity is the Church's greatest educational challenge.

Complementing the primary role of parents in educating their children, such schools, which should be accessible, affordable, and available to all, build up the community of believers, evangelize the culture, and serve the common good of society.

I would like to conclude this essay with a suggestion that might help to strengthen the Catholic identity of America's elementary and secondary schools. In the United States, various accrediting agencies monitor the institutional effectiveness of schools' educational activities. They look at outcomes that can be measured, using a wide variety of means, and ask the schools to show that they use the results of their assessment to improve their mission effectiveness. Quite simply, accreditors ask: *How do you know that you are achieving what you say you are? What steps are you taking to improve your effectiveness?*

Should not Catholic schools, precisely insofar as they claim to be specified by their catholicity, do something along the same lines? They too could engage in quality assurance—that is, assurance of their Catholic identity. How does a Catholic school know whether it is achieving its specific mission? What steps is it taking to foster its catholicity? Such a "Catholic" accreditation process would involve an internal review of the five benchmark indicators—as well as others that could be developed. Teachers, administrators, bishops, parents, and school-board members would all take part in the review. This collaborative and systematic exercise of assessing a school's catholicity would serve to identify, clarify, and strengthen its effectiveness in its service of Christ and the Church.

Review and Discussion Questions

1. In less than a paragraph, outline the thematic structure of this talk.

2. Miller opens his meditation by reflecting on the role of parents, then proceeds to name "five marks." Imagine you are asked to give a one-hour lecture on "Renewing the Identity of Catholic Schools." How might you structure your comments?

3. The Church argues that a "state monopoly" on education is unjust. On what basis does it make this claim?

4. Name and briefly describe Miller's "five marks" of a Catholic school. What others might you add?

BENEDICT XVI

Meeting with Catholic Educators

> First and foremost every Catholic educational institution is a place to encounter the living God who in Jesus Christ reveals his transforming love and truth.

In 1967 a group of American university presidents, administrators, religious superiors, and one archbishop, signed the Land O'Lakes agreement, a manifesto of the Catholic academy's radical independence from the tradition and teaching authority of the Church. The statement marked the start of the systematic dismantling of confessionally Catholic education across North America. In this talk, Benedict XVI replies. Future professors and college presidents will look back at Benedict's 2008 address as a turning point in the cultural battle for the soul of Catholic higher education in North America. Faith seeks understanding. Faith also frees the mind from endless floundering. Unlike postmodern skeptics, Christians can with confidence and joy affirm the most elementary of all faiths: that the mind was made for truth. The first task of a university is to draw its students into an encounter with Truth itself.

Further Reading: Benedict XVI, *A Reason Open to God: On Universities, Education, and Culture*, ed. J. Steven Brown (Washington, D.C.: The Catholic University of America Press, 2013); Joseph Cardinal Ratzinger, *Truth and Tolerance: Christian Belief and World Religions* (San Francisco: Ignatius Press, 2004); Tracey Rowland, *Ratzinger's Faith: The Theology of Pope Benedict XVI* (Oxford: Oxford University Press, 2009).

❖

Your Eminences,
Dear Brother Bishops,
Distinguished Professors, Teachers and Educators,
   "How beautiful are the footsteps of those who bring good news" (Rom 10:15–17). With these words of Isaiah quoted by Saint Paul, I warmly

greet each of you—bearers of wisdom—and through you the staff, students and families of the many and varied institutions of learning that you represent. It is my great pleasure to meet you and to share with you some thoughts regarding the nature and identity of Catholic education today. I especially wish to thank Father David O'Connell, President and Rector of the Catholic University of America. Your kind words of welcome are much appreciated. Please extend my heartfelt gratitude to the entire community —faculty, staff and students—of this University.

Education is integral to the mission of the Church to proclaim the Good News. First and foremost every Catholic educational institution is a place to encounter the living God who in Jesus Christ reveals his transforming love and truth (cf. *Spe Salvi*, 4). This relationship elicits a desire to grow in the knowledge and understanding of Christ and his teaching. In this way those who meet him are drawn by the very power of the Gospel to lead a new life characterized by all that is beautiful, good, and true; a life of Christian witness nurtured and strengthened within the community of our Lord's disciples, the Church.

The dynamic between personal encounter, knowledge and Christian witness is integral to the *diakonia* of truth which the Church exercises in the midst of humanity. God's revelation offers every generation the opportunity to discover the ultimate truth about its own life and the goal of history. This task is never easy; it involves the entire Christian community and motivates each generation of Christian educators to ensure that the power of God's truth permeates every dimension of the institutions they serve. In this way, Christ's Good News is set to work, guiding both teacher and student towards the objective truth which, in transcending the particular and the subjective, points to the universal and absolute that enables us to proclaim with confidence the hope which does not disappoint (cf. Rom 5:5). Set against personal struggles, moral confusion and fragmentation of knowledge, the noble goals of scholarship and education, founded on the unity of truth and in service of the person and the community, become an especially powerful instrument of hope.

Dear friends, the history of this nation includes many examples of the Church's commitment in this regard. The Catholic community here has in fact made education one of its highest priorities. This undertaking has not come without great sacrifice. Towering figures, like Saint Elizabeth Ann Seton and other founders and foundresses, with great tenacity and foresight, laid the foundations of what is today a remarkable network of parochial schools contributing to the spiritual well-being of the Church and the nation. Some, like Saint Katharine Drexel, devoted their lives to educating those whom others had neglected—in her case, African Americans and Native Americans. Countless dedicated Religious Sisters, Brothers, and Priests together with selfless parents have, through Catholic schools, helped generations of immigrants to rise from poverty and take their place in mainstream society.

This sacrifice continues today. It is an outstanding apostolate of hope, seeking to address the material, intellectual and spiritual needs of over three million children and students. It also provides a highly commendable opportunity for the entire Catholic community to contribute generously to the financial needs of our institutions. Their long-term sustainability must be assured. Indeed, everything possible must be done, in cooperation with the wider community, to ensure that they are accessible to people of all social and economic strata. No child should be denied his or her right to an education in faith, which in turn nurtures the soul of a nation.

Some today question the Church's involvement in education, wondering whether her resources might be better placed elsewhere. Certainly in a nation such as this, the State provides ample opportunities for education and attracts committed and generous men and women to this honorable profession. It is timely, then, to reflect on what is particular to our Catholic institutions. How do they contribute to the good of society through the Church's primary mission of evangelization?

All the Church's activities stem from her awareness that she is the bearer of a message which has its origin in God himself: in his goodness and wisdom, God chose to reveal himself and to make known the hidden purpose of his will (cf. Eph 1:9; *Dei Verbum*, 2). God's desire to make himself known, and the innate desire of all human beings to know the truth, provide the context for human inquiry into the meaning of life. This unique encounter is sustained within our Christian community: the one who seeks the truth becomes the one who lives by faith (cf. *Fides et Ratio*, 31). It can be described as a move from "I" to "we," leading the individual to be numbered among God's people.

This same dynamic of communal identity—to whom do I belong?—vivifies the ethos of our Catholic institutions. A university or school's Catholic identity is not simply a question of the number of Catholic students. It is a question of conviction—do we really believe that only in the mystery of the Word made flesh does the mystery of man truly become clear (cf. *Gaudium et Spes*, 22)? Are we ready to commit our entire self—intellect and will, mind and heart—to God? Do we accept the truth Christ reveals? Is the faith tangible in our universities and schools? Is it given fervent expression liturgically, sacramentally, through prayer, acts of charity, a concern for justice, and respect for God's creation? Only in this way do we really bear witness to the meaning of who we are and what we uphold.

From this perspective one can recognize that the contemporary "crisis of truth" is rooted in a "crisis of faith." Only through faith can we freely give our assent to God's testimony and acknowledge him as the transcendent guarantor of the truth he reveals. Again, we see why fostering personal intimacy with Jesus Christ and communal witness to his loving truth is indispensable in Catholic institutions of learning. Yet we all know, and observe with concern, the difficulty or reluctance many people have today in entrusting themselves to God. It is a complex phenomenon and one which I ponder continually. While we have sought diligently to engage the intellect of our young, perhaps we have neglected the will. Subsequently we observe, with distress, the notion of freedom being distorted. Freedom is not an opting out. It is an opting in—a participation in Being itself. Hence authentic freedom can never be attained by turning away from God. Such a choice would ultimately disregard the very truth we need in order to understand ourselves. A particular responsibility therefore for each of you, and your colleagues, is to evoke among the young the desire for the act of faith, encouraging them to commit themselves to the ecclesial life that follows from this belief. It is here that freedom reaches the certainty of truth. In choosing to live by that truth, we embrace the fullness of the life of faith which is given to us in the Church.

Clearly, then, Catholic identity is not dependent upon statistics. Neither can it be equated simply with orthodoxy of course content. It demands and inspires much more: namely that each and every aspect of your learning communities reverberates within the ecclesial life of faith. Only in faith can truth become incarnate and reason truly human, capable of directing the will along the path of freedom (cf. *Spe Salvi*, 23). In this way our institutions make a vital contribution to the mission of the Church and truly serve society. They become places in which God's active presence in human affairs is recognized and in which every young person discovers the joy of entering into Christ's "being for others" (cf. ibid., 28).

The Church's primary mission of evangelization, in which educational institutions play a crucial role, is consonant with a nation's fundamental aspiration to develop a society truly worthy of the human person's dignity. At times, however, the value of the Church's contribution to the public forum is questioned. It is important therefore to recall that the truths of faith and of reason never contradict one another (cf. First Vatican Ecumenical Council, Dogmatic Constitution on the Catholic Faith *Dei Filius*, IV: *DS* 3017; St. Augustine, *Contra Academicos*, III, 20, 43). The Church's mission, in fact, involves her in humanity's struggle to arrive at truth. In articulating revealed truth she serves all members of society by purifying reason, ensuring that it remains open to the consideration of ultimate truths. Drawing upon divine wisdom, she sheds light on the foundation of human morality and ethics, and reminds all groups in society that it is not praxis that creates truth but truth that should serve as the basis of praxis. Far from undermining the tolerance of legitimate diversity, such a contribution illuminates the very truth which makes consensus attainable, and helps to keep public debate rational, honest and accountable. Similarly the Church never tires of upholding the essential moral categories of right and wrong, without which hope could only wither, giving way to cold pragmatic calculations of utility which render the person little more than a pawn on some ideological chess-board.

With regard to the educational forum, the *diakonia* of truth takes on a heightened significance in societies where secularist ideology drives a wedge between truth and faith. This division has led to a tendency to equate truth with knowledge and to adopt a positivistic mentality which, in rejecting metaphysics, denies the foundations of faith and rejects the need for a moral vision. Truth means more than knowledge: knowing the truth leads us to discover the good. Truth speaks to the individual in his or her entirety, inviting us to respond with our whole being. This optimistic vision is found in our Christian faith because such faith has been granted the vision of the *Logos*, God's creative Reason, which in the Incarnation, is revealed as Goodness itself. Far from being just a communication of factual data—"informative"—the loving truth of the Gospel is creative and life-changing—"performative" (cf. *Spe Salvi*, 2). With confidence, Christian educators can liberate the young from the limits of positivism and awaken receptivity to the truth, to God and his goodness. In this way you will also help to form their conscience which, enriched by faith, opens a sure path to inner peace and to respect for others.

It comes as no surprise, then, that not just our own ecclesial communities but society in general has high expectations of Catholic educators. This places upon you a responsibility and offers an opportunity. More and more people—parents in particular—recognize the need for excellence in the human formation of their children. As *Mater et Magistra*, the Church shares their concern. When nothing beyond the individual is recognized as definitive, the ultimate criterion of judgment becomes the self and the satisfaction of the individual's immediate wishes. The objectivity and perspective, which can only come through a recognition of the essential transcendent dimension of the human person, can be lost. Within such a relativistic horizon the goals of education are inevitably curtailed. Slowly, a lowering of standards occurs. We observe today a timidity in the face of the category of the good and an aimless pursuit of novelty parading as the realization of freedom. We witness an assumption that every experience is of equal worth and a reluctance to admit imperfection and mistakes. And particularly disturbing, is the reduction of the precious and delicate area of education in sexuality to management of "risk," bereft of any reference to the beauty of conjugal love.

How might Christian educators respond? These harmful developments point to the particular urgency of what we might call "intellectual charity." This aspect of charity calls the educator to recognize that the profound responsibility to lead the young to truth is nothing less than an act of love. Indeed, the dignity of education lies in fostering the true perfection and happiness of those to be educated. In practice "intellectual charity" upholds the essential unity of knowledge against the fragmentation which ensues when reason is detached from the pursuit of truth. It guides the young towards the deep satisfaction of exercising freedom in relation to truth, and it strives to articulate the relationship between faith and all aspects of family and civic life. Once their passion for the fullness and unity of truth has been awakened, young people will surely relish the discovery that the question of what they can know opens up the vast adventure of what they ought to do. Here they will experience "in what" and "in whom" it is possible to hope, and be inspired to contribute to society in a way that engenders hope in others.

Dear friends, I wish to conclude by focusing our attention specifically on the paramount importance of your own professionalism and witness within our Catholic universities and schools. First, let me thank you for your dedication and generosity. I know from my own days as a professor, and I have heard from your Bishops and officials of the Congregation for Catholic Education, that the reputation of Catholic institutes of learning in this country is largely due to yourselves and your predecessors. Your selfless contributions—from outstanding research to the dedication of those working in inner-city schools—serve both your country and the Church. For this I express my profound gratitude.

In regard to faculty members at Catholic colleges and universities, I wish to reaffirm the great value of academic freedom. In virtue of this freedom you are called to search for the truth wherever careful analysis of evidence leads you. Yet it is also the case that any appeal to the principle of

Christ Risen from the Tomb

academic freedom in order to justify positions that contradict the faith and the teaching of the Church would obstruct or even betray the university's identity and mission; a mission at the heart of the Church's *munus docendi* and not somehow autonomous or independent of it.

Teachers and administrators, whether in universities or schools, have the duty and privilege to ensure that students receive instruction in Catholic doctrine and practice. This requires that public witness to the way of Christ, as found in the Gospel and upheld by the Church's Magisterium, shapes all aspects of an institution's life, both inside and outside the classroom. Divergence from this vision weakens Catholic identity and, far from advancing freedom, inevitably leads to confusion, whether moral, intellectual or spiritual.

I wish also to express a particular word of encouragement to both lay and Religious teachers of catechesis who strive to ensure that young people become daily more appreciative of the gift of faith. Religious education is a challenging apostolate, yet there are many signs of a desire among young people to learn about the faith and practice it with vigor. If this awakening is to grow, teachers require a clear and precise understanding of the specific nature and role of Catholic education. They must also be ready to lead the commitment made by the entire school community to assist our young people, and their families, to experience the harmony between faith, life and culture.

Here I wish to make a special appeal to Religious Brothers, Sisters and Priests: do not abandon the school apostolate; indeed, renew your commitment to schools especially those in poorer areas. In places where there are many hollow promises which lure young people away from the path of truth and genuine freedom, the consecrated person's witness to the evangelical counsels is an irreplaceable gift. I encourage the Religious present to bring renewed enthusiasm to the promotion of vocations. Know that your witness to the ideal of consecration and mission among the young is a source of great inspiration in faith for them and their families.

To all of you I say: bear witness to hope. Nourish your witness with prayer. Account for the hope that characterizes your lives (cf. 1 Pet 3:15) by living the truth which you propose to your students. Help them to know and love the One you have encountered, whose truth and goodness you have experienced with joy. With Saint Augustine, let us say: "we who speak and you who listen acknowledge ourselves as fellow disciples of a single teacher" (*Sermons*, 23:2). With these sentiments of communion, I gladly impart to you, your colleagues and students, and to your families, my Apostolic Blessing.

Review and Discussion Questions

1. Benedict claims that "first and foremost" a Catholic school is a place to encounter the living God. What alternative views of Catholic education does Benedict implicitly contradict?

2. What, precisely, "vivifies the ethos" of a Catholic school?

3. In Benedict's view, how can faith purify reason?

4. Name the corrosive beliefs which Benedict says Catholic educators must guard against.

5. How does Benedict reconcile "academic freedom" with the Church's *munus docendi*? On what grounds might a secularist disagree?

❖ SOURCES AND PERMISSIONS

1. Plato, *Republic*, trans. Benjamin Jowett (Oxford: Clarendon Press, 1888), opening of Book 7 (514a–521c).

2. Aristotle, *On the Parts of Animals*, trans. William Ogle (London: K. Paul, French and Co., 1882), from Book 1.

3. Quintilian, *Institutes of Oratory: or, Education of an Orator*, trans. J. S. Watson (London: H. G. Bohn, 1856), from Book 1.1.

4. St. Augustine, *On Christian Teaching*, trans. J. F. Shaw, in Nicene and Post-Nicene Fathers, vol. 2 (New York: The Christian Literature Publishing Co., 1890), book 2, chaps. 1–7.

5. Thomas Aquinas, *Of God and His Creatures: An Annotated Translation of Summa Contra Gentiles*, trans. Joseph Rickaby (St. Louis: B. Herder, 1905), Chapter 1.

6. Thomas à Kempis, *Imitation of Christ*, trans. Rev. William Benham, The Harvard Classics, vol. 7, part 2 (New York: P. F. Collier and Son, 1909–14), book 1.1–7; book 3.1.

7. H. S. Gerdil, *Anti-Emile,* trans. with notes by William A. Frank (South Bend, Ind.: St. Augustine Press, 2011), 30–48. Reprinted by permission from St. Augustine Press.

8. Blessed John Henry Newman, *The Idea of a University: Defined and Illustrated* (London: Pickering, 1873), Discourse 6.

9. St. John Paul II, *Fides et Ratio* (Encyclical Letter on the Relationship between Faith and Reason), 14 September 1988, paragraphs 1–15. © Libreria Editrice. All rights reserved. Used with permission.

10. Plato, *Republic*, trans. Benjamin Jowett (Oxford: Clarendon Press, 1888), book 3 (399e–405d).

11. St. Basil the Great, *To Young Men on the Reading of Greek Literature,* trans. Frederick Morgan Padelford in *Essays on the Study and Use of Poetry by Plutarch and Basil the Great, Yale Studies in English* 15 (1902): 99–120.

12. Hugh of Saint Victor, *The Didascalicon of Hugh of St. Victor: A Medieval Guide to the Arts*, trans. with notes by Jerome Taylor (New York: Columbia University Press, 1991), book 3, chaps. 3–19. Copyright © 1991 Columbia University Press. Reprinted with permission of the publisher.

13. St. Bonaventure, *Reduction of the Arts to Theology*, translation taken from http://people.uvawise.edu/philosophy/phil205/Bonaventure.html

14. St. Thomas Aquinas, *Summa Theologiae* I, q. 1, a. 1. Literally translated by the Fathers of the English Dominican Province, 1920.

15. Blessed John Henry Newman, selection from "Catholic Literature in the English Tongue, 1854–1858," in the section "University Subjects Discussed in Occasional Lectures and Essays," in *The Idea of a University: Defined and Illustrated* (London: Pickering, 1873).

16. Jacques Maritain, *Education at the Crossroads* (New Haven, Conn.: Yale University Press, 1943), 58–70 with a few exclusions. Copyright © 1960 Yale University Press. Reprinted with permission of the publisher.

17. Plato, *Meno*, trans. Benjamin Jowett (Oxford: Oxford University Press, 1892), selections.

18. St. Augustine, *On Christian Teaching*, trans. J. F. Shaw, in Nicene and Post-Nicene Fathers, vol. 2 (New York: The Christian Literature Publishing Co., 1890), from book 4.

19. St. Thomas Aquinas, *Summa Theologiae* I, q. 84, a. 6. Literally translated by the Fathers of the English Dominican Province, 1920.

20. Desiderius Erasmus, "Of the Method of Study to Christianus of Lubeck," from *The Colloquies*, vol. 2, trans. Nathan Bailey, ed. Rev. E. Johnson (London: Reeves and Turner, 1878).

21. Michel de Montaigne, "Of the Education of Children," trans. Charles Cotton, ed. W. Hazlitt (New York: Burt, 1892), annotated.

22. *Ratio Studiorum*, translated into English, with an Introduction and explanatory notes by Allan P. Farrell, S.J. University of Detroit, 1970.

23. H. S. Gerdil, *Anti-Emile*, trans. with notes by William A. Frank (South Bend, Ind.: St. Augustine Press, 2011), 48–57. Reprinted by permission from St. Augustine Press.

24. Maria Montessori, *The Montessori Method*, trans. Anne E. George, with an introduction by Professor Henry W. Holmes of Harvard University, 2nd ed. (New York: Frederick A. Stokes Company, 1912), 215–23, chapter, "General Notes on the Education of the Senses."

25. A. G. Sertillanges, *The Intellectual Life*, trans. Mary Ryan (Washington, D.C.: The Catholic University of America Press, 1987), 86–100. Reprinted with permission.

26. Pope Leo XIII *Aeterni Patris* (Encyclical Letter On the Restoration of Christian Philosophy), 4 August 1879. © Libreria Editrice. All rights reserved. Used with permission.

27. G. K. Chesterton, *Orthodoxy* (London: John Lane the Bodley Head Ltd., 1900), from chapter 3, "The Suicide of Thought."

28. Ronald Knox, "Christian Education," in *University Sermons of Ronald A. Knox—Together with Sermons Preached on Various Occasions*, with an introduction by Philip Caraman, S.J. (New York: Sheed and Ward, 1963). Reprinted by permission of United Agents, holders of the literary estate of Ronald Knox.

29. C. S. Lewis, "Learning in War-Time" (a sermon preached in the Church of St. Mary the Virgin, Oxford, Autumn 1939) copyright C. S. Lewis Pte. Ltd. Extract reprinted by permission.

30. Dorothy L. Sayers, *The Lost Tools of Learning*. Reprinted by permission of David Higham Associates, holders of the literary estate of Dorothy L. Sayers.

31. Christopher Dawson, *Crisis of Western Education*, introduction by Glenn W. Olsen (Washington, D.C.: The Catholic University Press of America Press, 2010), 99–110. Reprinted with permission.

32. St. John XXIII, *Veterum Sapientia* (Apostolic Constitution on the Promotion of the Study of Latin), 22 February 1962. © Libreria Editrice. All rights reserved. Used with permission.

33. John Senior, *The Restoration of Christian Culture* (San Francisco, Calif.: Ignatius Press, 1983), 30–43. Reprinted by permission of Andrew Senior and IHS Press.

34. St. John Paul II, *Familiaris Consortio* (Apostolic Exhortation On the Role of the Family in the Modern World), 22 November 1981; paragraphs 6–8, 36–40, and 59–62. © Libreria Editrice. All rights reserved. Used with permission.

35. Laura M. Berquist, *Designing Your Own Classical Curriculum* (San Francisco: Ignatius Press, 1998), 249–55. Reprinted by permission from Ignatius Press.

36. Michael O'Brien, *A Landscape with Dragons* (San Francisco: Ignatius Press, 1998), 70–91. Reprinted by permission from Ignatius Press.

37. Archbishop J. Michael Miller, CSB, *The Holy See's Teaching on Catholic Schools* (Manchester, N.H.: Sophia Institute Press, 2006). Reprinted with permission of Sophia Institute Press.

38. Pope Benedict XVI, *Meeting with Catholic Educators* 17 April 2008). © Libreria Editrice. All rights reserved. Used with permission.

❖ NOTES

Introduction

1. Aristotle, *On the Parts of Animals* 1.1.
2. Augustine, *Confessions*, 3.4.7.
3. 1 John 4:8.
4. Colossians 2:8.
5. Romans 12:2.
6. Augustine, *City of God*, 15.22.
7. Cicero, *Tusculan Disputations*, 5.10.
8. See their long meditations on this theme in, respectively, *Republic* book 7 or *Nicoma-chean Ethics* book 10.
9. John Paul II, *On Faith and Reason*, §43.
10. Leo XIII, *On the Restoration of Christian Philosophy*, §18.
11. Ockham himself still retained a version of natural theology. But he does not think, for instance, that we can prove that there is only one God. This we affirm merely by faith (cf. *Quodlibeta*, 1. Q.1).
12. See his Sermon on 17 January 1546.
13. Thomas Aquinas, *Summa Theologiae* I, q. 1, a. 8 ad 2.
14. G. K. Chesterton, *What's Wrong with the World* [1910] (New York: Sheed and Ward, 1942), 213.

Chapter 7: H. S. Gerdil

1. *Emile*, 2.35 (Bloom translation, p. 85).
2. *On the Social Contract*, 1.7; Norton ed., p. 95.
3. *Emile* 2.22 (Bloom, pp. 81–82).
4. *Emile* 2.60–61 (Bloom, p. 92).
5. *Emile* 2.33 (Bloom, p. 85).
6. *Emile* 2.36 (Bloom, p. 85).
7. *Emile* 2.50 (Bloom, p. 89).
8. *Emile* 2.49–50 (Bloom, pp. 88–89).
9. *Emile* 2.11 (Bloom, p. 79).
10. *Emile* 2.49 (Bloom, p. 89).
11. *Emile*, 1.152 (Bloom, pp. 65–66).
12. [Gerdil's note:] Rousseau himself says that children "will find a secret pleasure in catching you misbehaving.... One of children's first efforts ... is to discover the weakness of those who govern.... Overburdened by the yoke imposed on them, they seek to shake it off, and the shortcomings they find in the masters furnish them with good means for that" [*Emile* 2.170 (Bloom translation, p. 121)]. There is great truth in this remark, but then it proves in contradiction to the author that children are not devoid of all notions of morality. If they take a secret pleasure in discovering their master's faults, they then certainly know what a fault is, and can distinguish between moral good and evil. Here then Rousseau is confuted by himself. Nothing can be more ingenious than the subterfuge this writer has

contrived to screen himself from whatever contradictions may be laid to his charge; this is to acknowledge that "his expressions" clash, but not "his ideas" [*Emile* 2.120 (Bloom, p. 108)]. He says absolutely, in one place, that "[the child] does not know what it is to be at fault" [*Emile* 2.61 (Bloom, p. 92)], but in another part of his work [*Emile* 2.170 (Bloom, p. 121)] he says, children take a secret pleasure in detecting their masters in a fault. Is this contradiction merely in the expression, or does it not in some measure affect the ideas?

13. *Emile* 2.54 (Bloom, p. 90).

14. *Emile* 1.5 (Bloom, p. 38).

Chapter 9: St. John Paul II

1. In my first Encyclical Letter, *Redemptor Hominis*, I wrote: "We have become sharers in this mission of the prophet Christ, and in virtue of that mission we together with him are serving divine truth in the Church. Being responsible for that truth also means loving it and seeking the most exact understanding of it, in order to bring it closer to ourselves and others in all its saving power, its splendour and its profundity joined with simplicity": No. 19: *AAS* 71 (1979), 306.

2. Cf. Second Vatican Ecumenical Council, Pastoral Constitution on the Church in the Modern World *Gaudium et Spes*, 16.

3. Dogmatic Constitution on the Church *Lumen Gentium*, 25.

4. No. 4: *AAS* 85 (1993), 1136.

5. Second Vatican Ecumenical Council, Dogmatic Constitution on Divine Revelation *Dei Verbum*, 2.

6. Cf. Dogmatic Constitution on the Catholic Faith *Dei Filius*, III: *DS* 3008.

7. Ibid., IV: *DS* 3015; quoted also in Second Vatican Ecumenical Council, Pastoral Constitution on the Church in the Modern World *Gaudium et Spes*, 59.

8. Dogmatic Constitution on Divine Revelation *Dei Verbum*, 2.

9. Apostolic Letter *Tertio Millennio Adveniente* (10 November 1994), 10: *AAS* 87 (1995), 11.

10. No. 4.

11. No. 8.

12. No. 22.

13. Cf. Second Vatican Ecumenical Council, Dogmatic Constitution on Divine Revelation *Dei Verbum*, 4.

14. Ibid., 5.

15. The First Vatican Council, to which the quotation above refers, teaches that the obedience of faith requires the engagement of the intellect and the will: "Since human beings are totally dependent on God as their creator and Lord, and created reason is completely subject to uncreated truth, we are obliged to yield through faith to God the revealer full submission of intellect and will" (Dogmatic Constitution on the Catholic Faith *Dei Filius*, III: *DS* 3008).

16. *Sequence* for the Solemnity of the Body and Blood of the Lord.

17. *Pensées*, 789 (ed. L. Brunschvicg).

18. Second Vatican Ecumenical Council, Pastoral Constitution on the Church in the Modern World *Gaudium et Spes*, 22.

19. Cf. Second Vatican Ecumenical Council, Dogmatic Constitution on Divine Revelation *Dei Verbum*, 2.

20. Proemium and Nos. 1, 15: *PL* 158, 223–224; 226; 235.

21. *De Vera Religione*, XXXIX, 72: *CCL* 32, 234.

Chapter 16: Jacques Maritain

1. "… Since liberal education is the sort that enables each man to think as well as his native powers permit, it is by definition appropriate to all men. It is not for the rich alone, nor the intellectual elite alone…. A free society that limits it to a small fraction of its citizens, does so at the peril of its existence" (S. Barr, "Report of the President," July 1942, St. John's College, Annapolis, Maryland, p. 14).

2. "Since to live well, since even to earn a living, requires a man to think, liberal education is the basic preparation for life. But it is a full-time job and cannot be carried on adequately by institutions that attempt simultaneously to give occupational training and what they may call 'practical' knowledge. That kind of knowledge can be speedily acquired, whether on the job or in a post-graduate professional school, by the man who has learned to think. It can be acquired only with difficulty and inadequately by the man who has not. The penalty which contemporary society has paid for omitting this basic sort of education is the multiplication of highly trained specialists, who are, fundamentally, uneducated men and who are inadequate to the varied responsibilities of life" (S. Barr, "Report of the President," p.14). The same degree of rigorous study and progress in all items of the curriculum is most unwise. If the youth displays eagerness with regard to certain matters, even a natural apathy in regard to others will be a normal mode of differentiation. Laziness must be fought, of course, but encouraging and urging a youth on the ways which he likes and in which he succeeds is much more important, providing, however, that he be also trained in the things for which he feels less inclination, and that he traverses the entire field of those human possibilities and achievements which compose liberal education.

3. "The child-centered school may be attractive to the child, and no doubt is useful as a place in which the little ones may release their inhibitions and hence behave better at home. But educators cannot permit the students to dictate the course of study unless they are prepared to confess that they are nothing but chaperons, supervising an aimless, trial-and-error process which is chiefly valuable because it keeps young people from doing something worse. The free elective system as Mr. Eliot introduced it at Harvard and as Progressive Education adapted it to lower age levels amounted to a denial that there was content to education. Since there was no content to education, we might as well let students follow their own bent. They would at least be interested and pleased and would be as well educated as if they had pursued a prescribed course of study. This overlooks the fact that the aim of education is to connect man with· man, to connect the present with the past, and to advance the thinking of the race. If this is the aim of education, it cannot be left to the sporadic, spontaneous interests of children or even of undergraduates." Robert M. Hutchins, *The Higher Learning in America* (Yale University Press, 1936), pp. 70–71.

Of course, the rejection of the elective system does not imply that in addition to the essential (and therefore required) subjects of the curriculum other subjects should not be taught in optional courses, chosen by students according to their own preferences.

Be it noted that the age and degree of maturity of the student is a factor to be considered, and that any discussion of the· elective system would be made easier and clearer if college years began earlier than is the case today, and extended from sixteen to nineteen.

4. Supposing that the training in foreign languages begins at the age of ten, the youth will have a sufficient mastery of these languages after six years of training. At sixteen, in his freshman year at college, he will bring this knowledge to completion in regard to the sphere of the humanities, with a rational and logical analysis of what he has already studied more or less empirically.

5. Supposing that the period of the humanities were to last seven years, so that secondary education, which forms the transition between the period of rudiments and the college, and whose importance is therefore crucial, would comprise three years (from thirteen to fifteen),we might order these three years as follows:

The year of *Languages*, comprising: first, foreign languages, studied in connection with the national language; second, comparative grammar and the art of expression; third, national history, geography, and natural history (especially elementary astronomy and geology).

The year of *Grammar*, comprising: first, grammar, especially comparative grammar and philology; second, foreign languages and the art of expression; third, national history, geography, natural history (especially botany).

The year of *History and Expression*, comprising: first, national history, history of civilization, the art of expression; second, foreign languages, comparative grammar and philology, geography, natural history (especially zoology).

Thus the field of what I called in my second chapter the pre-liberal arts would be covered in the three years of secondary education (with the exception of logic which would be studied in the first year of college).

The general plan which I have in mind and which forms the background of my present considerations divides the main educational periods as follows: I. The rudiments (or elementary education): 7 years, divided into 4 years of initial elementary education (age: six to nine) and 3 years of complementary elementary education (age: ten to twelve). II. The humanities: 7 years, divided into 3 years of secondary education or high school (age: thirteen to fifteen) and 4 years of college education (age: sixteen to nineteen.) III. Advanced studies, comprising the university and higher specialized learning.

The B.A. would be awarded at the end of the college years, as crowning the humanities and making possible admission to the university. There, the time normally required for the M.A. would be 3 years; and for the Ph.D., roughly from 2 to 4 years. This general plan seems to be in substantial agreement with the reforms proposed by Professor John U. Nef in *The United States and Civilization*, chap. ix, and by President Robert Hutchins in *Education for Freedom*, chap. iv. Yet, since the four years of college would be hurried, the B.A. would be awarded at the end of the senior year, according to the tradition, and not at the end of the sophomore year. The result would be the same with regard to the age of the student.

6. As I indicate farther on, the curriculum of the last two or three college years would also comprise optional studies in theology.

7. According to our general scheme, comparative grammar and philology should be taught—as instruments rather than as sciences, and in a manner fitted to the sphere of knowledge of the young—before the college, during the years of secondary education.

Chapter 18: St. Augustine

1. Book I, chapter 1.
2. Cicero, *De Oratore*, 3.31
3. Cicero, *De Inventione Rhetorica* 1.1.
4. Book of Wisdom, 6:24.

Chapter 23: H. S. Gerdil

1. *Emile* 2.57 (Bloom translation, p. 91).
2. *Emile* 1.55 (Bloom, pp. 46–47).
3. *Emile* 1.33 (Bloom, p. 85).
4. *On the Social Contract* 1.2 (Norton ed., p. 86).

5. [Gerdil's note; Cohler trans.:] We add this passage from Montesquieu's *Spirit of Laws* Bk. 23, ch. 2: "Among animals this obligation [to nourish the young] is such that the mother can usually meet it. The obligation is much broader among men: their children partake of reason, but it comes to them by degrees; it is not enough to nourish them, they must also be guided; even when they can sustain their lives, they cannot govern themselves."

Chapter 26: Leo XIII

1. Matt.28:19.
2. Col. 2:8.
3. 1 Cor. 2:4.
4. See *Inscrutabili Dei consilio*, 78:113.
5. *De Trinitate*, 14, 1, 3 (PL 42, 1037); quoted by Thomas Aquinas, *Summa theologiae*, 1, 1, 2.
6. Clement of Alexandria, *Stromata*, 1, 16 (PG 8, 795); 7, 3 (PG 9, 426).
7. Origen, *Epistola ad Gregorium* (PG 11, 87–91).
8. Clement of Alexandria, *Stromata*, 1,5 (PG 8, 718–719).
9. Rom. 1:20.
10. Rom. 2:14–15.
11. Gregory of Neo-Caesarea (also called Gregory Thaumaturgus, that is, "the miracle worker"), *In Origenem oratio panegyrica, 6* (PG 10, 1093A).
12. Carm., 1, Iamb. 3 (PG 37, 1045A–1047A).
13. *Vita Moysis* (PG 44, 359).
14. *Epistola ad Magnum*, 4 (PL 22, 667). Quadratus, Justin Irenaeus, are counted among the early Christian apologists, who devoted their works to the defence of Christian truth against the pagans.
15. *De doctrina christiana*, l, 2, 40 (PL 34, 63).
16. Wisd. 13:1.
17. Wisd. 13:5.
18. 2 Peter 1:16.
19. Const. *Dogm, de Fid. Cath.*, c.3.
20. Const. cit., c.4.
21. Loc. cit.
22. *Stromata*, l, 20 (PG 8, 818).
23. *Epistola ad Magnum*, 2 (PL 22, 666).
24. Bulla *Apostolici regiminis*.
25. Epistola 147, *ad Marcellinum*, 7 (PL 33, 589).
26. *Const. Dogm. de Fid. Cath.*, c.4.
27. [Original note 34] Cajetan's commentary on *Sum. theol.*, IIa-IIae 148, 9. Art. 4; Leonine edit., Vol. 10, p. 174, n.6.
28. [35] Constitutio 5a, data die 3 Aug. 1368, ad Cancell. Univ. Tolos.
29. [36] Sermo de S. *Thoma*.
30. [37] Bucer.
31. [38] Sixtus V, Bulla *Triumphantis*.
32. [39] 1 Peter 3:15.
33. [40] Titus 1:9.
34. [41] 1 Kings 2:3.
35. [42] James 1:17.
36. [43] James 1:5.

Chapter 32: St. John XXIII

1. Tertullian, *Apol.* 21: Migne, PL 1, 394.
2. Ephesians 1, 10.
3. Epist. S. Cong. Stud. *Vehementer sane,* ad Ep. universos, July 1, 1908: *Ench. Cler.,* N. 820. Cf. also Epist. Ap. Pius XI, *Unigenitus Dei Filius,* Mar. 19, 1924: *AAS* 16 (1924), 141.
4. Pius XI, Epist. Ap. *Officiorum omnium,* Aug. 1, 1922: *AAS* 14 (1922), 452–453.
5. Pius XI, Motu proprio *Litterarum latinarum,* Oct. 20, 1924: *AAS* 16 (1924), 417.
6. Pius XI, Epist. Ap. *Officiorum omnium,* Aug. 1, 1922: *AAS* 14 (1922), 452.
7. Ibid.
8. Saint Iren., *Adv. Haer.* 3, 3, 2: Migne PG 7, 848.
9. Cf. CIC, can. 218, par. 2.
10. Cf. Pius XI, Epist. Ap. *Officiorum omnium,* Aug. 1, 1922: *AAS* 14 (1922), 453.
11. Pius XII, Al. *Magis quam,* Nov. 23, 1951: *AAS* 43 (1951), 737.
12. Leo XIII, Epist. Encycl. *Depuis le jour,* Sept. 8, 1899: *Acta Leonis XIII,* 19 (1899), 166.
13. Cf. *Collectio Lacensis,* espec. vol. III, 1918s. (*Conc. Prov. Westmonasteriense,* a. 1859); Vol. IV, 29 (*Conc. Prov. Parisiense,* a. 1849); Vol. IV, 149, 153 (*Conc. Prov. Rhemense,* a. 1849); Vol. IV, 359, 861 (*Conc. Prov. Avenionense,* a. 1849); Vol. IV, 394, 396 (*Conc. Prov. Burdigalense,* a. 1850); Vol. V, 61 (*Conc. Strigoniense,* a. 1858); Vol. V, 664 (*Conc. Prov. Colocense,* a. 1863); Vol. VI, 619 (*Synod. Vicariatus Suchnensis,* a. 1803).
14. International Convention for the Promotion of Ciceronian Studies, Sept. 7, 1959, in *Discorsi Messaggi Colloqui del Santo Padre Giovanni XXIII,* I, pp. 234–235 [English translation in TPS, V, 421]. Cf. also Address to Roman Pilgrims of the Diocese of Piacenza, April 15, 1959, in *L'Osservatore Romano* April 16, 1959; Epist. *Pater misericordiarum,* Aug. 22, 1961, in *AAS* 53 (1961), 677; Address given on the occasion of the solemn inauguration of the College of the Philippine Islands at Rome, Oct. 7, 1961, in *L'Osservatore Romano,* Oct. 9–10, 1961; Epist. *Iucunda laudatio,* Dec. 8, 1961: *AAS* 53 (1961), 812 [English summary in TPS, VII, 367–8].
15. Pius XII, Epist. Ap. *Officiorum omnium,* Aug. 1, 1922: *AAS* 14 (1922), 453.
16. Epist. S. C. Stud., *Vehementer sane,* July 1, 1908: *Ench. Cler.,* N. 821.
17. Leo XIII. Lit. Encyci. *Providentissimus Deus,* Nov. 18, 1893: *Acta Leonis XIII* 13 (1893), 342; Epist. *Plane quidem intelligis,* May 20, 1885, *Acta,* 5, 63–64; Pius XII, Alloc. *Magis quam,* Sept. 23, 1951: *AAS* 43 (1951), 737.

Chapter 34: St. John Paul II

1. [Original note 16] Cf. St. Augustine, *De Civitate Dei,* XIV, 28; CSEL 40, II, 56–57.
2. [17] Second Vatican Council, *Gaudium et Spes,* 15.
3. [99] Second Vatican Council, *Gravissimum Educationis,* 3.
4. [100] *Gaudium et Spes,* 35.
5. [101] St. Thomas Aquinas, *Summa Contra Gentiles,* IV, 58.
6. [102] *Gravissiumum Educationis,* 2.
7. [103] Apostolic exhortation *Evangelii Nuntiandi,* 71: *AAS* 68 (1976), 60–61.
8. [104] Cf. *Gravissiumum Educationis,* 3.
9. [149] Cf. 1 Pt. 2:5.
10. [150] Mt. 18:19–20.
11. [151] *Gravissumum Educationis,* 3; cf. Pope John Paul II, *Catechesi Tradendae,* 36: *AAS* 71 (1979), 1308.
12. [152] General Audience Address, Aug. 11, 1976: Insegnamenti di Paolo VI, XIV (1976), 640.

13. [153] Cf. Second Vatican Council, *Sacrosanctum Concilium*, 12.

14. [154] Cf. *Institutio Generalis de Liturgia Horarum*, 27.

15. [155] Paul VI, Apostolic Exhortation *Marialis Cultus*, 52–54: *AAS* 66 (1974), 160–61.

16. [156] John Paul II, Address at the Mentorella Shrine (Oct. 29, 1978): *Insegnamenti*, I (1978), 78–79.

17. [157] Cf. Second Vatican Council, *Apostolicam Actuositatem*, 4.

18. [158] Cf. John Paul I, Address to the Bishops of the 12th Pastoral Region of the United States (Sept. 21, 1978): *AAS* 70 (1978), 767.

Chapter 37: Archbishop J. Michael Miller, CSB

1. [Original note 5] Cf. *Renewing Our Commitment to Catholic Elementary and Secondary Schools in the Third Millennium*, 5.

2. [6] Kenneth C. Jones, *Index of Leading Catholic Indicators: The Church Since Vatican II* (St. Louis: Oriens Publishing Company, 2003), 36.

3. [7] Cf. Idem.

4. [8] John Paul II, *Vita Consecrata*, 96; cf. Congregation for Catholic Education, *Consecrated Persons and Their Mission in Schools: Reflections and Guidelines*, 29.

5. [9] Sacred Congregation for Catholic Education, *Lay Catholics in Schools: Witnesses to Faith*, 37.

6. [10] Ibid., 60.

7. [11] Second Vatican Ecumenical Council, *Apostolicam Actuositatem*, 25.

8. [12] Cf. *Gravissimum Educationis*, 3, 6; John Paul II, *Familiaris Consortio*, 36; *Lay Catholics in Schools*, 12; Pontifical Council for the Family,*Charter of the Rights of the Family* (22 October 1983), 1–3; *Code of Canon Law*, canon 793; *Catechism of the Catholic Church*, n. 2229; John Paul II, *Letter to Families*, 16; Pontifical Council for Justice and Peace, *Compendium of the Social Doctrine of the Church* (Vatican City: Vatican Press, 2005), n. 239.

9. [13] Peter Redpath, foreword in Curtis L. Hancock, *Recovering a Catholic Philosophy of Elementary Education* (Mount Pocono, Pennsylvania: Newman House Press, 2005), 19.

10. [14] Cf. *Code of Canon Law*, canon 796; *The Catholic School*, 8.

11. [15] John Paul II, *Letter to Families*, 16; cf. Benedict XVI, Angelus Address (28 October 2005): *L'Osservatore Romano*, English-language edition (2 November 2005), 1: "Parents are the primary and principal educators and are assisted by civil society in accordance with the principle of subsidiarity (cf. *Gravissimum Educationis*, 3)."

12. [16] *Lay Catholics in Schools*, 14; cf. *The Catholic School on the Threshold of the Third Millennium*, 16.

13. [17] *The Catholic School*, 13.

14. [18] *Gravissimum Educationis*, 6; cf. *Code of Canon Law*, canon 793 § 2.

15. [19] *Compendium of Social Doctrine of the Church*, n. 241.

16. [20] Cf. *Code of Canon Law*, canon 797; Jason Boffetti, *All Schools Are Public Schools: A Case for State Aid to Private Education and Homeschooling Parents* (Washington, DC: Faith and Reason Institute, 2001).

17. [21] Cf. *Renewing Our Commitment to Catholic Elementary and Secondary Schools in the Third Millennium*, 12.

18. [22] *Gravissimum Educationis*, 9; cf. *Consecrated Persons and Their Mission in Schools*, 69–72.

19. [23] *The Catholic School on the Threshold of the Third Millennium*, 15; *The Catholic School*, 58; *Consecrated Persons and Their Mission in Schools*, 70: "Sometimes, however, it is Catholic educational institutions themselves that have strayed from such a preferential op-

tion [for the poor], which characterized the beginnings of the majority of institutes of conse-crated life devoted to teaching."

20. [24] John Paul II, *Ad Limina* Address to American Bishops of the Ecclesiastical Provinces of Portland in Oregon, Seattle, and Anchorage (24 June 2004), 1: *Origins,* 34:14 (16 September 2004), 220-221.

21. [25] Cf. *The Catholic School on the Threshold of the Third Millennium,* 11.

22. [26] Michael J. Guerra, "Catholic Schools in the United States: A Gift to the Church and a Gift to the Nation," *Seminarium, 1, 2* (2004), 105.

23. [27] Cf. *The Catholic School,* 29.

24. [28] Cf. *Gravissimum Educationis,* 8.

25. [29] John Paul II, Address to Catholic Educators (12 September 1987), 7: *Origins,* 17:15 (1 October 1987), 270.

26. [30] Cf. Hancock, *Recovering a Catholic Philosophy of Education,* 34.

27. [31] *Lay Catholics in Schools,* 18; cf. *The Religious Dimension of Education in a Catho-lic School,* 63; *Consecrated Persons and Their Mission in Schools,* 35.

28. [32] Second Vatican Ecumenical Council, *Gaudium et Spes,* 22; cf. *The Catholic School on the Threshold of the Third Millennium,* 9.

29. [33] *The Catholic School on the Threshold of the Third Millennium,* 9; cf. *Lay Catholics in Schools,* 18.

30. [34] *The Catholic School,* 35.

31. [35] John Paul II, Message to the National Catholic Educational Association of the United States (16 April 1979) *Insegnamenti,* 2 (1979): 919-920.

32. [36] *The Catholic School,* 34.

33. [37] *The Religious Dimension of Education in a Catholic School,* 25.

34. [38] *Lay Catholics in Schools,* 41.

35. [39] John Paul II, *Novo Millennio Ineunte,* 43.

36. [40] *Lay Catholics in Schools,* 22.

37. [41] *The Religious Dimension of Education in a Catholic School,* 31; cf. *The Catholic School on the Threshold of the Third Millennium,* 18.

38. [42] *The Religious Dimension of Education in a Catholic School,* 40.

39. [43] Cf. *Lay Catholics in Schools,* 78.

40. [44] Cf. *Consecrated Persons and Their Mission in Schools,* 16.

41. [45] Ibid., 46.

42. [46] *The Religious Dimension of Education in a Catholic School,* 42: cf. *Lay Catholics in Schools,* 34.

43. [47] *Consecrated Persons and Their Mission in Schools,* 17; cf. 41.

44. [48] Ibid., 46.

45. [49] Cf. John Paul II, *Novo Millennio Ineunte,* 43.

46. [50] John Paul II, *Ad Limina* Address to American Bishops (28 October 1983), 7: *Insegnamenti,* 6/2 (1983), 891.

47. [51] Cf. *Code of Canon Law,* canon 375.

48. [52] Canon 794.

49. [53] John Paul II, *Pastores Gregis,* 52.

50. [54] Cf. *Code of Canon Law,* canon 806 § 1; cf. *Consecrated Persons and Their Mission in Schools,* 42.

51. [55] Cf. *Code of Canon Law,* canon 803 § 2.

52. [56] John Paul II, *Ad Limina* Address to American Bishops of the Ecclesiastical Prov-inces of Portland in Oregon, Seattle, and Anchorage (24 June 2004), 3: *Origins,* 34:14 (16 September 2004), 221.

53. [57] Cf. John Paul II, *Pastores Gregis,* 51.
54. [58] Cf. *Consecrated Persons and Their Mission in Schools,* 61.
55. [59] Cited in *Consecrated Persons and Their Mission in Schools,* 62.
56. [60] *The Catholic School on the Threshold of the Third Millennium,* 18.
57. [61] *Lay Catholics in Schools,* 33.
58. [62] *Consecrated Persons and Their Mission in Schools,* 62.
59. [63] *The Religious Dimension of Education in a Catholic School,* 27.
60. [64] Ibid., 25.
61. [65] Ibid., 29.
62. [66] Lay Catholics in Schools, 17; cf. *The Religious Dimension of Education in a Catholic School,* 99.
63. [67] *The Catholic School,* 55.
64. [68] R. Scott Appleby, "Catholicism as a Comprehensive Way of Life," *Origins,* 32:22 (7 November 2002), 370.
65. [69] "Dry Salvages."
66. [70] "Choruses from 'The Rock' 1934."
67. [71] Hancock, *Recovering a Catholic Philosophy of Elementary Education,* 77.
68. [72] Joseph Ratzinger, Homily for Mass *Pro Eligendo Romano Pontific* (18 April 2005): *Origins,* 34:45 (28 April 2005), 720.
69. [73] John Paul II, *Ad Limina* Address to Bishops from Illinois, Indiana, and Wisconsin (30 May 1998), 3: *Origins,* 28:5 (18 June 1998), 76.
70. [74] *The Catholic School,* 41.
71. [75] *The Religious Dimension of Education in a Catholic School,* 57.
72. [76] Cf. *The Catholic School on the Threshold of the Third Millennium,* 14.
73. [77] *The Religious Dimension of Education in a Catholic School,* 53.
74. [78] *Lay Catholics in Schools,* 20.
75. [79] *The Religious Dimension of Education of a Catholic School,* 34; cf. *The Catholic School,* 44.
76. [80] *The Catholic School,* 49; cf. 36.
77. [81] *The Catholic School,* 47; cf. *Gravissimum Educationis,* 8.
78. [82] *Lay Catholics in Schools,* 43.
79. [83] Cf. *The Catholic School,* 50–51; *The Religious Dimension of Education in a Catholic School,* 66–69.
80. [84] Cf. *The Religious Dimension of Education in a Catholic School,* 26; *The Catholic School on the Threshold of the Third Millennium,* 19.
81. [85] *Gravissimum Educationis,* 8.
82. [86] Cf. *Lay Catholics in Schools,* 37; cf. *The Catholic School on the Threshold of the Third Millennium,* 19.
83. [87] *The Catholic School,* 43.
84. [88] Benedict XVI, Address to the Participants in the Ecclesial Diocesan Convention of Rome (6 June 2005): *L'Osservatore Romano,* English-language edition (15 June 2005), 7.
85. [89] United States Conference of Catholic Bishops, *National Directory for Catechesis* (Washington, D.C.: United States Conference of Catholic Bishops, 2005), 231.
86. [90] Ibid., 233.
87. [91] John Paul II, *Ad Limina* Address to Bishops from Illinois, Indiana, and Wisconsin (30 May 1998), 4: *Origins,* 28:5 (18 June 1998), 77; cf. *Lay Catholics in Schools,* 32, 40.
88. [92] Benedict XVI, Address to the Participants in the Ecclesial Diocesan Convention of Rome (6 June 2005): *L'Osservatore Romano,* English-language edition (15 June 2005). 7
89. [93] Paul VI, *Evangelii Nuntiandi,* 41.
90. [94] *Lay Catholics in Schools,* 32.